Band Together

Band Together

Internal Dynamics in U2, R.E.M., Radiohead and the Red Hot Chili Peppers

MIRIT ELIRAZ

McFarland & Company, Inc., Publishers
Jefferson, North Carolina, and London

OCM 70839737

LIBRARY OF CONGRESS CATALOGUING-IN-PUBLICATION DATA

Eliraz, Mirit, 1974–
    Band together : internal dynamics in U2, R.E.M.,
Radiohead and the Red Hot Chili Peppers / Mirit Eliraz.
        p.   cm.
    Includes bibliographical references and index.

    ISBN-13: 978-0-7864-2620-1
    ISBN-10: 0-7864-2620-9
    (softcover : 50# alkaline paper) ∞

    1. Rock groups.   2. U2 (Musical group)   3. R.E.M.
(Musical group)   4. Radiohead (Musical group)   5. Red
Hot Chili Peppers (Musical group)   I. Title.
ML394.E43   2006
781.66—dc22   2006025061

British Library cataloguing data are available

Cover image ©2006 *Brand X Pictures*

Manufactured in the United States of America

McFarland & Company, Inc., Publishers
    Box 611, Jefferson, North Carolina 28640
        www.mcfarlandpub.com

For my sweet girls,
Monica and Lenore

Contents

Preface

Rock groups have always held a special allure for me. I am as intrigued by their camaraderie and chemistry as I am by their music. Over the years, I sought to learn more about the inner mechanics of various bands by reading rock biographies, but most afforded only the occasional glimpse into the relationships between the members and the nature of the group's communal life. Some three years ago, then, I decided to pick up a book on the subject of band dynamics in order to get a more in-depth account. The problem was, I couldn't find one. After thoroughly scouring the Internet and the shelves of many a bookstore, I realized that this topic hadn't been tackled—at least not in the way I envisioned. There have been no books whose exclusive focus is a particular band's dynamics, let alone any broader explorations of this topic, involving multiple groups, to provide more general insight into what characterizes these outfits. This came as quite a surprise to me, as it is both a noteworthy and topical theme. Films like *Almost Famous* and the Metallica documentary *Some Kind of Monster* have drawn a lot of attention to it of late. It also seems as if bands are talking more about what it means to be in a band—and in their band—than in the past.

Perhaps the only band whose inner workings have been given more than cursory attention is The Beatles, because everything connected with this most influential of rock groups, about whom countless books have been published, continues to fascinate the public. And considering the electric spark the coalition between the Fab Four produced, it's not surprising that there is a keen interest in determining how this particular band was wired internally. Most of the written material about other rock bands presents biographical information or discusses their artistic output, treating the unit almost as if it really were a singular being. But for the stray comment on their mode of operation or the occasional reference to a telling incident in a band's history, what typically goes on inside these groups and what are their principal attributes are essentially untouched subjects. Given how exceptional they are and how appealing is the fellowship they often manifest, I feel that rock groups merit discourse aimed at furthering our understanding of their essential nature and how they function. So I started dreaming up the kind of book I would like to see on the subject, and shortly thereafter, set about researching it.

To uncover details about the mechanics of these entities, the internal worlds of a sample set of bands, preferably those that have some features in common, need to be studied and compared. This is the agenda of *Band Together: Internal Dynamics in U2, R.E.M., Radiohead and the Red Hot Chili Peppers*, which takes an in-depth look at the four groups named in the title in order to provide insight into their inner workings relative to one another. The book describes the diverse interactions, relationships and forces that shape these bands, revealing what form they commonly take and how they vary from unit to unit. To this end, rather than focusing on particular events in the life of the collective, such as a major blowup or a unifying episode (subjects typically covered in rock biographies), it explores how each band regularly functions and identifies the constants that define it.

Anyone coming across this book might rightfully ask: why these bands? The answer is that once a decision has been made not to look at every handful of musicians who have ever split a royalty check, selection criteria need to be established in order to extract a suitable study sample from the general assembly of bands. U2, R.E.M., Radiohead and the Red Hot Chili Peppers are (more or less) contemporaries with representation in the same media outlets and, despite their respective sonic departures and differences, are all notable purveyors of guitar-rock. In terms of their internal organization, each of the bands collaborates on all possible levels, performing and writing music together, making decisions collectively and generally exhibiting a strong group identity. In addition to their reputed internal harmony and indisputable chemistry, they display an enviable brand of fellowship.

Having endured over a considerable length of time with the core of the group or a classic lineup in place, the unit's longevity and the continuous association of the band members ensure that these groups have well-established internal patterns to examine. As musical pioneers and innovators, they have each heavily influenced the current crop of bands, while constantly reinventing themselves and their sound. At times, their experiments have led them to challenge the collaborative paradigm, making them acutely aware of its limits and strengths. They are also some of the biggest acts to emerge from the most recent period in rock history—the last decade and early part of the new millennium. The combination of these shared features makes these four tight-knit outfits ideal candidates for *Band Together*.

It's true that there are other bands that could meet these criteria. In that regard, Radiohead, R.E.M., U2 and the Red Hot Chili Peppers are not far removed from many of their peers. But there is also the question of readership to take into consideration. It simply makes sense for a book discussing more than one band, but still only a few, to bring together under its single cover groups whose fans overlap to a certain extent, which is the case here. And, while the denominators common to the selected bands make it expedient to discuss them together, the differences between the four—such as the fact that the Chili Peppers experienced numerous lineup changes while U2 and Radiohead have had none—ensure that a fairly wide gamut of groups is represented.

Examining the internal mechanics of rock bands is admittedly tricky. For one thing, the dynamics within any group or relationship are, well, *dynamic*, subject to perpetual change—even when there is no turnover among the individuals involved. Certain patterns of behavior and interaction are more fundamental than others, as they are rooted in the intrinsic natures of the participants or the basic structure of the group, and are therefore relatively stable. It's possible, and more than that, worthwhile, to illuminate them. Still, it's necessary to be aware of the fact that the features of such alliances, including those we can reasonably call trademarks, are far from set in stone. As such, fluctuations in the inner workings of the bands are documented throughout this book. In fact, an entire chapter is devoted to describing the evolution of each unit.

This brings me to another complicated aspect of writing a book of this nature: some topics can fit equally well in more than one section or chapter. For example, conflict is discussed in Chapter 4 (as one of the consequences of a democratic group setup) as well as in Chapter 5 (which looks at the nature of arguments in the bands). In Chapter 3 I look at the shared artistic vision of each band but don't get to the members' musical influences, which shape this vision to some extent, until Chapter 6. The guiding principle I employed was that each segment should be in *the most* logical or prudent chapter in the book, even if it's not the only spot it could occupy. Where appropriate, I drew connections between related ideas presented in different sections or chapters.

Clouding the exploration undertaken in *Band Together* is the notion that band dynamics should not be anatomized. R.E.M.'s Michael Stipe views the matter in this light. He believes chemistry is the band's linchpin, but is concerned that picking it apart, "like a frog on an operating table," could destroy it.[1] During an *MTV.com* interview, Anthony Kiedis of the Red Hot Chili Peppers expressed similar reservations about looking too closely at the band's inner workings, particularly in an effort to identify its source of strength. He was reluctant even to respond to the suggestion that the group's sense of humor is what kept it alive in the face of frequent calamity. "It could be," he conceded, adding, "Just in case it is, let's leave it at that. Whatever's working for us, we don't want to mess with the secret sauce."[2] What both men seem to be saying is that attempting to figure out exactly what makes their band tick is a dangerous exercise. Implicit in their objections is the idea that there is something wondrous about these groups—what Kiedis once described as "an intangible and inexplicable mystery quotient"—that matter-of-fact accounts of their mode of operation might stamp out.[3]

However, logic dictates that if the source of that wonder is some indefinable factor, some essential element that defies explanation, then it is safely out of the reach of this and any other inquest. In other words, by gaining a better understanding of how bands work, we are by no means dispelling the inherent mystery underlying their operation. If anything, it will become even more apparent that there *is* an unspecified force, an unlabeled ingredient, at work here. That the whole is—somehow—greater than the sum of its parts is, after all, a conclusion arrived at only when one is thoroughly familiar with those parts; so *Band Together* should increase rather than diminish our reverence for bands.

The nature of this book and, indeed, the study of band dynamics, is such that it depends heavily on insights and descriptions provided by the members themselves, as well as associates who are familiar with the group's mode of operation. There is simply no other way to come by the relevant information. My task was to gather, interpret and then synthesize the various accounts to form coherent chapters and sections. In that sense, I functioned partly as an anthologist of sorts and partly as an author. With the aim of making my sources transparent and pursuable, endnotes are given for direct quotes, and in-text details identify the origin of significant points reported indirectly.

Ideally, I would have liked to speak with members of U2, R.E.M., Radiohead and the Red Hot Chili Peppers directly, but they declined my requests for interviews. Fortunately, there is so much data available about these bands that I was still able to write the kind of book I had in mind. For this, I am heavily indebted to the many talented journalists and show hosts (radio and television) who have interviewed these bands over the years, often asking the very questions to which I needed answers. Some sources proved particularly invaluable. They are: *Rolling Stone, Q, Hot Press, New Musical Express* (NME), *Melody Maker, Spin, Musician, Kerrang!, Mojo,* and *Addicted to Noise.* I am grateful for the many excellent articles and interviews I found in these publications, along with many others, documented in the bibliography (works cited and works consulted). The journalists and authors I contacted directly were all incredibly gracious and eager to help.

Without access to the band members, however, there were some topics I couldn't explore in as much detail as I would have liked, as well as certain contradictions that I had to resolve based on my own research and interpretations (and, in a few cases, left unresolved). My hope is that these and other bands will continue to speak openly about their dynamics, whether in general or in future books on this topic, so that we can gain even more insight into and clarity in regard to the workings of these communal enterprises.

Finally, there are a number of people to whom I owe thanks for their assistance: Steve Roeser (one of the kindest people I encountered on this journey), who provided me with copies of pieces he had written about these bands, advice, and answers to my music trivia questions; Professor Rob Bowman (Musicologist, York University), for a crash phone-course in the history of music that proved incredibly useful in writing the introduction; Paul Zollo, who generously offered me the benefit of his experience in soliciting interviews; Professor Kelly Quinn (English Literature, Western University), for clearing up my grammatical and writing dilemmas, for giving me the benefit of her sound judgment, and for many years of friendship; Jeff Silver, who filled in my musical gaps and let me bounce countless ideas off him, and who has always been an important musical mentor in my life; Drs. Mark and Sofia Weisman, for their myriad efforts on behalf of this book; my wonderful and dedicated parents, Ariel and Menucha, who back my aspirations in word and deed; my brother, Ted, who let me wear out his Supertramp records when I was a kid (he started it all); my sister, Dalit, who has always encouraged me to do what I love; Alex and Solomon Blumenfeld, for freeing up my time and giving me all the aid in their power to write this book; and last but certainly not least, my husband, Zohar, who was there for me every step of the way (as always), as a counselor, IT consultant, editor, morale officer, field research companion and all-around load-carrier (not to mention all the music he has introduced me to over the years). In every respect, he made this book possible.

Introduction:
On Bands

"The thing is, we're all really the same person. We're just four parts of the one."[1] This is perhaps Paul McCartney's most memorable statement about The Beatles, a group that, more than any other, epitomizes the musical ensembles we call rock bands. His now-famous remark has implications beyond its depiction of the legendary Liverpool quartet. It suggests that a kind of mystic fusion takes place when any collection of individuals bands together to form a symbiotic, long-term artistic collaboration. They are transfigured, in a sense, becoming a single organism greater than any one of them (or the sum of its parts), sustained by an intangible chemistry, deep-rooted interdependency, and, quite frequently, an intimate personal bond.

In this singular union, and the apparent camaraderie it often breeds, lies one of the sources of the widespread and prevailing appeal of bands. After all, the Beatles succeeded in capturing the imagination of generations not just with their incomparable music and lovable haircuts, but because they exhibited an enthralling interpersonal chemistry and endearing spirit of togetherness. There was a dazzling, inexplicable force at work whenever the four were in each other's company, not just when they joined forces to create music, that continues to captivate the world. We are drawn to what such a group represents: a surrogate family, an ideal fellowship, a band of brothers.

The most engaging musical groups are those that, in addition to their *esprit de corps*, strike us as a bonded-for-life gang, whether because the lineup has been in existence for a long time or because we have the impression—as we do even with some less stable outfits—that, in some grand cosmic scheme, the members of the band were meant to be together. One of the reasons the dissolution of a well-established or particularly synergistic unit, or the departure of one of its members, is so jarring for fans is because they cherish the notion that these people are somehow indivisible. As disappointing as the fact that the group will no longer make music is the end of what appeared to be a real, permanent, and predestined confederation.

With their unparalleled communal structure, bands are a unique phenomenon in popular culture. In no other artistic discipline do we commonly find outfits wherein the members congregate of their own accord to form an enclosed and enduring (i.e., not tied to a short-term project) collective that they then govern themselves. Yet, such groups play an integral role in modern music. And whereas bands, like acting ensembles, dance troupes or chamber orchestras, perform together, they differ from these other groups in that, in many cases, the participants also create in unison. This type of partnership has little to no precedent in the history of art. Artists, be they authors, painters or composers, nearly always worked alone. Sharing the task of bringing creative visions to life is a relatively novel concept and still rather rare outside of popular musical groups, and, on a broader scale, filmmaking (where a much larger team generally collaborates on a single project).

Consisting of bass, guitar, drum and vocals, the traditional four-piece rock band is essentially a stripped-down version (namely, the rhythm section) of the big bands that dominated the Swing era, which, on account of the numerous instruments and musicians involved, were no longer financially viable by the end of the 1940s. The spare and economical ensembles that replaced these populous groups provided the backing music for the rock and roll singers that rose to prominence in the latter half of the 1950s. Bill Haley was accompanied by His Comets, Gene Vincent by the Bluecaps, Buddy Holly by the Crickets, and Elvis Presley by the Blue Moon Boys. Collaboration within these units took a much more limited form than that described above. With the exception of Buddy Holly, who wrote most of his material, songwriters external to the bands scored their music, so the compositions were not generated within the confines of the group. Arrangement and performance of the songs were the bands' domains. Also, as their names imply, these outfits were comprised of two distinct parties: a famous solo performer and his auxiliaries.

In the early 1960s, groups like The Beatles and The Beach Boys surfaced, along with a somewhat different band ethos. They shared one designation, indicating (at least in title) that this was no superstar and his back-up band. For the most part, their material was original, its genesis within the group, although usually only one or two members partook in the writing—or so the credits indicated. (In some cases, the group's songwriter had a creative partnership with someone outside the unit, like Brian Wilson of The Beach Boys and non-member Gary Usher.) An even more collective mindset, which proved forward-thinking because it became increasingly common in the years to come, was manifested by The Doors.

According to an article written by drummer John Densmore about his days in the group, it was Jim Morrison who suggested in 1965, when The Doors was still a garage band, not only that every member have veto power over any decision, but that both profits and songwriting credits be split equally between the four. "Since [Jim] didn't play an instrument—literally couldn't play one chord on piano or guitar, but had lyrics and melodies coming out of his ears—the communal pot idea felt like a love-in," explains Densmore.[2] It made sense, since they worked very collaboratively. (Indeed, an episode of VH1's acclaimed *Storytellers* series that reunited Densmore with Ray Manzarek and Robbie Krieger emphasized this often-overlooked aspect of the band). This was the first group to credit its songs to the band, in recognition of the fact that The Doors was very much a four-man operation.

Other groups, such as Genesis in the early part of the 1970s, and Bauhaus in the latter part, acknowledged the teamwork at the heart of their music by crediting not individual songwriters but the entity they had formed. Nevertheless, this practice was rare, as most of the bands that loom large over the period, like Supertramp, Led Zeppelin, Pink Floyd, Queen, and Yes, continued to ascribe their compositions to particular members. But, gradually, the tide was turning. By the following decade, a growing number of groups identified the band (or all its members) as the source of their output, thereby exhibiting a more united front.

It's nearly impossible to pinpoint precisely what this change in the representation of the workload distribution within bands stemmed from. It may reflect an evolution in the *real* mode of operation of these outfits (i.e., they actually became more collaborative) or perceptual adjustments related to shifting views of what constitutes a group effort or a song. There seems to be an element of both involved. In other words, there were certain developments that changed what really went on in bands as well as how the members (and others) viewed the group.

Whereas at one time, a song—consisting of lyrics set to a melody and married to a series of chord changes—was the product of musical inspiration, studio recordings—often featuring overlaid elements—eventually became the primary artifact associated with popular music. This means that even in cases when the basic components of a song proceed from an individual or pair of writers, if the additions to the *recording* provided by the other musicians in the group are viewed as integral, categorized under the umbrella of songwriting rather than arrangement, then the finished product is considered the property of the band.

The groupwork identified in these cases lies in translating a song into a mutually-realized recording. And popular music indeed became increasingly complex throughout the '60s and '70s, as intricate and often sprawling compositions replaced the more straightforward sing-along songs that defined the genre before. In short, these developments forced band members to redefine songwriting contributions. Meanwhile, the complexity and sound layering possibilities of studio recording and the modern orientation of popular music were, in fact, conducive to collaboration in practice, since there were that many more bits outside of a song's elemental framework that could be added to the track, opening up opportunities for everyone in the group to contribute to a given piece.

Although they occurred so gradually that it's impossible to correlate them to any specific period, there were a couple of largely *conceptual* revolutions that are also worth noting in this regard. As popular musicmakers began writing their own tunes and the form started to gain cultural respect, songsters came to be regarded as artists rather than merely entertainers. This was a significant paradigmatic switch. In a way, it transformed band members from a set of affiliated instrumentalists into the fellow torchbearers of a shared artistic vision—a solidarity-enhancing model. Equally important is the fact that bands have, over time, become as closely associated with a particular sound and approach as they are with specific songs. This is a type of output the entire group can generally lay claim to, even if what they count as actual songwriting falls to specific individuals within the unit. Certain band members may take a backseat to others when it comes to penning lyrics or devising melodies but play a crucial role in formulating the sound with which the group is identified and on which its reputation rests. This realization, too, fosters the kind of all-for-one mentality progressively displayed by (some) bands.

The punk acts that stormed the stage in the late 1970s (re)introduced the idea that anyone can be in a band, regardless of musical ability—what is sometimes referred to as a do-it-yourself credo. Some of the outfits that formed in the wake of this "revolution"—like U2 and R.E.M.—were comprised of novices (at least one or two) whose music was, by default, a communal effort. By the early '80s, bands had also been around long enough to develop a history that current and future generations could draw upon. Newcomers who sought to establish an enduring and relatively conflict-free alliance were able to look back upon the factors that led to the demise of previous groups and take steps to avoid these pitfalls. Squabbles over money and battles for control frequently broke up bands, so a more isonomic approach was the natural remedy. This is not to say that, with the passage of time, *all* bands adopted an egalitarian and coactive structure, a more group-driven creative ethic or a perception of the group as a unified entity. But it seems as if a significant number did, ensuring that a band like The Doors wouldn't be an anomaly today.

Joe Carducci points out in *Rock and the Pop Narcotic* that the instrumental dialogue that takes place in any musical ensemble becomes a framework for creation in (some) rock bands, so the inherent interdependency of the musicians is a tremendous asset to this seminal form. In these outfits, the merging of the ensemble instruments serves as the basis not only for performing music, but also for the musicians to generate original material together—a process that demands a high degree of integration among the participants. The already formidable bond between the musicians in rock groups was deepened by the legacy of the punk movement.

Because it was acceptable for individuals with no prior musical training (and who hadn't spent hours alone in their bedroom mastering Jimmy Page solos) to form bands, the members of some groups ended up learning to play their instruments through working together. This explains why musicians in post-punk rock bands sometimes remark that their style is intertwined with the group's sound and not just vice versa. A collective in which the artists compose music together and also gain their own skills in the process embodies a truly remarkable creative alliance. If we carry forward the linguistic metaphor, each such band develops something of its own internal dialect, spoken only by its members, as it produces its instrumental dialogue.

The fact that bands govern their own affairs, albeit with ample guidance from managers, producers and record executives, separates them from outfits presided over by an external figure who calls all the shots. It also adds another dimension to the group by turning the members into business associates as well as artistic partners. In addition to these various intrinsic properties that differentiate bands from other ensembles found in the art world, the celebrity attained, and the subsequent media attention received by even moderately successful rock groups, is an external element that has serious repercussions in terms of the teamwork that takes place within them. Fame introduces a whole slew of issues for groups in this genre to contend with—from the pressure to stay on top to matters of ego and sharing the spotlight. Groups in less popular musical categories and in other creative disciplines rarely, if ever, have to contend with these peripheral challenges. Taken together, these circumstances and traits render rock bands a highly individual breed among collectives, quite unlike any of their counterparts in other genres.

This book examines the inner workings of four post-punk groups that are particularly close-knit and who operate as a team on every imaginable level. It begins with a brief biographical sketch of each outfit, followed by eleven chapters that discuss various aspects of their band dynamic—from the roles of the members to the obstacles faced by the group to the impact of external factors on the unit's inner workings.

1

"How the West Was Won and Where It Got Us": Band Bios

U2: ROCK'S INDIVISIBLE FAMILY
DUBLIN, IRELAND
PAUL HEWSON (BONO): VOCALS
DAVID EVANS (THE EDGE): GUITAR
ADAM CLAYTON: BASS GUITAR
LARRY MULLEN, JR.: DRUMS

As their good friends in R.E.M. often point out, U2 set out to become one of the biggest bands in the world—and, simply put, succeeded. But the Irish supergroup, as famous for its political outspokenness and grand gestures as its propulsive music, boasts another admirable distinction: it has had no lineup changes since its formation 25 years ago. In fact, its four founding members continue to enjoy a warm and functional relationship. Known for its remarkable chemistry, seemingly inviolable solidarity, and thoroughly democratic mode of operation, U2 has come to symbolize rock's ideal family. The quartet's ethics of togetherness and determination to battle through any strife within the unit serve as an inspiration for other bands.

During its long and illustrious career, U2 has weathered trials that would have rung the death knell for a less committed and inter-wired collection of individuals. The group was born inauspiciously in 1976 when 14-year-old Larry Mullen, Jr., an avid young drummer, posted a notice at Dublin's Mount Temple school requesting that individuals interested in forming a band meet at his home for a rehearsal. Among those who responded to the ad were fellow students Paul Hewson, brothers David and Richard (Dick) Evans, and Adam Clayton. None of these young men eager to form a band could play an instrument (even those

L-R: Adam Clayton, Larry Mullen, The Edge, Bono. The band's semi-official photographer, Anton Corbijn, likes to snap the four together and they obviously favor this approach. He says he likes to convey the band feeling and capture the force of the quartet's unity. Photofest (Anton Corbijn).

who had one), but the punk groups by which they were influenced had proven that virtuosity was no longer a prerequisite for rock stardom; passion and energy were sufficient.

The charismatic and outgoing Hewson, nicknamed Bono by some of his cronies, instinctively took charge of the band from the first meeting in the drummer's kitchen. Such a move could have capsized the unit, but the young men proved to be well-matched. The coup didn't bother Mullen; he was only interested in playing drums. Other matters soon fell into place, as Richard (Dick) Evans left after a short time to join another band.

Although the band was admittedly lousy at first—they started writing their own songs because they weren't sufficiently adept at covers—

L-R: Larry Mullen, Adam Clayton, The Edge, Bono. The unstoppable and unsinkable Irish quartet scooped up the Q Icon award in 2004 for an incredible career spanning a quarter century. Their uninterrupted and intense collaboration over this expanse of time is almost unheard of in rock. The force of their unity and chemistry comes across potently in photographs. CP/PA (Yui Mok).

when the four members combined their efforts, there was an intangible "spark" around which they built U2. Their friendship was what enabled them to fan the tiny flame. The quartet christened itself Feedback and then The Hype before settling on the name U2 in 1978.

Constant touring throughout the UK, a capable new manager, and the release of the EP *U2:3* finally landed the group a contract with Island Records in 1980. Later that year, U2 delivered its first full-length album, *Boy*, to critical accolades. No one was more amazed with the record than its creators. To this day, the band marvels at how four such unaccomplished musicians could have given birth to such a fervid and innovative piece of work, attributing the feat to the inexplicable alchemy of their union. From the outset, chemistry and ingenuity compensated for the group's lack of technical expertise. *Boy* evinced the quintessential U2 sound, namely The Edge's signature ringing guitar complemented by Bono's ardent vocals and an explosive backbeat.

Having got off to such a promising start, the unit floundered somewhat over the course of the next few years, as the members found themselves in a state of crisis. Everyone but the ever gung-ho Clayton began to wonder if the band was his true calling. Complicating matters, Bono,

Mullen and The Edge had become involved with a Christian sect known as the Shalom Group, which led them to believe that their occupation and faith might be mutually exclusive. As he didn't share the spiritual devotion of his bandmates, Clayton felt left out, and something of an unuttered rift opened within the group, which was effectively sealed (after months of underground tension) when Bono invited Clayton to serve as best man at his wedding, thereby affirming the band's allegiance to the bass player. Such demonstrations of friendship mitigated the general consternation within the group.

In the climate of uncertainty and moral conflict that pervaded U2 in 1982, the group recorded its second album, *October*, which embodies the prevailing mood. With the exception of the vibrant opening track, "Gloria," listeners found the brooding sophomore release inaccessible, so the record failed to carry the group far. The demons the band was wrestling had not all been slain even by 1983, when U2 recorded its breakthrough album, *War*, which reached the top of the UK charts and spawned two classic U2 singles: "Sunday Bloody Sunday" and "New Year's Day." Featuring martial drumbeats and aggressively political lyrics, *War* was a gutsy album for a young band to make, and even bolder was Bono's predilection for strutting around on stage waving a white flag during the supporting tour. *War* was an apt title for the record because, inside the group, the personal conflicts raged on. And the assurance the quartet displayed outwardly masked lingering ambivalence towards U2.

The year 1984 marked a new beginning for the group. Having vanquished their misgivings, the four men were at last wholeheartedly committed to the band. And Bono claims that U2's musical life really began at this point. For the recording of the band's next record, *The Unforgettable Fire* (1985), the quartet parted with producer Steve Lillywhite and brought in a fresh team comprised of the pop- and ambient-music icon Brian Eno and Canadian songwriter and studio wiz Daniel Lanois. This was to become a fruitful and lasting relationship, one of many in the broader U2 camp. With this more experimental album, featuring sprawling atmospheric tracks like "A Sort of Homecoming" and "Bad," the band inched closer to international superstardom. *The Unforgettable Fire* debuted at the top of the UK charts and went platinum within a year. "Pride (In the Name of Love)" gave the group its first Top 40 hit in the U.S., where the album peaked at number 12.

Meanwhile, the band's electrifying stage shows continued to be its most valuable asset, which explains why the live recording *Under a Blood Red Sky*, sandwiched between *War* and *The Unforgettable Fire*, became a bestseller. The group's bold Live Aid performance had an immeasurable impact on its career, boosting sales of its fourth album, and significantly raising the group's public profile. It set the stage for the global domination that was next in the cards for the band. With the release of its sublime fifth album, *The Joshua Tree* (1987), U2 achieved the stardom for which it was ripe. Instant classics such as "With or Without You," "I Still Haven't Found What I'm Looking For" and "Where the Streets Have No Name" turned U2 into a household name. The absolutely staggering success of this record (it was the fastest selling album in UK history, certified platinum within 28 hours) catapulted the group onto the front cover of *Time* and into stadiums around the world, but without overthrowing the staunch solidarity of its members. The new Fab Four, as they were hailed, remained dedicated to the collective they had formed in high school.

Rattle and Hum, released in 1988, was a double album comprised of mostly new material recorded live and in the studio. A motion picture by the same name accompanied the LP. It documented the band's journey through the American heartland as the members retraced the roots of rock and roll, capturing some of the highlights of their musical quest, including a jam with legendary blues guitarist B.B. King and a visit to Graceland. These segments were punctuated by footage that transmuted onto celluloid the thrilling energy and intensity of the band's live shows. Although it performed reasonably well at the box office, the movie proved to be something of a misfire. Perceived by critics and the public as an unabashed display of hubris by a band perched on the top rung of the rock and roll ladder, U2 was condemned for making a silver-screen picture in the first place and for using it to prove that they belong in the ranks of rock deities like Elvis.

The quartet was profoundly taken aback by such reactions to the film, insisting that their intention had been to present themselves as fans paying homage to some of their heroes. But the damage had been done and something of a U2 backlash set in. As the decade drew to a close, it was evident that U2 had reached a crossroads. The band knew it would have to fight for its musical life. Bono's last, and now-famous, public statement of the '80s, delivered to an audience at The Point Depot in Dublin (and broadcast to an additional 300 million viewers), made apparent which alternative the group had opted for. It was time, he announced, for the band to go away and "dream it all up again."[1]

Each member of U2 internally pledged his continued loyalty to the unit and ratified the decision to strike out in a new direction. The group decamped to Berlin in 1990 to record its next album but the mood in the newly reunified city was not what the band had anticipated. Nor did it expect the sessions that would eventually lead to the release of *Achtung Baby* in 1991 to be so beleaguered and tense as to threaten the group's survival. The band was divided on the question of how to update U2's sound, with the members pulling in different directions. When the dust settled, they opted to replace the group's characteristic sincerity with irony and to flesh out its conventional rock sound with electronic elements borrowed from dance, techno and industrial music.

Achtung Baby (containing some of U2's best-known tracks: "The Fly," "Mysterious Ways," and "One") was a chart-smashing sensation and represented a triumphant rebirth for the band. Not only was the edgy, dark, and heavy material on the album a risky sonic departure for the typically uplifting U2, the CD insert and original video for "One" featured the group—which had acquired a staid reputation—in drag. This was the first of many steps the band would take to doff its Quakerish cast and show some of its other colors (including pink). By fearlessly embracing contemporary influences and turning the group's image on its head, U2 was able to make the transition into the '90s and remain relevant while most of its peers fell by the wayside. It was a precipitous passage, necessitating the consensus of four strong-minded individuals on the weighty questions of the band's public face and artistic course, but this collective had the grit and all-for-one spirit to see it through.

The band next embarked on the highly theatrical and elaborate ZOO TV tour, which saw a persona-adopting Bono poke fun at the idea of rock stardom and make nightly phone calls to the White House from the stage. A far cry from the barren set of yore was this purposely prop-laden spectacle, which constituted yet another move to leave the old U2 behind. Somehow, the four found time during this relentless tour to begin recording another album, *Zooropa* (1993). Even more than its predecessor, this record drew on industrial and techno music, deliberately propelling the band further away from its familiar sound. "Lemon," with its dance-inspired groove, and "Numb," flaunting industrial noise, were the kind of songs that heralded an unprecedented musical orientation for U2. This record represented a moderate commercial and critical achievement for the band, but it didn't excite nearly the same adulation as *Achtung Baby*. After devoting 14 years entirely to U2, the group took an extended hiatus, though they composed an avant-garde movie soundtrack with Brian Eno, *Passengers* (1995), which never ended up accompanying a film and the merits of which the band members still disagree upon.

In 1997, the group reconvened to make *Pop*, an album that took to the extreme the notion of abstracting the traditional U2 sound and rock music in general, as the quartet continued to plunge deeper into the realm of computerized sounds. But suddenly disenchanted with the "trip-hop aesthetic" by which they had been captivated throughout the early half of the decade, the band did a U-turn partway through recording, trying to return to the sound of the four of them playing together, or what Edge calls a "rock 'n' roll performance aesthetic."[2] However, they didn't manage to pull the album back from its original tangent. Although the CD sold well in Europe, by U2 standards, it wasn't well received in North America. Acceptance of the album wasn't significantly boosted by the glitzy Popmart tour, riddled as it was with technical difficulties resulting from a satellite linkup with war-torn Sarajevo, which did little but dampen the spirits of the audience and lead to arguments within the band. The ties binding the group could have easily snapped at the culmination of all this turmoil, which coincided with the end of a decade during which the band had experienced gnawing internal friction due to its envelope-pushing agenda.

Some critics indeed wrote off the group, claiming it had strayed too far from its ordained course in its quest for novelty. But U2 demonstrated its staying power by making a gratifying comeback with the multi–Grammy scoring *All That You Can't Leave Behind* (2000). After spending most of the '90s exploring the limits of a rock band, this record was a fall-back to rock basics and the traditional practices of the four-piece. It bore the unique U2 imprint, though the group had previously striven to camouflage its unmistakable sound. "Beautiful Day" and "Kite," like most of the tracks on this album, push back to the forefront the sound of the four musicians playing off one another. The spirit of togetherness spilled over into the group's personal relationships, drawing the four men closer than they had been in recent years, thereby reversing a trend that had prevailed during the '90s, when the band members had, according to Bono, wandered apart too much. This return to form was seasonable, given that the frontman's increasingly time-consuming role as spokesman for the campaign to drop third world debt had begun to put a new strain on the band.

How to Dismantle an Atomic Bomb hit stores in 2004, and the quartet began receiving lifetime achievement awards in addition to its induction into the Rock Hall of Fame. Throughout this period, U2 continued to contend with Bono's frequent absences due to his auxiliary career as a political activist. But the singer's devotion to the group is unwavering and his bandmates have made every effort to accommodate him. We expect nothing less of a band that has demonstrated the oneness of U2.

R.E.M.: FOUR (NOW THREE) AGAINST THE WORLD
ATHENS, GEORGIA, USA
MICHAEL STIPE: VOCALS
PETER BUCK: GUITAR
MIKE MILLS: BASS GUITAR
(BILL BERRY: DRUMS 1980–1997)

No biography of R.E.M. fails to mention that the group was formed

L-R: Bill Berry, Mike Mills, Peter Buck, Michael Stipe. Stipe dominates this early shot of the band. Although the media spotlight often falls on him, internally R.E.M. has always been based on the principles of equality and democracy. And the singer is the first to own up to a profound dependency on the band. Photofest (Sanda-Lee Phipps).

in 1980 by four college students from the Southern university town of Athens, Georgia; was among a handful of American garage bands comprising the nascent post-punk alternative scene; and was one of the first bands to make the transition from the fringes of rock to its epicenter. A more notable achievement is that, over the course of its more than two-decade-long career, the band has enjoyed tremendous commercial clout coupled with universal critical acclaim. Determined to succeed on its own terms, the group consistently flouted industry conventions that didn't suit its members' inclinations. By rejecting offers to open for other acts, eschewing tours in favor of studio work, and generating enigmatic videos and album artwork, R.E.M. proved time and again that a group whose members stand shoulder to shoulder can chart its own course— and an auspicious one at that—even in the regimented music business.

A series of fateful encounters brought the members of R.E.M. together. Bassist Mike Mills and drummer Bill Berry, friends since their school marching band days, came to study at the University of Georgia in Athens to escape from small-town life in their native Macon. Meanwhile, an Athens record store clerk by day, student by night and wanna-

Front row L-R: Peter Buck, Mike Mills; back row: Michael Stipe. R.E.M. as a trio in 1999, minus drummer Bill Berry. His departure after 17 years with the group significantly altered the personal and creative dynamic within it. The difficult adjustment to the new configuration nearly resulted in a split. Photofest (Robert Sebree).

be guitarist named Peter Buck formed a friendship with one of his customers, Michael Stipe, an art student, music aficionado and aspiring singer. The two moved into an abandoned church where they began composing songs together. At an opportune soiree, they became acquainted with Berry, who introduced them to Mills. Although the rhythm players were relatively experienced musicians and the corresponding pair untrained novices, collaboration on a few pieces of music proved to both parties that they could develop a good working relationship and that they had a solid basis for a band.

They dubbed their outfit R.E.M., after the dream-laden slumber typified by rapid eye movement, and began playing gigs wherever Berry could book them. There was, in addition to the personal connection the members developed, a quickening and indefinable force suffusing their union; they perceived it and so did others. Jefferson Holt, who later became the band's manager, spoke about "a miracle of chemistry between the four members" that was apparent to him when he first met them in 1980.[3] As the group gained bookings and support, the four decided to drop out of college and tour the South, Kerouac-style, in an old van. Venturing into the studio for the first time in 1981, they recorded "Radio Free Europe" and issued the single on the independent Hib-Tone label. College radio stations took to the tune, which also won plaudits from local reviewers.

In 1982, R.E.M. signed to the independent I.R.S. records and released a promotional five-song EP entitled *Chronic Town*, procuring the group further critical approbation. The band's first long-player, *Murmur*, was delivered in 1983 and topped *Rolling Stone*'s critic's poll as album of the year. Quite an accomplishment for an unknown cult band from a remote town. "Talk About the Passion" and "Perfect Circle" were just a couple of the incomparable tracks which demonstrated that the three years the group spent touring before gaining the confidence to make a debut album had indeed been beneficial for its creative evolution. But it came as no surprise that the praise heaped on *Murmur* far exceeded the sales it garnered. The distinct sound forged by Buck's much-ballyhooed "jangly" strumming, Stipe's famously mumbled vocals and cryptic lyrics, combined with the rough-edged strokes of the Mills-Berry rhythm section, was very much against the grain of the slick and pellucid music that permeated the airwaves during much of the '80s. Only campus disc jockeys championed this "arty garage band," as Buck referred to it, and spun its first record incessantly.[4]

Meanwhile, the band continued to crisscross the country, winning over audiences one dive bar and pizza parlor at a time. Set apart from other live acts largely by Stipe's natural magnetism, commanding stage presence and quirky dance moves, R.E.M.'s shows also benefited from their unpredictable sets and the foursome's eloquent devotion to playing music. These stirring performances (and some fortuitous industry connections) landed R.E.M. a seven-date slot opening for The Police. While these stadium shows promised the Southern quartet unequaled exposure, they proved to be a miserable experience and, at least in the band's estimation, of little value to its career. Always marching to its own tune rather than the industry's common beat, the band resolved to find more agreeable, if less conventional, ways of expanding its audience and getting its music heard.

With *Reckoning* (1984), the foursome solidified their status as the reigning kings of American indie rock, a genre R.E.M became virtually synonymous with. Recorded in just 12 days, the second album smacked of the sessions' intensity, spontaneity and "drunken party" atmosphere.[5] Critics continued to be impressed with the group's output and the record begot more R.E.M. converts. It was a hit, but only in the underground scene. *Fables of the Reconstruction* (1985) was the group's next studio project. A stark and morose album, *Fables* reflected a troubled period within the unit. Ironically, R.E.M. chose wintry London in which to record a collection of songs about the decline of the American South. The resulting sense of dislocation and infelicitous working conditions had a major impact on the album's sound and creation. Cold, broke and suffering from tour-induced fatigue, the four couldn't collaborate very effectively, and their lack of cohesion marred the album. Considered a failed experiment by some, *Fables* nonetheless represented a breakthrough of sorts for R.E.M. in terms of its peak chart position (in the U.S. Top 30) and the number of copies it shifted. *Life's Rich Pageant* came out the following year (1986) and continued the band's slow but steady climb towards fame, while the rousing "Cuyahoga" and "These Days" displayed its growing interest in politics.

Document (1987) gave R.E.M. its first taste of future spoils and a large contingent of the American public its inaugural acquaintance with the group, as the oft misinterpreted "The One I Love" became a Top Ten single and the album went gold in its first week of release. "It's the End of the World as We Know It (And I Feel Fine)," which saw Stipe's cynical lyrics set to a chipper tune, also contributed to the band's increasing appeal and has since become one of its concert standards. Suddenly, the group's work, which had previously been the well-kept secret of a select few, was being consumed by the masses. This album also represented the beginning of the band's decade-long partnership with producer Scott Litt.

Document's successor, *Green*, came out in 1988, taking the band past the last mile of the ascent to celebrity. It sold two million copies, yielded hits such as "Stand," "Pop Song '89" and "Orange Crush," and put R.E.M. on the cover of *Rolling Stone*. A grueling year-long global campaign in support of the record, coming on the heels of nearly a decade of constant touring, drained the band completely. When the tour was over, the four made a brave decision to stay off the road indefinitely, though they had just cracked the mainstream and risked a backward slide with this abdication. This was no marketing ploy or attention-getting strategy, explains Stipe, "it was survival."[6] It was also time for R.E.M. to moderate its breakneck pace of releasing an album every year, so the group took a much-needed sabbatical during which the members engaged in numerous side-projects, then spent a year recording the blockbuster *Out of Time* (1991).

The first single off the LP featured a mandolin as the lead instrument. Not exactly standard MTV fare. However, a brilliantly evocative and groundbreaking video helped the catchy "Losing My Religion" become one of the most memorable songs of the '90s, and had an undeniable hand in driving *Out of Time* to the top of both the U.S. and UK charts. A year later, the band outdid itself once again with the moody and masterful *Automatic for the People* (1992). Selling some 15 million copies, this album also reached the top of the charts on both sides of the Atlantic, enabling R.E.M. to join U2 on the pedestal reserved for the biggest rock acts on the planet. Given that R.E.M. once again abstained from setting out on a global trek to push the record, this achievement was all the more remarkable. It was attributable both to the momentum the group had built and the diverse but powerful collection of songs featured on *Automatic*, ranging from the edgy "Drive," to the buoyant "Man on the Moon" and the tearjerker "Everybody Hurts."

The group was aware that this might be the perfect high note on which to end R.E.M. Mills and Berry both felt that if the band didn't resume touring, there was no point in carrying on. But, instead of packing it in and letting *Automatic* become the capstone of the group's career, the four decided to pack their bags for a tour. First, they agreed to record a new album that lent itself to live interpretation and would be fun to take on the road. It was to be made quickly and intuitively, and would constitute the full-tilt rock collection R.E.M. had been threatening to put its name on for years. According to the plan, a rollicking tour would follow. But this wasn't how the real events unfolded. *Monster* (1994) was, without question, the most straightforward rock the group had ever set to disc. But the band nearly fell apart putting it together. In fact, the album's title suggests what an unruly beast it was to rear. Factors ranging from illness to the deaths of Kurt Cobain and River Phoenix (both close friends of the band) resulted in delaying the completion of *Monster*.

In addition to these external factors, there were internal stumbling blocks hindering the album's progress. The band members were having trouble seeing eye-to-eye about anything, and each flitted in and out of the studio according to the dictates of his personal life. They weren't really functioning as a unit at all. The four eventually agreed that they need to buckle down and start operating collectively again, enabling them to complete the album without further holdups. Though *Monster* received mixed reviews and baffled many of the band's devotees, it sold well and added "What's the Frequency, Kenneth?" to the group's growing list of venerated singles. R.E.M. took to the road for the first time in five years, but, as if the foursome had been put under an insidious curse, every member of the band suddenly faced a health problem requiring a surgical resolution. Berry's affliction was the most serious. In Switzerland, he suffered a brain aneurysm that nearly killed him, but was able to resume the suspended tour when he recovered.

Only a band as determined and defiant as R.E.M. would decide to make another album during the tour from hell (or, as the band referred to it, The Aneurysm Tour). Comprised of songs composed largely during soundchecks and rehearsals, *New Adventures in Hi-Fi* (1996), unlike its predecessor, came about quite naturally and without any notable intra-group friction. It was less about sonic experimentation and channeling compositions into a certain genre than it was about simply writing solid songs and recording them in unconventional ways. U.S. sales of the album were disappointing, but the band considered *New Adventures* its crowning achievement, the optimal output obtainable from the four of them jamming together. According to Stipe, with this record they reached the "zenith" of what they could do with the "group feeling."[7] It was clear to the quartet that the next R.E.M. project would be a radical departure from its last two "group rock" albums. Little did they know in 1996 what a dramatic transformation awaited the band.

During the '90s, the tightly woven R.E.M. network began to unravel somewhat. Over the period of a few years, R.E.M. gradually ceased to be the inseparable gang of yore, turning into a looser unit that periodically convened to record and perform. Abstention from touring was one factor, but there were others. Stipe became heavily involved with the two film production companies he had started a few years earlier and the other band members were involved in numerous extracurricular musical activities. Of more significance was the fact that in 1992, Buck moved away from the group's Athens homebase, taking up residence in Seattle with his family. The four had always believed that if any one of them left Athens, it would be fatal to the band. Yet R.E.M. came through this potentially sundering crossing with its solidarity (within the new paradigm) intact, only to weather an acrimonious split with the group's manager of 16 years. However, R.E.M.'s real trial was just approaching.

In 1997, Bill Berry announced that he was quitting, after 17 years behind the drumkit, to pursue a more peaceful existence on his Georgia farm. Naturally, the three remaining members considered throwing in the towel at this juncture, but only for a brief moment, for they had new material for the band's next studio venture that they were excited about. It was fortunate that Berry made his move after the group had begun to lay the groundwork for this next effort, rather than at the conclusion of the tour, before the four had spun new musical fibers to keep them interwoven. The group let him go, promising that R.E.M. would prevail. There was to be no replacement sticksman recruited. The thought of hiring another drummer, a "fake Bill," didn't appeal to the remaining members of the band, who felt it would be disrespectful to their longtime friend.[8] Besides, Berry's departure was fortuitous in that it gave the group license to explore the territory of machine-generated sounds, which was the direction the band had been headed anyway. In a sense, then, his absence and the attendant collapse of the traditional four-piece unit were liberating for R.E.M., which set about redefining itself as a trio. Stipe likened the post–Berry band to a three-legged dog that has to learn to walk again. The members knew that a painful adjustment awaited them, but they didn't realize the full extent of the permutation R.E.M. would undergo.

Instead of taking time off to reconfigure in calm waters, the streamlined R.E.M. plunged straight into recording its eleventh album. By trying to redesign the band and make a record at the same time, the band members put enormous pressure on themselves. Communication broke down and mutual resentment sprung up, until the three found themselves completely estranged from one another. As the situation went from bad to worse, for all intents and purposes the band ceased to exist. "I had to get used to the idea that we had completely split up," Stipe later confided to *Q*. "I was working on what I thought would be our last will and testament." He adds that it was "awful" to witness relationships so important to him "fold and collapse," and that he gradually forced himself to come to terms with the thought of a life beyond R.E.M.[9]

But this resignation to his new lot proved premature. An emergency summit was held to see if the group could be salvaged. Stipe, Buck and Mills were prepared to walk away from this meeting as solo artists in the event that the fissures in the band could not be sealed, but they emerged reunited. "In the end, we had to bring ourselves back together as friends and as musicians because we're not ready to be torn apart," Stipe remarked about the ultimate outcome of the fracas.[10] The trio adjusted its approach, and managed to pull the album together, despite additional problems like Stipe's writer's block. Proving the old adage that what doesn't kill you makes you stronger, the band declared that the ordeal had availed their friendship.

Up took fans and critics by surprise because it deviated so dramatically from R.E.M.'s earlier material, and sales were alarmingly weak. Stipe believes that the record was such a shocker because Berry's absence forced the band to mutate at an accelerated rate. It would have taken R.E.M. two or three more albums to arrive at *Up* if they had continued as a quartet, he postulated in *The New York Times* (1998). The group certainly felt that *Up* was as good as any of its other records, though conceded that it could have been even better had it been conceived in a less fractious environment. Accentuated by lush arrangements and Beach Boy harmonies, *Reveal* (2000) was the band's next LP. Reflecting the relaxed and enjoyable atmosphere in which it was created, this album contained more sunny and uplifting songs. Clearly, R.E.M. was settling into its new iteration and evolving as a trio. "Imitation of Life," the first single, was a big hit in the UK, but *Reveal* didn't provide an antidote for the lackluster North American sales of the band's post–*Monster* releases.

According to all three members of R.E.M., the relations within the group have never been better, and, commercial viability aside, they feel that they can still make worthwhile music together. Having faced the prospect of the band's end, they have gained a new perspective on how fortunate they are to be in it. In 2004, they confirmed with the politically-charged *Around the Sun* that they continue to find their collaboration inspiring. The trio has taken flak for going on without Berry, but this is a band the members describe as unusually insular, finding in solidarity the strength to rely solely on their shared internal barometer. Says Stipe: "Ranks cannot be broken; when we get in a huddle, that's that. It's served us well. We've forged our own path. We've made horrible mistakes, but we can't blame them on anyone else."[11]

THE RED HOT CHILI PEPPERS: THE INDESTRUCTIBLE BAND
LOS ANGELES, CALIFORNIA, USA
ANTHONY KIEDIS: VOCALS
MICHAEL "FLEA" BALZARY: BASS GUITAR
JOHN FRUSCIANTE: GUITAR (1988–1992; 1998–PRESENT)
CHAD SMITH: DRUMS
(HILLEL SLOVAK: GUITAR 1983–1988)
(DAVE NAVARRO: GUITAR 1992–1998)

In its infancy, the Red Hot Chili Peppers was essentially a party band that music industry insiders believed wouldn't last long or even make a blip on the mainstream radar. Fast-forward a couple of decades and it turns out that these oft-labeled "Hollywood ruffians" have become renowned musicians, with top-selling albums, scores of imitators, and legions of fans. Few of those familiar with the group's story fail to be impressed by its ability to overcome obstacles and turn virtually any setback into an advantage, earning the L.A. outfit a reputation for being indestructible. Over the course of its 20-year existence, this band has experienced a series of surprising and seemingly destiny-directed personnel shifts that shed unique light on chemistry, group dynamics and the fact that some lineups are simply meant to be.

L-R: Jack Irons, Hillel Slovak, Flea, Anthony Kiedis. A classic shot of the original Red Hot Chili Peppers lineup. They were enamored with the idea of four close friends unleashing their unusual brand of funk-rock on the world, but this dream was to prove short lived, as guitarist Hillel Slovak died tragically of an overdose and drummer Jack Irons departed immediately afterwards. The band would become adept at rebuilding. Photofest (Nels Israelson).

Four high school friends formed the band somewhat inadvertently in 1983. From their earliest days at Hollywood's Fairfax High School, Anthony Kiedis, Michael "Flea" Balzary and Hillel Slovak were an inseparable trio, sharing a special bond and sense of brotherhood. Flea was a talented trumpet player who hoped to make it as a jazz musician while the Israeli-born Slovak had dedicated himself to the guitar. When they were 16, Slovak taught Flea to play bass, at the same time introducing him to some of his musical idols, like Kiss and Jimi Hendrix. The two started a band together with another close friend of Slovak's, Jack Irons, on drums. Sometimes serving as emcee at his friends' gigs, one night Kiedis assumed a more central role for what was supposed to be a one-off performance billed as Tony Flow and the Majestic Masters of May-

L-R: Chad Smith, Anthony Kiedis, John Frusciante, Flea. Shortly after reuniting with Frusciante, the Chili Peppers began reaping the benefits of the group's restored chemistry, picking up numerous awards for 1999's *Californication*. The band members' closeness and mutual affection are clearly evident in this candid shot. They have never been chary of openly expressing their brotherly love for one another. CP (Kim Johnson).

hem. He joined the others onstage, speed-reading a poem he had written as the band played in the background.

The event was a turning point in more ways than one. From this single impromptu experiment, the group and its genre-bending sound blending funk, punk and rock with rapid-fire rap-style vocals emerged. This unprecedented hodgepodge drove the crowd wild, and Kiedis was transformed by the thrill of performing. The owner of the club at which the legendary event took place begged the band to return with more of this incendiary material and the four agreed. They dubbed their outfit the Red Hot Chili Peppers and began writing songs shaped by their unorthodox views about music and life. While the band members clearly gelled musically, the ties of friendship between them provided the foundation for a strong unit. From the outset, the rabble-rousing quartet displayed an unmistakable gang mentality, referring to themselves as the "Four Motherfuckers from Fairfax."[12] Their brotherhood has, in fact, often been celebrated in the group's music, where it figures as a prominent lyrical theme.

The band's galvanizing live shows, erupting with energy and peppered with all manner of outrageous capers (including the famed socks-on-cocks routine), quickly gave it a strong local following. It took only a few months for the band to get signed, with EMI snapping it up in 1984. That year, the Red Hot Chili Peppers put out a self-titled debut album. This record did not feature Slovak or Irons, who opted to stay in the group they had formed long before the Chili Peppers materialized, What Is This (which had also been taken on by a label). So Jack Sherman and Cliff Martinez, on guitar and drums, respectively, were hired to replace the members missing from the Chili Peppers for the band's first studio effort.

Despite the fact that most of the songs were already written, with only half the band present to record them, the album failed to capture the magic evoked by the live shows in which all four members had participated. A contentious atmosphere also marred the sessions. Producer Andy Gill proved surprisingly conservative, provoking animosity in Kiedis and Flea. Adding to the tension and strife were the rancorous relations between Kiedis and Sherman. Their wrangling reached a crescendo on the subsequent tour, at the end of which Sherman was sacked. It was obvious that neither Sherman nor Martinez truly shared the inherent spirit and vision of this band. This was the first, but by no means the last, time that Flea and Kiedis would encounter the limitations involved in working without their preferred lineup.

For the group's next effort, *Freaky Styley* (1985), Slovak returned to play guitar but Martinez continued on drums. Venerable funk maestro George Clinton took over production duties, bestowing on the band a sense of legitimacy and consequence, while bringing to bear his expertise in the genre the quartet wanted to explore more thoroughly. The happy months the quartet spent in Clinton's Detroit home resulted in a lifelong friendship with the father of funk and a sophomore effort head-and-shoulders above its forerunner. In 1986, Irons returned to the fold, restoring the Chili Peppers' founding lineup in time to contribute to the group's third studio album, *The Uplift Mofo Party Plan*. Released in 1987, this record fared better than its predecessors, even eking out a spot on the Billboard chart (No. 148). It was followed a few months later by the *Abbey Road* EP, containing tracks from the group's back catalogue, which the mini-album was meant to promote. Combined with their frank sexual commentary and predilection for performing in as little clothing as possible, songs like "Catholic Schoolgirls Rule" and "Party on Your Pussy" stamped the Red Hot Chili Peppers as sex-obsessed, artistically lightweight misfits. It was an extremely tenacious image that would often serve as grounds for dismissing the band in later years. But, at this juncture, it didn't look as if the Chili Peppers had a future at all.

Flea has said that the band was formed "out of music and friendship," but it was drug use that shattered the group just as it started to gain momentum.[13] Slovak and Kiedis had developed hardcore heroin addictions that began to put their lives in jeopardy and take a grim toll on the band. The two made a pact to lay off all ruinous substances and watch each other's backs. United in their resolve, they found the strength to stay clean, and were aided by the structure and routine provided by touring. They soon discovered that it took the group's support to keep them on the straight and narrow. Upon returning home from an exhausting round of European dates and going their separate ways, both Kiedis and Slovak slid back into heroin abuse. In the case of the 26-year-old Slovak, this relapse proved fatal. An overdose ended his life abruptly in June 1988.

Slovak's untimely death left his friends with a hole in their hearts and a vacancy in the band. While the emotional void resulting from his loss would never be filled, the remaining Chili Peppers decided to find a guitarist to take Slovak's place and carry on. But before long, they were to find themselves short of a drummer as well. Devastated by the loss of his friend and fearing that Kiedis was on a similar path to destruction, Jack Irons bowed out of the band following Slovak's death. Flea and Kiedis were now the only remaining members of the Red Hot Chili Peppers, and the singer was still in the throes of drug addiction. It was a desolate period in the group's history, but the tragedy that had truncated it also instilled a new resolve in the two old friends to focus on their music and prove its worth to the world. Rather than call it quits, the pair moved forward in the face of adversity, keeping the band going through the sheer power of determination. They began looking for musicians to replace those they had lost, knowing that they needed to do more than just put together a band; they needed to form another gang. Though Irons and Slovak were gone, nothing had changed in terms of the Chili Peppers' definition of a band, which is rooted in "friends sharing their lives," not "strangers coming together to make music."[14]

It wasn't easy, but the search eventually yielded two new members who would ultimately fit into the Red Hot Chili Peppers like perfectly chiseled puzzle pieces, though, on the surface, they were dubious choices. Chad Smith was a metalhead from Detroit who had never listened to the band's music. Nevertheless, in typical drummer fashion, he was both down-to-earth and laid-back, bringing to the group what Kiedis has called "simple, powerful rhythms" that had a "monstrous" impact on its sound and appeal.[15] The other gem the Chili Peppers picked up at this time was guitar prodigy John Frusciante, a die-hard fan who was a mere teenager when he joined the already-seasoned band. He displayed such promise and was so thoroughly familiar with the group's material that he was asked to join it despite his youth and inexperience. Fortune had clearly smiled upon Frusciante, now performing with the band whose shows he had zealously attended night after night, but the others were equally lucky to have stumbled upon the talented guitarist, with whom they felt an instant chemistry that revitalized the group. The newcomers created a different outfit altogether but one with a similarly cohesive unit and creative force at its core. In the years to come, this was to become the definitive Red Hot Chili Peppers lineup, though the group was not yet through with personnel changes.

Fully staffed for the time being, the band made two albums that elevated its trademark sound and also took its music in fresh directions. Smith and Frusciante, no mere accomplices to veterans Flea and Kiedis, became half of the band's songwriting team from the moment they came on board. *Mother's Milk* was the first fruit of their union, and it brought the group more notice than it had hitherto received. On the strength of tracks like the pummeling "Knock Me Down" and a breathtaking cover of Stevie Wonder's "Higher Ground," the LP went gold. It was with its next record, *Blood Sugar Sex Magik,* that the band realized its promise and finally gained mainstream appeal. This album, the group's first on the Warner label and with über-producer Rick Rubin at the helm, captured the Chili Peppers' now well-honed funk at its early peak and effectively showcased the foursome's growing versatility as songwriters. In addition to the poignant ballad "Under the Bridge," which went on to become a huge hit and signature anthem, *Blood Sugar Sex Magik* spawned a number of well-known singles, including "Breaking the Girl" and the Grammy-winning "Give It Away." Selling over three million copies in the year following its release and peaking at N0.3 in the U.S., the record turned the Red Hot Chili Peppers into a headlining act. "We knew it was a watershed for us," says Kiedis.[16]

In the shadows of *Blood Sugar Sex Magik*'s public success, another height had quietly been scaled. As a unit, the Chili Peppers had developed an exceptional solidarity. During the making of *Mother's Milk,* the members of the reborn group were still in the process of connecting with and adapting to one another. They were also dealing with issues in their personal lives that made it difficult to concentrate on cementing the bonds within the group. The follow-up album, benefiting from the protracted tour that preceded it and exerted a centripetal force over the group, was created in an atmosphere of harmony and fellowship, with the band not only working together but also living together for several months in a Hollywood mansion-turned-studio. This era was immortalized in the *Funky Monks* documentary, which contains footage of the recording sessions and portrays the band at the apex of its closeness. In Rubin, the Red Hot Chili Peppers had found an ideal producer, and in each other, an inspiring kinship and transcendent musical telepathy. Both had an obvious impact on the band's music.

The fraternity forged during the recording of *Blood Sugar Sex Magik* only made the events that followed more shocking, although Kiedis revealed a decade later that "the seeds for destruction" were being planted even while the four reveled in the brotherhood and burst of creativity that resulted in the record.[17] In 1992, when the band embarked upon a global trek in support of the album, these seeds were sown. The camaraderie between the bandmates rapidly disintegrated under the pressures of their newfound celebrity, and, partly as a result, John Frusciante announced before taking the stage in Japan that he was leaving the band. To outsiders, most of whom were unaware of any tensions in the group, the announcement was a surprise, but to insiders, his decision was not entirely shocking. Alienated by rock stardom, frustrated with the more commercial direction in which the band was going, lamenting the fading bond between the band members and fed up with touring, Frusciante was a guitar-slung time bomb.

During their last year on the road together, Frusciante became conspicuously apathetic and failed to relate to the group on any level. The Chili Peppers consequently found themselves operating in a state of fractiousness that is absolutely stifling for a group in which an emotional intimacy is the mandatory prerequisite for artistic creation. As the tour wore on, this intimacy, which they had established with Frusciante with surprising ease, palpably diminished. Some musicians choose to carry on under such circumstances, but the situation was unbearable for Frusciante, and the band, too, was cracking under the strain of internal division. Still, no one wanted to see the guitarist leave. On the contrary, for the group, having found its missing link in Frusciante, his departure was absolutely wrenching. Once again, the Chili Peppers had an incomplete unit on their hands. Worse still, this was the second time in four years that they had lost a kindred musical spirit and close friend. But, with typical doggedness, the drummer, bassist and singer resolved to keep going. Shortly after Frusciante left, Kiedis declared to *Rolling Stone* the band's intention to replace him: "He is one of the most deeply soulful guitar players that we've ever been connected with. Also, he's a good friend, and we had something going that was cosmic and special. And we're going to have to find that elsewhere."[18] This would prove more difficult than they imagined.

The search was once again on for a new Chili Peppers guitarist. Several added their name to the list, including Arik Marshall, with whom the band headlined the 1992 Lollapalooza tour, and Jesse Tobias, who joined briefly after Marshall's departure. None of these musicians were ultimately right for the group. Finally, the band recruited Dave Navarro, formerly of the vanguard alternative outfit Jane's Addiction. The newest Chili Pepper was an inspired musician, a star in his own right, and got along well with the rest of the band. Aside from the fact that he disliked funk, he was a great catch, and, with his dark, edgy aesthetic, a seemingly ideal match for a group eager to expand its musical vocabulary. But Navarro's troubled stint with the Red Hot Chili Peppers was relatively short, and, defying expectations, far from sensational. *One Hot Minute* (1995), the title of the sole album they recorded with him, strangely prophesied its own fate. Released four years after *Blood Sugar Sex Magik,* the laboriously completed record was regarded as an unworthy follow-up to its predecessor. After a falsely encouraging start, it quickly slipped off the charts. It had been so difficult to complete the project, with Kiedis back on smack and groping for lyrics while the musicians in this latest incarnation of the group struggled to find common ground, that the Chili Peppers were in no hurry to embark on another.

In 1998, having spent nearly six years together, Navarro and the Red Hot Chili Peppers parted ways, citing artistic differences as the reason for the split. Though he had come closer than anyone else to filling the void in the group and completing the circle, the singular dynamic the Chili Peppers had with Frusciante was obviously missing, and its absence was strongly felt. It was evident that Frusciante belonged in this band in a way that no one else did. But reinstating him was practically mission impossible. He had spent the six years since exiting the Chili Peppers a virtual hermit, filling his days with painting, writing, and ingesting extraordinary amounts of drugs. He seemed bent on self-annihilation.

As if his condition weren't a sufficiently immovable obstacle, there was also lingering animosity between Frusciante and Kiedis that could not but get in the way of a reunion. Incredibly, the band overcame these snags, and not a minute too soon, since, by 1997, it seemed as doomed and debilitated as its former guitarist. On his part, Frusciante managed to kick his life-threatening drug habit, making a miraculous return to mental and physical health. Flea, who had kept in touch with the recluse throughout his junkie period, learned of this and suggested making a bid to get Frusciante back. To this end, he invited the guitarist to jam with the band of which he had once been such a vital member.

No one expected the meeting to go smoothly. There was remaining resentment and hurt that would need to be healed with time and discourse. As for the magical musical understanding the four had once shared, that might be gone forever. "What are the odds the chemistry will work for a minute?" Kiedis recalls thinking.[19] But upon convening in Flea's garage, the quartet discovered that, from both a personal and artistic perspective, they had barely skipped a beat in six years (not counting the fact that Frusciante's command of the frets had considerably deteriorated, an impediment his bandmates disregarded). The hard feelings they had harbored towards one another for most of the decade melted away, replaced by a profound joy in renewing their partnership. "[F]rom the first time we got together to play, I felt completely levitated," Kiedis remarked in 1999.[20]

Reunited, the band embarked, as they had done once before with Frusciante, on a path of trailblazing musical discovery and commercial reward. The multi-platinum *Californication* was released in 1999, earning the quartet another Grammy award for the chart-dominating single "Scar Tissue." The Chili Peppers went on to complete a triumphant tour in support of the group's biggest album to date, and followed it up with 2002's highly-acclaimed *By the Way*, which saw the quartet experiment with a new palette of sound that considerably broadened its fan base. By the summer of 2004, when the Peppers performed for a record-breaking throng during three dates at London's Hyde Park (preserved for posterity on a live double-album), they were arguably the biggest band in the world. In 2006, they released a double album, *Stadium Arcadium.* They revealed that the *By the Way* sessions had been quite fractious, as they each tried to dominate the creative process, but the friction diminished when they recorded the follow-up with a greater team spirit.

Although the Red Hot Chili Peppers have been blessed with a once-in-a-lifetime lineup twice, it's been a rough ride to the top. But, rather than wondering what they could have achieved without all the vicissitudes along the way, they accept the fact that this was the path they had to travel to arrive at their current position. Kiedis put a typically positive spin on the band's epic journey in an interview on AOL *Sessions*: "Maybe it's been good for us that we haven't had some sort of stagnant consistency. Maybe it's the way it was meant to be for us, that we'd have a lot of peaks and valleys, triumphs and tragedies."[21] Their experiences with band formation and disintegration, particularly the loss and reacquisition of Frusciante, have given the Chili Peppers uncommon insight into the extraordinary mechanics of rock bands and what it takes to make these enterprises work.

RADIOHEAD: ADVENTURES IN COLLABORATION
OXFORD, ENGLAND
THOM YORKE: VOCALS, GUITAR, PIANO
JONNY GREENWOOD: GUITAR
COLIN GREENWOOD: BASS GUITAR
ED O'BRIEN: GUITAR
PHIL SELWAY: DRUMS

Despite being dismissed as a one-hit wonder when their infectious anthem "Creep" hijacked radio stations the world over in 1993, Radio-

L-R: Ed O'Brien, Jonny Greenwood, Thom Yorke, Colin Greenwood, Phil Selway. An early publicity shot. Radiohead gained instant fame at this time with its first album, putting the five school friends in a high-pressure situation that nearly tore the group apart. Ultimately, they decided not to strangle the band at birth and found a way to move forward. Photofest (Tom Sheehan).

head, in the decade following the release of its debut LP, has risen swiftly to the rank of legend, establishing itself at the same time as a resilient and resourceful unit. Since advancing from a practice room at school to the world stage, there has been enormous pressure on the band to prove itself time and again, and it has often come close to being crushed by the weight of these expectations. By making onerous demands upon themselves, the band members have often added to this load. Indeed, one of Radiohead's monumental accomplishments, but one that nearly tore the group apart, has been redefining the parameters of collective musical composition in pursuit of a fresh sound and approach.

Officially, Radiohead came into existence in 1991, but the five founding members had been playing together since their early teens. Although

L-R: Ed O'Brien, Phil Selway, Thom Yorke, Colin Greenwood, Jonny Greenwood. Looking glum in 1997, despite the fact that the band had a lot to smile about at this time. Things would get worse before they got better, as the five friends started to push against each other as soon as they stopped fighting the world together. CP/Rex Features (Roger Sargent).

they weren't all in the same year at the boy's school near Oxford where they met, Phil Selway, Thom Yorke, Colin Greenwood and Ed O'Brien shared an interest in music that led to their association under the matter-of-fact banner On a Friday (signifying the group's weekly rehearsal date). Colin Greenwood's younger brother, Jonny, a budding musician and jazz enthusiast, was a constant presence during the Friday afternoon jams until he was finally admitted to the group. The gifted and prolific Yorke wrote most of the unit's material. His bandmates were both impressed and motivated by the quality of his songs. As each of the five young men graduated in turn from school, they duly went off to university. They were scattered throughout the country during these years, but kept the group alive during holidays and the occasional weekend rehearsal, demonstrating their incredible passion for and dedication to the band. From the outset, they wanted the group to have a future and did not waver from that purpose.

In the summer of 1991, their university degrees secured, the band reformed as planned and began gigging around Oxford. Shortly afterwards, Parlaphone signed the group, which adopted a new moniker: Radiohead. The label uptake was quick—a matter of months—but the quintet was ready to play in the bigger leagues, with the members having spent years as a schoolboy band honing their skills and nurturing a group sensibility. Still, nothing could have prepared them for the startling events that followed the release of their debut album, or the effect they would ultimately have on the band and its future trajectory.

Radiohead first hit the airwaves in 1992 with the EP *Drill*. The British press promptly derided it as the unworthy product of an upstart outfit that had not paid its dues. This was the opening salvo in the British music tabloids' love-hate affair with Radiohead that caused the fledgling quintet a great deal of angst. *Pablo Honey* (1993) was Radiohead's first long-player. Preceding the album's release was the single "Creep," a song not particularly representative of the record or Radiohead's general oeuvre. It went nowhere upon its initial appearance in September 1992. Without warning, months after its release, and just as Radiohead arrived to play some North American dates, "Creep" took off in the U.S.

Radio stations suddenly discovered they had been sitting on a goldmine, a tune featuring the trendy Nirvana-esque theme of the outsider's self-flagellation, and began playing the song relentlessly. The group's victory in the U.S. with "Creep" was a blessing and a curse for the band in many ways. On the one hand, "Creep" launched the group's mainstream career with one stroke. It gained Radiohead recognition on both sides of the Atlantic, since the track made the UK top 10 when it was re-released there at the end of the year, marking its conquest of America. Owing to the hit single, *Pablo Honey* was a commercial blockbuster in the U.S., far outselling the debut albums of other contemporary British bands.

However, pegged as the "Creep" band, Radiohead became synonymous with this track and was saddled with the dreaded one-hit-wonder label. "Creep" overshadowed the rest of Radiohead's work and came close to eclipsing the band itself. There were also implications for the band's career progression. Shortly after completing *Pablo Honey*, the quintet realized that they could put together a far better album. They felt that this first effort had been hampered by their inexperience in the studio, awkward track sequencing, and lack of true group cohesion. By the time "Creep" erupted, the five were itching to record new material that would do more justice to their aptitude and sound. Instead, they ended up having to tour the U.S. extensively, first on the crest of the single's success, and then in an attempt to prove that the group was more than just that one song. What ended up being a two-year tour of an album the band wasn't fully behind dragged on, leading to significant internal strife.

Not surprisingly, Radiohead came close to calling it quits at this time. The whole situation was enough to make any serious and ambitious band disintegrate. According to Colin Greenwood, the group suffered a collective "breakdown" rather than a "breakup."[22] While it's possible to recover from the former and move forward, the latter spells the end. As Yorke points out, having a hit as big as "Creep" would normally kill a band just out of the start gate. But Radiohead survived. Undoubtedly, the group's ability to rise above the complicated situation stemmed from the fact that, though *Pablo Honey* was its first release, the five had been together for nearly eight years and were bound to one another by friendship and a long-nurtured, shared determination to make it—no matter what.

When the band was finally able to get off the road and back into the studio, it faced a predictable dilemma. What could Radiohead do to certify, given recent events and media sneers over the fluke success of "Creep," that it was a band of substance? Not knowing in which direction to go, although they had many new tunes to work with, the five shilly-shallied for several fruitless months. They had to get as far away from the hit single as possible, but how to do so became the million-dollar question. The impasse at which the band found itself did not benefit from the fact that relations within the collective were shaky, and communication between the members had by and large broken down. Doubt and anxiety plagued everyone, but they kept their feelings hidden from one another. According to Jonny Greenwood, this was an "insidious" and "depressing" period for the group.[23] Escaping from the mounting pressures and unproductive recording sessions, the band checked out of the studio and hit the road again to resume what it did best: perform live. During the brief tour, the quintet recaptured the enthusiasm and confidence that had always sustained it.

Many of the problems within the unit were also resolved during this trek, when the five finally had it out with each other in Mexico. There was a major blowup between the longtime friends in which issues that had been brewing, but had never been dealt with, were dragged into the light and confronted. When the shouting subsided, the band members were on much better terms and able to speak openly with one another for the first time in years. It made a world of difference. Returning to the studio with their musical and personal wrinkles ironed out, Radiohead completed the album in a matter of weeks.

Yorke had this to say about the band's turning point: "Years and years of tension and not saying anything to each other, and basically all the things that had built up since we'd met each other, all came out in one day." They confronted all the issues they had neglected to discuss in the past during this nasty fight, which cleared their path. "I think that completely changed what we did and we all went back and did the album and it all made sense."[24] Containing hauntingly beautiful tracks, such as "High and Dry," "My Iron Lung," and "Street Spirit (Fade Out)," underscored by intricate guitar-work, *The Bends* (1995) is now widely considered one of the finest releases of the 1990s. With this album, Radiohead earned the critical respect it deserved, but not, at least initially, the public attention such an outstanding rock record merited. It took nearly a year, the cumulative effect of several singles, a slot opening for R.E.M., and many citations on "Best of 1995" lists before the album began to catch on. Finally, in 1996, *The Bends* began to climb both the U.S. and UK charts.

In the fall of 1996, after another extended blitz of live shows, the group began work on its third album. Given the impression *The Bends* had made on critics, there were great expectations for Radiohead's next project, and the band couldn't help but feel their oppressive weight. Having decided to produce the new record themselves, there was even more pressure on the five members, since they had a lot to learn in a short time and needed to rely on each other more than ever. Radiohead surpassed even the highest hopes by turning out what was deemed its most brilliant work to date. The lofty and elaborate *OK Computer* was hailed as a masterpiece by critics, and made the group, until then a relatively marginal sensation, a hugely important act virtually overnight. The album peaked at number one on the UK charts and at 21 on the U.S. Top 200. Although songs like the six-minute, three-part "Paranoid Android" hardly conformed to radio standards or popular tastes, they won over a broader mainstream audience for the band. At the 1998 Grammy ceremony, Radiohead was honored with the award for Best Alternative Rock Performance.

Everything seemed to be going their way. Radiohead was held up as the saviors of guitar-rock and heirs of the stadium-bound-best-band-in-the-world mantle from U2. Inside the Radiohead camp, however, the outlook was anything but rosy. The band didn't aspire to the messianic status conferred upon it by the press; the five were frustrated with the relentless album-tour-album cycle; and they were nearly leveled by a grueling live schedule and an endless stream of mind-numbing media engagements. Yorke, who, in addition to these issues, was growing increasingly disenchanted with both guitar-driven music and melody, was particularly downcast. In interviews, he cites anger, self-doubt, and a sense that his life had spun out of control as the feelings that practically paralyzed him. Filmmaker Grant Gee's documentary of the tour, *Meeting People Is Easy* (1999), captures the band's mood during this period and sheds light on some of the elements that gave rise to it—too many hotels, handshakes and hollow interviews.

There was unprecedented hype surrounding the follow-up to *OK Computer* because of the group's inflated status and retreat from the public eye after its homecoming. And, of course, everyone was waiting to see if the band could top its magnum opus. Even Radiohead had never before faced this much pressure. *OK Computer* was not only a tremendous musical landmark for Radiohead; its members had reached a higher collective ground while making it. They were working more effectively and seemed to have found their footing, but, when it came time to write the music that would eventually comprise *Kid A* and its sister-release *Amnesiac*, Radiohead's fourth and fifth albums, the group bravely walked away from both the sonic and collaborative breakthroughs it had achieved—even in the face of the frenzied fan and media anticipation.

After virtually disappearing for nearly two years, Radiohead re-emerged in 2000 with the controversial *Kid A*, produced by Nigel Godrich, who was rapidly becoming the band's sixth member in the studio. The quintet's desire to get off the conventional rock treadmill while taking time to reconnect with friends and family after years of touring partly explains the long wait for the new album. Yorke's depression and a severe bout of writer's block also contributed to the delay. Factor in a lengthy gestation for the new material as the band essentially rewired itself, and it becomes clear why *OK Computer* and its successor were delivered three years apart.

Recording of *Kid A* commenced in 1999, but the initial period was spent painfully and, at first, aimlessly, deconstructing both the group's sound and creative process. The quintet began experimenting heavily with electronic equipment and new songwriting approaches in the hopes of deviating from its now-familiar guitar-oriented sound. The five had no real sense of direction, little prewritten material and, having moved into a studio under their own proprietorship, plenty of time to tinker. The first few months of what would be a protracted year-long odyssey were reputedly hellish, nearly proving the group's downfall. Panic and frustration led to frequent crisis meetings, and, as Yorke informed *Rolling Stone* in 2001, there were huge arguments. If no music worth releasing emerged from the chaos, the band members agreed to admit defeat and go their separate ways. But they eventually figured out a new way of composing electronic-inspired music together, and got on such a roll that they ended up with enough material for two albums.

They whittled down the mass of music to 10 songs for a single record, which was released to dramatically opposing reviews. Not only did *Kid A* not sound like anything the band had done before, it didn't resemble what any of its counterparts were doing at the time and didn't fit neatly into any musical categories. Some critics called it courageous and groundbreaking; others saw it as a cop-out and commercial suicide. But, with the record entering the Billboard chart at number one and reaching the top spot in the UK upon its release, the public's vote was unquestionably favorable. The industry later came around as well, as the LP was nominated for a Best Album Grammy. Radiohead did little to promote sales of *Kid A* or tickets for the limited live dates (which sold out in minutes). Short blips took the place of videos, while interviews and appearances were kept to a minimum. When the band did reach out to the masses, performing "Idioteque" and "The National Anthem" on *Saturday Night Live*, new fans zealously joined the existing loyal base.

As for the group, it not only remained intact throughout this arduous metamorphosis, but, as is often the case, the members were unified by the tribulations they had surmounted together. Eight months after the release of *Kid A*, in June 2001, Radiohead introduced another album, *Amnesiac*, featuring additional tracks from the *Kid A* sessions. It consisted of further irregular pieces, such as "Spinning Plates" and "Life in a Glass House," alongside more tuneful numbers like "Knives Out." In 2003, the group unleashed its sixth studio album, *Hail to the Thief*. This time, recording seemed to be relatively stress-free for the quintet, which was determined not to go through another harrowing studio experience. New songs were tried out on a live audience and then, in a matter of weeks, the band cut optimal versions of the ones that met with the most positive response.

Since Thom Yorke is such a strong figurehead for the group and a highly accomplished songwriter, some observers have remarked that the others in Radiohead are nothing more than his backup band. Any member of the group will admit that Yorke is quite often its main mover and shaker, but would also point out that none of them would be content to ride on his coattails, which is another way of saying that their contribution is absolutely crucial. Acknowledging the singer's rare creative gift, O'Brien points out that it's the band that gives the music "soul."[25] And Yorke has always maintained that the interdependency of the group extends to all involved, including himself.

2

"Begin the Begin": Reasons for Forming the Band

Understanding the reasons these bands came into existence provides tremendous insight into their unity and the foundation of their group dynamic. Why did the members join a band in the first place and what was it about their particular group that hooked them and seemed right?

Mutual malcontent

For Radiohead, U2, and R.E.M., one of the primary motivations for starting a band was to alleviate boredom and escape from the even more mundane future the members believed awaited them. Getting into a band was their way of opting out of the "real" world, a ticket to freedom—albeit an uncertain one. Mutual malcontent is what brought the members of U2 together, confesses Bono. They were disenchanted by school and didn't relish the bourgeois prospects beyond it. "We didn't want to get a job in a factory or work for the government. We didn't want to be schoolteachers or join the army or whatever." Like a street gang, the band members weren't initially drawn together by a shared musical mission but by "their sense of what they are against more than what they are for."[1]

Adam Clayton makes joining U2 sound like signing up for the Peace Corps. For him, the main attraction wasn't the idea of writing great songs, but the very notion of being part of a group unified by an overriding goal, the "whole experience of being a band of four people with the one cause; a cause you could develop and become emotionally involved in."[2] However, Bono stressed to *In Fashion* that this noble cause had more to

43

do with saving their own asses, and not, as people tend to think, the world. He isn't ashamed to concede that naked ambition and fantasies of rock stardom played a role as well. "You want to play to the crowd rather than be in the crowd. I wanted to own up to all this because people look at U2 and see all these pure motives—but we started off being in a band for the most impure motives."[3] What the band seemed to bestow upon the four, particularly Bono, who had grown up in a lower-middle class Dublin neighborhood, was a sense of destination, the singer told author Niall Stokes, because even if they had little hope of getting anywhere individually, together, they were a formidable force—and they knew it. Even when they were still messing up Ramones covers, Bono and Clayton believed the band had what it took to go all the way.

R.E.M.'s founding four may have come from slightly more middle class backgrounds than their Irish contemporaries and been on a college career path when they hooked up, but staving off ennui was for them, too, a significant motivator. Small-town life appears to have been the culprit in this case. The band was "nothing more than something to do [to] maybe annihilate a little of the boredom that you get around here," proclaimed Bill Berry in 1983.[4] Like Bono, Michael Stipe has owned up to the fact that he didn't want to join a band for entirely noble reasons. He confessed in *The Independent* in 2003 that he was enticed in part by teenage fantasies of superstardom, travels and bedding groupies.

Fairly prosperous backgrounds and a preppy boys' school outside of Oxford left five students, who would eventually form Radiohead, equally unsatisfied with their lives. The private school they attended was far from fun, bassist Colin Greenwood conveyed to *Request,* so they used music to carve a space for themselves away from an environment they found stifling and monotonous. The band was their private entertainment, and presented a more appealing career option than any others open to them. There is a long history of British teens with a similar upbringing forming such gangs and turning to music as a reaction to the middle class treadmill, notes Ed O'Brien. Where once they may have fled their homes to join the circus, says Yorke, they later started eloping with bands to escape from an oppressive reality. (U2 drummer Larry Mullen, in fact, told *The Sunday Times* in 2004 that joining the group felt like running away to the circus.) And there's an element of Peter Pan to it as well, since being in a band represents a refusal to grow up, claims the Radiohead frontman. Joining a band is a last desperate attempt at a different kind of life, he once explained to *NME* (1993), before you give up and take a job like everyone else.

Misfits unite

Another factor that led these individuals to join forces was their inability to fit into the mainstream. To a large extent, these bands represented a refuge for misfits, in the positive rather than pejorative sense that the members were, in many cases, artsy, sensitive, deliberately rebellious, or inherently nonconformist. "We were four completely different people, four people going nowhere," says Bono, "and we decided to go there together. Four rejects, on all different levels, from the system. Four people—four intelligent people—who probably wouldn't be accepted for the E.S.B. or the Civil Service."[5] With the exception of the steadfast Larry Mullen, the three schoolmates who filled out the band were truly different from most of their fellow students. Clayton was a downright outcast, who had been expelled from many a strict boarding school and was later ousted even from the liberal Mount Temple for streaking across campus in his birthday suit. He even looked the part of the freak, sporting a conspicuous peroxide-blonde Afro and long Caftan coat. Paul Hewson, aka Bono, was a fairly infamous character in his own right, part of a street gang called Lypton Village comprised of oddball artsy types. A quieter, brainy sort, Dave Evans, aka The Edge, was no less of an outsider in his own way. According to a *Rolling Stone* interview he gave in 1987, it was this that led him to pick up the guitar.

Regarded by both the media and the public as endearingly eccentric, Michael Stipe is credited with popularizing the figure of the enigmatic rock star. Even among the unconventional students at the art school he left in order to focus on the band, he stuck out and was considered strange, not merely because he was painfully shy and had a very idiosyncratic fashion sense. If Stipe can be described as something of a beatnik, Peter Buck was simply offbeat. Instead of concentrating on his studies, he took a job as a record store clerk, which was the closest he believed he'd ever get to a musical career. When he wasn't busy stashing out of sight the best punk albums in the store's inventory, he would sit behind the counter in a leather jacket strumming a guitar. Berry and Mills were in completely different camps at college—the latter ran with the nerdy set and the former with the pot-smokers—but both were, in their own way, on the social periphery.

The members of Radiohead have always felt like outsiders, both collectively and individually. They wrote a song about it ("Creep") which catapulted them to stardom. But perhaps no band is, in essence, more a league of misfits than the Red Hot Chili Peppers. Anthony Kiedis said it best when he remarked about Flea and himself: "He was a freak and I was a freak, so we decided to freak together."[6] The clowns of Hollywood's Fairfax High School, the two were known for wearing outlandish clothes and performing outrageous deeds, signifying the extent to which they stood out from the crowd. In 2002, Kiedis recollected in *Guitar World* that he deliberately wanted to stand out from the masses so he dressed differently and perversely steered clear of the music most of the kids in his school were listening to. Flea admits that his friend's attitude rubbed off on him and he became similarly defiant about his deviance and strove to accentuate it. Hillel Slovak and Jack Irons were less visible and notorious, primarily because they had been absorbed in playing music from a young age and worked at it seriously (which made them anomalous in one sense). But they shared with the other pair an uncommon lust for life and freedom of spirit.

The love of music

Having said the above, the obvious motivator must not be omitted: these bands were established because of the members' love for music. According to Colin Greenwood, for the Radiohead clan (with the possible exception of Yorke, who had been writing songs since his early teens), this took the form of a desire to play specifically with one another. "We were people who picked up their respective instruments because we wanted to play music together, rather than just because we wanted to play that particular instrument."[7] For them, the whole concept of making music revolved around the collective. With the exception of Anthony Kiedis (who landed the lead vocalist's role in the band by accident), the founders of the Red Hot Chili Peppers were dedicated musicians who honed their chops in numerous L.A. outfits and who had always worked towards playing professionally. Yet, they, too, were especially enamored with the notion of the four of them propagating the unique sound they had forged in unison. "It was just a matter of us being friends and what a fine idea it would be to have four close friends as bearers of the zany new funk we had in our minds and bodies," explains Kiedis.[8] In other words, the three yearned to play music in general, but were particularly passionate about doing so with their Fairfax brothers.

Of the students who responded to Larry Mullen's invitation to form a band, none had an unquenchable thirst to play music individually, let alone with the other bunglers that showed up. But the concept of a band intrigued the four who stuck around, and, when they saw what they could do together under the banner of Feedback (later U2), they became excited at the prospect of both making music and working with one another. "It became an obsession pretty quickly," recalls The Edge. "We all realized that we really liked doing it. We loved playing together and writing songs together."[9] What inspired them to *commit* to this collaboration, once it was in place, was the spark that their combined efforts produced. Once they added some skill to the chemistry, it suddenly dawned on them that there wasn't such a gulf of ability or talent between themselves and bands with recording contracts, so they decided at that point to go for it.

The members of R.E.M.—primarily Peter Buck and Michael Stipe— were also committed to the notion of a musical career and knew that they wanted to be in a band, but didn't immediately find suitable partners. After hearing Patti Smith's *Horses* when he was 15, Stipe had decided to become a singer. But he was 19 and enrolled in a college art program by the time he met Buck. His efforts in the vocal arena had, until then, been limited to the occasional gig fronting for a local band. On his part, the 21-year-old Buck had been waiting patiently behind the counter at Wuxtry Records for a worthwhile opportunity to come along. "I just figured that you'd meet the right people, then you'd get in a band, then you'd make the good music, and people would come and see it."[10] (What neither of them understood, and realized only much later, was that most aspiring musicians spend their entire lives searching for that ideal combination, usually without success.) Mills and Berry had always had a keen interest in playing music but they had essentially given up on the idea and resigned themselves to studying for other professions. Their passion was reawakened when Ian Copeland, a booking agent with industry connections, befriended them and turned them on to new music. Shortly afterwards, they relocated to Athens along with their instruments (which they had sold to and then bought back from Copeland), where they met Stipe and Buck.

A worthwhile alliance

The impetus to form a band together and stick with it boiled down to the simple fact that these artists liked what the other members had to offer, both in terms of their musical skills and what they contributed to compositions. Half-convinced that he would never find a band he would want to perform with because most people can't sing—and "who wants to back up a guy who can't sing?"—Peter Buck was willing to append himself to Stipe because he felt that this was a vocalist worth supporting. "I thought he was good the first time I saw him. He wasn't a Rod Stewart-type frontman, but I thought he had something that, vaguely, most singers don't have. He could sing, for one thing, and that's 90 percent of it right there."[11] Mike Mills may have been a more proficient guitarist than Peter Buck, but the latter's jangly style, reminiscent of the '60s, greatly appealed to him. By the same token, the songs that the rhythm players introduced at the first session were received warmly and enhanced effectively by the other pair. "I really enjoyed what Michael and Peter were doing with the songs Bill and I brought, and it was clearly working," Mills remarked with regards to their first jam.[12] As with U2, the decision (if it can be called that) to stick with this bunch wasn't long in the mulling. The two parties started playing and writing songs together, and a couple of days later, says Buck, they were a band. They didn't even have to try anyone out, he boasts in Tony Fletcher's epic band biography.

Enthusiasm for Thom Yorke's compositions led his four school-friends to devote themselves to Radiohead. Explaining why he made the effort to regularly return to Oxford for band rehearsals while attending Cambridge University, Colin Greenwood remarks: "The important thing for me, apart from the friendship, was the quality of Thom's songs." After listening to an acoustic version of "Creep" that Yorke gave him in 1987, Greenwood recalls thinking: "This is what I want to do. This is my destiny: to help disseminate this music and propel it directly into contemporary popular culture because it's so important."[13] Jonny Greenwood had analogous feelings. He was blown away by the fact that a teenager in his own school could write songs that he felt were well-nigh on par with those of his idol, Elvis Costello. To the same degree that Yorke's friends felt he is a songwriter deserving of support, he recognized that his music benefited from the collaboration with them. At 16, his compositions were, by his own admission, "half-formed."[14] A big step forward for him, he says, was starting to work with the others.

Hillel Slovak, Jack Irons and Flea were masterful musicians who would have been welcomed into virtually any band. And they were, in fact, involved with a number of outfits, some of which had tremendous potential. Aside from their enthusiasm for a band consisting of their gang of friends, what appealed to them about the untried, unknown and less-than-promising Red Hot Chili Peppers? Creative freedom and a high comfort level seem to have been the big attractions. As bassman for the then up-and-coming L.A. hardcore punk band Fear (circa 1982 or 1983), Flea was reaching larger audiences than he had with any of the other groups he'd moonlighted with, was making money for once, and learning how to stage a searing live show. But, as he mentioned in one of his "Fleamails" to the Chili Peppers' official website, he was never really comfortable in Fear, and didn't feel like he could be himself. He attributes his malaise partly to the age gap between him and his bandmates. As time went by, it also became clear that, in this outfit dominated by singer Lee Ving, he would never have the autonomy or influence over the band's vision that he craved, Flea explained to *Bass Player* (1992).

On top of that, Fear had begun to gravitate towards heavy metal, a genre the jazz-bred and punk-loving Flea had little interest in exploring.

After two years with the group, he quit. Although he was invited to join another rising band (PiL), he had had enough of being an accessory player. Once the option of forming a band with his high school buddies presented itself, he didn't hesitate to jump on board, eschewing all other options. The high-voltage funkrock they performed was close to his heart, and he knew that here he could be an active participant in shaping the group and its sound. Similar factors seem to have propelled Hillel Slovak to return to the Chili Peppers after pitching his tent in the What Is This camp when both bands went pro and he was forced to choose between them. Slovak's girlfriend told Jeff Apter when he interviewed her for his biography of the Chili Peppers, *Fornication,* that What Is This was, ultimately, too much frontman Alain Johannes' band. Under the circumstances, the guitarist must have felt that in the company of his "brothers," Flea and Kiedis, his input and therefore his creative satisfaction, would be greater. According to Apter, drummer Jack Irons also came around to the belief that his role in the Red Hot Chili Peppers would be more significant than it was in What Is This. Collective "ownership" over the band was what these musicians sought (and got) in the Red Hot Chili Peppers.

3

"Pyramid Song":
Friends, Collaborators,
Business Partners

Within their single cells, the four bands in this book, like many others, embody three distinct relationships: a friendship, overlaid by an artistic collaboration, overlaid by a business partnership. Of these three relationships constituting rock groups, friendship is the only one that can be dispensed with—at least in theory. From a purely logical perspective, a group of musicians can collaborate and run the business end of their band without more than basic civility between them, and many a group has done with even less. Yet, given that so many bands—these four included—are, in fact, rooted in a deep friendship, and that it quite often serves as the unit's basis and ballast, this relationship is undoubtedly consequential. All three relationships will be examined in this chapter.

Part I: Friendship

FRIENDS FIRST

The original members of the Red Hot Chili Peppers were friends long before they became a band. Music may have strengthened their bond and given them another reason to keep company, but it wasn't what brought them together in the first place. It was, in a sense, just a glorious by-product of their closeness and shared passions. "When friends hang out and truly love each other, cool shit ends up flowing down the river," is Flea's account of how the band evolved from their brotherhood.[1] Before they were the Red Hot Chili Peppers or even Tony Flow and the Majestic Masters of Mayhem, they were a gang of friends, the Four Motherfuckers from Fairax, as they thought of themselves. In the three other groups—R.E.M., Radiohead and U2—the members initially congregated for the purpose of making music, but established meaningful social ties while (or before) cementing their creative alliance. As schoolboys at a private institution near Oxford, the members of Radiohead knew one another, but, with the exception of Thom Yorke and Colin Greenwood, didn't develop a relationship until they began collaborating in On a Friday and became firm friends in the process.

In U2, it was Larry Mullen's schoolboard notice that brought himself, Dave Evans (The Edge), Paul Hewson (Bono), Adam Clayton and a few stray instruments into the same room. They had convened to start a band, but lacking any significant musical training or ability, Feedback was naturally more of a clique or club than a rock group in the early days. After they met, they wanted to hang out together and the instruments (which they couldn't play) were really just an excuse, according to Bono. Clayton concurs, explaining that when they got started "music was very much the secondary thing. We liked each other and got a lot of fun out of it as a social situation."[2] Enjoying one another's company eventually led to the artistic collaboration they had sought in the first place. "The ideas came before the music. We were together, so it just, sort of evolved into music."[3]

Indeed, Bono often stresses the fact that it was four *people*, rather than four *musicians*, who assembled in Mullen's kitchen and plugged into the one amplifier they had between them. "The group was there, before anything," he notes, implying that the *band* grew out of a *nonmusical entity* the four had already created, neither of which would have existed, however, had it not been for the music.[4] They were united first on a personal level and only later on a creative one. However, as he pointed out in a 1983 interview with *Hot Press*, it was music that forged their friendship rather than the other way around. According to Mullen, it wasn't a proper working band until '78 or '79.

Clayton attributes the formation of these early bonds to the fact that he and the others in the group were Dublin schoolboys who teamed up without a defined agenda and without taking a strictly pragmatic view of the band that superseded its fraternal aspect. He presents an alternate scenario in which friendship might not have become the band's bedrock. Had they met in their mid-twenties in London, and tried to form a group out of a desire to get into showbusiness, they would have developed a different kind of relationship, he postulates. In that scenario, the musicians don't necessarily pull together, they just try on the group for size or use it as a stepping-stone. It's not that they weren't ambitious, the bassist clarifies, "it's just that we got together when we were very young—and there was nowhere else to go, that was the nature of those friend-

ships."[5] Bono has remarked on more than one occasion that U2 fits into
a unique band paradigm alongside some of the greats precisely because
they were adolescents, rather than seasoned musicians, at the outset.
That puts U2 in the tradition of The Rolling Stones or The Beatles in
the sense that the members grew up together, contended the singer in
a 1982 interview with *NME*, going on to argue that it's the resulting
process of learning off one another, turning into adults and musicians
collectively, that makes such bands special.

Although they began writing songs together not long after they met
across the counter at Wuxtry Records, Michael Stipe and Peter Buck
clearly shared a strong rapport in addition to their common love for
punk and mutual desire to pursue music. Stipe has often said that in Buck
he found someone he could really talk to, putting an end to his previous solitude. The duo then hooked up with Bill Berry and Mike Mills,
whom they encountered on the local party circuit. Like U2, they got
together to play music, but forged a personal connection from the outset. According to Berry, this has to do with the coincidental and organic
way in which they met (just as the circumstances of U2's formation determined the type of relationships cultivated within that unit). They didn't
find each other through newspaper clippings, he once pointed out, "it
was just something that happened. It overrides everything else in the
band right now. We're friends first, professional musicians second."[6] In
Documental, Buck likens putting together a band and then figuring out
if you can be friends to marrying a stranger. It works out sometimes, but
even so, it's not something he would have wanted for himself.

BONDING

For the sake of practicality, or out of necessity, many young bands
end up living together, which often strengthens their internal bond.
With the exception of U2, all the groups discussed in this book lived
under the same roof early in their career. When they first joined forces,
R.E.M.'s Stipe and Buck occupied an abandoned Episcopal church,
which made a great rehearsal space and even had a stage. It wasn't long
before their rhythm section moved in as well, with Mills taking up residence on the couch. This became the band's base during its formative
period, as well as the historic location of R.E.M.'s first gig. Essentially
street-kids, various members of the original Red Hot Chili Peppers lineup
(particularly Flea and Kiedis) often ended up in the same dwelling
(sometimes as squatters).

After graduating from their respective university programs, the
members of Radiohead regrouped in their hometown, promptly moving en masse into a rented semi-detached house. Although Colin Green-

wood claims they didn't socialize much and tried to avoid one another (presumably, outside of band work), Thom Yorke recalls in *Select* (1998) cozy evenings spent listening to records together and concocting experimental pesto delights in the kitchen. Like any group of friends who become roommates, they enjoyed in-jokes and learned how to deal with the frictions attendant to enforced togetherness. The singer admits that these experiences prepared them for the close quarters of a tour bus. Interestingly, when the band built its own studio, Yorke described it as essentially a throwback to their erstwhile tenement (at least in terms of the mess and clutter).

Aside from sharing a pad on occasion, Flea, Kiedis, and Slovak of the Red Hot Chili Peppers—who formed a close trio—had plenty of opportunities to bond as teenagers by going on camping and skiing trips together. Kiedis stated on VH1's *Behind the Music* that it was these excursions that turned the friends into lifelong soulmates. Coming from broken homes, the three were like family, recounts Flea. "We were so close; we did everything together. First sex, first drugs, first time listening to Gang of Four or Echo & The Bunnymen.... All the most intimate experiences I had."[7] These adventures and the common feelings they engendered made their way directly into the band's music. As a result of the personnel changes that followed the disintegration of this lineup, the Chili Peppers had to do more purposeful bonding than other bands in order to integrate new members. To foster closeness and solidarity with Dave Navarro before going into the studio, the band members spent three months together in Hawaii engaged in intimacy-building activities such as scuba diving and hiking. The rest of the time, they just hung out, with the aim of getting to know each other well. Each of them bought a Harley Davidson and they formed their own riding gang called The Sensitives. These were all deliberate strategies to forge a gang mentality through shared experiences and membership signifiers.

When the chemistry in a group is right and a friendship in place, intentional efforts to cultivate an intimate connection are often unnecessary. The personal bonds are maintained and strengthened by the group's collective life and work, without the members having to actively encourage them. Musicians in bands don't have the kind of conversations people probably think they have, says Yorke. "You click together in the studio or whatever and that's enough to make you feel close to each other. There are no long nights of bonding where you tell each other your innermost fears."[8] This goes for Radiohead, in any event. Guitarist Ed O'Brien concurs, telling *NME* in 1995 that he and his bandmates don't feel the need to discuss all their problems with one another in order to feel mutually attuned. He attributes their lack of interest in this kind of exchange to their upbringing and the type of school they attended, but doesn't feel that their relationship requires more soul-to-soul outpourings.

Even U2's Adam Clayton says that the close-knit members of the quartet are not "hugely intimate" with one another, although he implies that there is less backstage bonding going on now that they are older and have full lives outside of the group. "There is intimacy, but a lot of the time it is a work situation and then everyone goes back to their families. It's more adult."[9] Chad Smith of the Red Hot Chili Peppers notes that he and his three partners can lead fairly separate lives and have completely different interests without weakening their profound sense of attachment to one another. "I don't feel I have to go to yoga meditation class with Flea to feel connected."[10]

FRIENDSHIP SEPARATE FROM BAND-HOOD

Not unexpectedly, the line between friendship and band-hood can become blurry. Clayton's remark, as well as Yorke's comment about clicking mainly in the studio, suggests that personal connections are reinforced primarily by the group's professional activities. Jonny Greenwood also remarked in *NME* in 1993 that since Radiohead became their job, he and his four schoolfriends started seeing each other chiefly within rather than outside of work. But this was not necessarily, I would submit, because they were now more bandmates than buddies or grew sick of one another. There was suddenly a lot more work to be done and what wouldn't have constituted work before, like hanging out and discussing plans, now fell under that banner. The friendships in all four groups do, in fact, seem to transcend the band, and, in most cases, the members don't converge solely for work purposes. In other words, the friendship is not entirely co-opted by the creative partnership.

Despite Clayton's claim that most of the encounters with his U2 cohorts are now work-related, Edge declared in *Spin* (2001) that, at parties, they are frequently found huddled together in a corner by the end of the evening. They also own vacation homes in the South of France and take holidays there together. There are indications that in Radiohead, the five also continue to seek each other out when band business isn't in the picture. Ed O'Brien told *The Musician's Exchange* that, following a long tour, the band members go their separate ways to catch up with friends and family, but, by their second week into a long break, they're already phoning one another up. Anthony Kiedis admitted to *CDNow.com* in 2000 that after spending so much time together in the studio and on the road, he and his three partners generally prefer to be apart when they're not working, but added that their friendship runs deeper than the band. In 2006, the band members remarked that they spend even less of their leisure time together than before, especially now that Flea and Smith have families, but still feel like buddies.

For R.E.M., much has changed over the years because Peter Buck now resides in Seattle while his bandmates have remained based (for the most part) in Athens. The three have few opportunities to fraternize when the band is inactive, quite unlike the early days. By Bill Berry's account, they would regularly hit various clubs in Athens together throughout the '80s, but Stipe admits that he doesn't see Buck and Mills much anymore unless they're working. It's not a problem, insists the singer, because of the stage they're at in their relationship. "You have to remember, we've been doing this for 21 years," he says. "Our friendships and our relationships are intact. A phone call or an email or note and dinner every other month is just fine."[11]

IMPORTANCE OF FRIENDSHIP

The Red Hot Chili Peppers and U2 insist that the personal bonds within their collective are paramount and that the unit must function on this level in order to function at all. For them, friendship is the glue that holds the band together and makes possible everything they do, more so, even, than the chemistry binding the musicians. According to Edge, a real band is not just a "working unit but something that works socially."[12] The band is rooted in their friendship, Larry Mullen affirmed in *Time* (1987), and insisted that the group would have failed if it had originally been based on a professional rather than personal alliance.

The Red Hot Chili Peppers have always averred that the group revolves around their amicable rapport. "I wouldn't be able to make music with the band if we weren't all friends," says John Frusciante.[13] There's no doubt he practices what he preaches, as the guitarist left the Chili Peppers in 1992 largely because those bonds had broken down and bad blood divided the band members. But such statements hold true for his bandmates as well. When they couldn't establish with other musicians the requisite brand of personal intimacy, the group ceased to function effectively. In 1988, Chad Smith auditioned for the group and, although Flea and Kiedis didn't doubt that he was the best drummer for the job, they weren't so sure he was the right *person* for this unit. "We had to ponder the situation for a couple of days to see whether we could live with this guy. Whether we could marry this guy and spend the rest of our lives with him," Kiedis confided in 1990.[14] (Ultimately, the sticksman was too good to let go of, though it took time, and turned out to be a surprisingly ideal companion to boot.)

Constant association with one another is what makes friendship a prerequisite in Flea's view. "When you're with someone all the time, on a bus or in the studio, wherever you are, you have to love that person. You have to be able to live inside their energy and love it."[15] On the simplest level, the experience of being in a band just isn't a positive one unless the members enjoy one another's company, Frusciante points out. A deep personal bond serves other purposes in this context. As Flea observed in *The Washington Post* when speaking of his decades-long connection with singer Anthony Kiedis, the situations in which people hurt those closest to them—as the two of them often do—can be very difficult in a band, but there's an underlying bond that transcends any rift and keeps the relationship intact. As we'll see further on, the Chili Peppers also believe that friendship is an essential part of the group's chemistry.

On the surface, there seem to be divergent opinions in Radiohead on the question of whether friendship is imperative to the group's operation. "I've always maintained that our friendship is absolutely crucial," says O'Brien, adding that the singer does not share this conviction unreservedly. "I think Thom has thought it hasn't been crucial—at times."[16] The coda points to shifting views on this issue, which other band members have owned up to. Speaking for the group, Colin Greenwood reports that, when Radiohead was first signed, the members believed their professional relationship was now the priority and their friendship very much secondary to it. But the longer they are in the business, he continues, and meet bands they admire (like U2 and R.E.M.), the more they appreciate the relevance of their personal relations in keeping them happy and sane (Baktabak Interview CD). Yorke claims that even before landing the contract with Parlaphone, the band was never really "about being friends or anything." It was about the music, and getting together was simply beneficial. "We were playing our instruments in our bedrooms and wanted to play them with someone else and it was just symbiotic."[17] There is evidence to suggest that his attitude has changed since then and O'Brien identifies a specific incident—the group's 1994 fallout in Mexico—as a pivotal turning point in the group's relations *and* the members' perspective on them. That unsavory episode made them all realize, as O'Brien explained in *The Barrie Examiner*, that their friendship weighs equally in the band's fortunes as the music they make together.

Whether they all acknowledge it or not, the quintet's personal bonds have, in fact, always played an important role in the group. Although Yorke's cohorts made the effort to keep the band going throughout their university years because they believed his songs had merit, their longstanding friendship was an equally influential factor, claims Colin Greenwood, who cited both as a motivation in a 2001 *Mojo* interview. He has also noted in *Request* that the members' ongoing dedication to the band is bolstered by their sense of fellowship. On camera for the MuchMusic series *The Story of ... [Radiohead]*, he made another noteworthy point: that the band members don't want to let one another down because of their friendship. More than any external source, their friendship puts more pressure on them to do well and give the band their all, he added. Having found many aspects of the entertainment industry disconcerting and unpleasant, camaraderie has also made it easier for the band members to contend with the ramifications of their position. "Thank fuck we all get on and have been doing this a long time and work with people we love because it's a completely insane existence," declared the guitarist in 1997.[18]

Similar sentiments have been expressed by Peter Buck, who proclaimed in *Mojo* (1994) that life in R.E.M. would be unbearable if the members hated each other. In fact, when the band was mired in the tortuous *Monster* sessions, he reflected cheerily that the situation would be far worse if they weren't such good friends. Others in the band have always insisted that their personal ties take precedence over their relationship as collaborators and expressed how dearly they cherish those connections. But after years of upholding the virtues of band friendships, Buck sent a ripple of shock throughout the rock world when he told *Q*'s Tom Doyle in 1999 that he would want to maintain R.E.M. so long as he felt that the alliance yielded great music, even if he and his bandmates weren't particularly thick anymore. "It just wouldn't be as fun," he said.[19] Whether or not he meant it in earnest, it hasn't come to that with R.E.M., nor does such a development seem likely.

FRIENDSHIP AND THE MUSIC

So far, this section has explored the significance (real and perceived) of friendship within these groups in a general sense, without looking specifically at its artistic implications. The Red Hot Chili Peppers insist that they are able to write music together only on account of the depth of their relationship. This is partly because the group's original mission and approach to its art descended directly from the communion between the founding foursome. There is also the band's jam-based method of composition, which demands that the musicians be attuned to one another on various levels, to take into consideration when accounting for how a personal bond facilitates the quartet's creative efforts. Comity undoubtedly renders cooperative composition easier in U2 and R.E.M., but there is no indication that their professional efforts depend upon it. In Radiohead, the music doesn't hinge on the state of the band members' interpersonal relations, but vice versa. "If we're creatively happy, then we're also very very happy all together," says Ed O'Brien.[20] For the Chili Peppers, harmony within the unit is a starting point for collaboration, and for Radiohead, more a final product of (or, a relationship reinforced by) its art.

In any band, work-related problems and disputes often seep into the friendship. How can they not? The extensive questioning Radiohead went through while making *Kid A* was hard to bear particularly because the members perceived how their friendship was being altered and marred by this creative struggle. Likewise, when R.E.M. encountered serious bumps in the creative process during the *Up* sessions, their personal relationships suffered. They were still friends, joked Mills; they just didn't know it.

A remark by Radiohead's Phil Selway adds another dimension to the discussion of the link between friendship and collaboration in bands, as he maintains that the inter-relations in the collective directly impact its sound. In his view, *Hail to the Thief* has a warmer tone than the two Radiohead albums that preceded it precisely because there was more warmth between the band members during the period in which it was recorded. "You can't fake how you're feeling when you're making music together," is the conclusion he draws.[21] The group's art will ineluctably reflect the degree of affinity between the members. On his part, Yorke has often alluded to the tense and fragmented state of the group during the recording of *The Bends* and how he can hear its impact on the album, which, he said in *The Trigger*, captures how they were functioning as a band at that time.

Fables of the Reconstruction similarly captured R.E.M. during one of the band's most fractured periods. The four members were miserable and sick to death of one another. And despite the fact that they were alone in London, with only their bandmates for company, they were, as Peter Buck confessed to *Bucketfull of Brains* in 1987, quite mean to one another, which clearly affected the music they committed to tape together. "We weren't sure if we really liked each other or not and that was really reflected in the record," says Stipe.[22] There was no way around it, according to the singer, because "in the studio, what comes out and what gets stamped down for eternity is the result of what we are when we go into the studio, what state of mind we were in, what the situations were like."[23] That includes their personal relations. Buck has gone so far as to aver in *Q* (1994) that if he could go back and change anything about *Fables*, he would make the band see a group therapist. Had the four been getting along and communicating more effectively, they could have made a much better album, in his view.

It's a simple equation for John Frusciante. The music is a product of all that goes into it. And how the authors feel about one another is a palpable ingredient. "We love each other, and that love comes out in the music."[24]

Part II: Creative alliance

INTERDEPENDENCE

As musical collaborators, the relationships between the friends that constitute U2, R.E.M., Radiohead and the Red Hot Chili Peppers feature a host of other attributes that have never been fully explored. Interdependence is one of the most intriguing facets of these alliances. In any musical ensemble, the performers are dependent on one another to a certain extent, but in certain post-punk outfits where the members master their instruments, write songs as a group, and develop an individual style by playing together, their creative integration is particularly profound.

In a sense, they are guitarists, drummers and singers only within the context of the group. This is a difficult idea to get across, but U2's Larry Mullen conveys it brilliantly with a keen observation that brings to light a subtle distinction. "We never learned how to be musicians. We only learned how to work together." Since none of them are virtuosos, he explains, they find it difficult to play with other people or even play other people's songs, "because we're so tuned in to each other."[25] In the absence of technique or craft, they have always had to rely heavily on the collective, knowing that their *combined* ability is their only strength. Musically, they got by on very little, says Clayton. "But we were always able to make something of it, just in the way we played together."[26] (It's no wonder their early recordings, which seemed like the product of some inexplicable voodoo, amazed them.)

In the past, that interdependence didn't end with the band's enabling chemistry, as they also looked to one another to palpably compensate for their own shortcomings as musicians. Clayton pointed out in a 1983 *U2 Magazine* article that Edge's guitar style evolved partly as a result of having to cover up for an inexperienced rhythm section. At a 1989 press conference in New Zealand, the bassist stated that the four thus have a real *need* for the band and for each other, so they can't work apart very effectively. Their friend and producer Brian Eno surmises that the members' recognition of the band's necessity to their own musical career is the wellspring of their celebrated dedication to one another. They seem to realize, he observed in *The Los Angeles Times* (2004), that none of them would have become a musician without the others, which has rendered them understandably loyal to one another (especially since they remain, to this day, insecure about their individual abilities).

Speaking for himself, Jonny Greenwood shrugs off the general title of "guitarist" and, instead, appears to prefer something more contextual and limited, to the tune of "plays guitar in Radiohead." It's another slight but significant distinction that emphasizes the interconnectedness between him and the group in which he first took up the instrument. "My style is so tightly tied in with our songs," he says, "that I don't think you could even ask me to quit Radiohead and play guitar for another band. I don't think I could do it. It would probably reveal me to be the bluffer that I believe I am."[27] His feeling is that he's only a guitarist within, and not outside of, Radiohead. This perception derives largely from the fact that, in his case, he was in the band before he strapped on a guitar, so his playing is inextricably, and explicably, bound up with the group.

Even band members who might not subscribe to the rather radical notion that they wouldn't be able to play outside of their band acknowledge that their individual style and/or their ability to write music is largely contingent upon the collective. Possessed of a unique vocal approach that's instantly recognizable and known the world over, Stipe modestly credits R.E.M.'s musical treatment with occasioning it. "I'm not sure that without a real melodic bass and background vocals and Peter's guitar I would be a very good vocalist. I think if the band didn't sound the way it does I would probably sing in a different way. The vocal sound came out of there being a necessity for a vocal sound like that."[28]

Even more humbly, Stipe decrees that he's not terribly special and would be nowhere as an artist and musician if it weren't for his bandmates. "I've got a nice voice and good cheekbones, but without those guys writing songs with me, I don't know that anyone would ever hear what I have to say."[29] He told *The Los Angeles Times* in 2003 that he relies on the support and approval of his bandmates in order to write, and when he didn't have it during the difficult *Up* sessions, he couldn't make any headway with the lyrics. On his part, Mike Mills insisted in *NME* (1984) that if Peter Buck didn't play what he terms a constant solo, he wouldn't have developed his well-known melodic bass approach (as the music would likely require more of a conventional thumping technique).

John Frusciante similarly stresses that he forged his guitar style through working with Flea, and, in the process, altered the band's bass sound. When he first joined the Chili Peppers, the young guitarist confesses he had difficulty finding his own artistic expression, so he began to imitate Hillel Slovak's chops in order to at least establish a groove with the adroit and energetic bass player. He was then able to build his own musical vocabulary out of that style, and Flea's playing started changing to match it, he informed *Guitar One*. Frusciante's approach was shaped by the need to gel with Flea and Smith, who then, all together, generate compositions that Kiedis, specifically, can sing over. Thus, when he was no longer in the band the guitarist lamented the fact that, through this collaboration, he had developed a whole range of sound and style of playing that were now defunct. "Without these people to play with I had no place to play this style I had worked so hard to develop."[30]

Realizing musical ideas with the aid of the group is the type of reliance on the others to which Bono most often refers. Without U2, the melodies he hears in his head don't have an outlet. He needs the band to help him actualize them and recalls the frustrating years during which he could do nothing with the tunes that came to him because the band was not yet in existence. Even now, when he finds himself outside of his artistic cradle, he experiences the same, for lack of a better term, creative constipation. He told *The Guardian* in 2000, after spending a year dedicated primarily to non-musical pursuits, that he kept coming up with tunes during this period and getting really frustrated because the band wasn't around to help him capture them. And it's not simply a matter of his not being proficient at an instrument that can serve as a songwriting tool (he's capable of accompanying himself on the guitar). His need for the band, for the three collaborators he has in it, is not entirely practical; they complete Bono the songwriter on a much more fundamental level. In Oprah's *O* magazine, he defended the dependency he has developed on his bandmates, claiming that it's a strength rather than a weakness to lean on others in this way. Expressing his gratitude for the band and what he owes to it, he remarks elsewhere: "I don't think of myself as a great singer but I sing from a great place. That place is U2."[31]

A multi-instrumentalist and born songwriter, Thom Yorke nevertheless depends on his colleagues in Radiohead to complete his compositions—as does the band's other songwriter, Jonny Greenwood. Both of them always get to a point with a song where they can't take it any further on their own and need the band's input, explained the singer in an edition of *Q* dedicated to Radiohead. Yorke says that playing the guitar is a "totally functional" activity for him and he doesn't rate himself the world's most interesting guitarist, so he finds it more exciting to respond to what other musicians come up with.[32] Hearing another approach to the instrument is a way of overriding his own "limitations" and advancing the song. Phil Selway claims that he's a reactive musician and told *Access* in 2003 that he finds it extremely difficult to generate ideas on his own, since his contributions to the music generally take the form of a response to what the others in the band are doing. On their own, then, the band members are each missing some essential building blocks that they rely on the others to provide them with. "There are no budding solo artists in this band," Jonny Greenwood stresses. "We're holding each other up."[33]

FANS OF ONE ANOTHER

Obviously, mutual respect is necessary for any group of people to work effectively together, and particularly for artists in a creative partnership. It's the price of entry into a fruitful and enduring collaboration. But, in these bands, respect has swelled into genuine admiration for each other. You could say that they are fans of one another. Peter Buck, for instance, perceives R.E.M.'s charismatic and vocally-gifted frontman as an extremely valuable asset to the band. As he sees it, R.E.M. made it big while other alternative guitar bands that rose to prominence (well, cult status) along with them fell by the wayside because he and his bandmates worked a lot harder and had more interesting melodies. More to the point, the other groups "didn't have Michael."[34] This footnote implies that Buck believes Stipe annexed himself to a rather generic, albeit talented, bunch, and, because he's so extraordinary, rendered the group exceptional. This is precisely the theory Bill Berry advanced by holding that the singer, who "definitely marches to a different drummer," took "three fairly ordinary guys and made a unit that's pretty acceptable."[35]

As we'll see later, the members of R.E.M. don't discount the paramount importance of their combined chemistry, but they view Stipe as their X-factor when it comes to distinguishing their group from other bands. As for the singer, he holds his bandmates, as they hold each other, in high esteem. "The stuff they throw at me," he marvels, delivering a superlative compliment that underscores his veneration for Buck and Mills, "is challenging not only for me and them, but for the people out there."[36] To the bass player, who shares music-writing duties with Buck, his partner's compositions seem so electrifying, he credits them with motivating him to get up each day and work on new songs. In a 2005 interview with *Uncut*, Buck returned the compliment, claiming that he is blown away by what Mills can do on a four-string, and ranked him alongside some of the world's greatest bassists (including Paul McCartney).

It's already been established that Radiohead's Thom Yorke is revered by his bandmates. They proudly extol his gifts, particularly as a wordsmith. O'Brien referred to him as "the finest British lyricist of our generation" during a discussion in which he and Selway expressed their astonishment at Yorke's linguistic achievements on *OK Computer*. "On this album, the lyrics opened me up to stuff that I hadn't necessarily noticed before or maybe felt but couldn't put into words," continues the guitarist. "And I think it's amazing that he can do that." They were "completely floored," he adds, when Yorke first played them "No Surprises."[37] Speaking to *Hot Press* in 2001, Colin Greenwood tendered what he loves the most about Yorke's verses, concluding with the observation that his great gift as a songwriter is his ability to transport listeners and affect them on a visceral level. The singer himself shrugs off such encomiums, stressing that the music, written collectively by the group, "sends you far beyond the words."[38]

Nevertheless, the group's homage for his work helps the super-critical songwriter appreciate its assets. He told *The Toronto Star* that he felt nothing for his *Hail to the Thief* demos until the band's contagious enthusiasm infected him. Meanwhile, the musical prowess of his bandmates bowls the singer over as well. Jonny Greenwood mentions a rehearsal during which a greatly impressed Yorke had to stop the other four in the middle of a song in order to express his amazement with the group forthwith, lauding them for their excellent contributions to the piece. On a humorous note, Colin Greenwood implies that this professional regard enables the band members to put up with one another's foibles. "Jonny's a great fucking guitarist," he says in reference to his younger brother, "which makes up for a lot of his unsavoury personal habits."[39]

No less in awe of each other are the members of U2. In *Muse*, Bono called Adam Clayton the only bass player one would miss if he weren't there and, in the same sentence, boasts that Larry can do beats like no other drummer. Edge similarly avers that it would be silly for him to ever leave U2 for a new band because it's clear that he'll never find another singer or rhythm section of the same caliber. When it comes to Bono, the band seems particularly in awe of his willingness to take artistic risks and push the envelope. Mullen, Clayton and Edge also admire Bono on a personal level, lauding his humanitarian achievements, his drive and his discipline. "He's all going forward, and it's amazing how much he achieves," raves Edge.[40]

The same types of comments are made by the Red Hot Chili Peppers. In the liner notes to the reissued *Red Hot Chili Peppers* album, Flea claims he was so excited when Kiedis wrote the lyrics to "Green Heaven" that he called up everyone he knew and read the words to them over the phone. The bassist noted in *Oor* in 2002 that his old friend, whose work obviously thrilled him before, has grown a great deal as a musician and now comes up with even more astounding lyrics and melodies. Kiedis feels, reciprocally, like he's playing with the most talented musicians in the world, and often showers them with praise in interviews. Frusciante, the prodigious guitarist, garners the most effusive panegyrics from the other three.

TAKING EACH OTHER TO NEW HEIGHTS

Indeed, what all this inter-group adulation leads to, from an artistic perspective, is that the band members are not only challenged by their partners, but, as Mike Mills put it in *Flagpole* (1999), pushed to new heights and inspired by one another. This is the mark of a successful creative alliance, when it enables the individuals to take their craft to a higher level than they could have done on their own. "That's where the dynamic of the band is so vital," says Stipe, "our ability to rope each other back in, to pull out the best from each other, is what's so significant about this group."[41] But this is not the only type of animus the band members derive from one another.

While John Frusciante's guitar wizardry and musical acumen galvanize his bandmates to be in top form as well, his spirit suffuses the group and elevates it. "John is a very pure artist," explains Flea, "and that inspires the most pure part of our band."[42] His dedication to music, rhapsodized Kiedis on *MTV.com* (1999), is also heavily contagious, making all of them more eager to write and perform than ever before. Frusciante's entrance into the Chili Peppers as a zealous fan—a real one—was particularly uplifting. His youthful and un-jaded perspective rubbed off on the somewhat demoralized crew. He reminded them how important their music is and of the profound effect it can have on the lives of others, Kiedis revealed in *MusicMakers*.

It's not only inspiration that brings out the best in each other. Living up to the standards set by the group promotes individual excellence. Ed O'Brien commented on *The LiNK* that industry and audience expectations are not as difficult to deal with as those originating within the unit. His bandmates expect a lot from one another and none of them wants to let the group down.

ADDED EXCITEMENT

The collaborative relationship within these bands heightens the excitement inherent in any creative endeavor. Bouncing ideas off one another and witnessing their mutation is a great thrill. It lies in seeing what someone else, who has an equal stake in the band and is well respected by all parties, will do with a particular piece of music or a song. For Jonny Greenwood, being in a band is most electrifying when they have what they suspect is an amazing song, but nobody knows, initially, how he's going to approach it, let alone what the others will do with it. Each of them plugs into an amp to come up with something and, before long, ideas are flying around the room. "It's the best part of being in a band in a way." So exhilarating is this collective brainstorm scenario that it's Greenwood's version of heaven, a "big empty room with the band and all these half-written songs."[43] Yorke says he gets chills from the same scenario. The element of surprise inherent in writing collaboratively is key.

Equally exciting is the act of unveiling one's ideas to the group and seeing the reactions of the others. Who isn't familiar with the feeling of coming up with something fantastic that you can't wait to share with your friends? But in this case there's the added rush of watching what the band does with it. Mike Mills confesses that he gets really pumped when he composes music on his own, and then gets an additional rush from presenting it to his partners and receiving their input. "I realised that I still get incredibly excited every time I write what I think is a good song. And then, when we meet up as a group and see what we can do it's incredible, and as long as that is there then we will have no problems making records."[44] There's the double wallop of flexing the band's collective muscles in addition to one's own.

PASSING THE CREATIVE TORCH

Passing around the creative torch is one of the greatest benefits of a collaboration such as that which exists in these bands. To start with, sharing the artistic burden with one's bandmates takes some of the pressure off of everyone. *The Bends* featured more group compositions than Radiohead's first album, which was a huge relief for Thom Yorke because he wasn't on the spot nearly as much as before, when he was responsible for producing the bulk of the band's material. He didn't have that crushing sense of "'Ohmigod, I've got to come in with something,'" which made Radiohead seem "much less of a job and much more of an enjoyable being-in-a-band thing."[45] By 1997, Jonny Greenwood was introducing not just parts but full-fledged songs to the group, the first of which to appear on an album was *OK Computer*'s closer "The Tourist." For Yorke, having a second songwriter in Radiohead affords him even more breathing space. Asked to comment on Greenwood's new role, the singer said simply that he's happy to spread the load. "Whenever I am tired, he is there and awake."[46]

U2's longtime producer Daniel Lanois noted on *CNN.com* (2000) how the creative energy in that group shifts around. As inevitably happens, the person leading the musical onslaught at a given moment runs out of steam, he explains, but there is always someone else willing and able to take the tracks to the next level. This teamwork is crucial for maintaining high musical standards, notes Mike Mills. Songs and pieces of songs originate with any number of people and are then pulled together by the whole band, providing two safeguards against poor quality due to a paucity of ideas or inspiration. "That dynamic helps you avoid slumps," says the bassist.[47] In *The Sunday Times* (2003), Stipe posited a third screening mechanism arising from this mutual effort, in that several people are charged with the task of judging the merit of the songs, deciding which to leave on the cutting-room floor and which to put on the album. Kiedis pointed out in an interview with *Risen* that it's highly unlikely all four members of the band could be having a bad idea at the same time, so there's a reliable "failsafe mechanism" inherent in their collaboration.[48] That's why he's glad not to have to write songs on his own which, presumably, leaves more space for slip-ups. In Peter Buck's view, this is one of the reasons the group dynamic can't be beat.

CHEMISTRY

Chemistry. There's no discussion of bands or the creative relationship within them that doesn't invoke this key concept. It's the *je ne sais quoi* that makes rock groups—well, those that have it—alluring, mysterious, rare, successful, and, some might say, possible. It is, according to many musicians, the intangible element that separates one outfit from another, or to put it another way, a band from a musical ensemble. "The thing that makes the difference between a *band* and a group of musicians," proposes Mike Mills, "is the chemistry between the people."[49] Indefinability is, however, the only definitive quality that can be attributed to chemistry. Anything else is mere guesswork. As Edge rightly points out, there is no way to describe what it is when a certain set of musicians is playing together and it's clear that there is something special going on. Yet, various attempts have been made by members of the four bands to pin down this elusive force, Adam Clayton, for instance, referred in *U2 Magazine* (1985) to chemistry as a certain *spirit* pervading the band due to the combination of the individuals involved.

Perhaps the best description is offered by Kiedis, who tags chemistry quite simply as "the way you affect one another creatively."[50] For some unknown reason, you put a certain set of people together and that union has a profound impact on their individual efforts. In a way, this theory equates chemistry with the more mundane notion of bringing out the best in one another. And then, with each molecule supercharged, so to speak, by the others, the whole does become greater than the sum of its inherent parts. Still, it's impossible to explain why some people have this effect on each other while others don't, and why the removal of one individual from this equation can completely change the flow of creative energy. "If there's one U2 in the room, or two of us in the room, or three," quips Bono, "we have our individual weight. But when there's four of us in the room, it changes the molecules a little bit."[51]

The Chili Peppers are also of the persuasion that there are different levels of chemistry, and that, underlying their creative alchemy is "a spiritual chemistry that brings it together in the first place" (which makes friendship a critical ingredient).[52] In that sense, how the parties affect one another creatively has a lot to do with their interpersonal impact on each other. *Addicted to Noise* correspondent Gil Kaufman correctly pointed out that part of the mystique of the Chili Peppers derives from this spiritual and brotherly love the quartet shares, to which Flea responded: "The truth is, that's the intangible thing that makes the band be what it is."[53] He essentially equates the group's chemistry (or one aspect of it) with the band members' bond of fellowship.

Since chemistry depends on the individuals constituting the group, it is generally not nullified by role swapping, stylistic shifts or instrument changes (i.e., the use of keyboards instead of guitars) that occur within the unit. It also transcends genre and methodology. The special energy in U2, says Adam Clayton, has always been there, no matter what the band has experimented with. Edge intimates that the elasticity and tenaciousness of this dynamic makes the four curious to explore just how far they can go with it. "That's the thing that keeps us interested in what we might be able to do," he told *CNN.com*,[54] referring to the "spark" the band has always had. John Frusciante similarly contends that the Chili Peppers' chemistry is one of the factors that impels the band to seek out new ground to cover. "I will continue to explore other territories in the future," he says, "it's just because it's fun to play around when you have such a chemistry like that in the group you know."[55]

Chemistry can also bear long interruptions, as the Red Hot Chili Peppers discovered. When the idea of reinstating Frusciante first came up, the band wondered if that ineffable ingredient might have evaporated after the six-year pause. To their surprise, they felt it again, instantly. The change in the group was perceptible, Kiedis reported in *Interview*. Suddenly, it became easy to write songs and feel connected to the music. Outsiders also noticed the transformation in their dynamic, since one notable attribute of chemistry is that it's apparent on the surface. Many early supporters of all these bands were struck by the sense of an extraordinary force at work in the group. On account of all the lineup changes the band endured, the members of the Chili Peppers are in a better position than anyone else to understand that the dynamic they have is extremely rare, cannot be forced, and should never be taken for granted.

SHARED VISION

A shared artistic vision or philosophy is another feature—perhaps the most notable one—of the professional alliance constituting a band. It's a broad, overarching concept that applies to more than one project or more than one aspect of the band's work (i.e., stage versus studio) and is a tremendously unifying force. This vision is perhaps best described as a sense of "this is what our band is all about," not just "this is what our band sounds like." It is not limited to an *artistic* doctrine, nor is it related only, or even primarily, to common musical tastes. Indeed, quite often, a concordant attitude or outlook binds the band members as individuals and forms the basis of their aesthetic.

With the Red Hot Chili Peppers, who were a group of friends for several years before they established the band, the collective vision emerged from the members' liberal and nonconformist perspective on life—views that bound them first on a personal level. They had something akin to a club credo that became a creative direction when the circle of friends turned into a band. Since Kiedis, Flea, Slovak and Irons were like brothers, there was little need for them to put this vision, which took the form more of a mutual feeling and mindset, into words. But, once newcomers infiltrated the lineup, at a time when the Chili Peppers were still largely unknown, Kiedis and Flea had to find a way to articulate this zany and radical creed to outsiders, which proved extremely difficult. "What we originally set out to do," begins the singer in an oft-quoted remark on this subject, "was to be complete and utter perpetrators of hardcore, bone-crunching mayhem sex things from heaven. To try and describe that to another musician, and have it mean something, is nearly impossible unless you've grown up with that person."[56] Some musicians (like Chad Smith) got it, but most didn't.

John Frusciante was a completely unique case. Shortly after joining the group, he explained to *Musician* that he was drawn to the Red Hot Chili Peppers as a fan because they were an extension of his own take on the world, music and how he wanted to live his life. He felt spiritually aligned with the band members and in tune with their overall philosophy before he ever met them. Still, he revealed in a 2003 interview with *Guitar One* that when he came on board, his new bandmates made a point of reviewing the Chili Peppers manifesto with him. The guitarist admitted in an online interview with Fender Guitars that, though he felt deeply connected to the band's values and passion for music, he misjudged its creative scope and potential. His view of what the group was trying to do and what kinds of ideas his bandmates were open to was very limited. Only when he got to know them better and learned that their tastes were wide-ranging and their appetite for growth keen did he truly comprehend their artistic orientation and begin exerting an influence over it. By the time Dave Navarro stepped in, the Chili Peppers were famous and their gospel well-known. From the sounds of it, all they needed to do was get the guitarist up to speed on funk basics, to which end they equipped him with some Meters and Funkadelic recordings.

An equally pronounced collective vision was present in U2 from the band's earliest days, shaped by the members' particular strengths and inclinations, as well as their aspiration to embody certain features they admired in other groups. "Even from the beginning we wanted something like the power of The Who and something that was as sensitive as say, Neil Young," said Bono in 1980. What the band was after, he went on to state, was an "aggressive power," and a range of different effects rooted in emotions.[57] Exploring and eliciting potent feelings was one of U2's main precepts because they felt that the group, and Bono in particular, had uncommon insight into human emotions and an ability to convey them honestly. But, while the band had this aesthetic in mind, the singer claims it never amounted to a calculated plan. There was almost a subliminal quality to it. "We don't say: 'let's be aggressive, let's really communicate and be passionate.' Sometimes to think about it is to destroy it," he remarked in 1982.[58]

Exposing raw emotions can be dangerous (even in art), but it fits in with another of U2's founding tenets: taking risks. Edge has often stated that he hates the idea of U2 as a nice safe band. He explained to *Guitar World* in 1997 that simple perversity isn't the reason they have always tried not to play to public expectations, debunk myths about the group, seek out new territory, take chances and reject the norm. It's part of the band's governing ideology. Even the quartet's most cautious member, Larry Mullen, regularly applauds the ballsy frontman for sticking his neck out, and though he openly criticizes some of U2's boldest campaigns (like Popmart's controversial satellite linkup with Sarajevo), he adds that he's proud to be in a group willing to take such chances. It's what U2 is all about.

Turned off by the mainstream music scene, the members of R.E.M. saw little worth emulating in any of the big acts of the day. Their allied vision for the band seemed to grow out of their dissatisfaction with what was out there and a consequent conviction that popular music could offer more. Neatly cataloging the contemporary musical schools, Peter Buck defines R.E.M.'s intent against them. "There was the post-punk thing with guys with Les Paul guitars doing three-chord fast songs, new wave which was just dumb disco dance with skinny ties and then there was dinosaur rock. We were trying to invent a more literate, evocative and more harmonically complex structured kind of rock 'n' roll."[59] Like many of its fellow bands in Athens, R.E.M. also subscribed to the notion that it's deplorable to sound like any other outfit and that every group should strive to express itself in an unprecedented fashion.

In keeping with the desire to be both unconventional and inscrutable, on top of a marked disdain for rock lyrics, R.E.M. decided to aim for ambiguity on the vocal front. Hence the largely incomprehensible mumbling characteristic of the band's early albums. Whenever the approach was criticized, which happened quite frequently, Stipe's bandmates defended him staunchly, making it clear that the muffled enunciation reflected a deliberate artistic decision they had made together. They ended up repeatedly elucidating their position and describing their shared philosophy regarding lyrics to the discombobulated music press.

Buck talked abstractly about short-circuiting the accepted code represented by literary language while Stipe expounded upon his yen for making listeners interpret songs on their own. The four had, after all, settled on the cryptic moniker R.E.M. in order to avoid being pigeonholed or summed up too easily, which was obviously an essential element of their group concept. Outsiders, like Jay Boberg of IRS, were impressed by the strength and clarity of R.E.M.'s vision. According to *Documental*, producer Don Dixon, in fact, found this well-developed sense of purpose rather surprising given the quartet's limited musicianship, when, in actual fact, it largely made up for what they lacked in formal training and experience.

Thom Yorke was not only Radiohead's chief songwriter during the band's formative years but also (since the two often go hand-in-hand) its prime conceptualist. Richard Haines, who worked with Radiohead on some early demos, provides the most concrete insight into this matter in Mac Randall's band biography, *Exit Music*. According to Haines, Yorke was the man with the vision, possessing a definitive and unswerving view of the overall picture that helped focus the entire group. Although this differs from the situation in the three other groups discussed in this book, there are plenty of historical parallels, such as The Beach Boys (largely Brian Wilson's brainchild) and The Who (whose guiding spirit was Pete Townshend). But it's natural that when the songwriting is more of a group effort—as, by most reports, it became in Radiohead by the time they made their second album—the vision takes on a more collective aspect as well. Of course, sharing a broad vision for the band doesn't mean that individual members don't have their own ends to realize both for and through the group. On the contrary, as Colin Greenwood testifies in *The Guide*, they each have a different agenda in terms of what they want to do in Radiohead. Presumably, however, it's subservient to the common agenda.

Thom Yorke captures the value of the creative coalition in bands with one pithy deposition that makes a spectacularly apt conclusion for this section: "We always had this idea that the good thing about being in a band was people clicking, keeping one another's interest going—all the stuff you can't do in a bedroom by yourself."[60]

Part III: Business partnership

GOALS

The band's artistic vision can be described as the sum of its creative goals. But there are career-related objectives shared by the band members that form the basis of their business relationship. "We might disagree about what to play, when to tour, or what the cover should look like, but we certainly don't have goals that aren't in common," says Buck, intimating that this is critical.[61] The band members all want to get to the same place and that unites them on a corporate level. When they don't, the repercussions are severe. Both Bill Berry and John Frusciante left their respective groups partly because they had more modest ambitions for the band than their cohorts.

A goal doesn't constitute a master plan outlining the band's every move. Sometimes, as with U2, it can be as concrete and long-range as becoming the biggest and best band in the world, and even then there's no map or blueprint to follow, just a lofty target. Since R.E.M. moved steadily up the industry ladder with each album and tour, it looked as if the foursome knew exactly what they were doing and where they were going. But Buck vowed in *The Cleveland Plain Dealer* that their only priority was to do what's right for the band at any given moment, like taking a break from touring when they got sick of it or continuing without Berry because they wanted to carry on. They didn't always agree on which course of action was in the band's best interest, but they all had that same goal at heart.

In Radiohead's case, the goal essentially comprised a shared determination to stick together and give the band a serious shot. Like many high-schoolers who start a band, they spent much of their time as teenagers hanging out in pubs and coffee houses formulating plans and fantasizing about the future, reminisced O'Brien in *The New York Times Upfront*, but that was the extent of their strategizing. Throughout their scattered university years, they remained committed to the band and to pursuing a career with it, which enabled them to maintain their cohesiveness and focus despite the lengthy physical separation and pursuit of higher education. They were dead set on making it work. This tenacity owes much to the peer pressure within the group, Colin Greenwood imparted to *Nightshift*. The five friends compel one another to keep reaching for their common goals, making it difficult for any one of them to feel discouraged for long. But, by O'Brien's account, the band derives much of its collective drive and determination from the resolute and aspiring Yorke. Left to his own devices, the guitarist admitted to *Rolling Stone* in 2001, he probably wouldn't have achieved anything because he lacks the internal impetus that spurs Yorke on, and in turn, spurs on the band.

Despite their determination to succeed (whatever success meant to each), in none of these bands has that goal overridden the members' loyalty to one another, largely because they are friends and recognize that they have been blessed with a rare alchemy. But there also seems to be an honorable allegiance or gentleman's agreement underpinning their unflappable mutual commitment to one another, a sort of unspoken pact that they will make it together or not make it at all. As U2 scrambled to gain the attention of record companies and eke out a living, a number of third parties suggested that one member or another be replaced in order to strengthen the band's musicianship. The thinking was that the band would be signed more quickly if its technical proficiency improved. However, all such suggestions were categorically rejected.

Competence was hardly an issue for the Red Hot Chili Peppers, but drugs were a formidable problem. At various times the group's two heroin aficionados, Hillel Slovak and Anthony Kiedis, clearly stood in the way of the band's artistic and professional progress. The singer was regularly AWOL and both he and Slovak often gave less than their best. For the most part, everyone bit the bullet and soldiered on. Only when the fiercely addicted guitarist became an unbearable burden did the band consider letting him go. But, as Kiedis recounts in his autobiography, Fishbone frontman Angelo Moore talked him out of that idea by reminding him that solidarity is paramount, and once convinced himself, Kiedis took that argument back to the band. Apparently, it was the singer who ended up getting fired when he became, as he describes it, like a gangrened foot that had to be amputated. Hindering the band's career is one thing, and it was a handicap the band was willing to live with, but he was threatening its very survival. (They took him back as soon as he cleaned up.)

Once a band turns pro, it becomes a commercial enterprise. Bono likes to say that U2 is a corporation of five (counting the manager). Unlike many of their predecessors, these four bands claim to be heavily involved in the operational aspects of their musical venture, rather than leaving everything up to the record executives or their managers. So there are endless business decisions to be made by the members in their capacity as joint CEOs. This is yet another relationship they need to maintain, but one they are fairly mum about in interviews. Having multiple decisionmakers only complicates matters. This topic is covered in the next chapter because the band's regulatory structure prevails over both creative and corporate issues.

4

"Trip Thru Your Wires": Governing Structure and General Relations Within the Bands

Understanding how a band is internally "wired" involves decoding its form of governance, its overriding structure, the nature of the general relations within it and the types of interactions that typically take place between the members. The *implications* of these arrangements in terms of each group's communal life also need drawing out.

Part I: Democracy

THE WAY IT WORKS

R.E.M. and U2 refer to themselves as democratic organizations. And they *are* democratic in the sense that the members are all equals and each has a say in every matter. Their contributions and roles vary, but everybody is afforded the same respect within the group. "We've held onto this idea that it is an equal situation, even though every element of what we do is not necessarily equal," observes Edge.[1] In other words, they have a perception of the band and one another that isn't tied to what actually goes on. Just because one person carries a heavier load or seems to play a more significant part in the whole doesn't give him any ascendancy over the others, win him more privileges, or afford him greater control over the group.

When it comes to actually making decisions and passing resolutions, these bands operate like a jury, requiring not a majority vote but unanimous agreement, which essentially gives each member of the band veto

power over any decision. (While it's not a subject they touch upon frequently, the Red Hot Chili Peppers seem to have a similarly über-
democratic structure. Chad Smith told *Batteur* in 1995 that one of the
greatest challenges for his band also lies in having to constantly reconcile the divergent desires and stances of four individuals.)

Indeed, it's no easy feat for three or four people to reach a consensus. And the democratic debate that precedes the exacting vote can be
very cumbersome. The main disadvantage with this system is that it's
ponderous and time-consuming. Hearing out every band member is a
lengthy process, Stipe acknowledged in *Jam!*, while Buck simply pro-
pounds that democracy is "the hard thing about bands."[2] Adam Clayton
and Paul McGuinness have similarly owned up to the fact that having
five opinions of equal weight to take into consideration makes band
meetings excruciatingly long. After each stakeholder makes his position
clear comes the difficult part. Since no one has the final say-so, intense
and often protracted negotiations commence in the interest of reaching a verdict that pleases everyone. They have fine-tuned the strategy in
U2 over the years, notes Mullen, but it can still be a "real pain because
everybody's got opinions."[3] What makes it work, he points out perceptively, is that they're usually fighting for the same end (like making great
music), only disagreeing about the means.

As for veto, it's a power the band members exercise with great pru-
dence. There's an all-for-one spirit and a dedication to compromise in
the groups that promotes cooperation even in cases when one person
isn't keen on a particular course of action. He will often go along with
a plan favored by the others unless he is violently opposed to it. The
reputedly no-nonsense Mullen may not have been overjoyed at having
to camp up for the "Discotheque" video or wear a dress for the "One"
shoot, but he deferred to his bandmates when he could have vetoed
these ideas. They also trust one another's judgment, Bill Berry pointed
out to *Musician* in 1991. Often, if he's opposed to something and his
R.E.M. cohorts assure him it's a really good idea, he figures he must be
wrong and defers to their point of view. In general, it's important, he
concluded, to constantly bear in mind and be concerned with how others in the band feel about a certain issue.

Mike Mills illustrates how the veto needs to be used sparingly, only
when the situation truly warrants it. The rule of thumb is to back down
whenever you can, instead of sticking to your guns in every disagreement. "If someone in the band has really strong feelings about something, then you should definitely go with them unless you have equally
strong feelings against it," he advises, and then alludes to the give-and-
take involved. "If you don't feel that strongly about it, then that is the
time to let that one go. Then when the next issue comes around that

you do feel that strongly about, maybe you will prevail."[4] If someone does decide to stand his ground in a dispute, the others must capitulate to him. Where it gets really weird, as Berry noted in the *Musician* interview, is when the four band members are split down the middle (two and two) on an issue. Presumably, they either duke it out between them or someone else (a manager or producer) gets involved.

IMPLICATIONS

The democracy-plus-consensus approach is onerous not just because of its inherent exigencies but also because the whole gang (or, as Bono likes to refer to it, the *Politburo*) has to OK *every* maneuver from the momentous to the trifling. U2 has made it no secret that the band's policy is to discuss absolutely everything—and this takes up a lot of their time. Their own manager calls them "obsessively—sometimes annoyingly—democratic."[5] It's no different in R.E.M., where every resolution is passed collectively. They sit around and vote just about as much as they write songs, grumbles Buck. "We vote on where we're going to play, where we're gonna make the records, who's gonna produce it."[6] Of course, not every single issue raises debate within the band. The unit couldn't possibly function that way. Many of their decisions, artistic and "political," are based on what Adam Clayton calls a collective instinct and Stipe has often referred to as a shared internal barometer that guides them.

Obviously, the arrangement has significant benefits, otherwise the bands would have scrapped it long ago. For one thing, says U2's bespectacled bassman, it leads the group to make better decisions because they're not taken lightly or for the wrong reasons (like ego). He goes so far as to ascribe U2's success and longevity to its collective government. On his part, Michael Stipe told *Jam!* that, as hard as it is to live with this regime, he and his partners in R.E.M. have managed to preserve their friendship much longer than the members of other bands precisely because they all have the right to speak up and each of them wields veto power.

But this mandate for consummate cooperation between equals who don't always see eye to eye brings with it, in Bono's words, "the grief of constantly having to convince the others of [one's] point of view."[7] When each member of the band has a strong opinion and doesn't back down easily, the situation can become explosive, with more dramatic consequences than an extended debate. There are shrill arguments, sulking matches and the occasional brawl. R.E.M. is comprised of admittedly stubborn and headstrong individuals, so the democratic rule has frequently resulted in fierce confrontations. Buck pleads guilty to wrestling with Mills on the ground during a particularly passionate disagreement, and confesses that the band members have cursed at one another and even thrown things at each other (the guitarist once launched a jug at Stipe's head). They get very heated at times in U2 as well, says Edge, as no one in the group gives up without a major fight. His three bandmates are impossible people, Bono stressed to Alastair Campbell, each with set ideas about how to live life, run the band and play music. The guitarist reinforces this characterization, declaring with blunt candor that there are "four evil motherfuckers in U2." Surprisingly, however, he adds that they would have broken up years ago if there had been any "pansies" in the band.[8]

His statement contains a key insight that emerges in relation to this subject: that the disagreements *made possible* by the democratic system have a positive flipside that abet the group. It's these disputes between resolute equals that keep the band members sharp. No one champions this theory more than Bono, who is its most vocal supporter. Conflict, which he gets plenty of in U2 from the sound of it, is healthy, he argues, because it keeps you on your toes and in touch with what's really important. "I like to be around a row," says the singer, "I always think you're as good as the arguments you get."[9] He firmly believes that dealing with clashing perspectives is one of the great benefits of being in a democratic collective. Only highly evolved individuals want to be in this type of equal partnership and put up with vehement opposition, Bono stated in *Vanity Fair*. As they get older, most people find having equals who don't always agree with them increasingly grating. They try to avoid arguments and get rid of anyone who questions them in order to become the uncontested king of the castle. But surrounding oneself with yes-men is a mistake. It's what the singer refers to as "the classic rock and roll star disease," one that adversely affects the artist's life and work.[10]

Sometime R.E.M. producer Don Dixon seems to be in agreement with Bono, pointing out that a delicate balance between strife and accord is what makes the Athens quartet great. He remarks of R.E.M.'s stint with him in the studio, during which he witnessed many a confrontation: "They got along well enough while still retaining enough tension to be worth a shit."[11] For the recording of *OK Computer*, the Radiohead quintet rented actress Jane Seymour's serene mansion nestled in the pastoral English countryside, partly in the hopes of avoiding the discord they experienced while laying down tracks for *The Bends* in a traditional recording studio. It didn't work out as they anticipated, but it taught the band that creative tensions aren't necessarily bad, that they, in fact, signify the merit of the work. "We now know that there are always going to be clashing moods whenever we make anything worthwhile," says Selway.[12] Recognizing the value of disputes makes them more bearable while being prepared for their occurrence minimizes their significance and impact. Some of the fights and screaming matches are unnecessary, but alternative forms of government are even more unappealing and may eradicate the productive side of disputes, says Stipe. "We realize that without debate and without democratic decision you have oligarchy and none of us is interested in that."[13]

In Bono's view, discord is at the very heart of a rock group's essence and the anvil on which the music is forged. "When you're in a band, that's your situation. You're just going to be with all these people that you love and scream at each other. And the racket that comes out of the friction is called rock 'n' roll."[14] So while our natural instinct is to see the output of these bands as a product of the *harmony* between the members, the fact of the matter is that, quite often, *conflict* is an equally important progenitor.

THE UN

What separates Radiohead from R.E.M., U2 and the Red Hot Chili Peppers is that the British band has a leader in Thom Yorke. He doesn't call all the shots, but he is the only one with veto power within an otherwise democratic setup. He famously compared Radiohead's method of governance to that of the United Nations in a *New York Times* interview (2000), implying that he is to the band what the U.S. is to that organization. Chris Hufford, one of the group's three managers, confirms that this is a fitting analogy for how Radiohead works, given that Yorke has the ultimate authority in the band, though, in every other respect, it's a democracy. "When all five of them say, 'This is great,' then it's great. If just two of them—say, Ed and Phil—say it's great and the other three say it's rubbish, then it's not going anywhere. And Thom definitely has the veto."[15] Phil Selway insists that the decisions reached by the band reflect the input of all five of them. It's just that Yorke "has the biggest voice in that."[16]

With an uneven number of people in the band, someone ends up casting the deciding vote when the other four are divided. In these cases, they generally defer to the singer, who says it's a difficult spot to find oneself in. During an interview with KCRW's (Santa Monica) *Morning Becomes Eclectic*, Yorke talked about the arguments the band had over which tracks to put on *OK Computer* and which to leave out. As it happened, it frequently fell to him to say yea or nay, which was, he insisted, quite hard on him. Yet, at other times, he has been unreservedly imperious, and indeed, confesses to having abused his position.

Yorke's power within Radiohead was absolutely unbalanced, he conceded in 2004, and he took advantage of it to "subvert everybody else's power at all costs."[17] Likening himself to Stalin (!), he claims to have created a climate of fear because he was worried that he would lose control over the band otherwise and not get his own way. These days, the structure of the group is somewhat more equitable. Yorke is still leading the band but the power is distributed more evenly between him and his four partners, he told *The Age* in 2004, adding that it's a healthier setup. What triggered the change? He simply realized that he's not right all the time. Following this line of thought, if he's not infallible, then it's better for the band to make decisions collectively. Five (Radio)heads are better than one. But given that he retains the authority to settle disputes, it's likely that arguments play out differently in Radiohead than in the other bands. Per the democratic mandate, everyone's voice is heard but there is, perhaps, less opinion-reconciliation activity if the final decision ultimately rests with Yorke.

Exhibiting admirable solidarity, Yorke's bandmates, who have undoubtedly found his domineering behavior irksome from time to time, have always publicly stood by him and defended his sovereignty. In *Rolling Stone* (1997), O'Brien applauded Yorke's apt comparison of Radiohead to the UN and indicated that he believes the singer rightly deserves to be the group's alpha. Since Yorke has the most demanding role—that of communicator—and the pressure on him is enormous, it's only fair to let him take the driver's seat.

Part II: Proceeds division

When it comes to allocating royalties and songwriting credits, equality prevails in R.E.M., U2, and the Red Hot Chili Peppers, again, without direct relation to the actual contributions of individual band members. Although Edge is considered the architect of U2's sound while Bono writes most of the lyrics and melodies, the group has always split the credit for the music (minus the lyrics, which are attributed to Bono, or more recently, Bono and Edge), as well as the loot, five ways (one portion going to McGuiness). It's a bit of a sacrifice for Bono, Clayton admitted to *People* in 1985, but the practice makes everyone feel equally valued and eliminates financial fallouts.

Despite the fact that there is typically a primary writer on each song, the members of R.E.M. have always attributed their output to the group. When the band started out, Mills campaigned to credit only the lead composer of a track. "I was thinking, well, if I wrote the song, I want my name on it because I wrote it and, by god, put my name behind the song."[18] But Peter Buck, well versed in rock history and cognizant of the royalty-related breakups of bands like Creedence Clearwater Revival, made the others realize that this was the quickest route to a greed- or jealousy-induced rift. Besides, since they would develop their individual songs together, they were all entitled to the recognition and rewards. Another selling point for the guitarist's approach, especially in a band so devoted to quality, was that it's easier to maintain high standards and serve the music if the proceeds are shared equally. "I remember reading an interview where the drummer for a famous '60s band said, 'The money's in songwriting, and I am going to get three of my songs on the next album no matter how bad they are,'" a horrified Buck recalled in 1994.[19] He thus insisted on distributing the songwriting credits and money four ways in what Mills calls one of the best decisions the band ever made.

According to Buck, there is simply no other way to make a band like R.E.M. work except by splitting everything evenly because each of the members has a big ego. Saying who wrote what and paying people accordingly would only lead to a battle of egos instead of neutralizing them, he informed *Guitar* in 1998. The kibbutz-like arrangement also reinforces the group's inward sense and outward appearance of solidarity. Likening the band to a family business, Buck argues that it's counterproductive to give some participants more credit than others, adding: "I like the idea of the four of us indivisible; you can't drive a wedge between us. That's how we stay together."[20] In other words, proceeds-sharing bolsters and emphasizes the band's collective ethos. There's certainly less inimical pressure on and competition between the musicians to come up with songs in order to secure lucrative songwriting credits, as Bill Berry stated in a 1987 interview with *Modern Drummer*.

The most enlightened and enlightening point the R.E.M. guitarist makes in relation to this topic is that songwriting is only a small part of what the band members do. As they each contribute to and sustain the band in various ways, their compensation needs to reflect the myriad indirect efforts that are no less important than coming up with a lyric or hook. What counts is simply being in the band, with all the sacrifices hardships and demands entailed by that affiliation. The songwriting revenue they share isn't necessarily for writing the songs, clarifies Buck in setting out the band's holistic doctrine. "It's for sleeping on the floor for ten years while we toured, it's for the eight hours of rehearsal we used to do, when we were making forty dollars a month."[21]

With their improvisational method of composition and frequent lineup shifts, the Red Hot Chili Peppers had to adopt a slightly different system to maintain fairness and avoid financial squabbles. Jeff Apter reports in *Fornication* that the band's original stance with respect to credits and royalties was that all band members be treated uniformly (without regard for the term of their tenure in the group) and songwriting credits be extended to any musicians jamming on a particular track. Presumably, then, anyone who was in the band when certain songs were written shared equally in the spoils (notwithstanding his degree of participation in the writing). True to form, when Frusciante joined the group, it was clearly as an equal member, because the others explained to him that his ideas will have the same weight as everyone else's and that he is entitled to the same remuneration.

A different strategy is implemented in Radiohead, in keeping with that band's unique configuration. Asked if they divide the group's profits equally, Yorke responded that they do, with the exception of the songwriting income, which is apportioned according to who wrote what (although, interestingly, all songs are officially credited to Radiohead). While the process takes "ages," the singer claims that the policy is not a source of contention in the group. They are aware that such unevenness has been the downfall of many a band, but, on their part, they've found a practicable way of going about the allocation of the funds in question. "I think we're pretty sorted out," Yorke assured Q.[22] To some extent, this proves that such an approach isn't inherently flawed. In certain outfits and with a particular modus operandi in place, it can succeed.

Part II: General interactions

SUPPORTING AND PROTECTING ONE ANOTHER

So much for the formal organization of these groups. But there are other constitutive elements that need to be examined in the context of this discussion. Among the subjects covered in the previous chapter were the predominant characteristics of the artistic alliance in these bands. In the following pages, some of the *general* relations and interactions within the groups will be described.

A strikingly supportive structure exists in the four bands. This support takes many forms. During personal crises, the members of U2 rally emphatically around whichever one of them is in need of encouragement and see him through the rough patch. When Clayton was arrested on drug charges in 1988, his bandmates stuck by him until the storm blew over, just as, two years later, they lent Edge the fortitude to get through his divorce to wife Aislinn. These examples of how the band members come to one another's aid and are there for each other when any one of them is faltering or bruised bears out Mullen's contention that U2 is a four-legged table, and "if one leg gets dented, the whole thing doesn't fall down; the other three support it."[23] Being such close friends, they also understand what the other is going through. Indeed, the band was so keenly aware of the guitarist's suffering after his marriage ended that *Achtung Baby*, the album they were working on at the time, contained endless references to broken relationships and the cruelties lovers inflict on one another—not because Edge asked Bono to explore these themes, but merely because the singer was in tune with his friend's emotions (not to mention the fact that the band, too, was divided).

Owing to the strength and comfort the members of U2 derive from the group, the four feel profoundly dependent on it. The bassman indeed expressed to *The Sunday Times* in 2001 how much he felt the need for the band's succor when his addictions got out of hand and he felt as if the world was crashing down on him. As a musician, says Bono, he needs the others in U2 more than they need him because, on his own, he lacks the ability to translate the melodies in his head into real music. But, as he confessed to *Vanity Fair*, he also needs them emotionally. They rely on one another for moral support not only when experiencing crises in their personal lives, but also when it comes to dealing with the pressures of their position. Bono reveals that Clayton helped him overcome his early insecurities about performing and to figure out what's really expected of him on stage. Indeed, sometimes he would get so frustrated by failing to reach his unattainable performance ideals that he would instruct the band to give the members of the audience their money back! Fortunately, Clayton was there to talk to him about it, late into the night on occasion, until the frontman grew more comfortable with his approach. "He's responsible for me being me" is Bono's grateful tribute to the bassist for his backing.[24]

By producer Nigel Godrich's account, Radiohead operates along the same lines. The five members get a lot of support from one another, he says, providing the gloss that "when one of them feels bad, the others readjust, gather around him."[25] The reputedly sensitive and fragile Thom Yorke appears to have avoided a few mental collapses thanks to the solace he derives from his bandmates. He informed *Alternative Press* in 1995, for instance, that he nearly had a breakdown in New York while touring *The Bends*. What brought him back from the brink (and made him withdraw his request to fly home) was simply discussing his distress with the others in the group. They are not only his bandmates, he noted, but his closest friends, so it's natural for him to turn to them, and they need to know when something is wrong.

Group support has been called for in the Red Hot Chili Peppers over the years primarily because Anthony Kiedis, Hillel Slovak, John Frusciante and Dave Navarro all wrestled with drug problems. Their efforts to stay clean have often meant keeping an eye on one another, as Kiedis and Slovak did quite effectively while touring Europe in the spring of 1988 (the guitarist's tragic overdose took place shortly afterwards, when the band dispersed upon returning to L.A.). As recently as 2002, the singer admitted (to *The Australian*) that the band bolsters his clean regime because they are all partners in sobriety. As noted earlier, the band members, particularly Flea and Kiedis, felt like they had no one but each other in the early years of their friendship, so they got into the habit of supporting and looking out for one another. On occasions when the band members have been remiss in understanding what someone in the group is going through or in lending him aid, the consequences have been dire. John Frusciante received little support from the other Chili Peppers, each immersed in his own problems and the first flush of fame, at the onset of his emotional tribulations in 1992 and ended up abruptly quitting the band.

A protective relationship seems to germinate around the more vulnerable band members. Journalists interviewing these groups have reported observing such behavior. In the Red Hot Chili Peppers, Kiedis and Flea exhibit a desire to shelter John Frusciante, described by many people as somewhat childlike, from some of the harsh or unpleasant realities of the music business (such as unscrupulous journalists). Jon Regardie noted in *Alternative Press* that Kiedis acts like a big brother towards the guitarist. A reporter for *The Guardian* (1997) discerned a similarly protective attitude among the four members of Radiohead when the conversation turned to Thom Yorke. And there have been numerous comments about how vigilant the three musicians in U2 appear in relation to Bono. In U2's case, the watchful mien turned into bona fide bodyguard action on one occasion. The frontman relates how, during the 1987 Joshua Tree tour, he was being threatened by a lunatic and was afraid of being gunned down at the L.A. show during the band's rendition of "Pride." When it came time to perform the song, Bono crouched down and closed his eyes. Upon opening them, he discovered the stolid bass player standing between him and any potential missiles emanating from the crowd.

THE CONFIDENCE TO DO IT

Many untrained rookies found their way into post-punk groups because they imbibed the no-experience-required ethos of the late 1970s. A prime example is U2, a band formed by four teenagers who were utterly ill-prepared, from a technical perspective, for the occupation they had chosen. Other notable novices include Peter Buck (who joked in *The Memphis Flyer* that at the outset he got by on three chords and a cloud of dust) and Anthony Kiedis. Complete lack of training or preparation can lead to fairly acute feelings of self-doubt in an aspiring musician (even one who subscribes to the punk ideology). So unsure of his abilities was Buck, for instance, that it took some persuading to rope him into R.E.M. Ultimately, joining forces with Stipe gave him the confidence to follow what had seemed like an unrealizable dream. The Red Hot Chili Peppers' frontman has made it no secret that he was, for many years, very self-conscious about his vocal abilities.

It's hard to imagine that these individuals would have had the guts to embark on careers as professional musicians were it not for the band. Jonny Greenwood, who, as we've seen, considers himself something of a bluffer, has indeed stated that he wouldn't have the confidence to "do anything but this [Radiohead]."[26] The group provides a support network in that the contributions of others—however unschooled themselves—can render one's own limitations less glaring. Working with people who are equally untaught can also help one feel less alone, part of an underdog team, while playing with more experienced musicians is an opportunity to learn. Finally, having partners who believe in you inspires assurance in oneself.

There are other circumstances that give rise to insecurity among the members of these groups, but they are fortunate in that their bandmates are there to inspirit them. Lineup changes have been a source of despondency in the Red Hot Chili Peppers, often leaving one party or another racked by doubts as to the future of the band. By receiving encouragement—directly and indirectly—from one another, they have overcome their misgivings and guided the band safely through some unimaginably turbulent periods. During the hard times of 1995, Kiedis openly expressed his gratitude for Flea's presence and waxed poetic about the fortitude he derives from their relationship. "Knowing that he exists, that he's my artistic partner and my friend for life gives me confidence to know that everything will be all right."[27]

A very extraordinary situation ensued when the Red Hot Chili Peppers invited John Frusciante to rejoin the band after his six years of exile, which had been devoted primarily to drug experimentation. It's an extreme example of the self-belief that can be instilled in even the most doubtful musician by a supportive band. In his heyday Frusciante had been a phenomenal guitarist, but the extended timeout put him in the position of a virtual beginner vis-à-vis the instrument. It didn't take long for him to regain his skills but his confidence might never have returned if his bandmates hadn't cheered him on. It's their sincere faith in him that the recovered addict credits with getting him on-track with music again. They looked past his deficiencies and perceived his potential. It didn't matter that his fingers were weak and he couldn't think as quickly musically, he said in describing their attitude. "They didn't see any of that stuff. They saw in me what I was capable of, and for that I'll always feel indebted to them."[28]

Yet—and here's the key—while championing his future promise, Frusciante's bandmates never made him feel inadequate, or that they only welcomed him back because of what he could become rather than what he was. Although they clearly looked forward to greater contributions from him down the road, they were delighted with what the guitarist brought to the band even in his feeble state. With Frusciante's reinstatement, the symbiotic creative element that had been missing from the group was restored—and this mattered far more than his competency. "They just thought the sound of us playing together is the greatest thing in the world," exclaims the guitarist with an amazement that comes across even in print. "I don't think they were thinking, 'Oh, in five months he'll be good.' They were thinking, 'This is the greatest thing in the world right now.'"[29] Other people Frusciante played with at this time neither accepted him as he was nor foresaw his growth. To practically everyone besides his bandmates, he goes on to relate, he was a loser. Were it not for Kiedis, Flea and Smith, he humbly confesses, he wouldn't be making music at all.

Collective lack of confidence is a trait exhibited by Radiohead. The band as a whole is often insecure. Surprised that so many people actually "get" the band, Yorke confesses that he's always paranoid about whether he's the only one who understands what he's trying to do. It's the same with his partners, he claims, adding that they cope with their qualms by emboldening one another. "We need to tell each other that what we're doing is good."[30] Part of the problem, explains Selway, is that they were a school band for many years before they became professionals, which generates insecurity. They feel somewhat like imposters who could be unmasked at any moment.

Yorke, in particular, seems to doubt himself and his decisions regularly. His anxiety peaks when the band takes what he considers to be a big risk, but his colleagues generally manage to talk him out of backpedaling or just assuage his anxiety. Having chosen the poignant but controversial title *Hail to the Thief* for Radiohead's sixth album, Yorke says that he was at peace with the decision initially, but became nervous as the record's release date drew near. He might have retracted the headline had his bandmates not bolstered his mettle. "I smashed my head against the wall about it for ages. The others steered me back," he said simply.[31] Along the same lines, when *Kid A* met with pockets of public outrage because it was regarded as such a radical departure for the band, Yorke was relatively unshaken by the response because his partners had prepared him for it, enabling him to face the situation coolly. In fact, when asked if he would have made *Kid A* as a solo album had the band rejected his electronica-centered vision, Yorke insists that he wouldn't have had the confidence (*Mojo* 2001). (By 2006, he felt self-assured enough and sufficiently comfortable with the electronic medium to release a solo effort in this vein.)

A coda to this discussion is that members of the group who are younger than the others—or in Frusciante's case, both younger and, at one time, a newcomer to an established lineup—are sometimes afflicted with timidity brought on rather than alleviated by the presence of their bandmates. Jonny Greenwood worried that his bandmates wouldn't take him seriously or accept his input, so at first he struggled to muster the courage to present his ideas to his fellow Radioheads. He was diffident about his songwriting abilities (and the fact that he can't sing a note), but he was also intimidated by the simple age gap between himself and the other four. In 1994 he reminded an *NME* journalist that his bandmates are the older kids he went to school with, who were his seniors in every respect and basically in charge of everything. Frusciante's bandmates tried to put him at ease when he first joined the Red Hot Chili Peppers by assuring him that he's their equal in every way, but the young guitarist didn't have the nerve to be himself around them. Impressing his idols, eight years older than he, was his chief agenda and one that clearly stemmed from reservations about his worthiness and fear of falling short of their expectations. He recalled in *Guitar* in 1991 that it took a while for him to really express himself, as opposed to showing them what he could do.

KEEPING ONE ANOTHER IN CHECK

Sometimes, support or a boost of confidence *isn't* the response a situation calls for, but a kick in the teeth *is*, and there's generally someone in the group to deliver it. All four bands cite keeping one another in check as a key constituent of their dynamic. It's the equality in the group, the fact that the members are partners, which gives them warrant to frown upon—and thereby curb—the wayward behavior of any in their ranks with impunity. Preventing one another from becoming too arrogant or taking themselves too seriously, what Buck calls falling for the typical rock and roll garbage, is the most common objective. Stipe doesn't think that's likely to happen in R.E.M. given how tough they are on one another. "One thing we have going for us is that none of us is afraid to slap the other if he starts getting a big head."[32] The ego stroking accorded rock stars by many of those surrounding them doesn't extend to the band, which is like a sealed-off hothouse with a completely different climate inside that is more conducive to mental and creative health. "When it's just the four of us and we're working," says Mills, "there's no coddling."[33]

Buck confirms that they monitor themselves and one another very effectively in R.E.M.: "We mock each other so much none of us could get away with being a real pompous, pretentious person. I've never seen

a group of people so quick to deflate egos as this band and our manager."[34] As one rather comic story goes, an unwitting *Rolling Stone* critic
stated in his review of *Reckoning* that Peter Buck does everything on the
record. Little did he know to what torment he had condemned the guitarist as a result of this overblown praise! Buck was certainly in no danger of becoming smug, what with his bandmates jeering him at every
opportunity. He told *The Los Angeles Times* in 1984 that whenever they
stopped at a gas station, for instance, Stipe, Mills and Berry would chime,
"Peter Buck does everything. Why don't you go pump the gas, Pete?"

In U2, measures are taken to ensure, quite simply, that the members don't turn into jerks. Well, not for too long, at least. Each of them
goes down that path once in a while, and after giving him some space,
the others start reining him in. "Every time, in this group's life, someone's gonna be a bollox," submits Bono. "You have to give him enough
room, and then when they go too far, take them out of that."[35] The singer
often wonders how solo artists manage to keep their head on straight,
when everyone is on their payroll and no one is in a position to criticize
their actions. This situation would make him awfully nervous, he confessed to *Sonicnet.com*. For Bono, then, it's reassuring to be in a band like
U2. With four of them, there's a limit to what any one individual can do,
he explains while pondering an alternate scenario. "I can't imagine what
that's like, without someone to occasionally tell you you're a prick."[36] His
assertion that the bandmates keep each other in order is borne out by
Edge, who swore to *Rolling Stone* (1992) that none of them will ever be
allowed to become an asshole because the other guys in the band won't
let him get away with it. While there's a lot of mutual criticism in U2,
the band members give each other plenty of leeway, Edge informed *USA
Today* (2002), drawing attention to the need for balance.

Failing to point out the error of one's ways can be detrimental to
the group. So it's essential, claims Anthony Kiedis, for the band members to carry out this duty ruthlessly. According to the singer, his objectionable conduct made his bandmates literally hate him on occasion. But
they only exacerbated the situation by not confronting him about it. "I
need my friends and I need them to tell me 'Excuse me but you are
being an asshole' ... 'Oh thanks I didn't realize!'"[37] He depends on them
to keep him in line. Their willingness to pull each other up also pro-
hibits the band members from becoming sloppy or indifferent about
their work. Gigs can become boring and meaningless in the midst of an
extended tour (and a long career). It's easy to lose sight of the fact that
each night is special—and even easier to surrender to indolence. In U2,
if any of the four takes the attitude that one night's performance is "just
another show," one of the others will grab him by the scruff of the neck,
says Bono, knock him against the wall and make him realize how momen-

tous the occasion is and that second-best won't cut it. No one in the band has to fight this kind of tour sickness, or any other incitement to sloth, on his own. "We've learned to pull each other up when one of us is getting lazy," remarks the singer.[38]

In addition to being on equal footing, the members of these bands have, for the most part, grown up together, and that also gives them license to censure one another. Asked if he and his cohorts in U2 continue to act like schoolboys when they're together, Larry Mullen quips that they still beat each other up (figuratively speaking, one presumes). "Obviously there's respect, but there are limits. We all have to take a battering sometimes!"[39] Bono confirms that they enjoy a lot of laughs together, "as well as kicking the shit out of each other."[40] Having been friends since they were 15, says Thom Yorke of himself and his bandmates, "how can you not mercilessly rip the shit out of each other? It's just like when you're a kid; it's no different."[41]

They make fun of each other all the time in R.E.M. because they're such good friends, says Buck, who once remarked that the band calls him "Mister Rock 'n' Roll" and Mike Mills "Mister Musician." Whether or not it dates back to their juvenile days, this type of communal mockery undoubtedly adds to the fun of being in the band, and, at the same time, has a powerful grounding effect. In some cases, direct criticism with no attached element of humor is employed to curtail undesirable behavior. That seems to be a predominant dynamic in U2. Each member of the band has three equal peers criticizing him all the time, Paul McGuiness stressed to *Vogue*.

Each group also has its own moral code (spoken or unspoken) that the members are, to some extent, compelled to adhere to. There are undoubtedly moments when the tenets of this code need to be actively enforced, but the knowledge that it exists is enough to keep the band members on the approved path most of the time. As Bono revealed to journalist Michka Assayas in an interview for the latter's book about the singer, although Adam Clayton's front-page-worthy failure to show up for a Zoo TV concert in Sydney was more self-betrayal than band-betrayal, it still represented a completely unacceptable offense by U2 standards, but might have been perfectly legitimate in another outfit where partying regularly interferes with band business. It wasn't unusual, after all, for Anthony Kiedis to miss Chili Pepper rehearsals in the heyday of his drug addiction, but he knew he had to make it to the shows. In an interview with *Vox*, Ed O'Brien revealed that he didn't take advantage of a beautiful groupie who propositioned him after a gig in Dallas because the seedier elements of rock culture are generally frowned upon in Radiohead (which he regards as a very moral group) and he wasn't sure what his bandmates would think of him.

From a creative standpoint, there is a similar dynamic of keeping one another in check. Everyone in the band has the freedom to experiment, explore and propose ideas, knowing the others won't let him get carried away. "If you get too far off into one tangent, there's someone else to pull you back to ground zero," R.E.M.'s Michael Stipe shared with *Addicted to Noise* (adding that if you get too close to ground zero there's someone else "ready to take a left turn").[42] In Radiohead, U2 and R.E.M., there is, in fact, a visionary "ideas man" who would be in serious danger of going adrift if his more earth-bound partners didn't keep him anchored. Alluding to this concept, Thom Yorke claims that one of the reasons he benefits from being in Radiohead is because his bandmates provide him with indispensable "points of reference." Were he working alone, he muses, he'd wind up in "lala land."[43] Not only might his ideas be radically offbeat, but his ability to execute them would be compromised in the absence of his bandmates' restraint. (This is, of course, another aspect of his dependence on the band.) With his obsessive and perfectionist tendencies peaking during the recording of *Kid A*, the singer confesses that he would have continued tinkering in the studio forever if Jonny Greenwood hadn't called time on the sessions and forced everyone to wrap up (*Mojo*, 2003).

In R.E.M., the musicians make it possible for Stipe to spread his artistic wings (knowing how much this freedom to fly enriches the band), but at the same time, they also put the fetters on his wilder flights of imagination. Stipe says as much when he remarks that Mike Mills and Peter Buck are "really solid people, supportive of my flights off," which are, he insists, "essential to my contribution to what we do." Knowing that "those guys are always there to pull me back in" enables him to "go off" when he feels the need.[44] Kate Pierson of another famous Athens band, the B-52's, confirms that Stipe's bandmates hold down the fort, which allows him to "step out and be the wild thing that he is."[45]

U2 seems to have a comparable dynamic, Bono with his head in the clouds while the others keep his feet planted on terra firma. Adam Clayton emphasizes that this system avails both the band and the visionary singer. "For every mad idea of Bono's, he drags us somewhere interesting. And he benefits when we hold him back from where the ice is thin."[46] However, they have also learned over the years that not every one of the singer's fanciful notions is as mad as it seems. Edge recalls how, when the band was recording "The Wanderer," Bono picked up the microphone to sing, and suddenly proposed inviting legendary country artist Johnny Cash, who was visiting Dublin, to provide vocals for the track. Far from receiving the suggestion enthusiastically, the guitarist claims he, Clayton and Mullen thought this was just another of the frontman's ludicrous schemes. But they've learned, over the years, to bite their tongue in these situations, Edge admitted to *Hot Press* in 2003, because many of the singer's ideas that strike them as crazy or improbable actually come to pass (as was the case when Cash agreed to appear on the track). Rick Rubin told *Rolling Stone* in 2006 that Frusciante is the ideas man in the Chili Peppers, the one who takes the track over the top, but has his bandmates to rein him in when necessary.

Bono's three partners have, in the past, also curtailed some of his more reckless or caricaturist behavior, particularly some of his stage antics, such as waving or wrapping himself in a white flag. Like Yorke, Bono is grateful for the limitations imposed by his bandmates because he realizes that his own efforts at self-restraint would be inadequate. He'd be in deep trouble as a solo artist, he confided to *USA Today* in 2001, so he's lucky to have the band. He tries, for example, not to let his political views figure too prominently in the band's music, but can't always censor his lyrics appropriately himself, so he relies on the others to perform this function.

PROMPTS

It sometimes happens that the band members have to be prompted into action by one another. Both Stipe and Yorke have confessed that they developed a quasi-fear/quasi-loathing for touring following particularly long and draining campaigns (respectively, the 1988 *Green* road trip and the 1997 *OK Computer* trek) that they might not have overcome had it not been for their bandmates' prodding. Berry insisted that R.E.M. return to the road in 1995 after its controversial five-year seclusion in the studio. As Buck and Mills also proved eager to set out again, the band managed to overcome Stipe's lingering reluctance. In 2000, when *Hot Press* asked Thom Yorke point blank if he ever wanted to play before a live audience again after the previously exhausting outing, he confessed that even the idea of a short and pleasant summer jaunt filled him with horror. But his four partners in Radiohead urged him to consider it and convinced him that it would be fun and laid-back. He confesses that he wouldn't have ventured out again had they not worked hard to persuade him. That was after the band forced Yorke to get past his trepidation about finishing the album, which meant releasing it to the public and starting the daunting cycle (press, promos, performances) all over again. Had it been up to him, says the singer, he would have continued delaying the moment of truth, as he did for a good six months before his collaborators pulled the plug.

COMPETITION

Internal rivalry can be a dividing and destructive force in bands—or any team effort, for that matter—but not always. The Red Hot Chili Peppers' inimitable energy and spirit derives at least in part from the fraternal competition between Anthony Kiedis and his longtime friend, Flea, who have what Kiedis calls a "real scrapping-brother-type relationship."[47] They always drove each other in a competitive way, explains the singer, each trying to outdo the other's crazy antics. It was competitive but healthy at the same time, he insists. This friendly rivalry continues to be an important part of the group's essence even now that the two are cognizant of it. "We're a little more subtle, and less egotistical, about it. But it never dies, that sort of thing that brothers have. There's always, you know, 'I'll kick your ass.' 'No, I'll kick your ass!' But at least now we recognize it and can laugh about it. Back then, we tried to masquerade it and pretend like [sic] it's not there."[48] Implicit in this statement is the notion that when this sort of antagonism, even of a non-hostile variety, is acknowledged and out in the open, it's not a problem, but it can become one if is concealed or ignored.

Adam Clayton has made numerous statements indicating that there was an undercurrent of competitiveness running through U2 in the early days, though there is nothing to suggest that it resembled the kind of one-upmanship driving the Red Hot Chili Peppers. It was more a jockeying for position arising from an adolescent lack of confidence. "For the first couple of years we were like a gang of guys fighting with each other. I think there was the same kind of competitiveness and insecurity within all of us and everyone wanted to be top dog," says the bassman.[49] They were struggling for dominance over the unit. At the same time, however, Clayton claims that they were such poor musicians when they started out that there wasn't even a remote possibility of anyone having an artist's ego. Thus, when it came to their musical abilities, the four, far from vying with one another, reveled in seeing their partners improve, because, the bassist notes humorously, they all "started with minus points."[50]

If, in the band's infancy, any possibility of *creative* rivalry was tempered by the members' undisguised weaknesses, it has since been kept at bay by the aptitude each of them has developed on his instrument. They have developed individual strengths, so there is no real competition, Edge asserted two decades into the band's career in an interview with *Muse.* It's easy to see why both scenarios repel skill contests: when the four musicians were equally inept, they had nothing to envy in one another, and the same is true now that each has established an adroitness he can take pride in and for which he is respected by his bandmates. With the passage of time, then, the initial strain of competitiveness in the group became less pronounced, says Clayton, and Bono reminded *Hot Press* (2001) that U2 is, in any case, not a group that thrives on the sort of sibling rivalry that fuels a band like Oasis.

Some creative competition exists in Radiohead owing to the fact that there are three guitarists in the band. Each of them scrambles to come up with the best line first, Yorke notified *Select* in 1995 (facetiously adding that Jonny Greenwood always comes out on top). Not denying that there's an element of rivalry among the guitarists, Selway refers to it as spurring each other on and observes that it is secondary to the desire each member of the band feels to do what's best for the song. In an interview with *Consumable Online* in 1995, the drummer also drew attention to certain positive outcomes of the contest between Yorke, Greenwood and O'Brien. It leads the three of them to come up with very interesting arrangements and broadens the scope of what Radiohead can do as a guitar band.

5

"Feeling Gravity's Pull": Obstacles to Band Unity and Survival

The most appropriate way to kick off this chapter is with Bono's observation that bands are miracles because they "defy gravity" (which seems to signify, in this case, the forces that tear people asunder) and "basic human needs" such as the desire for independence.[1] Indeed, the taxing group dynamic has shortened the lifespan of countless bands who just couldn't hack it. There are so many obstacles in the way of collaboration and unity, it's a wonder any band can hold together for decades. Those who do manage it invest a lot of effort in the group, facing down both predictable and surprising challenges in the process. In order for the group to survive and function effectively, certain behaviors have to be *kept out of it* (the don'ts) and others must be *brought to bear on it* (the do's). This chapter outlines the major points that fall under each category. It also discusses the nature of conflicts in these groups and why the members are determined to make the band work.

Although the affection and musical connection shared by the members of these four rock groups sprung into being naturally, keeping the peace and overcoming obstacles to the band's unity demands significant ongoing effort. Flea acknowledges that the Red Hot Chili Peppers require "a lot of focus and discipline all the time, and not letting up, and not letting things unravel."[2] He specifically mentions that a lot of energy goes into maintaining the cohesiveness in the group. Brotherhood, love and camaraderie may be what the band is all about, he commented in *The Boston Globe* when the Chili Peppers were struggling to keep it together in 1996, but these are ideals that they cannot reach all the time. In the same article, Flea admitted that his relationship with Anthony Kiedis requires the most work—more than any romantic liaison—precisely because the two friends are so close and have the ability to hurt each other deeply. The contentious nature of their friendship also means they must actively avoid ruptures.

Staying cool with the other band members requires daily diligence, according to Kiedis' testimony in the Red Hot Chili Peppers edition of *Kerrang!* They end and begin each day on a harmonious note, no matter how sticky things get in between, because they are willing to do what it takes to sort out their differences. No member of the band can escape from the onus of maintaining the relationships within it. In the year leading up to John Frusciante's severance from the group, the guitarist refused to make any attempt to mend his rapidly deteriorating relationship with Kiedis. Although Flea urged Frusciante to seek reconciliation, the latter decided to let the problems slide, which was a cardinal mistake. He has since revealed that he just didn't care enough about his friendship with the singer to do what was necessary to rehabilitate it.

Part I: Why do they do it?

"A band is a very difficult thing to keep going," corroborates Edge, who likens U2 to a four-way marriage, "and when you're in a good one, you try to make it work whatever way you can."[3] Here, then, is the primary motivation (aside from friendship, the obvious inducement) for investing all this energy in maintaining the collective: the recognition that you're in an optimal collaboration. There are two distinct admissions involved in arriving at this conclusion: first, understanding that you're made to work with others; second, acknowledging that you've found the ideal artistic allies, which is where mutual respect and admiration enter the picture. When the going gets tough, says Edge, he asks himself if he wants to be a solo performer, and inevitably comes to the conclusion that he prefers working with other musicians in a collaborative setup, which means that he has to be in a band. He then ponders who he would want to be in a band with, and, because he regards his bandmates as incomparable creative partners, ends up reinventing U2 in his head. "'Well, Bono! He's such a great singer, I couldn't imagine working with a different singer. And Adam and Larry, what a rhythm section!'"[4] Since he can't conceive of another outfit that could offer an equally challenging and exciting creative environment, declared the guitarist in 1995, he probably wouldn't be interested in making music at all if he weren't in U2. A few years later, he reiterated this statement in *Time Out*, introducing an additional incentive to stick with this unit—the band members' profound and unparalleled understanding of one another.

For Bono (who once joked that it's just fear of their manager that has kept U2 together), the determination to uphold and abide in U2 starts with loving the band life for its fraternity and frolics. So, like Edge, he'd always opt to work in a group, but for slightly different reasons. The second part of the equation is the same for both men: no other group could measure up. If you're going to be in a band, U2 is the best one to be in, Bono insists. But, in his case, it comes down to the personal relationship more than the creative one. He couldn't possibly have more fun with anyone else, since his bandmates (and manager) are some of the only people in the world who really make him laugh, he explained to *Rolling Stone* in 1987. These, then, are the points he keeps in mind when he gets restless or fantasizes about hooking up with other artists.

In an interview with Radio 1, Mullen cracked that, at least for him, there's also the horrible realization that he's not actually qualified to do anything else. Not only are he and his partners in U2 unprepared for other careers, they are ill-equipped to join another band. As they aren't virtuosos, the drummer believes, as we've seen, that they manage to make music *together* because they learned how to play with one another rather than to play in general. So the resulting sense of profound interdependency is a significant factor underlying their fidelity to U2. Making his point with equal wit in *Time Out,* Adam Clayton expressed his lack of interest in trout-fishing, the prototypical pursuit of washed-up rock stars. When he considers that this is the alternative to being in the band, he is convinced of the fact that, despite all the hardships, there's no better gig for him out there.

Like Edge, Thom Yorke readily admits that he's built to work with other people because, he remarked in *The Observer* (2000), they provide the reality checks without which he would get lost, bored or frustrated. His right-hand man, Jonny Greenwood, is compelled by the other half of the syllogism. "I'd feel really fraudulent going and playing guitar, or any other instrument, on something else, because I know it wouldn't be anywhere near as good. It's a Radiohead thing."[5] The Red Hot Chili Peppers, who have always shown dogged perseverance in the face of critical challenges, remark that they haven't given up on the group because they believe in one another and in what they are doing. Chad Smith reveals, in addition, that he is mobilized by the immeasurable investment he has made in the Chili Peppers and how bound up he is in this outfit. "It's part of my identity. That's not to say I couldn't do other things, but I *live* the RHCP."[6] (Still, if the group started cranking out music just to make money, he insists he would feel differently.) Another imperative for adhering to the group is that the band's improvisational method of composition demands an emotional closeness and mental telepathy that take time—not to mention a hearty dose of chemistry—to develop.

Certain individuals have, on occasion, thought the group was done for and that it should just end, reflects Kiedis, but the key is that they've never come to that conclusion *as a band*. They have also seized every opportunity the universe has thrown their way to keep the Chili Peppers going. "Maybe there's been passing phases of 'Holy shit! This is going nowhere, I've got to move on' in the past. But then, lo and behold, something would happen, a little crack in the sky would open up, and it becomes, 'Maybe I'll give this just one more try.'"[7] These sudden reprieves inspired the band members to continue exerting themselves on behalf of their collective.

In a group with three songwriters who could conceivably go it alone, the reigning belief among the members of R.E.M. is that their solo efforts would fall short of what they achieve together because their collaboration pushes each of them to new heights. It's the best situation for any of them to be in, Mills declared in *Addicted to Noise* (1998). As for ditching R.E.M. in favor of another outfit, the pragmatic Buck doesn't see the point in breaking up a solid band and going through the pain of putting together a new one. According to Stipe, they also realize they wouldn't get any more out of another outfit. "R.E.M. has provided each of us with just about everything. Abandoning it doesn't make sense."[8] Having been in R.E.M. since he was 19, added the singer, he is greatly attached to the group because it's the only life he knows. After Bill Berry left in 1997, the remaining band members had to decide if they should carry on and followed essentially the same logic that Edge put forward. None of them were ready to stop making music, Stipe revealed in *AllStar*, and they couldn't think of anyone else they prefer to work with, as they find their partners more inspiring than anyone else, so they moved forward as a trio.

When the band effectively split and reunited in 1999, Stipe said they discovered how much R.E.M. really means to them. There's a spiritual aspect to being in the band. "Getting back together was like church," he declares. "This band is my church, pure and simple."[9] According to a quote in Johnny Black's biography, *Reveal*, at times like this Mike Mills explains that he doesn't necessarily need to remind himself how great R.E.M. is or that he prefers his existing partners to any other collaborators. He claims that the questions he asks himself have to do with how much he's willing to put into the band and whether he thinks it's worth the investment. In other words, that it's an ideal alliance goes without saying, but does that offset the costs of sustaining it?

What ultimately makes it worthwhile for him, he remarked in an interview with *The Herald*, is that they love each other, the work that they do together and what each of them brings to it. Furthermore, he told *Addicted to Noise* (1998) that the band members are determined to stick to R.E.M because of the realization that it's their life's work and will forever be their highest accomplishment. Finally, they are also—and this is key—willing to make any changes necessary (like touring less and recording infrequently) to ensure a workable future for their collaboration. "We do whatever we have to do to keep the band going on a level that we can all stand."[10] They're not rigidly tied to a certain setup or usage that can put off members of the band if it becomes unsuitable, unsustainable or simply unappealing.

When it comes to keeping a band together despite all the hardships, nothing is as important as an unswerving commitment to the collective. That has prevented the members of U2 from becoming overwhelmed by even the fiercest fracas that erupts in the unit. Internal friction can split up bands that have "less of a sense of being a band," says Edge, adding that this involves loyalty, a deep friendship, and, above all, an unshakable dedication to the group. It would take "a hell of a lot," he declares, to threaten the relationships in U2 and overthrow the members' devotion to the group.[11] The responsibilities and commitment to the band run so deep, alleged Mullen in an interview for the Zoo TV tour program, that there's no escape—a slightly sinister way of acknowledging that their allegiance to U2 is too inveterate for any force to crush it. Not only has this stance helped the band tolerate strife but also to persist in the face of what Edge euphemistically calls some "less-than-perfect-endeavors" that could easily destroy another group.[12] Surviving failures is tremendously challenging for bands because it's tempting for the members to blame one another and easy for them to lose faith in the benefits of the partnership.

Part II: The don'ts

THE SOUND OF SILENCE

None of these bands are notorious for feuding in public, but, as Bono puts it, "We have our moments and things can get pretty rough out there."[13] Just because they are friends and their love for each other deeper than anything that comes between them, confirms Mullen, doesn't mean there aren't "scraps and bust-ups" in U2.[14] They both seem to refer to patent clashes between the members, but there are various forms of internal division. Strife, Jonny Greenwood ruminates, infers arguments and raised voices and hurled objects. In reality, malaise is just as clearly manifested in stony retreat from one another. During the wearisome Pablo Honey tour, there were never any real arguments between the members of Radiohead, Greenwood informed *B-Side*, just a custom of withdrawing into themselves, which he deems worse than open warfare. The band members essentially stopped talking to each other. They made small talk and spoke of trivial matters, but exchanging words doesn't constitute genuine communication (a lesson many a band has had to learn).

It's a problem Radiohead has faced time and again, where, in an effort to avoid confrontation, concerns and frustrations weren't tabled. In some cases, on top of a characteristic reserve, the perceived fragility of the band led the quintet to keep thoughts and feelings bottled up, Selway divulged in *Kulturnews*. As a result of their reluctance to speak openly with one another, there have been numerous stretches when they should have thrashed out contentious issues, but didn't, allowing grievances to brew until they reached a dangerous boiling point, as they did during the 1994 tour of Mexico. The consequent showdown between the five friends was cathartic, but the band members would be the first to admit that it wasn't wise to let the situation reach this almost-irreparable stage.

Lack of communication and its corollary, withdrawal from one another, is often at the root of problems even in bands more seasoned than Radiohead and whose members aren't nearly as reticent. They're pretty good at clearing the air in R.E.M., boasts Buck, but they consistently neglected to reach out to each other when they were making *Up*, and the band narrowly escaped extinction. They dealt with the crisis engendered by Berry's departure like typical guys, Stipe said in *The Mirror*, each retreating into his own corner. By the end of recording, the situation was so far gone that an iron curtain had fallen between the three longtime collaborators. It got to the point where they didn't even know how to talk to each other anymore, he recalled in *Q* (1999). Fortunately, their manager stepped into the breach, calling for a formal summit to re-establish a dialogue between the band members. It was a drastic measure by any estimation.

The complete communication breakdown between Anthony Kiedis and John Frusciante during the *Blood Sugar Sex Magik* tour was more a symptom than the cause of the rift between them, but it served to widen the distance considerably. Divisions and beefs giving rise to tension between the four members were swept under the carpet instead of addressed as everyone tried to pretend that nothing was going on—another trap bands can easily fall into, especially when they're on the road, Kiedis points out. In retrospect, the singer marvels at how ineptly they dealt with the palpable discord on the fateful 1992 tour that ended without Frusciante.

The Chili Peppers never stopped to assess the situation or talk about the issues, concentrating instead on getting from one week to the next, which didn't create a healing environment. "Considering the severity of the dysfunction being displayed, it's strange for me to look back and think that we didn't realize things couldn't go on like this," Kiedis disclosed in his autobiography.[15] Thanks to the eleventh-hour summit R.E.M. managed to pull up in time; the Red Hot Chili Peppers did not. Simply put, poor communication, whether it ultimately provokes shouting matches or puts distance between the parties involved, is the kiss of death for any relationship if it goes unchecked.

THE BIG EGO

Ego aggrandizement is right up there with lack of communication and financial squabbles as a classic bandbreaker. So constant vigilance to keep egos in check and out of sight is an idea that surfaces repeatedly. It's true that the band members help one another keep a lid on their egos, but it takes more than that. Mike Mills says that in R.E.M., they hold the sanctity and importance of the group above their individual egos. Similarly, the members of U2 reveal they have learned to sublimate their egos and ambitions to a *band* ego and a *band* ambition. "We've long since stopped worrying about our personal space or reward in terms of ambition or effort," says Edge. "We see it as a group ego."[16] It's not surprising that they developed a collective ego given Adam Clayton's earlier claim that they were so awful when they started out that it wasn't possible for any of them to be full of himself. In Radiohead and the Red Hot Chili Peppers, The Song reigns supreme, with the band members seeking to elevate their work, rather than themselves, to lofty heights. That means doing what's right for the music, Phil Selway clarified in *Modern Drummer* (1996), rather than trying to stamp one's ego all over it. The idea here is not to eliminate ego gratification by cultivating humility, but to find it in collective accomplishments or to channel it into the work.

CONTROL FREAKS NEED NOT APPLY

Harmony within the group can be disrupted (or its very survival threatened) by less documented behaviors, practices and circumstances. An enormous challenge lies in curbing natural proclivities that make collaboration difficult or downright impossible. As little room as there is in a rock band for egomaniacs, control freaks are even less welcome. (It might be considered puzzling that anyone so disposed would choose to be in a band in the first place, where, by default, you have to give up much of your individual authority. But there are the obvious benefits, and in many cases, the need for the collective to take into consideration.)

Peter Buck identifies the individual's yearning for domination as a human trait that must be cautiously managed in a band in order to avoid disparities in influence and the strife that accompanies them. "We have a very delicate four-way balance," he says of R.E.M., "and we're always careful about not assuming too much control over things."[17] This was a steep learning curve for the band, given that each member is a song-writer in his own right; it was hard for them to adapt to the idea of relin-quishing control over their own compositions. "None of us gets exactly what we want. It's something that I would never have believed I'd be able to do when I was twenty-four," says Buck. "I used to be like, 'God-damnit, this is *my* song. I don't like that verse. Either you change it or I will.'"[18] Kiedis and Yorke are self-confessed control freaks who have had to learn to regulate this impulse in order to collaborate effectively with their bandmates. Yorke was, in fact, a control freak with actual control over Radiohead, which is a particularly bad combination. Not only was his sway within the band unbalanced, but he recalls moments in the studio when he wouldn't let anyone else do anything because he wanted to be in sole command of the creative process.

Even equality and comradeship don't necessarily rule out hazardous power struggles, which can creep into any collective in some form and undermine its solidarity. This is not the case in U2, contends producer Brian Eno, noting in *Propaganda* (1992, issue 16) that none of the four members are out to dominate their bandmates, as often happens in other bands. In the same interview he remarked that other groups he's worked with also have a covert diplomatic scene (this person won't do this unless that person does something else) that takes up a lot of the musicians' energy and ultimately hurts the music. A band is no place for petty pol-itics. That U2 has managed to keep these elements out of the relation-ship between the four of them is one of the band's greatest strengths in Eno's view.

OBSTINACY

Collective obstinacy has been a boon to R.E.M.'s career but when it's turned inwards and the individual band members visit their stubborn natures on one another, the repercussions are noxious. Discussing with *Q* (1988) how fights get started in R.E.M., Buck identified his own and bandmate Stipe's inherent stubbornness as fairly frequent culprits. Stipe attributes the band's near collapse in 1998 in part to his own pighead-edness, which he was forced to curb once he grasped its consequences. "When it all came to a really ugly head, I realized I wasn't ready to let it fall apart because I had my arms crossed over my chest and was being stubborn."[19] It's not that everyone has to relent easily (and they don't), but it's another matter to stand your ground in situations when you can bear to budge, as Mills explained in the preceding chapter. That's when resolve can turn into baneful intransigence that ends in strife.

CLIQUISHNESS

In the Red Hot Chili Peppers, cliquishness has sometimes created an unhealthy dynamic. While Chad Smith tends to stand on the sidelines, Frusciante, Flea and Kiedis have had difficulty forging a three-way friendship in the past. Instead, one pair would become bosom buddies, making the third person feel left out. First it was Kiedis and Frusciante who formed a close relationship from which Flea was excluded. Later, during the recording of *Blood Sugar Sex Magik*, Frusciante took to smoking pot with Flea on a regular basis, but Kiedis, then a teetotaler, was marginalized by his unwillingness to join in. The singer's resulting sense of loneliness had a positive outcome in that it inspired the lyrics to the band's best-known song, "Under the Bridge," which came to him while he was driving home from a particularly alienating rehearsal. But the groundwork for the hostility that surfaced during the subsequent tour was laid by these scrimmages. According to Frusciante, Kiedis and Flea were always at loggerheads, which forced the guitarist to align himself with one or the other. "It couldn't just be the three of us all being friends equally, which is what it is now," he remarked in 2000.[20] There's nothing wrong with some band members being more intimate with others and for that to change constantly, says Kiedis; it's an inevitable part of being in a group. It's when partiality leads to segregation that tensions arise and the band suffers.

Similarly, religious differences made Adam Clayton the odd man out in U2 during the band's early days because he didn't share the Christian zeal of his reborn bandmates and they couldn't relate to his hedonistic lifestyle. "I was in the wilderness for a few years," says the bassist, "so there was a natural antagonism within the band that people picked up on."[21] It wasn't a healthy state of affairs, but the band closed ranks in time to salvage the alliance. A twist on this theme is the act (or perceived act) of ganging up on one another, which Buck felt Stipe and Mills were doing to him during R.E.M.'s first venture as an uneven-numbered trio. It's likely that any time a member of the group doesn't share the views of the others, who then try to bring him onside, he feels somewhat as if his partners have launched a joint offensive against him, which can lead to indignation and resentment if the situation isn't navigated carefully.

DRUGS

Drugs, booze and rock bands have always gone hand-in-hand, but, as the Red Hot Chili Peppers can attest, enslavement to alcohol and other substances, whatever they may or may not do for the group's creativity, can grievously obstruct its ability to function. During the periods when Kiedis was heavily into heroin, he regularly missed band rehearsals. Worse still, his contributions on the songwriting front were often impoverished, as when the band recorded *The Uplift Mofo Party Plan,* or tardy for *One Hot Minute.* He was also incapable, in his ravaged state, of challenging the others in the band the way they needed and wanted to be challenged by one another. With copping a hit rather than making music with the band topping his list of priorities, the strung-out singer was often a liability instead of an asset.

Kiedis' destructive behavior engendered substantial intra-group friction. Hillel Slovak managed to minimize the impact of his equally acute drug dependency on his participation in the Red Hot Chili Peppers, but the band suffered nonetheless. In his memoirs, Kiedis describes how Slovak became increasingly detached and aloof. After shows, for instance, he would quickly slip out of the venue searching to score while his bandmates convened to analyze the evening's performance, which, in his case, was frequently underwhelming. An overdose eventually took the gifted guitarist's life and chased away the band's disconsolate drummer, strikes from which few bands would have recovered.

Part of the problem with drug use in the Red Hot Chili Peppers in particular is that it has been restricted to certain members of the band at certain times. When Kiedis and Slovak were using, Flea and Irons weren't. Later, when Kiedis cleaned up his act, Flea and Frusciante took to smoking pot together and Frusciante began dabbling in heroin shortly before he left the band. In the mid 1990s, with Flea sworn off narcotic substances, Kiedis relapsed and Navarro brought his own struggles with addiction to the group. Beer and cigarettes, meanwhile, have reportedly been Chad Smith's only vices. There has been a great deal of unevenness in the unit with all this asynchronous and non-universal drug-taking.

As a result, the members' all-important dedication to the group has, at times, been incommensurate and they routinely found themselves occupying incompatible headspaces. Kiedis felt relegated to the sidelines when his two bandmates were getting high without him, and they, in turn, resented his holier-than-thou attitude and imperious brand of asceticism. Frusciante told the French magazine *RockSound* that the singer exhibited blatant disgust whenever anyone lit a joint or had a drink in his presence. The guitarist consequently feared (and perhaps began to despise) Kiedis as one would an overbearing father. A few years later, sparks flew between Kiedis and Smith when the latter openly expressed his frustration with the singer for essentially putting the band on hold by disappearing into a cloud of dope again.

Speaking to *Modern Drummer* in 1999, Smith revealed that his attitude had since changed, as anger with the self-absorbed drug fiends who held back the band turned to compassion for their predicament. Indeed, demonstrations of clemency rather than expressions of outrage can be credited, to a large extent, with saving the band. Frusciante recalls in *RockSound* how kind and sympathetic the formerly stern Kiedis was towards him during a chance encounter at a concert when the guitarist was deep in the throes of his addiction. This sympathy and concern for his well-being warmed his heart and undoubtedly paved the way for the pair's reconciliation. Whenever Kiedis was ready to return to the band following a relapse, he felt no trepidation at the thought of facing Flea, he wrote in *Scar Tissue*. At times like these, his old friend was supportive and nonjudgmental, neither condemning nor lecturing the prodigal singer, who has come to the conclusion that dope doesn't mix well with band life. "It's a lot easier to be in the band when people aren't screwing their minds with drugs. It's a lot easier to make rehearsals and to be supportive of each other," announced a reformed and enlightened Kiedis in 2002.[22]

WHEN ONE PERSON GOES ASTRAY

While researching this book, I filed various "complications" under the nonspecific heading "When One Person Goes Astray." What this refers to is a psychological or mental state affecting one or more members of the band in a way that interferes with, jeopardizes or threatens it. Bono, for instance, confided in Michka Assayas' book that members of U2 have, on occasion, lost themselves or lost their way in the music, and while it's important to allow people to do that, it's upsetting nonetheless.

To take a more concrete example, for three years following Radiohead's OK Computer tour, Thom Yorke experienced a period of intense internal turmoil. Not mincing words, he declares: "I was a complete fucking mess."[23] His consequent ill-humor at times made it very unpleasant for the five to work together. Meanwhile, his confusion, disillusion, and disenchantment with everything slowed the group down and demoralized his bandmates. The quintet weathered this trial but it was one of the shakiest periods in its history. Emotional disturbances have also rocked the Red Hot Chili Peppers. Many of the low points the group has survived were precipitated by an individual member's precarious mental state (often, but not always, associated with drug addiction).

Flea describes the rough patch he and Kiedis went through over the years spanning from *Blood Sugar Sex Magik* to *One Hot Minute*. For the bassist, this represented the darkest period in his life. "I went into a two-year down, just bottomed out," he confided in 1996.[24] His friend Kiedis was wrestling with his own demons and, according to Flea, both men were confronting some ugly truths about themselves. Accounting to the press for the long gap between albums, Kiedis indeed imputed the holdup to his personal struggles. "I've been on a blistering roller-coaster ride of mental-health ups and downs. Germs of psychosis knocked me out for a while" was the justification he offered *Rolling Stone*.[25] Flea confessed during a *VH1.com* interview that the psychological perturbations both men experienced also knocked out their friendship for a while, as they were not on very good terms during this difficult stage in their lives. The group was virtually out of commission until Kiedis and Flea were on their feet again.

WAVERING COMMITMENT

Each of the bands has weathered at least one phase in which the members (or most of the members) had doubts about carrying on with the group or about continuing to work together. This isn't about loss of faith in the band or its merits but about the musicians questioning whether or not they want to be in it. Bono and Edge were physically in U2 during the *October* and *War* years, but confused by their fervent religious beliefs, their hearts just weren't in the right place. That they initially formed the band rather inadvertently also came back to haunt them at this time, because they had yet to define its purpose or why they were in it. "Having thrown ourselves into this thing we were trying to make some sense of it," the guitarist remarked in retrospect.[26] They made the records, but the band wasn't their priority at this time, the singer revealed in 1987, saying they must own up to this lack of commitment. "The Edge and myself left the band for a while, certainly in our heads," is his fitting description of the situation.[27]

Bono recalled in *Spin* (1987) that, once he became a born-again Christian, he lost interest in the group and was eager to explore other sides of himself. Being in a rock band seemed like a waste of time and the young frontman thought he could do something more productive with his life. Only when he came to terms with the idea that he is better at writing songs—and could contribute to the greater good with his gift— than anything else was his ardor for music and U2 restored. Meanwhile, Edge wrestled with the notion that his vocation conflicts with his spiritual beliefs, but discounted it after much soul-searching. This period of doubt and detachment nearly put an end to the band, and, in Bono's view, impeded its development to some extent because he and Edge weren't as focused on U2 as they might have been otherwise. "After *Boy*, the next two albums were almost made in our spare time. We weren't even sure we wanted to be in a band. So we were actually quite retarded on other levels."[28]

Eventually, they quelled these uncertainties and realized that they want to be musicians and want to be in U2. Reportedly, as the three Christians in the group struggled to figure out what to do with their lives, the others were sympathetic and understanding. Their ultimate decision to stick with the band can be credited at least in part to the support they received from one another. In a 1987 interview with *Rolling Stone*, the singer stated that, finally, all four of them are *simultaneously* excited about being in U2, indicating how crucial it is for their level of interest and involvement to be in sync.

In R.E.M., the quartet's dedication to the group and one another faltered when they recorded *Fables of the Reconstruction* in 1985. Mirroring the doubts the young Irish group had just laid to rest, Stipe, Buck, Mills and Berry weren't convinced at this juncture if they wanted to continue being in a band—but the reasons were entirely different. Stipe revealed that he had misgivings about the position the band was in and felt worn out enough to call the whole lifestyle into question. He and his bandmates were beginning to grow weary of being incessantly on the road and were sick to death of one another from touring, Buck divulged to *Bucketful of Brains*. They weren't even sure they liked each other anymore, he concedes. Moreover, R.E.M. was on the verge of becoming a bona fide career for the four and each of them had to decide if he was ready to make the kind of commitment that entailed.

"We could stay home and tour once in a while, or make a full commitment to be in a rock 'n' roll band. None of us were really sure," said Buck in 1988, retracing their earlier thoughts. "We'd been on the road for three years, so we wanted to stop before we got so sick of it that we didn't want to do it again."[29] Another issue was that the four were spending far too much time together, with just an annual two-week break between touring, recording and rehearsing. They were never out of each other's company, the guitarist remarked in *U*. They ultimately came to the conclusion that R.E.M. is worth pursuing. But only later would the band implement strategies to avoid claustrophobia, such as taking longer breaks and sidestepping touring. Radiohead went through a similar experience while recording *The Bends*. They had some reservations about the group and, as O'Brien told *NME* in 1997, for a while, they too weren't certain they actually liked one another.

Both the Red Hot Chili Peppers and R.E.M saw one member's fidelity to the group wane inexorably, with serious consequences. In his final year with the Chili Peppers, John Frusciante just didn't want to be in the group anymore, which made him disruptively and perniciously indifferent towards it. Although his bandmates mourned his eventual departure, there was a concurrent sense of relief among the remaining three because they no longer had to deal with what Kiedis calls the "day-to-day drama" of having the morose and apathetic guitarist in their midst.[30] As Frusciante himself later pointed out, his behavior dampened the others' pleasure in the band and its newfound fame. His disinterest also translated into poor performances, which the other, dedicated, musicians in the group couldn't abide.

When Bill Berry told his bandmates that he was hanging up his drumsticks, the shock was mitigated by their awareness that he hadn't really been into R.E.M. for some years. Despite their best efforts to gloss over it, they noticed that his interest in the band had gradually waned, evidenced, for instance, by his hasty egress from rehearsals and recording sessions. They knew all along that something was going on but Berry was perpetually reluctant to sit down and discuss it. This situation was hard on the group, says Buck. "It feels like you're forcing someone to work. It probably took some of the pleasure out of it for all of us. I knew Bill wasn't enjoying himself and that kind of bummed me out."[31] It was also difficult to collaborate with a drummer who always seemed anxious to get out of the studio. Berry's emotional distance, like Frusciante's, was followed by his outright extrication from the band. In 2006, Flea revealed that he nearly quit the Chili Peppers during the *By the Way* era. Frusciante completely dominated the sessions, making the bassist feel that his contributions weren't important. But Flea was deterred by the thought of announcing his intentions to Kiedis and later made peace with the contrite guitarist.

Part III: The do's

TOLERANCE AND TRUST

Tolerance and acceptance of one another, faults and all, is not a concept that the bands harp on, perhaps because it's so elementary. Stipe acknowledges that he's not the easiest person in the world to work with and thus appreciates the fact that his bandmates are willing to put up with him in such close quarters. You just "have to learn when to sublimate yourself to other people's foibles," he says.[32] The same open-mindedness has prevailed in U2. Clayton explains that it has been a never-ending process of adapting to one another and not getting hung up on someone's less appealing attributes. "You have to get used to being with people, being with them for a long period of time, and they become very tolerant of you and your little quirks, and you become tolerant of them and theirs. And you just try to see the positive in every situation."[33]

Trust is another self-evident prerequisite for a functional unit. Edge told *USA Today* (2002) that there's little need for any member of U2 to watch his back, primarily because of their friendship. Fellowship generally brings forth this trust and renders it impervious to virtually any assault. Any band whose members feel they must be on their guard in one another's company is bound to fall apart sooner rather than later. In the meantime, the musicians expend valuable energy that should go into the music worrying about treachery.

COMPROMISE: IT'S NOT A DIRTY WORD

Of course, no relationship or team effort can succeed without compromise. It's a concept that Bono, as both a band member and political activist, thoroughly comprehends and has taken to promoting. It's not a dirty word, he assured the audience at one of U2's 2001 homecoming shows in Dublin (available on DVD). His definition of surrender and, by logical extension, compromise, is positive and inspirational. In his view, it's not about giving up, but about "being open to bending your spirit in a wise way."[34] Such an affirmative perception undoubtedly renders concessions easier to make when they're called for. It also harkens back to Mike Mills' insistence that it's prudent to give ground in a disagreement whenever your feelings allow. Phil Selway observes that he and the others in Radiohead regard their albums as essentially the product of the compromises they've made along the way, and, being happy with their work, the fact that things don't always go as one would like doesn't seem so bad.

EMOTIONAL REGULATION

Thom Yorke has frequently ruffled Radiohead's serenity by inflicting his variable moods on the others in the band. After the *OK Computer* tour, to take one example, he descended into an especially acute funk that his bandmates bore the brunt of. "Nobody could say anything to me without me turning round and launching a vicious tirade at them."[35] These outbursts and Yorke's spirits in general have a tremendous impact on the atmosphere in the band. But any type of and any person's overreaction can be deleterious to the group. There's no place for drama queens in a band, Phil Selway intimated in *Consumable Online*, after admitting that they've all been tempted to stomp out of the room in a big huff at times, but, obviously, that's not a constructive way to handle disagreements so they make the effort to restrain themselves. Individual emotions and responses must be regulated, to some degree, to maintain the equanimity that is crucial to the band's operation.

Touchiness and oversensitivity fall into this category as well. Stipe brings up this notion in relation to the idea of not permitting oneself the indulgence of taking offense. "The essential thing is that you've got to realize that the band is more important than your hurt feelings. And if it comes to the point where the band is not more important than those particular personal feelings, then maybe it is time to move on."[36] Even with everyone attempting to react moderately in any situation, a gruff or callous manner can do a lot of damage. Confessing in *Q* (1988) that he has an untoward tendency to be insensitive and trample on his bandmates' feelings, particularly during fights, Buck, it seems, has regularly put temperance to the test in R.E.M.

EMPATHY

The Red Hot Chili Peppers cite an inability to empathize with one another's feelings as a stumbling block the band has had to clear. Frusciante testifies that during the 1992 tour, one of the issues was that they weren't "bending to feel things the way the other person was feeling."[37] Kiedis indeed divulged to *Q* in 1999 that he was too self-absorbed at that time to even begin to understand Frusciante's experience of the band's celebrity turn or anything else the guitarist was going through, which contributed to their alienation from one another.

Understanding the demands weighing on various band members and being able to put their selves in another's shoes prevents blowups originating in misconceptions about their position. Chad Smith, for instance, professed in *Batteur* that he admires lyricists because he realizes how difficult it must be to come up with words and melodies for 20 pieces of music. Being cognizant of the amount of work that requires, as well as the fact that he wouldn't be capable of it himself, disposes him to be more diplomatic and principled with Kiedis than he would be had these challenges not been apparent to him. Owing to this knowledge, the drummer says he would never cavalierly scorn any lyrics the latter comes up with.

FEELING VALUED

Each member of the band needs to know that the others perceive his worth. "If you feel good about yourself, you will be honest and generous toward other people," explains Ed O'Brien, asserting that no one in Radiohead is replaceable (or more importantly, they don't *feel* as if they are). "We are all individually essential."[38] Bands in which certain members feel like interchangeable parts generally break up as a result, he opines. Indeed, John Frusciante felt disconcertingly underrated by his bandmates during his first spell with the Chili Peppers, especially on the 1992 tour. They didn't seem to notice the effort he was putting into his performance every night. Six years later, it was a different story. Upon asking Frusciante to rejoin the band, the others conveyed to him that they consider his place in it one of great importance. Kiedis attested in *The Sunday Herald* in 2003 that they made it clear the group would actually disappear without him.

Their understanding of the part they all play in the whole has changed. In the past, Frusciante explained in *The Dayton Daily News,* each of them believed that he was the most important member of the band and failed to appreciate the significance of his partners. Now they value one another a lot more. In U2, Adam Clayton says they have always borne in mind each member's indispensability, realizing that "without any one of us the fragile uniqueness and specialness of U2 would be gone forever."[39] Just as it's necessary to remark each member's creative contributions to the band, it's crucial to treasure one another's friendship. Anthony Kiedis confessed to the *Associated Press* that, for many years, he neither nourished nor held dear his friendship with Flea. Had it not been inherently strong (and upheld by Flea's greater efforts), it might have disappeared, possibly taking the band with it. The singer recently stated that he's making a greater effort to connect with Flea.

By the same token, the band should never be taken for granted. One of the reasons R.E.M. has stayed together is that the members have never lost sight of how fortunate they are to be in this outfit, claims Buck. One of their greatest strengths, he stressed to *The Los Angeles Times* in 1995, is that they have never taken the band for granted. Looking around them, confirmed Berry in 1994, they're constantly reminded that what they have is wonderful, rare and priceless. They realize how lucky they are to actually get along and have fun, in addition to enjoying a fruitful creative partnership. For Frusciante, appreciation of the band's chemistry is paramount. As he put across to *The Boston Herald,* none of them really cherished it or acknowledged that they are ideally matched musicians when he left the Chili Peppers in 1992, but they do now. He told *Addicted to Noise* in 1999 that they have also realized that without this band their lives would be far less meaningful.

Losing faith in the band altogether is an even bigger threat to its survival than underestimating its value. Just before Radiohead recorded *The Bends,* Thom Yorke's belief in the band was dangerously undermined by the internal problems the group was experiencing and some disappointing performances. "I just decided that it wasn't true. I decided that live Radiohead wasn't some fantastic combination. I said to myself, 'This is not working, it's falling apart.'"[40] Focusing on the group's problems made Yorke overlook its assets and doubt its alchemy, which could have had dire consequences had these doubts extinguished his commitment to the group. But he hung around long enough for the issues to be resolved, restoring his belief in the band and leading him to perceive how attuned to one another he and his four partners actually are.

MAKING ROOM

Maintaining a group of this sort without crowding or smothering one another is tricky. It requires an understanding that everyone needs his own space alongside the fraternity. They know how to stay out of each other's way as well as how to be together, Paul McGuiness states pithily in relation to U2, implying that both modes of operation need to be mastered. It's a street gang mentality, clarifies Mullen. "We hang out together and we're friends and all those things, but we keep our distance."[41] As noted in the previous chapter, they also give each other plenty of leeway. Producer Mitch Easter says he believes R.E.M. has held together for so long because the members don't get in each other's way. One reason the Red Hot Chili Peppers' dynamic has been healthier in the years since Frusciante's return is because the four are now able to "breathe in each other's space," something they weren't able to do in the past, says Kiedis.[42] What exactly this means in a band, as in most relationships, is too elusive to really pinpoint, but it seems to include making it possible for individuals to pursue other projects, and giving them an opportunity to do their own thing and handle situations in their own way, as well as ceding physical space (affording them time alone). Creative space can be interpreted as leaving one another ample territory for diversification, experimentation and personal expression within the context of the group.

Anyone who has ever been in a close relationship knows that each person must also be allowed to be an individual within it. So conforming to the requirements of the alliance must be balanced by sufficient latitude to preserve one's distinct self. That they've been able to do just that is one of the keys to R.E.M.'s longevity, Stipe informed fans during an online chat session with *Zoogdisney.com*. John Frusciante has spoken on a number of occasions about how crucial it is for him to feel like he can be himself in the Red Hot Chili Peppers. His previous dissatisfaction with the band was driven in part by a sense that he had to pretend to be someone else in order to ingratiate himself with Kiedis and fit into the group. These days, he doesn't feel pressured to alter his behavior on any account and is happy to be in a band where everyone knows he can be himself, he remarked in *Interview* (2002).

Part IV: On conflict

FIGHTING CAREFULLY

Conflict is taken in stride by these bands because they know it comes with the territory, especially in a democratic collective, and that any intense relationship has its ups and downs. However, with so much at stake, battles must be chosen circumspectly as well as contained so that they don't assume dangerous proportions. Being in a band is a lesson in diplomacy, claims Bono. "You're living in each other's pockets. You have to know when to have that row or not. Or else you'll destroy the thing you've all been working on."[43] Paul McGuinness states that the members of U2 (including himself) have learned to argue very carefully and with an eye to diplomacy. "Nobody wants to start discussions by saying 'well, this is my point of view and anyone who wants to disagree with me can fuck off.' That would paralyse our operation, so they never start like that."[44] If you do fly off the handle and behave badly, he adds, it's best to just apologize right away.

Indeed, one of the problems the Chili Peppers had in the past, Smith revealed to *Rolling Stone* in 2002, is that they would be horrible to one another for no reason, then fail to apologize or make amends later. The R.E.M. trio makes an effort not to let arguments escalate to shouting and swearing (although they frequently have). They realize that losing one's temper is counter-productive, says Mills, because it leads people to say things they don't mean and later regret, while making the group's collective objectives recede into the distance (*Q*, 1999). Scott Litt also reported that they don't argue unless they're vehement about an issue, which goes back to the point Mills made about knowing when to let something go and when to insist on your position.

But the Radiohead clan learned that keeping a tight lid on conflict is a policy that, like any other, can be taken too far, to the detriment of the band. In the past, the quintet tried to camouflage disputes so as to downplay them and keep the situation under control. Yorke remarks facetiously that there used to be a lot of "serious infighting under the guise of reasonable discussion," which prevented the bandmates from being honest and real with each other at critical moments.[45] They later discovered that a measure of unrepressed yelling can aid in resolving problems because it enables everyone to speak frankly and address issues head-on. "It's sort of like a marriage where you learn to shout at somebody and that's a good thing."[46] Like competition, disagreements can be more cankerous if they aren't recognized for what they are and dealt with as such.

Regardless of how far a dispute goes, the band members certainly can't afford to hold grudges because they need to work together again the next day. Figuring out how to reconcile easily is essential and R.E.M. mastered the art early on, according to Buck, who says they can shout at each other but, afterwards, no one is angry. Minutes after they've been fuming at each other, they can head down to the pub for a beer together, Bill Berry confirmed in 1988, in an interview with *Q*. This didn't come as naturally to the Red Hot Chili Peppers, but in time, they've learned that they must be cool with one another at the start and end of each day. In a 2002 MuchMusic interview, Kiedis revealed that one of the costliest mistakes the Chili Peppers made in the past was harboring grudges against and evil thoughts about one another.

CREATIVE VERSUS PERSONAL DISAGREEMENTS

One of the most interesting questions in relation to this topic is whether fights and disagreements center more frequently upon creative or personal issues. Given that several relationships exist in tandem in these bands, it's clear that conflict will arise in each one, but there may be predominant areas of strife. The primary disputes in the Red Hot Chili Peppers are not generally related to the music, Chad Smith informed *Batteur* in 1995. While that may seem foolish, he proceeds, it's better this way because it's most important for the four of them to get along when they're playing together. They discuss musical matters effectively, which helps the unit function more smoothly on a creative level. Although the *Kid A* sessions were fraught largely because Radiohead was in the midst of a massive creative crisis, Thom Yorke apprised *Mojo* (2001) that few of the actual arguments were to do with music. Sadly, he says, much of it was just fall-out. Indeed, most of the periods of discord that these groups have openly discussed seem to be rooted in the resolution of personal beefs.

Conversely, the only real clashes in U2 occur when the band is actually recording, claims Adam Clayton, because they end up fighting over how the music will turn out. "So it's kind of professional clashes as opposed to personal ones," he clarifies.[47] It's tough, explains the bassist, to balance everyone's feelings and all the input each of them has into the tracks. In another interview, he elaborated on the kind of creative conflicts the group tends to have. The music's potential and where to set limits seem to be the controversial issues. "They're always rows based on the belief of what we *can* do, where the music's going."[48] When one thinks of the (very few) highly publicized altercations within the U2 camp, typically creative differences, such as those that nearly divided the band in Berlin during the making of *Achtung Baby*, come to mind. Squabbles in R.E.M., be they creative or personal (Buck doesn't specify), "always come out of little things," often the result of someone being stubborn or insensitive.[49] In 1984 Buck pointed out that they rarely have violent creative disagreements because they all have good taste and respect one another's judgment. Their major clashes, especially those that ended in a brawl, were born out of the frustration of constant touring, he clarified in *Musician* (1991).

Bono believes that personal friction and certainly financial wrangling pose a greater threat to a band than artistic disputes. When notified by a journalist that Radiohead nearly broke up (a slight exaggeration) over *Kid A*'s track sequencing (one of several music-related skirmishes the band *did* have at this time), the U2 singer responded that it would at least be a noble reason to part ways, as opposed to splitting over royalties, adding that bands tend to break up due to greed, not passion for their work.

What all four groups really believe is that it won't be a dispute of any sort that spells their end, but simply the expiration of their collective artistic vitality. Each band offers up a unique description of what constitutes a dearth of creative vigor, ranging from a shortage of fresh ideas to a stale musical partnership, resulting in music that is just mediocre or holds little significance for the members. "I think we will exhaust all the ideas the band has," ruminates Yorke. "And then we'll exhaust the band."[50] If there comes a day when he, Stipe and Mills cease inspiring one another and R.E.M. starts churning out lousy records, he'll quit no matter what, declared Buck in 1992 (*Pulse!*), adding that he's still learning a lot from his bandmates. Bono insists that making a record they don't believe in would lead to U2's demise because, he explained in *Live!*, it would signal the disappearance of their passion. "To be vital, and to write music that means something, or means something to me, and means something to the band, and that is exciting to play, is kind of a challenge," Kiedis told journalist Steve Roeser. "And I think whenever that stops is when we'll stop playing."[51]

Since the groups tend to view creative dissension as a sign of artistic vigor, it seems more likely that they'll call it quits when they *cease* disagreeing about the music. Or if other factors come into play. Their personal lives, rather than aesthetic differences, will lead the members of Radiohead to drift away from one another, augured Colin Greenwood in *The New York Times Upfront*.

RE-EVALUATING THE BAND

Neither crises nor conflicts have (thus far) severed these groups, but they quite often lead to a re-evaluation of the band and its dynamics. Deconstruction takes the place of self-destruction. Many of the episodes described in this chapter and in previous pages resulted in band members stopping to reassess the group in their minds. Responding to the rumor that Radiohead was frequently on the brink of collapse while making *Kid A*, Ed O'Brien set the record straight by suggesting that these incidents revolved around finding new ways to band together rather than preventing the alliance from falling apart (a subtle distinction). "I don't know whether it's splitting up, but it's like re-addressing the balance or re-addressing things."[52] It just has to be done once in a while, he points out.

Both R.E.M. and Radiohead refer to periods of doubt about the band and significant conflicts within it that have ended in renewed allegiance to the group as mid-life crises, because, says Colin Greenwood, you think about whether you want to be in the band and how you work together, as well as "whether you still like each other, or are you happy making compromises and stuff like that."[53] For R.E.M., these moments arrived (most notably) when they were making *Fables of the Reconstruction*, after Bill Berry opted out, and when the newly-born trio reached a pinnacle of dysfunction during the recording of *Up*. For Radiohead, periods of doubt attended the Pablo Honey tour and subsequent making of *The Bends*, as well as the early *Kid A* sessions (when they were so at odds they nearly disbanded). U2 had this experience during the band's first few uncertainty-drenched years and tense recording of *Achtung Baby*. The big tests for the Red Hot Chili Peppers came after Frusciante's departure and following the release of *One Hot Globe*, when the band seemed destined to vanish.

Questioning the band and/or rethinking the way it operates gives the members a fresh perspective on what they're doing and why. There's a rediscovery of why the group came into existence in the first place. It's an awakening that typically brings about a rededication or recommitment to the group. In that sense, even major fallouts or dilemmas have a positive outcome. Thom Yorke says that he and his four friends in Radiohead have a much better understanding of why they're in the band ever since they questioned everything (in 1999–2000) and then made the decision to carry on, he remarked in *The Face*. Likewise, had he not had second thoughts about U2 and taken stock of what the band was doing back in the early '80s, says Edge, his perspective on it wouldn't be nearly as healthy as it now is, and that might have led him (and the group) into serious trouble (*Rolling Stone*, 1987).

What doesn't kill you makes you stronger, goes the old adage. Naturally, bands are no exception. Adversity overcome not only heightens the connection between the individuals in such groups, but also instills in them a collective and individual confidence that they can triumph over any roadblock (particularly as they appear less daunting after you've tackled a few). But groups that have survived this long know it's best to keep a tight lid on any divisions within the unit in order to prevent others from exploiting them. Whatever is happening internally, the bands strive to maintain a united front. Later, when the fray has ended and the threat of schism has passed, they don't mind telling the rest of us what happened (and even what *nearly* happened).

6

"One": Merging Diverse Elements Into a Productive Whole

Bands often constitute a very disparate crew. By their own admission, this is true of R.E.M., U2, Radiohead and the Red Hot Chili Peppers. So how do such different people merge into a productive whole? What are the overriding qualities the band members have in common that lend the group its unique character and internal climate? These are some of the questions tackled in this chapter, which also discusses diverse musical influences and their impact on the band, and the characteristics the unit, as a whole, possesses.

Part I: One, but not the same

DISPARATE CREWS

Larry Mullen pointed out in *Dazed and Confused* that one of the biggest fallacies about U2 is that they are four men who think and act alike, rather than distinct individuals with unique characteristics and different tastes. Nothing could be further from the truth, insist the band members. What you have in U2, says Bono, is a combination of four individuals who, apart from the band, have little in common insofar as personality. They are four completely different people, the singer frequently swears, in an effort to dispel the myth to which Mullen alludes. Having arisen, as Brian McCollum of *The Detroit Free Press* remarks, amid a different paradigm than that which prevailed in the '60s, when rock groups (though the members often dressed and strove to look alike) were regarded as multi-headed monsters comprised of singular characters (George Harrison was The Quiet Beatle, John Lennon The Clever

Beatle, etc.), U2, R.E.M., and their peers didn't really play up their distinct personalities, which may account for their agglomeration in the public mind.

If any of these groups is perceived as an undifferentiated pack—with the notable exception of Yorke—it's Radiohead. *The New Zealand Herald* claims, for instance, that the band is widely regarded as an alliance between the angst-ridden singer and "four relatively normal young men from Oxford."[1] Yorke shrugs off this image of the quintet as little more than an occupational hazard. Looking at bands from the outside, the public naturally doesn't see separate individuals, only a melded front, he theorized in *The Trigger*. But his bandmate Jonny Greenwood insists that the appearance of parity in Radiohead is primarily their own doing, as the band members have studiously cultivated personal anonymity. They don't wish to stand out from the Radiohead entity. "Radiohead is something that we push forward instead of ourselves," he explains, calling the band a "big badge to hide behind."[2]

In reality, the five are a motley crew. They're like the *Odd Couple*, quips Ed O'Brien, except that there are five of them. He extrapolates in another interview: "We are a weird bunch, we are very disparate. We are different people—you get a different take on the band whoever you speak to. Somehow, at the end of it, it goes through the filtering process and out comes the Radiohead thing."[3] That filtering process produces the Radiohead entity, but it has not done so by effacing these differences. It can be likened to emulsion rather than dissolution. And, having met in school, they have not grown more similar on account of their longtime association, Colin Greenwood muses. It's true that, with the passing years, they have come to know one another better, but they have not merged into some amorphous "musical blob."[4]

R.E.M. is one group that hasn't been dogged by the false impression that the members are very much alike. That this is a gang of "galvanically mismatched individuals," as Warner Brothers referred to the quartet in an official press release, has been an integral component of the band's image and mystique.[5] For one thing, it's an aspect of the group to which attention has regularly been drawn. To take just a couple of examples, journalist John Harris wrote, after interviewing the group in 2001, that Stipe, Buck and Mills are so dissimilar it's as if someone inserted a coin into the "rock one-arm bandit" and came up with the members of three very different groups.[6] Don Dixon, who produced the band's first two albums, says that what struck both him and co-producer Mitch Easter was "how complete each guy was as a character, each almost a caricature of themselves. All really really distinct personalities."[7] For some reason, the discrete qualities of the R.E.M. foursome shone through quite forcibly and became legendary. Stipe is the

shy and artsy one, Buck the slightly cynical and outspoken rock and
roller, Mills the affable and somewhat nerdy bassist while Berry was the
down-to-earth drummer (but a bad boy in the early days).

Perceptions aside, tales of bands who were eventually crushed by the
actual contraposition of the personalities involved abound in the annals
of rock history. But, no matter how heterogeneous the members, what
counts, of course, is that their relationships with one another are harmonious, which is precisely the case in the Red Hot Chili Peppers. "Not
one of us has that much to do with each other in a lot of ways," marvels
Frusciante, "but we get along absolutely perfectly."[8]

WELL-MATCHED IN DIVERSITY

Ultimately, the contrasting personalities in these groups are also
well-matched. They merge effectively into a productive whole, which may
explain both how they work well together and why their union is so
advantageous. Flea contends that if he and singer Anthony Kiedis weren't
polar opposites who, in a sense, complete one another, the Red Hot
Chili Peppers would lose its equilibrium. "We each fill a place [in the
band] that the other one couldn't fill," he explains, adding, "John fills
an equally important space that we needed and that we didn't have when
he was gone."[9] Greg Kot, music critic for *The Chicago Tribune*, made a similar observation about R.E.M., specifically that the members of the group,
though hardly alike as people, manage to fill one another's gaps both
musically and personally. U2 works so well, Bono informed *NME* in 1993,
precisely because Edge is calm, rational and tasteful, and, in short, everything that he is not. The Special Edition of *Q* dedicated to Radiohead
contains more detailed insight into the delicate equilibrium in this particular unit. O'Brien, for instance, brings to the group an unflagging
optimism that the others lack. The Greenwood brothers are the intellectual answer to Yorke's eccentricity while Phil Selway's quiet and cool-
headed nature is "a perfect antidote to the raging artistic egos in
Radiohead."[10]

To emphasize how divergent are the natures of the band members,
but how well they fit together, O'Brien stated in *Access* that Radiohead
works like all the elements (five rather than four in this case). Anthony
Kiedis makes a similar point about the Red Hot Chili Peppers by relay-
ing to *Interview* that each of the four blood types is represented in the
current lineup. Both depictions convey a sense of wholeness in the group
despite (or rather, because of) the lack of uniformity within it. This could
be the basis of the band's chemistry, suggests Kiedis, the fact that,
together, these diverse elements form a complete microcosm. Chad
Smith supports the hypothesis that the Chili Peppers' chemistry is tied

not just to the combination of certain individuals, but to the hodge-podge of that configuration. "We are very different people. We all have strong ideas and personalities and that's what makes the chemistry what it is."[11] The same holds true for R.E.M., argues Stipe: "We're four very distinct and very different people. But I think that push me/pull you has always been part of our indefinable chemistry."[12] These points seem to support the theory that chemistry boils down to the way the musicians affect one another creatively, with the added explanation that the effect revolves around their complementary differences.

BRIDGING THE GAPS

Along with balance there's a sense of camaraderie in tight-knit bands that helps the members bridge the chasms between them. There are, of course, also some essential commonalities that provide a meeting ground for the variegated players (aside from the music, of course). R.E.M.'s lawyer-turned-manager, Bertis Downs, told *Q*'s Danny Eccleston that his three charges have a lot of core values in common. They also share an analogous worldview, says Buck. "We all have the same thoughts on the way to live and the same acceptance of what goes on around us. We don't find ourselves at philosophical odds very often."[13] So, while there's little conformity in their individual traits, the band members appear to be bound by a certain like-mindedness. Their extreme stubbornness is another mutual trait. U2's foursome are joined primarily by their sense of humor and irony, claim Bono and Edge. Even as kids, says the guitarist, he (a very quiet person) and Bono (comparatively bold and brash) were exact opposites. But since they could always share a laugh, it was natural that they would get on with one another, he informed *Rolling Stone* in 1987.

THE BENEFITS OF NUMEROUS VIEWPOINTS

It's not always easy to accept the polarities in a unit. Thom Yorke claims he used to worry about the fact that he and his four partners in Radiohead constituted such a disparate crew and O'Brien says it's precisely the sort of circumstance that got to them in the past. Over time, the band learned to embrace and exploit this reality, particularly after observing, while touring with R.E.M., that this is a medium other successful rock groups inhabit, Yorke relayed to *The Trigger*. As Radiohead and other bands have learned, their dissimilarities can be a benediction rather than a curse. Along with a highly mixed bag of attributes come manifold creative viewpoints that pull the music in numerous directions. Because the four U2s are so unlike one another, Edge explained in *The*

Chicago Sun Times, there's a good counter-argument to every argument (the advantages of creative opposition were broached earlier), which forms the backbone of their creative relationship.

One obvious example is *The Joshua Tree,* the band's 1987 blockbuster album. It represents a delicate equilibrium between the very different directions in which he and Bono were pulling, says the guitarist. Owing to his fascination with America, Bono was trying to make an album rooted musically and lyrically in that continent, which contrasted sharply with Edge's Euro-Pop leanings. "But it is a democratic band, and neither my nor Bono's feelings came through completely," says Edge.[14] By Clayton's assessment, the "tension between directions and opinions resulted in an album of great variety and contrasts, and great depths."[15] This ties in with Phil Selway's comment about Radiohead's music essentially representing a compromise between the members' idiosyncratic slants.

Although they are united by shared values and broad views, the members of R.E.M. bring varying vantage points to bear on the music. Stipe puts it this way: "That's part of the beauty of it is that two of us can be looking at exactly the same thing and see something totally different and where those two meet, and you double that by two—where those four meet, is the little magic ... that makes R.E.M., R.E.M."[16] Again, the singer essentially ascribes the unique force at work in the band to the polarities within it. Whether or not he agrees, Buck is simply convinced that it would be boring to work with people who think as he does, and he knows the music would be correspondingly bland. Palpably, but seamlessly, the work is elevated by the presence of ideas that pull in different directions. "If you don't have that, you're Chicago," he adds in his typically outspoken fashion.[17] However, the profusion of miscellaneous and often opposing ideas can get in the way of the music when the band can't see the forest for the trees, noted Mills on *MTV Online,* so it's a matter of being able to reap the benefits of diverse opinions without getting bogged down.

Jonny Greenwood believes that he and Thom Yorke work effectively together because they come at songwriting from contrary angles. While Greenwood says he's keen to learn all he can about music and musical theory, he explained to author Jonathan Hale that Yorke prefers to capitalize on his lack of formal training. The union of these approaches strengthens Radiohead's work. R.E.M. similarly benefits from the marriage of musical idiot and savant, according to Stipe. Although Mike Mills, who has more of a proper musical education than anyone else in the group, is very knowledgeable when it comes to arrangement, Stipe's untutored contributions are essential because he manages to take the tracks in highly unusual directions. "I have a musically dumb standpoint that I'm looking at the song from. That Mike doesn't have, because he's musically trained and knows what's too stupid. And I'm not."[18] In other words, their perspectives are ideally balanced. Indeed, R.E.M. united two distinct band paradigms. Mills and Berry came from the tradition of apprenticeship in cover bands while Stipe and Buck subscribed to the "just-do-it" punk ethic. Far from disapproving of one another, the singer and guitarist appreciated the experience the other pair brought to the group and the rhythm players, on their part, liked the unconventional styles of the corresponding faction.

DIVERSE MUSICAL INFLUENCES

The Red Hot Chili Peppers ascribe their music's broad appeal to their personal diversity. He and his three partners are practically from opposite poles of the earth, writes Flea in the liner notes to the band's *Greatest Hits* release. "For that reason, for us all to agree on a piece of music's validity, that piece of music must cover all the blood types, all the seasons, and all 4 corners of the globe."[19] They also attribute the group's stylistic range to their diffuse musical tastes. In fact, the hybrid sound that the Chili Peppers are credited with pioneering was just the band's wide-ranging mix of influences in action, Kiedis put across to *Rock & Folk* in 1996. Surveying the group's musical landscape schematically, punk and funk were common threads, but the singer was into rap, Hillel Slovak a devotee of Jimi Hendrix, and Flea's roots in jazz. When the four started playing music together, a natural fusion of these diverse elements occurred. Later, Smith came into the picture with his rock-metal leanings (Black Sabbath, Led Zeppelin) and John Frusciante brought his myriad muses (including Frank Zappa and Lou Reed) to bear on the group (though the Chili Peppers were his chief inspiration).

Being all over the map when it comes to their respective musical backgrounds and tastes doesn't seem to interfere with the Chili Peppers' ability to collaborate. Though their inspiration for playing music had divergent origins, what's most material, at least for Frusciante, is that they pursue their art for similar reasons. What needs to be simpatico in this group is the musical animus (in the sense of an energizing force) of the members, more so than their inclinations. That becomes clear when comparing the fates of Dave Navarro and Chad Smith. It's often assumed that one of the main reasons the former Jane's Addiction star didn't gel with the Chili Peppers was because his musical sensibility was so at odds with that of the other three. But so was Smith's, and he blended into the group successfully. As Kiedis posits in *Scar Tissue*, the difference is that Smith's musical *spirit*, his passion and energy, matched the band's.

Kiedis makes two astute observations that stress the relative irrelevance of common musical preferences in this group. For one thing, musical influences are just one stimulus amidst a host of others, "emotional and comical and just life, art, love and weirdness." Secondly, "it's our chemistry that makes us what we are rather than what we listen to," he points out, clarifying that musical inspirations fluctuate but the immutable essence of the individuals involved in the band plays a more important role in shaping the songs.[20] These days, their veneration for Frusciante and his insatiable musical appetite has the quartet admiring many of the same recordings—those he, as the group's backstage DJ, spins for them. Frusciante also told *Wall of Sound* in 2001 that the Chili Peppers are likely to begin incorporating more programmed elements into their music because he and his three partners share a love for German electronic groups like Kraftwerk, Cluster and Harmonia. Since these are common influences, they will probably find their way into the band's future work, he concludes.

R.E.M.'s musical influences are, according to Thom Yorke (a friend of the band's), "about as disparate as you can get."[21] This was particularly true at the outset. Berry and Mills were bred on country music (though Ian Copeland brought groups like The Ramones and The Damned to their attention just before they moved to Athens, reigniting their fading passion for music) while Buck was into more cosmopolitan acts. Both he and Stipe also shared a love for British and New York punk. It's astonishing that the four had common musical ideals around which they could rally given their diverse preferences. But, as we saw, there was enough music they all *disliked* equally to bring them together and provide the group with a coherent vision.

What's more, there was a wide variety of artists that turned them on to music as a career, but they weren't necessarily aiming to write in that vein. In fact, when it came to songwriting, said Mills in *Q*'s R.E.M. edition, they all looked to legendary tunesmiths like The Beatles, Bob Dylan and The Byrds for inspiration. At any rate, Buck puts more of an accent on respecting the judiciousness of one another's selections rather than necessarily enjoying the same music. "I think we all have pretty good taste, so no one's gonna violently disagree with anything."[22] (The remark was made with respect to their own work and the creative arguments that arise between them, but it applies here because they trust one another's judgment when it comes to music in general).

Reconciling different musical leanings has posed challenges for both U2 and Radiohead. The Irish group found it difficult in the late '80s to integrate the American bluesy rock Bono favored with the ambient Eno-style pop that Edge gravitated towards. While working on *Achtung Baby* at the beginning of the following decade, they had to figure out whether to build on Bono and Edge's newfound zeal for industrial and techno dance music, considering that Clayton and Mullen's playlists during the group's downtime had been radically different. Reportedly, the drummer was rediscovering Cream and Hendrix while other members of the group were getting into contemporary avant-garde groups like My Bloody Valentine and Ozric Tentacles.

This proved to be a major hardship for U2, particularly since the bassist says the band members do feel the need for a common musical foothold, as they had when they first started (The Beatles, The Who, The Sex Pistols, Television, Patti Smith). He explains: "Our shared tastes give us a way of judging things we can still trust. So if everyone in the band is saying they don't like something, you know why, since you know their frame of reference. And every time we make a new U2 record, we bring along that frame of reference."[23] With new influences emerging all the time, the band is constantly required to re-establish this common ground the members need, which has occasionally been problematic. In recent years, they have relied on producer Flood and others in-the-know to introduce them to new music, which, vicariously, provides them with collective influences.

Comparable inspirational divides have, at times, hampered Radiohead. The quintet started out collectively enamored of guitar-rock (à la The Smiths, R.E.M., The Pixies), but gradually the members branched out into acts their partners in the group didn't necessarily appreciate to the same extent. By 1999, the situation came to a head, with the band struggling to reconcile a bevy of miscellaneous new influences (in *Nightshift*, Colin Greenwood reeled off a list that included Warp Records, Curtis Mayfield, Alice Coltrane, Humphrey Littleton, Kristin Hersh, Dr Dre, Kraftwerk, and Low) and concur on a direction. Can and Neu were the only artists they could all agree are brilliant, says O'Brien. Disparate influences don't prevent the five from writing music together, Yorke told *Addicted to Noise* in 1996, because the band isn't out to copy anyone's sound. At the same time, Jonny Greenwood pointed out in *The New York Times Upfront* that when they do find artists or recordings that intrigue all of them, it helps in shaping their collective vision for the project at hand. It gives them a general sound or concept to aim for together, knowing that their limitations and individual style will thwart their efforts to attain it, resulting (hopefully) in something unique. That's part of the reason they struggled to settle on a sound to even explore for *OK Computer*'s follow-up.

To sum up, diverse influences aren't generally a barrier to formulating a shared artistic vision or collaborating effectively in groups where the members respect each other's tastes and possess a congruent artistic spirit, especially when other factors represent an even more seminal influence. But when there is virtually *no* common ground in terms of their *current* musical interests, the group can lose focus and find it difficult to move forward. It's important for the band members to be collectively enthused, especially when generating new material, by a few select artists or recordings that they find worthy of emulating to some extent. The fact is that Radiohead, U2 and the Chili Peppers do spend time listening to music as a group or bringing artists to one another's attention, establishing, if nothing else, some crucial common reference points, and often, a mutual attraction that serves as the band's compass for a time.

Part II: Collective characteristics

The next step is to examine the attributes of each group as an entity and how its mode of operation is indicative of them. In the manner that people speak of family traits, the band members tend to use an inclusive "we" when drawing attention to what are essentially features of the *group.* Thom Yorke, for instance, once characterized himself and his bandmates as hypercritical. On another occasion, he commented, "Sabotage I think is very important in the way we operate. I think we are unhealthily paranoid about complacency to the point where it is just silly."[24] In reference to the exorbitantly frantic discussions about the group's future the five had in 1999, O'Brien remarked dryly that they can be quite hysterical at times (*Spin,* 2000). Concluding a rather comic portrayal of Mrs. Greenwood's concern over the prospects of her two sons (should this music thing not work out), the elder remarks: "Very Radiohead, that. We're all worriers, you know. Even when there's nothing to worry about."[25] In Yorke's view, the band's biggest downfall could be the members' collective penchant for taking everything about their lives, their music and their relationships with one another too seriously and overanalyzing it, so he affirmed in *B-Side.*

The Radiohead microcosm seems to be typified by neurosis, exorbitant scrutiny, paranoia and not a little self-induced gloom. Bearing this iconography in mind, when Jonny Greenwood revealed to *The Calgary Sun* that they chose to record *Kid A* in wintry Copenhagen because they felt that Radiohead is best-suited for sunless Northern European studios, one tends to agree with the correlation and what it says about the band's nature. However, recent reports suggest that the quintet had loosened up a great deal by the time they knocked out *Hail to the Thief* with relative ease (in sunny California, of all places). If that's really the case, Radiohead is in the process of shedding some of its fundamental, but sometimes detrimental, characteristics, and turning into a more easygoing unit. As O'Brien informed *The New Zealand Herald,* the incessant questioning lent the band momentum during the 1990s, but the unit was also slowly imploding as a result of having taken the penchant for analysis and fear of complacency too far.

In many ways, R.E.M. is the antithesis of Radiohead. Where members of the latter group tend to ponder and fret over every move and every note, the Southerners leap forward after their gut. "R.E.M. intuit as a band much more than they analyse," states Stipe, by way of explaining that the trust he places in his "reptile brain" over his "rational thought process" is typical of the band's collective approach.[26] R.E.M.'s other conspicuous collective trait, familiar to every serious fan, is a defiant obstinacy. Mills says, "We're all contrarians in this band. We're all independent thinkers, we're all very stubborn. None of us like to be told what do to do."[27] One of the corollaries of this shared disposition is that the band stays unwaveringly true to itself. It's out of the realm of possibility for them to follow a trend, Stipe declared in 1995, not because they're born leaders, but because they're so pigheaded, both individually and as a group. Mills notes in *Scene* that R.E.M. also tends to have a more sedate temperament than other bands, chiefly because the members seek to comport themselves with a certain amount of dignity and self-respect—especially as they get older.

The lineaments of the U2 profile include boldness and insatiability, as the group is perpetually on a quest to push the envelope farther than it's been pushed before (even by themselves). "We've always been greedy as a band" is how Edge serves it up, adding that they're not turned on by anything easy and thrive on being out of their depth.[28] During a 2002 radio interview, Bono reiterated this idea, professing that the quartet likes to take on what it can't handle because it makes the four feel like they're on the edge (not to be confused with The Edge!). They were the first group of their generation to play the big stadiums, with the massive Zoo TV tour they were on the verge of financial collapse, and they sold tickets for the Popmart tour before they had completed the album. He concedes that, in taking a negative view of this venturesome attitude, one could say the group stirs up its own problems.

Indeed, on some level what comes across is that the quest to avoid complacency and stasis has driven the group to some perilous, perhaps unnecessary, extremes—not that it hasn't ultimately served U2 well or that the quartet doesn't deserve kudos for its enterprising spirit and what that spirit has enabled it to accomplish. Although it's a mutual trait, Larry Mullen claims that the band owes the scale of its intrepidity to Bono, in whose nature it is amplified to the nth degree. "He's got an extraordinary capacity to deal with blows and to rebound, an incredible instinct. There are very few people like that, and there are very few bands who are prepared to take the risks that U2 takes, and that's because of the way [Bono] is."[29]

A group spirit is what the Red Hot Chili Peppers talk about rather than delineating specific characteristics of the band. Despite many personnel changes and stylistic shifts, Anthony Kiedis revealed in an online interview for the French music channel MCM that there is a persistent and collective state of mind in the Chili Peppers that has been present from the moment of the band's birth. It's what brought the singer and his high school friends together to play music in the first place. Although he leaves it at that, it's probably best described as a lust for life reflected in explosive energy, disdain for etiquette and liberation of the senses, along with a passionate belief in the power of music. If R.E.M. is driven by pure instinct and a dominant streak of contrariness, Radiohead by a kind of intellectual excess bordering on neurosis and U2 by a bold desire to swim in the deep end, it's fair to say that the Red Hot Chili Peppers is what it is because of a shared yearning to experience life and music as fully as possible, in addition to the members' collective pursuit of enlightenment (be it sexual, artistic or spiritual).

Cultural norms and proclivities color the complexion of each band. Who could deny, for instance, that there's an element of pure Californian hedonism in the Red Hot Chili Peppers? In recent years, the band has also adopted a New Age-y, Zen-like cast closely associated with this region. Certainly the drug use that wreaked so much havoc in the group and the whole party lifestyle that went with it had its roots in the licentious Hollywood Strip scene, which the founding members of the Chili Peppers imbibed. Probably more than any other band, the U2 quartet view disagreements in a positive light, as an indication of sincere passion. Bono claims that the Irishman's delight in a good row is at the heart of this creed and prepared them for life in U2. "I love the din of argument. We Irish go insane if there is accord," the singer comments gleefully.[30] Dublin is an excellent training ground for being in a band, he says, because you are accustomed to people haggling with or shouting at each other, which is what much of band life is about.

The members of Radiohead constantly ascribe behaviors that ultimately affect how their band operates to their British upbringing. Their reserve with one another and reluctance to share their feelings are traits that descend directly from the quintet's heritage. "The thing you have to remember is that we're English," Jonny Greenwood consoled a journalist with whom Yorke had not been forthcoming. "We're not raised to talk about ourselves or to be overly emotional or sincere. Especially in public—or even in private."[31] On top of this reserve are their British manners, which might explain why the group had, at least at one time, a tendency to politely avoid confrontations.

Social graces are an integral part of the Southern American upbringing of the R.E.M. clan. Much of the friction that marked the turbulent

Up sessions wasn't very apparent. "We're Southern, so everything is under the surface," explains Stipe. "There's always a patina of politeness."[32] On the one hand, their attempts to remain genteel prevented the three from confronting some of the issues that needed to be addressed at this time, which only made the situation worse. But, since they know each other all too well, they are able to see beneath that veneer and sense when one of their partners is pissed off. That only heaped annoyance with one another on top of poor communication. "There's a definite edge beneath Southern politeness that can be infuriating," remarks the singer.[33] Another aspect of Southern life that has come into play in R.E.M. is, as the singer informed *Melody Maker* in 1986, the relatively high tolerance for people's eccentricities. This is indeed a band that puts a heavy emphasis on accepting and accommodating one another's quirks.

7

"Where I End and You Begin": Role Divisions

Emerging from the discussion of divergent personalities is the notion of formal and informal roles within the band. Who is officially responsible for what job is one question. But there are, in addition, unofficial functions that certain band members fulfill on account of a strength they possess or a character trait that makes them well-suited to play the part in question. These can be equally or even more important to the group than any titular responsibilities.

Part I: Formal roles

WHO DOES WHAT

Let's start by examining official duties. Every band member plays an instrument from which he derives his formal title. There is a primary vocalist in each band, as well as a back-up singer—John Frusciante in the Chili Peppers, Mike Mills in R.E.M., Edge in U2 and Ed O'Brien in Radiohead. The instrumental portions of the songs are generally composed by all the band members, but fall chiefly to the musicians (Kiedis and Stipe, for instance, do not play instruments). Lyrics and vocal melodies are the domain of the singer while song arrangements are handled collectively. Where this is overlap, as there often is with guitarists, they have different designations. The Edge plays lead guitar in U2 and Bono, on occasion, plays rhythm guitar.

In Radiohead, it's more complicated because there are three guitarists, but it's generally accepted that Jonny Greenwood is on lead, Thom Yorke on rhythm and Ed O'Brien produces the flourishes and splinters of sound that enrich Radiohead's music and have become a band hallmark. It's perfect, says O'Brien, because he's never been keen on lead guitarists and their blistering solos. "I've always been into sounds, layerings, melodies things to pick out," he says, noting that another distinction between himself and Greenwood is the fact that he is self-taught and the other more versed in formal musical theory.[1] That's not to say the guitarists never trade places or perform overlapping functions. Both Greenwood and O'Brien, for example, have come up with the stunning arpeggios that dominate various Radiohead tracks, such as "No Surprises," "Street Spirit," and "Creep."

There are no rigid guidelines or artificial limitations, O'Brien clarifies, noting in *Total Guitar* (1997) that Greenwood, with his more schooled background, would never bar another guitarist in the group from playing anything by insisting that he's more capable. Yet, because there are numerous guitarists in the band, each of them is very conscious of the need to actively carve out a role for himself: "There aren't any rules, but if someone's down at the bottom of the fretboard, you get up to the top. You try and find a space for what you do—you learn that. It can get very covered. It's tricky having three guitars to get them all to come out. That's why you have to sonically find a space for each one."[2] There are times when it becomes competitive, he informed *Guitar World* in 1997 (and as we saw earlier), but they've come to terms with the idea that there may be songs on which one of them doesn't get to play (the next chapter discusses serving the song, a notion that is also relevant in this context).

Radiohead aside, the four-piece configuration works so well for bands and has stuck over the years partly because each musician has a role that is both vital to the group and highly defined. There's no need to eke out a spot for any of them. "I'm grateful this was never a band with a keyboard player and another guitar player," remarks U2's Adam Clayton, "because then what chops would I have ever needed?"[3] Although they nearly always augment the guitar, bass and drums with other instruments, these are merely accents rather than the foundation of the U2 sound.

ROLE-SHUFFLING

With some band members enlisting in the absence of musical training or a defined area of expertise, there was some initial role-shuffling in U2, R.E.M. and Radiohead. Bono fondly recalls that he wanted to be the lead guitarist of the band, but Edge, though no great axeman himself at that time, was obviously the stronger candidate. So Bono made a bid to become the singer. He wasn't very adept at that either, and the others tried to persuade him to serve as the group's manager instead, but he drew the line there and clinched the vocalist's spot by obtaining a working microphone. Functions were defined in the fledgling group largely by the equipment people had and the impression they made, rather than their skills. Adam Clayton couldn't play bass guitar, but he *had* one, pretended fairly convincingly that he knew what he was doing and threw around musician lingo to boot, so he qualified for the position. He was also the only one who showed up at Mullen's with an amp, that everyone then plugged into, so they couldn't very well chuck him on account of his musical shortcomings.

The four college students who got together in a dilapidated Athens church had to figure out what to do with diamond-in-the-rough Peter Buck. When the band started no one was really sure what instrument he would play, hc recalls. It was through a process of elimination that he ended up as the group's guitarist. "Mike could play guitar better than me, and I knew I wasn't going to play the drums. It was suggested that I play bass, but I could never work it out, so in the end I became a guitar player."[4] Radiohead had a similar problem with Colin Greenwood's younger brother Jonny, who desperately wanted to be in the band with his sibling's older friends. They had their four-piece, however, and Jonny didn't really play anything. Somewhat grudgingly, they eventually admitted the tenacious (not to mention, precocious) teenager to the group, first on harmonica, then on keyboards until one fine day he stumbled onstage with a guitar in his hands. He had found his niche and Radiohead now had three guitarists.

ROLE-SWAPPING

While the musical roles in U2 and the Red Hot Chili Peppers are more or less static, there has traditionally been a lot of instrument-swapping in R.E.M. It's a practice that began when the band was making *Out of Time*, on which Berry played bass instead of drums, Mills played organ instead of bass and Buck played anything but electric guitar. They simply wanted to get away from their standard roles in a four-piece band and avoid getting into a rut, Buck explained in a Warner Brothers press release for the album. This exercise was liberating, educational and put the group's chemistry to a revelatory test (it not only survived, it thrived). Instrument-trades in R.E.M. also make sense on account of the fact that each of the members is a multi-talented full-fledged songwriter. "There's no reason to keep Bill on the drums because he writes great songs on the guitar and mandolin," Mills remarked at the time.[5]

The quartet was at it again when recording *Up*. With Mills concentrating on keyboards, Buck usurped his four-string for most of the album. The arrangement pleased both parties. Sharing the bass frees him up to play other instruments, says Mills. Buck leapt at the opportunity to walk in the latter's shoes for a while, claiming that he loves to play the four-string but doesn't get a chance to because Mills is such a gifted bass player. "It's not like I'm going to take over his spot or anything," he stated with assurance in 1998.[6] As we'll see in Chapter 12, in this case the two ended up going beyond their usual habit of merely dabbling in one another's craft and nearly did trade places, which led to some role-confusion.

MULTI-INSTRUMENTALISM
AND PERCEPTION OF ROLES

Each of the four bands has at least one member who is accomplished on one or more instruments—keyboards, trumpet, Ondes Martenot—outside the primary colors of rock, so incorporating them into the band's music doesn't necessitate even temporary role-swapping. This is a way in which the musicians can branch out so they don't feel constricted or bored in the band, but without encroaching on anyone else's territory.

Quite often, roles are also broadly defined within the group, so the individual doesn't perceive himself to be limited to a narrow and inescapable function. Colin Greenwood, for instance, doesn't consider himself Radiohead's bass player. "I'm just in a band with other people," he says. The British quintet started out, as we saw, because they wanted to play music together, not because the members had an affinity for a particular instrument. "So it was more of a collective angle, and if you could contribute by having someone else play your instrument, then that was really cool."[7] The members of Radiohead have really pushed this collective philosophy since they began experimenting with computerized and electronic music, adding many new colors to their musical palette. Their basic approach now is that any member of the band can play any instrument the song seems to require, (although they seem to have stuck largely with their original functions).

It's likely that John Frusciante would be able to relate to Radiohead's current approach. He may have once seen himself as the Red Hot Chili Peppers' guitarist, but these days he is redefining his position in the group in much less restrictive terms. "I see the band as more of a free place where I mold and shape and expand my role to be what I want it to be—whether that means using a modular synthesizer, or playing piano or a glockenspiel or the harpsichord, doing a bunch of guitar overdubs, or writing beautiful chordal things."[8] In other words, it doesn't matter what instrument he has in his hands or what he's doing with it. The important thing is that, in one way or another, he's creating music with the band.

In his excellent introduction to *U2: The Complete Songs*, Bill Flanagan observed that when watching U2 compose and record music, he was particularly struck by the way in which they switched roles as needed, sharing in the responsibility for each part of the song. He paints a picture of a band without boundaries, at least in terms of cross-suggestions. Mullen came up with a melody for Bono to try out, Edge demoed a beat in the drummer's absence, Adam proposed some chords to the guitarist, and Edge worked on the lyrics when Bono departed for the night. "It is almost impossible for an outsider to tell where one leaves off and the next begins. The songs truly come from all four of them," the author concludes.[9] That's why Larry Mullen says he doesn't think of himself as U2's drummer but more generally as "a contributor to the U2 sound."[10]

NON-MUSICAL RESPONSIBILITIES

The band's business doesn't end with writing and recording songs. There are myriad concomitant tasks that the members divide between them. Thom Yorke works closely with his friend Stanley Donwood on Radiohead's album artwork. Similarly, in R.E.M., the artistically-oriented Stipe has traditionally been heavily involved in shaping the visual representations of the band. He also came up with the concepts for the group's earliest videos and was practically the only one in the R.E.M. clan to appear in them. His three cohorts had little interest in any of these activities. At that time, the bulk of the press duties devolved upon the verbose Buck, just as in Radiohead the affable Colin Greenwood (who is less media-shy than the other four) is frequently deployed to meet with journalists on behalf of the group (which is why he has been decorated by his four friends as the band's secret weapon).

U2's pragmatic Larry Mullen is in charge of the band's substantial merchandising operation. Bill Berry was R.E.M.'s de facto manager before Jefferson Holt came on board, a position Adam Clayton also filled before U2 hooked up with Paul McGuinness. Collecting the proceeds for a gig from crooked club owners was one of Anthony Kiedis' notable nonmusical jobs in the nascent Red Hot Chili Peppers. But success brings with it a paid staff that can tackle jobs (such as running the fan club) that were once the province of the band members. And there are also changes over time. "We have a group dynamic and it's really undefined," Peter Buck states on the topic of the labor division, musical and otherwise, in R.E.M. "I think if it had been defined at this point everyone would be so sick of it. The workload shifts around."[11]

Part II: Informal roles

MEET THE DRUMMERS

The behind-the-scenes functions of group members are numerous and varied. They are as important, if not more essential, than the "real" duties carried out by each individual. That's why a band member who may not appear, on the surface, to contribute as much as others, may actually be meeting some critical needs of the unit that only insiders are aware of. The duties that he and Mullen perform on stage and in the studio are "really just a very small amount of the responsibility that we have overall," stresses Adam Clayton, who, along with U2's drummer, is sometimes regarded as a second-rate citizen compared with Bono and Edge.[12] Many is the time the public has wondered why a band is shattered by the loss of an individual who isn't deemed key to the enterprise. "He was only the drummer" is a common refrain (one that R.E.M. is all too familiar with). It's appropriate, therefore, to launch into this section by looking at the drummers in each of these groups and what unseen role they play(ed).

Many drummers, including the four pertinent to this discussion, don't exhibit the flightiness, eccentricity and volatility that are often part and parcel of the creative temperament. So they tend to be stabilizing and grounding forces within their respective outfits. But this means something different in each band. The Red Hot Chili Peppers' Chad Smith is the epitome of the solid and reliable drummer who holds down the fort. Kiedis explains that Smith, probably an asset in any group, is absolutely indispensable to the Chili Peppers because he's the only one of the four who is not a "wild card in the deck." What he means by this characterization is that Smith is "the least likely to go off the deep end at any given time. Whereas pretty much everybody else in the band could disappear into a cloud, and you're not exactly sure when they're going to re-emerge."[13] In a band where squeaky wheels frequently threatened to fall off for one reason or another, Smith has always been the linchpin.

On his part, Smith makes a sincere effort to act in this capacity on behalf of his bandmates and live up to the expectations he believes come with the stool behind the drumkit. "It's part of my role in the band, being the drummer. I like the other guys to feel like they can always count on me."[14] In a 2000 interview with *Kerrang!*, he explained that he's had his fair share of personal problems but, knowing what's expected of him as a drummer, he has never let them get in the way of the band (as the other three have). He understands that having too many eccentric or screwy musicians in the group creates an impossible situation and the one trusty member is thus a source of comfort for everyone. "They know I'm always going to show up, I'm always going to perform to the best of my ability, and when they look back there, I'll be banging away and everything will be okay. Uncle Chad is there and they can count on me."[15] Although less never-failing than Smith, it should be noted that the highly dedicated Flea often held the band together along with the stalwart drummer.

Born more than a year before Yorke and O'Brien, Phil Selway is the oldest member of Radiohead and something of a father figure in the band. He is reputedly the most laid-back and level-headed member of this hypersensitive, hyperanalytical and supercritical bunch. One can only imagine how volatile the high-strung group would be in the absence of his relative unflappability. Bill Berry was the no-nonsense one in R.E.M., the down-to-earth Southern boy who enjoyed being out on his tractor in the sunlight more than he did being under the media spotlight or the dim lighting of a limo interior. These qualities helped keep the group anchored. He had a collateral musical sensibility that kept R.E.M. carefully toeing the pop line. It's no wonder, then, that the unit effectively came unhinged, creatively and in other ways, when he left. In his biography of R.E.M., David Buckley explains that, without Berry to keep the group focused and prevent his partners from getting carried away by experimentation, the three remaining musicians wandered unchecked in disparate artistic directions, barely finding a way back together again.

While he is, like Smith, Berry and Selway, a steady and reliable pillar in U2, Larry Mullen also, in Bono's famous words, *polices* the group. Explaining the meaning and implications of this label, Mullen informed *Dazed and Confused* in 1997 that before casting his vote in favor of something he needs to be convinced it's the right step to take. Every move the band makes needs to be justifiable in his view because he doesn't like to play games and studiously avoids delving too deeply into Art so as not to alienate the band's fans or make them feel like they've been swindled. Bringing his so-called bullshit-detector to bear in his policeman's role, Mullen's guardedness with respect to anything too artsy has severely restricted the quartet's forays into flaky or self-indulgent territory (with the possible exception of *Passengers*, which he has practically disowned).

This perennially chary approach has rendered him an effective counterpoint to the more capricious spirits in the group (namely Bono). In an interview with *Q,* the drummer protested, however, that people tend to misinterpret his attitude and function. He's not a thoughtless naysayer; more like the voice of reason or the sensible foot on the brake. "The perception is that if you say, Hold on a minute, it means, No. It's not about that. I suppose I think differently from the other three guys in the band. I don't like to make decisions quickly. In the excitement of a moment people agree to do things that are not good for the band and not good for them and I try to protect the band as much as I can."[16]

CONCEPTUAL INSTIGATORS

R.E.M., U2 and the Red Hot Chili Peppers each have a member who meets the description of Conceptual Instigator. As the label suggests, this isn't about offering a complete vision, but merely kicking off a new venture and/or nudging the band in a particular creative direction. The Edge actually refers to himself as U2's musical instigator in a *Hot Press* interview conducted in 2002, explaining that he's the one who will go through reams of tape (soundcheck recordings and the like) and pull out interesting bits for the four to work on. These snippets frequently serve as the band's starting point when it comes time to generate new material. The guitarist makes it quite clear that he doesn't dictate which pieces the group will pick up and run with, nor what should be done with them. His role ends with putting some options (such as a chord progression) before his bandmates in order to get the collective songwriting ball rolling. What began as an archeologist's job, digging through the proverbial sludge for long-forgotten or overlooked gems, has turned Edge into the driving force of new musical ideas in U2. It was a natural evolution from sound-hunter to sound-instigator. On account of these activities, Edge has variously been referred to as U2's quarterback or the group's backstage conductor.

Operating in a slightly different fashion, Buck typically sets R.E.M.'s creative agenda by recording demos that indicate where he wants to go with an album and presenting that to his bandmates as a more or less done deal. He likes to lead from behind, he explains. "It's like, 'Here's a bunch of demos, this is where I'm going,' as opposed to saying, 'This is what I'm gonna do, what do you think?' I'm always the one who has the first ideas, that's my job."[17] He charts a course on the map and provides some of the basic gear needed to get the expedition underway. It requires a lot of work in advance on his part, says Buck, in order to come up with songs that will get the others excited about the game plan.

Either he does a great job or they're very open-minded—probably both, because they generally follow his lead. He rarely objects to what Peter has in mind, explains the easy-going Mills, because he enjoys playing many different types of music. "If I ever have any strong desires to suggest a direction we should go in, I would certainly do that but I enjoy Peter's creativity and I enjoy the directions in which Peter wants to go."[18] The bass player admitted to *Q* in 1999 that he's more of a reactive musician anyhow, so having Buck in the vanguard works out well because it provides him with a necessary creative springboard. Mills respects Buck's ability to fully envision the tracks in his head early in the process and come in with very developed ideas, but that's in stark contrast to the way he operates: he tends to figure out what the songs need once he's playing them.

Always itching to move forward, Buck frequently announces the band's (or rather, his) intentions regarding a new album to the press before studio time has been booked or any songs written. The public was forewarned, for instance, that the successor to *Green* would have an orchestral flair (this came to be on *Out of Time*) and that the Monster tour would yield a semi-live album of new songs (what became *New Adventures in Hi-Fi*). It's almost always been up to Buck to pace the band as well, especially now that the three members are scattered in different cities, not tied down to a fixed schedule and engaged in numerous side-projects. So he's the one who approaches the others with new material and suggests getting to work on another R.E.M. album. A self-confessed workaholic, he's usually raring to go well ahead of everyone else. Half the time, Mills and Stipe roll their eyes at overtures that strike everyone but himself as premature and say, "'Oh God, didn't we just do that?'"[19]

Flea spearheaded some of the Red Hot Chili Peppers' albums, notably *One Hot Minute* (partly because there was no one else to take up the reins), but more often than not, especially since rejoining the band, Frusciante is the driving conceptual force. Kiedis, for instance, once referred to the guitarist as the "cosmic wizard" of the group.[20] In the press, he's been called its musical soul. It's his utter engrossment in all things musical that makes Frusciante an ideal guiding spirit (musically, if not in any other sense) for the Chili Peppers. He is, says Kiedis, the most disciplined and inspired member of the band, so he serves as its musical pillar. "In any moment of doubt or concern we kind of focus on John, because he's so into this and nothing else, because he is giving all of his energy to this and it's contagious that way."[21] Speaking for himself, the guitarist admits that he more or less shapes the sound of the albums because he always has a creative angle in mind before the quartet gets to work, but protests that he gets far more credit in the actual songwriting department than he actually deserves.

A lot of the time, pieces that people think he wrote are really Flea's, Frusciante told *Magnet* in 2004. It's one thing to acknowledge that the lush Beach Boys-inspired harmonies that define *By the Way* bear the stamp of Frusciante's influence, but it's quite another to assume that he single-handedly steered the band towards the pop signatures—heavy melodic hooks and mellifluous chord changes—that it now incorporates master-fully into virtually every song. That was where the band was heading when he joined, claims Frusciante, adding that his bandmates display equal prowess when it comes to this type of music. Also modestly rejecting the notion that he revitalized the Chili Peppers, the guitarist insisted in an interview with *The Toronto Sun* in 2002 that the band's undeniable renaissance has little to do with him as conceptualist *per se* and a lot to do with the restoration of a fertile chemistry.

Until recently, Radiohead's primary musical catalyst was Thom Yorke. He still performs this function—it's he, after all, who stoked the group engine for *Hail to the Thief* by sending out demo tapes to his bandmates. He was certainly the main mover behind *Kid A* and *Amnesiac*. O'Brien confessed to *Q*'s David Cavanaugh that Radiohead's discovery of new musical frontiers on its fourth and fifth albums was made possible only by Yorke's doggedness and artistic leadership. It's true that he didn't know exactly what he *did* want, but, O'Brien remarks, he knew very well what he *didn't* want, which was anything that smacked of a rock band or old Radiohead. "He's got a low boredom threshold and is very good at giving us a kick up the ass," concluded the guitarist, indicating that this is what qualifies the singer to serve as Radiohead's conceptual instigator (though a somewhat gentler approach is sometimes in order).[22]

But, increasingly, Jonny Greenwood is taking a turn in the pilot's seat, especially since his horizon-expanding appointment as BBC composer-in-residence. "I get these enthusiasms which can drive the band crazy," is how he describes his method of guidance, "but I just say: listen, French horns are amazing, we've got to find a way of using them. Or I'll say, it would be great if this song sounded like [Krzysztof] Penderecki, or Alice Coltrane."[23]

OF CHEERLEADERS, TASKMASTERS, DIPLOMATS AND OTHERS

Other members of the band perform functions that proceed from their own unique attributes. Ed O'Brien, for example, has been referred to as Radiohead's cheerleader, because of his indefatigable positivism, which has often lifted the spirits of his bandmates. According to Joe Boyd and other band associates, the sanguine Mike Mills similarly buoys R.E.M. He is also the peacemaker in the current trio, when the hot-headed Buck and occasionally intractable Stipe butt heads. In U2, this is Adam Clayton's commission. He is known as the group's diplomat, the one who will arrange for the quartet to discuss issues that need to be resolved. Flea has often found himself attempting to reconcile warring parties in the Red Hot Chili Peppers. He was the one who urged Kiedis and Frusciante to work on their relationship when it was falling apart in 1992 and later brought the guitarist, with whom only he had stayed in touch, back into the fold. *The Age* reported that Cambridge-educated Colin Greenwood is Radiohead's "chief diplomat and peacemaker."[24]

Alongside the musical instigators, certain individuals have a talent for instant incidental inspiration when the work is already underway. It's been said about both Thom Yorke and Bono that one of their fortés is setting off or igniting others. Yorke claims that he's an expert at "walking into a situation cold" and "sparking people off," which is consequently one of his main functions in the group.[25] After spending time in the studio with U2, Flood reported that Bono, similarly, has a tendency to "come in and vibe things up."[26] Characterizing the singer in broader terms, Adam Clayton remarks that Bono has a way of making people face up to daunting challenges, or get over their torpidity if that is the source of their inaction. "When you think you don't want to climb this mountain, Bono's the type of person who'll hit you in the ass and get you going."[27] With the possible exception of R.E.M., each of the four groups seems to contain one or two individuals who are notably ambitious and drive the group with their unflagging determination to succeed. Anthony Kiedis, Bono, Adam Clayton and Thom Yorke fall into this category. Flea told *Q* (2006) that the Chili Peppers is what it is today because of Kiedis' adamantine Will.

Taskmasters can also be found in some of the bands. Kiedis revealed in his memoirs that Flea is a stern drillmaster. In his case, this involves making sure everyone is diligently learning their parts, and playing with unfailing accuracy. He doesn't need to crack the whip much in the current Chili Peppers lineup, but some previous incarnations of the group have demanded it. Keeping everyone on schedule is Smith's business, since he deplores unnecessary delays. "It's been my job to bitch at the little guys when they get out of line," he joked in 1995, when the band had fallen severely behind schedule.[28] U2's Adam Clayton doesn't lash his partners into shape but he doesn't hesitate to lay it on the line to the others when a reproof is called for. Yorke's bandmates report that he is constantly putting them to the test and forcing them to prove themselves. The now-famous first words he directed at Phil Selway were "Can't you play any fucking faster?"[29] It's likely (one hopes) that he has become more tactful over the years, but he continues to be in charge of conditioning the group. If Yorke is the leader of Radiohead, it's not merely because he furnishes the bulk of the raw material the band molds into songs, but also because he simultaneously plays a number of key parts in the group, including conceptual instigator, chief motivator and taskmaster.

While the nuts and bolts of recording are generally left to producers and studio engineers, each band appears to have one member who matches the profile of a studio vulture. In the midst of the promotional junket for *By the Way,* John Frusciante was still approving final track mixes in between interviews. Michael Stipe admits that he spends a lot of time in the control room hanging over the engineers and paying attention to every detail. Likewise, Edge tends to babysit U2 albums into their final hour, long after his bandmates have fled the studio, or in Bono's case, developed an allergy to it. At the end, says the singer, "when everybody else is fading, he's the guy who's up all night for weeks."[30] Edge is also the unit's mad scientist, who tinkers incessantly with equipment to produce unusual sounds. A friend of the band describes how Edge and his brother once bought six echo boxes and connected them together to elicit a highly original sound. "There was always this Nutty Professor element going on, like a quiet genius at work."[31] John Frusciante and Jonny Greenwood have also been typecast as the mad scientists of their groups, thanks to their interest in and experiments with hardware (such as recording gear and arcane instruments).

An interesting, if somewhat baffling, title has been assigned to Adam Clayton by Bono, who referred to the bassist on more than one occasion as U2's conscience or the musical conscience of the family business. While Mullen is busy keeping U2 out of schmaltzland, Clayton maintains a kind of quality control over the music, ensuring that it is up to spec—*his* specifications. "The kind of music that I'm interested in is the stuff that transports you to a different place. That's a certain thing, and not everyone's doing it; so I guess that's what I look for in our own music," he explains when asked about the equivocal label.[32] In a sense, he keeps U2 honest, endowed with what Bono has called an "ear equivalent to a third eye."[33] Together, Clayton and Mullen make quite a duo, a comprehensive constabulary that Bono has dubbed the Rock Police. They are a hard-to-impress committee, "always reasonable and usually correct," says the singer, who admits that he occasionally finds their exactitude maddening.[34] Edge focuses on another of Clayton's capacities, christening him the group's jazzman, the one they can always count on to throw them a musical curveball. On his part, the bassist styles himself the confidence-booster in the band.

Perhaps U2 wouldn't require such strict monitoring by the Rock Police if it weren't for Bono's self-appointment as band risk-taker. He believes it's his job to ensure that U2 remains a rock group (i.e., unpredictable, untamed, unrefined), instead of becoming a Broadway act (i.e., slick, polished, rehearsed), by constantly shaking things up. In 2004, Mullen told *The Sunday Times* that the singer's fearlessness makes him, in a sense, the mother of the band because he's larger than life and will take on anything. (Incidentally, since he's such an effective decision-maker, Bono thinks Mullen is the paternal figure). The singer is also, like all frontmen, the band's arch-communicator. That's why Edge says his post as sideman is not just to play guitar in the band, but also to support Bono and make him look good because the frontman is the band's face. A clever illustration by Bono clarifies how all these various predispositions pan out in the actual operation of the band. "If we're in the studio trying to build the rocket, Edge is under the hood with his slide rule, I'm trying to become fuel, Larry is pointing out the reasons it'll never fly, and Adam's asking, 'Do we really want to go there?'"[35] But, early in the band's career (1983), he presented an equally valid depiction in *Rock!* of Mullen and Clayton as the group's feet, Edge as its head/brain and himself as its heart.

Obviously, these informal roles aren't fixed. Everyone plays the mediator or conceptual instigator once in a while. But there's no denying that some lots fall to certain individuals more than others. Now, a final note on this subject that both looks backward to the chapter on obstacles and forward to a section on side projects. The relative stability and harmony in these groups owes much to the fact that the members appear satisfied with their respective gigs. They aren't casting covetous glances in one another's direction or harboring secret (or not-so-secret) desires to usurp someone else's place. "We've avoided jealousy because we all know our positions," says Edge, speaking of both concrete and perceived roles. "I'm a sideman. Bono is the frontman. Adam and Larry are the rhythm section. We all know what we do."[36] In terms of their aspirations as well as their personalities, then, the various parties are well-matched. A broad view of one's role combined with the option of picking up other instruments and the absence of rigid rules governing who can do what are all factors that undoubtedly boost everyone's level of contentment and minimize the sense of being pigeonholed. But when anyone does feel the need to take on a role (extensively) that isn't available to him in the band, he can (and some do) get involved in ventures outside of it where he can be cast differently.

8

"2+2=5": The Collaborative Process

In most cases, the life of recording artists encompasses both studio and roadwork. Their job is to compose music and play it live (photo shoots, interviews and party attendance notwithstanding). Creation and performance, however, have very little in common. They require a completely different mentality and set of skills. For a band, each task demands, and no doubt inspires, a unique group dynamic and working relationship. In the studio, the collective and the interactions that define it take one shape, but on tour, they are likely to have a significantly different aspect. In this chapter, the dynamics involved in *composing* music as a group will be the focus of attention.

Part I: Songwriting methodology and implications

CREATING (AND RECORDING) TOGETHER

There is no shortage of articles in which the bands talk about how they write new songs. Two rather unsurprising facts are revealed therein. The first is that none of the bands has boiled songwriting down to a consistent formula that represents the genesis of every track. Within each group, the approach to the collaborative composition effort changes quite frequently and from piece to piece. That said, the second fact is that each band seems to have developed a methodology that is *most typical* of its songwriting process, or more typical than others. And, of course, each group works in its own fashion—one that carries with it a variety of compelling particulars.

The Red Hot Chili Peppers tend to lay down the basic framework for tracks through group jams. This is not, as one journalist pointed out, a sit-down-and-write-a-song kind of band. The mentality is essentially that of a garage band, observes Flea, because the songwriting process entails nothing fancier than a bunch of guys picking up instruments and rocking out together. They just start making noise and come across a promising groove that is then developed—through further jamming—into a song. Sometimes someone brings a snippet (drum fill, bass line, guitar riff) to rehearsal and if everyone agrees that it's worth trying to build a song around, the others fall in and play whatever it inspires them to play or try to match it up with a part they have already come up with. Aside from that, "there's no preconceived anything," says Smith.[1] Just being in one another's presence is a sufficient catalyst to get the creative juices flowing. "The music that we write, it's never something we plan on or think about," insists the bassist, "it's just something that happens when we get together."[2] They don't even decide on a general direction for a song—slow, funky, heavy—before laying into their instruments, remarked the drummer in a band interview with *Guitar*. It's just down to however they're feeling that day. The band's indeterminate approach supports the claim that its genre-bending sound was not premeditated.

If the band is missing a part—a bridge or chorus, for example—they'll often resort to a unique jam variant, an exercise they call a Face-Off, which involves Frusciante and Flea retreating into separate corners for five minutes to work up a part to fill the gap. The band then listens to the fragment each of them has devised in isolation and decides which one makes the cut. Occasionally, one of the four will come in with a fairly complete song strand—like Kiedis' lyrics for "Californication," or Frusciante's guitar parts for "Cabron" and "I Could Die for You"—and the others then flesh it out by adding their own parts. There have also been times when Kiedis and Frusciante have gotten together on their own to work on a song, but this is not a habitual or dominant practice. Recently, Frusciante explained to *Guitar One*, he has striven to bring a little more structure to the freewheeling jams by challenging himself to try different styles and channeling his own efforts in a particular musical direction, though his bandmates continue to come and play whatever they like. Instinctively, the four of them recognize when they've stumbled upon something worthwhile, and that's when they develop the jam into a song, working out the duration and arrangement of the piece together.

Flea pointed out in *Guitarist* that since freeform improvisation is the customary basis of the Chili Peppers' music, no one can be singled out as the main creative force or predominant songwriter in the group. Rather, it's a true four-way effort and, as Frusciante observed in *The Toronto Sun* (2001), a completely democratic songwriting method. To render the interplay between them fluid and organic, the band members need to be able to get inside each other's heads in some sense, which they are able to do when there's a special connection between them. "It's not like listening to another guy and hearing what he's playing, and saying, 'Oh, that's bitchin.' That's gonna make me do this,'" says the bassist. "When it's at its best, there's no thought involved. It's just like energy in the air."[3] This is what they often refer to as a telepathic kind of communication between musicians that allows them to play off one another effortlessly. An engineer who has recorded with the Chili Peppers reports that, to facilitate this psychic exchange, the three musicians in the band set up close to one another so they can see and hear what each of them is doing. But the basic ingredients for a creative communion at this level (what other bands might call being "tight" or simply "attuned to one another") are chemistry and/or longevity.

This extensive reliance on jams sets the Chili Peppers apart from other bands, Frusciante revealed to *Australian Guitar* (1999). The group's long-serving producer, Rick Rubin, seconds his opinion, contending that this approach is indeed unwonted and demands a sophisticated brand of interaction between the musicians. He intimates that it represents the zenith of collaboration in a band. There are few, if any, other big bands that really jam, he contends. "A lot of bands, people just play their parts, but the Chili Peppers are truly an interactive band, kind of in the way that musicians might have been in the '60s."[4] This interactivity takes the shape of creating music by listening and responding to one another— essentially playing off of one another while playing together. What is also special about this method of composition is, as Smith pointed out in *Batteur*, that the songs arising from it truly capture a communal feeling that prevailed at a particular moment in time.

Radiohead represents a very different collaborative paradigm because the band, not unlike many others, has one principal songwriter. In this case, what happens is that the members build together on skeletal tunes, lyrics or sound bites Thom Yorke has conceived. As Jonny Greenwood puts it: "Thom does the lyrics and usually kicks off the song, writes the majority of it or a tiny part of it. Things just get extended, altered and butchered by the rest of us."[5] It's important that the demos presented to the band be neutral and sparse, the songs stripped-down, so that the five can then work together on fleshing them out. So Yorke must take care to leave room for contributions from his bandmates. He says himself that it's not difficult to present the songs in roughhewn form because the collaboration with the other musicians evolved from his own limitations. Since he's not the most intent or sophisticated guitar player, what he has to offer are simple three- or four-chord compositions, to which the band adds the meat. As we've seen, he also frequently reaches a point in a song where he just doesn't know how to go on without the input of his bandmates. And while Yorke often writes on his own, some of the band's best songs have been inspired by his partners. With "Lucky," for instance, the unearthly sound O'Brien makes on the guitar at the beginning got Yorke going.

Though Yorke provides the basic framework for virtually every track, Radiohead's songwriting process is very much a "communal affair," according to O'Brien.[6] Selway says the band employs a technique of layering sounds until a mix that they all respond to emerges. This is one area in which teamwork comes into prominent play. Arranging songs is the part the quintet enjoys the most, and Jonny Greenwood claimed in *IC Coventry* that they devote a great deal of time and energy to this step in the process, which is one that demands mutual effort. Ideas count as much as riffs in songwriting, and the entire Radiohead clan gets involved in this aspect of composition. So, while his direct and immediately tangible contribution to the band's music, says Colin Greenwood, may be his bass lines, that's not where it ends. "Our ideas and suggestions in certain areas, as to where the music should go or develop, are listened to. We are very much a band."[7] John Harris, a source close to the group, revealed to band biographer Mac Randall that it takes Radiohead a long time to record an album precisely because each of them has so many ideas, all of which are taken into account. As Selway describes it in *The New Yorker* (2001), Yorke gives the group musical puzzles that must be solved collectively.

Working in this fashion, particularly given the quality of Yorke's compositions, puts the other members of the group in a peculiar quandary. Their part in the creative process is simultaneously facilitated and complicated by having tunes handed over to them, their role perhaps less demanding but more daunting. Jonny Greenwood explains that while it's a "luxury" having York come up with stunning tracks for them to work on, "the pressure is to not fuck up this great song rather than the pressure being to write this great song." They have to make it sound better than him playing it by himself, "which already sounds amazing, so that's our nightmare in a way and our motivation."[8] Consequently, Yorke's bandmates sometimes have a difficult time deciding whether they should touch the song at all, particularly if it's more or less complete, or to leave it as is. The fear of mucking up a great track can be as intense as the allure of enhancing it. But, while Yorke does turn out the occasional song, like "Fake Plastic Trees," that requires little embellishment, most of his material cries out for the input of his co-writers. "For every song like 'I Will,' which arrived fully formed and was immediately perfect," says Jonny Greenwood, "there are songs like 'Sail to the Moon,' which weren't great."[9] It was basically half an idea, he proceeds, which came together only after the whole band worked on it (and after Selway had a revelation about the arrangement).

Since Jonny Greenwood has a low boredom threshold, it takes more than a good song to hold his attention, he informed *Rolling Stone* in 1995. This impels him to shake up even some of the more fully-realized tracks Yorke brings in, counteracting, one supposes, any misgivings he might otherwise have about tampering with them. The general rule of thumb, especially when it comes to a piece that doesn't need dramatic alteration, is to make contributions that take the track in a novel direction, Ed O'Brien said in *Total Guitar* (1997), giving the example of the quiet mellotron sample Jonny Greenwood added to the chorus of "Exit Music." It requires a lot of discipline and intensifies the pressure, adds the guitarist, who doesn't seem terribly concerned about ruining a song (you could put an out-of-tune banjo over Yorke's vocals and they'd still sound good, he jokes) but is very alive to the challenge of actually bettering it, rather than merely throwing in an extraneous bit that neither adds to nor detracts from the piece.

"Nice Dream" is a track that Yorke often refers to as an example of why his songs benefit from the collaborative setup in Radiohead. "For me this song was just these four chords going round and round and I was quite happy with that." But his bandmates added all kinds of bits that took the track to places he would never have thought of on his own. "And that's the whole point of Radiohead, I think, really."[10] Sometimes, he doesn't have a firm idea about where to go with a song, and there too, the collaboration is invaluable because his bandmates step into the void. "If I have a direction, fine. If I don't have a direction, it's someone else's thing."[11] (All of this harkens back to the notion of interdependency and sharing the creative burden).

Usually, once Yorke has delivered the raw goods, the other band members have time to digest the songs and come up with suggestions about how to develop them before the group convenes to work as a unit. The subsequent show-and-tell session adds sizzle to an already exciting creative relationship. Even once they're in the studio together, the band members will often work independently, deliberately keeping to themselves, until one of them comes across something worth submitting for the consideration of his bandmates. He then turns up his amp so the others can hear, explains O'Brien, and they all get off on that and jam. But Yorke and Jonny Greenwood tend to be more effective when they work together rather than apart. They achieve the most when they sit down with two guitars and bounce ideas off one another, Yorke said on Australian radio station Triple J in 2004. Ever since Radiohead recorded *OK Computer*, the pair has enjoyed a fertile partnership—somewhat separate from the rest of the group—that they rely upon to turn half-formed compositions into more substantial songs to which O'Brien, Selway and Colin Greenwood can add their own parts and ideas.

Since *The Bends*, Radiohead's songwriting has, in fact, become an increasingly inclusive and broad-based endeavor. Jonny Greenwood, in particular, has assumed a more prominent role in the composition of songs. He is the author of a number of album tracks ("The Tourist" on *OK Computer*, "A Wolf at the Door" on *Hail to the Thief*), and has masterminded entire song sections, such as the strings on "How to Disappear Completely." The singer informed *The Age* in 2004 that all the band members now have home studios and have begun using computers as primary composition tools. So Radiohead feels like a new band in many ways, because "now ideas come from all over the place, which is good, much better."[12] This means that everyone is much more involved in the process of preparing material for the band to develop collectively.

In R.E.M., we find yet another creative model, a band boasting a number of different songwriters, since Mills, Buck, and in the old days, Berry, all bring in their own songs for the group to work on. Like The Beatles, three members out of four can each lay claim to certain tracks in the group's discography; the difference is that they don't, because they feel that the final product featured on the album represents a communal effort. What is unique about R.E.M. is that each band member regularly writes songs on his own, but they all recognize the benefits of working together. "It takes equal parts of all of us to make great records," Mills pronounces.[13] In Paul Zollo's groundbreaking book *Songwriters on Songwriting*, Buck similarly stated that they each have the ability to write songs independently, but the collaboration between the four of them makes a big difference (presumably, in the quality of the material). Notably, Mills politely refused to identify any of "his" songs or even single out those where his creative stamp is most apparent, telling *Scene* (1995) that he doesn't like to think in those terms. Initially, as we've seen, each of them wanted his name attached to the track he composed, but Buck persuaded them that it's wiser and more accurate (given the cooperation that actually occurs) to attribute all the songs to the band.

For the most part, especially now that the three bandmates don't reside in the same city, they write on their own and develop their individual compositions as a group—much like Radiohead except that there's no primary songwriter. They each enjoy the best of both worlds: the gratification of writing on one's own and the exhilaration of enhancing the pieces with the aid of the band. The fact that they work independently before they convene to tackle the tracks together has undoubtedly played a role in making it possible for the group to carry on even with the members living apart. The tunes arrive in various stages of readiness for recording. "Some songs we bring in are just about complete," says Mills, "but some songs are just the very germ of an idea. One person brings in anywhere from five to 100 percent of a song."[14] That explains why, as Stipe told *Flagpole* in 1994, it can take all four of them to pull a piece together, while at other times, they just need to add little bits here and there. Even the more fully-realized tracks (i.e., that have most or all of the important parts in place), such as those Buck tends to bring in, are often (by his own admission in the documentary accompanying the making of *Up*) shallow and rough, smacking of the home studio and in dire need of refinement.

Typically, the final track represents a significant collective effort, as the ideas get "dissected and changed and shaped," by everyone, notes Mills.[15] If Buck comes up with a chorus for a piece Mills has brought in, then it changes and becomes a completely different song, elucidated the guitarist in *Addicted to Noise* (1996). On top of that, each band member is responsible for his own part. Both arranging and mixing are protracted and highly collaborative activities in R.E.M., which may be another reason they view their songwriting as a communal effort—they work very much as a team during these critical moments in the realization of a track. Compromise becomes essential at this stage, because everyone wants to put in his two cents for every decision that needs to be made. This is a major pressure point in the creative process, Mills told *Guitar* in 1993, one that is riddled with friction as everyone competes to have his voice heard.

Sometimes, the band members just jam and find a song buried amidst the noise. They play their instruments without listening to each other and, all of a sudden, the parts start to fit together, explains Mills, who referred to this in *Pulse!* as the Chaos Method of Songwriting. "Finest Worksong" is one example. That's one that could never have been created by any one of them alone at home with his guitar, the bassist apprised *East Coast Rocker* (1987), because the tunes they come up with by improvising as a group are very different from those they produce in their more habitual fashion. The songs that aren't labored over, that just appear in the room seemingly out of thin air, claims Berry, are those that arise in this way. But, when it comes down to it, they don't come from nowhere; they are borne out of "the interplay of four people."[16]

With a chord progression or some other bit to get the creative wheels turning, new U2 material typically emerges from group jams, a system Bono has famously dubbed Songwriting by Accident. In the absence of any musical training the foursome were as clueless when it came to songwriting as they were with respect to their instruments, which is how they wound up with their haphazard methodology. "A lot of other people sit down and write songs in a much more disciplined fashion," the singer said in 1986, but U2 were compelled to form tracks by essentially sewing together the good bits of various jams.[17] Edge explained in 1997 that a sound would get thrown out in rehearsal and they would then start improvising, gradually becoming more conscious of what they are doing and trying different tacks, then molding the best fragments into a cohesive whole. "That's a technique that we used a lot, and it worked really well for us because none of us were really schooled musicians. So it was the spontaneous bouncing of ideas off of each other that created a lot of the things."[18] These days, it's more or less the same except that Edge takes it upon himself to provide the four with a jumping-off element—either a part that he's come up with or a sound elicited from the archival material through which he patiently sifts. Then, as a group, they develop a song around that snippet, which involves—and this is a notable band trademark—long discussions about its philosophical and musical possibilities in addition to the actual playing.

Given the band members' limited knowledge and abilities, the improvisational approach thus evolved out of necessity rather than a conscious artistic choice. (Despite their technical proficiency, the Chili Peppers' founding lineup also lacked songwriting savvy—Flea, Slovak and Irons were more musicians than songwriters while Kiedis was a complete ingénue—so it was natural for them to gravitate towards jams as well.) Not being virtuosos had other implications for U2 in the studio. Ironically, given that their collective effort was their only strength, being amateurs interfered with the foursome's ability to play together effectively.

Asked in 1987 if he and Clayton lay down backing tracks jointly, Mullen replied that, until then, they had found working together very difficult because neither of them knew how to play in a band. The fact that Clayton wasn't playing the way a schooled bassist would and Mullen wasn't hitting the skins like a typical drummer didn't help, so in the early stages of the band's development, the two rhythm players couldn't figure out how to bend their conflicting styles to complement one another. It was a battle to get it right and they spent many years working on becoming a tight rhythm section. They studied dance music grooves and, at some point in the mid–1980s, Clayton decided to take his cue from the beats Mullen comes up with and emphasize them with his bass lines, which resulted in greater congruence between the two instruments, they explained to *Musician* in 1987.

Since the band members didn't really know what they're doing, it also took U2 longer than other groups to write and record music, the drummer informed *Hot Press* in 2000, and tensions would arise simply because the entire process was so foreign to them and even the basics incredibly challenging. Indeed, the simplest aspects of the craft that other bands take for granted, like playing in time, he and his partners in U2 struggled to master, Bono remarks in this context (*Sound and Media*). But, ultimately, as they repeatedly assert, what they lacked in technique, they made up for with inspiration, personality, good instincts, hard work, and team effort—all of which have been integral to U2's success. In many ways, then, the four turned their limitations into creative tools.

Brian Eno and Daniel Lanois have also helped the four compensate for their dearth of skill by capitalizing on their erratic and extemporaneous songwriting practices. They believe that the moment the band stumbles upon something in the midst of a jam has an irreproducible potency. So, instead of going into the studio ready to record tunes they had composed and rehearsed beforehand, the quartet was advised to arrive without songs in hand and let the music take shape with all the people and equipment in place to capture its gestation. When the four of them are in the process of playing around with a beat or guitar lick, and building up from that together, explains Edge, everyone "is listening in a different way because they are genuinely uncertain of what is going to happen next. You're able to work off the sense of discovery. There's a feeling you can only get from playing something for the first time."[19] As they don't know what their bandmates will do next, there's a sort of breathless anticipation that can really bring a track to life.

While molding a composition out of a formless jam is thrilling and unpredictable, the inherent disorder can be nerve-wracking and the process seemingly or genuinely unproductive. For U2, it's always been a notoriously slow and frustrating way to work. It gets to them sometimes. In 1984, the foursome came to the conclusion that just bashing out ideas with Bono singing something on top isn't the optimal method of realizing a track's potential, especially as they were now cognizant of the difference between making music and writing the structured pieces known as *songs* that they heard on the radio. So the band decided to explore the less arbitrary, good old-fashioned craft of collective songwriting in place of the improvisation the band had hitherto relied upon. Working in this style, Edge comes up with a chord sequence, then Bono produces a vocal melody and some lyrics to go with it. Once they have these rudiments of a song in place, Clayton and Mullen plug in the rhythm portions.

However, only a couple of the numbers on *The Unforgettable Fire*, which is where they first tried the system out, survived this treatment, according to Clayton. The situation seemed stilted and forced. "This band cannot play other people's songs and it was almost like that with Bono and Edge saying: 'Here's the song, here's the demo.'"[20] This more systematic approach still doesn't suit the band. Speaking to *Bass Player* in 2000, Clayton explained that they find it very difficult to try and arrange a song that's already been laid out. When they start with a few bits and develop the piece together, they end up with something far more interesting. Edge agrees. U2 is at its best, he says, when the four members are simultaneously exhilarated by a breakthrough. Even if that means working in total chaos. They've simply had to make peace with the communal songwriting paradigm that works for them. "When we're making the records," says Bono, "it always feels a bit like we're drowning, and you do wonder if there's an easier way. But we seem to need some chaos to bring us together."[21] On occasion, they employ the more traditional songwriting technique, which they haven't abandoned, but certainly haven't converted to.

This section has thus far illustrated how starting out as novices shaped U2's approach to songwriting, but it's important to note that U2's approach has also had a tremendous influence on the band's sound. Without a musical heritage or years of playing other people's chops behind them, it was up to the four to define themselves individually and collectively, Clayton expressed to *Creem* in 1983, proving that Bono has a point when he claims that their main influences were each other rather than any musicians outside the group. Since they didn't play their instruments seriously (or at all) before joining U2, they hadn't styled themselves after anyone else. In developing their individual musical ability together, and bouncing ideas internally around the band, they ended up creating a highly distinct collective sound.

Getting on the Same Wavelength

By the time the members of U2 are actually playing their instruments in the studio, it's no wonder that the desultory nature of jam-based composition seems discombobulating. When working on a new album, the band spends the initial period engaged in endless discussions and debates, so it's usually down to the wire with actually writing and recording the songs. The term "groping" comes up frequently. What they grope *for* is a singular vision for the project. It's about dreaming up the kind of record they want to make and getting on the same wavelength (which, like the overarching vision for the band is rooted partially, but not entirely, in musical influences). So they sit in a room together and, instead of playing, evaluate concepts by which to get a handle on the sound they're aiming for.

Adjectives that characterize the target material are proposed so that everyone has a common reference point. *Achtung Baby*, for instance, was defined by a vision that encompassed the terms "trash" and "throwaway." Edge admits: "We've always wanted our albums to have a sense of unity, of a single direction—sonically or lyrically—some kind of unified creative direction behind the songs."[22] But it can take months for the band to settle on a course. And sometimes they don't succeed in rallying around a single notion, as was the case when U2 recorded *The Joshua*

Tree. Yet, the divisions in the band in 1990, as the four delved into *Achtung Baby*, had implications that the quartet couldn't work around without reconciling everyone's perspective first.

The other bands don't seem to require quite as much verbalizing of ideas as U2 in an effort to get on the same page, though they also tend to have a general aim in mind when embarking on a new project (with the possible exception of the Chili Peppers). It may take some deliberation to arrive at it, but in some cases it just happens naturally. When R.E.M. convened to make a record in 1994, they had worked on new songs separately yet found, to their surprise, that they were all headed in the same direction. They all wanted to record an album the exact opposite of the slow and moody *Automatic for the People*, recalls Stipe. Once again, when a dinner discussion turned to how they wanted *Up*'s successor to sound, they were quite astonished to learn that they were naturally on the same wavelength. They all wanted the next record to be essentially an extension of its predecessor while taking that aesthetic further, the singer said on XFM radio. Of course, quite frequently there's a conceptual instigator to propose an angle for the next album that everyone can then rally around.

Needless to say, even when the band members share an understanding on a broad level, they each have a different mental picture of how the songs and the album will actually sound. "The images that we all have in our heads are all completely different," confirms Frusciante. "We'll be doing something, and I'll be thinking it should be a ska thing, and Chad will be thinking T. Rex, and Flea will be picturing Led Zeppelin."[23] That, says Mike Mills, is the reason every record is such an arduous undertaking for a band, because generally "there's not a singular vision pulling it together"—beyond, perhaps, a very basic aspiration.[24] But, as we've seen, the tension between the divergent ideas of the band members can result in remarkable music. And the final product frequently surprises everyone, turning out quite differently than *anyone* had expected. Even for someone like Buck, who tends to have a long-range vision for the songs, the input of his bandmates makes it practically impossible to determine what the record will ultimately sound like.

WORK HABITS AND PREFERENCES

Accommodating diverse working methods and preferences is a challenge for all the groups, but primarily, it appears, for R.E.M. and U2. It might be easier on the band members if they at least approached their craft in a congruent fashion, but the fact is that here, too, we find a lot of miscellany. Some band members are proactive, others more reactive; some compose music with a trained eye and some from a novice's standpoint; some work in a very structured manner and others are quite offhand. These contrasting styles obviously don't preclude groupwork (except, for instance, in the case of Dave Navarro, whose methods really didn't fit with the Chili Peppers' jam-band orientation), but they are an important aspect of the group's creative dynamic and therefore deserve to be documented.

From the minute he starts writing a song, Buck can project where he's going with it, which is completely different from how his bandmates, particularly Stipe, function. "I've always wanted to be one of those people who had a complete vision and then simply carried it out," Stipe confesses. "It's not like that at all; a lot of the time I'm grabbing around and bumping into things. I'll throw them together and something will come out that's a combination of conscious and subconscious. A lot of times I figure something out after it's happened."[25] Buck claims that he also tends to work round the clock and then extracts the worthwhile bits from a morass of music while throwing out a lot of unsatisfactory material. His view is that you never know when inspiration will strike, so it's best to plug away at the music constantly. But Stipe prefers to wait for the moment of inspiration because he feels that his best ideas are the ones that hit him over the head unexpectedly, the guitarist revealed about his bandmate in an interview with *Neumu*. The hours they keep are equally at odds. Buck punches in relatively early; Mills and Stipe opt to show up later in the day and, in the bassist's case, stay late into the night. When Berry was around, he would report to the studio around the same time as the guitarist and they worked alongside one another until the others made their way in. After he left the group, Buck found himself *sans* bandmates for much of the day, so it felt like a solo gig, but the band has since taken steps to restore a more collaborative environment.

Whereas Stipe and Mills like to create in the studio, Buck is more inclined to arrive with a bundle of songs the band has already worked out and press record. He told *Neumu* that he doesn't have the nerve to go into the studio with nothing written. (Typically, they arrive with three-quarters of the writing done.) Having frequently observed the band from the producer's chair, Scott Litt remarked in *Addicted to Noise* (1994) that Buck usually takes a very straight-ahead approach to recording songs, focusing on getting all the parts in place and then laying down the track. But Mills greatly enjoys the overdubbing process and tinkering with the gear in the studio. Consequently, he and Buck not only work differently but have often disagreed about a song's state of completion, with the guitarist feeling that, on occasion, they smooth the music out too much before it's deemed finished. That's one of the reasons they decided to record *New Adventures in Hi-Fi* on the road, so there would be little opportunity to polish the tracks in the usual manner, he pointed out to *Guitar World* in 1996.

Bono and Edge differ from one another in a manner similar to their counterparts in R.E.M., in that the guitarist requires a fair amount of preparation and tends to plug away at his parts endlessly while the singer relies mainly on instinct. Edge is a very disciplined and deliberate artist, the one who patiently wades through reams of tape looking for an inspiring sound; Bono is much more impromptu. Contrasting the singer's style with his own, Edge explains that Bono creates in a very spontaneous fashion. "He doesn't slave for weeks on the nuances of a lyric or a melody. He comes in and kind of leaps, and that can be an incredibly inspiring thing to see." The guitarist characterizes himself as a much more methodical artist, one who builds up his parts slowly and painstakingly. "I circle things for a long time before finally moving in and finishing them off."[26]

The angle from which the band members regard the songs is quite individual as well, which is one of the advantages of collaboration, as Brian Eno points out. Since it's necessary to oscillate between detail and big picture, or zoom to wide angle, working in company means you don't have to do both yourself. "With U2 it's very rare that *everyone* in the room is using the same lens at the same time," he says. "Larry and Adam are reliable wide anglers when things start to lose perspective or become too narrowly focused."[27] Edge is keener on details than the overall picture— the guy with the screwdriver, as Bono referred to him in a *Rolling Stone* interview (1993).

APPROACHES TO RECORDING

While bands like U2 and the Red Hot Chili Peppers believe that jamming is the best method of collaborating, they also think it's essential to record tracks as a group. There is no way that recording each instrument in isolation and trying to blend them back together again from tape results in the same sound as when the musicians are playing together, Edge declared in *Musician* (1987), adding that you don't capture the band's chemistry that way. John Frusciante definitely agrees that recording each element on its own is too "clinical" an approach. "If we all record separately and every part is perfect, it can never be as good as each one playing together, and each person hearing little nuances that can happen at the moment."[28] Just looking at the expression on one another's face can make the musicians play differently, he notes.

Alternating between different recording techniques has worked for R.E.M. They started out tracking every song as a band, but once they became more familiar with the studio, they realized that there are other ways of recording, Buck said on XFM radio. So on *Green* through *Auto-*

matic for the People, it was "less and less a band and more and more one or two people playing together and then layering stuff on top."[29] In fact, the guitarist once described *Automatic* as a four-person solo project rather than a band album and remarked in *Documental* that, in this sense, it was like The Beatles' *White Album.* Ultimately, however, he agrees that there's a warmth and vitality to laying tracks down together than can't be replicated and shouldn't be undervalued, as he noted when discussing *Reveal* with *Rolling Stone* in 2001.

There seem to be varying opinions on this matter in Radiohead. Ed O'Brien thinks tracking live is the best way to go, partly for the same reasons presented above, he told *Guitar Player* in 1997. For him, it also has to do with the fact that it took Radiohead many years to master the art of playing as an ensemble, so they ought to take advantage of the tightness they invested so much effort in developing. In his opinion (which he expressed to *Total Guitar*), what's ultimately great about Radiohead— a sentiment shared by the other bands—is the way they play together. Following that logic, by recording individually, they are ignoring their core strength. Jonny Greenwood walks a sensible middle road, contending that the collective approach is appropriate in some, but not all, situations. "It's not something that we worship as being the only way, but it's a great skill that we realise that we have [sic], and for some songs, it's a great way to work."[30] Since recording is an artificial process, it's best at any rate, says the guitarist, to let go of the notion that you're trying to somehow reproduce the live experience. "People worry too much about combining the two," he says.[31]

More reactive musicians, like Mike Mills, Adam Clayton and Dave Navarro, appear to have an understandable preference for fiddling with their parts on their own once elements of the track are already in place to guide them. And as much as U2 gravitates towards an interactive recording environment, in the early years, when the four were still learning to play (and to play together), Clayton had the much-needed luxury of putting his basslines down after Edge and Mullen had prepared the backing track, which supports the notion that this debate rests partly on the band's *readiness* for live tracking, not just personal preferences. Recording collectively using a performance approach doesn't preclude overdubs, but what many of these musicians would argue is that the song benefits from a live foundation, on top of which additional elements can then be layered.

LYRICS

The frontmen in R.E.M, U2 and the Red Hot Chili Peppers don't play an instrument (at least not to speak of) so their tangible contribution to the tracks, consisting of lyrics and vocals/vocal melodies, typically occurs once the instrumental elements are more or less in place. This is not to say that they aren't involved in scoring the music. They are present during the initial sessions and participate by listening, responding, making suggestions or trying out vocal ideas. Anthony Kiedis starts dancing when he hears a promising refrain, which fires up his bandmates and alerts them that they're onto something. Occasionally, the music sparks a melodic idea that Kiedis will sing or hum as the band plays. He also listens to recordings of the rehearsals and identifies bits that he feels the group should use or expand upon, Frusciante described to a German guitar magazine in 2002. "Bono-eze" is how the U2 clan refers to the improvisational muttering Bono produces at the microphone when they're working on the music. Though it's often incomprehensible jibberish, his visible response to what they're playing, like Kiedis', has tremendous influence on the material. Mullen: "If he's doing something very intense, it might not even be what he's saying, but the way he's behaving, the way he's throwing the microphone around. The energy and intensity helps shape the song."[32]

R.E.M. prefers to give the musical ideas some form in early rehearsals from which Stipe is excluded then pass them on to him for the addition of lyrics and vocals. Otherwise, his commentary derails the process. The band experimented with getting Stipe involved at an earlier stage in the music-generating process but it didn't work out. "If he sits there, it can be deleterious," says Buck. "He's like 'Oh, that's real great. Now speed it up twice as fast, throw away the chorus, write a new bridge, and change the key."[33] But, as Stipe told Paul Zollo, it's not uncommon for a vocal idea to emerge when he's listening to a piece in its raw state. The band then rearranges it, if necessary, to suit his part.

In all three cases, the singers wield a great deal of power in that they determine which pieces are completed and which end up being filed in the "unfinished" drawer. Basically, the band prepares a clutch of tunes, too many for a single album, and the singer then goes through them and writes lyrics for those that inspire him the most (or for which he has suitable verses). It can be quite trying for the musicians in the band to see songs that they are rooting for (and have slaved over) fall by the wayside. There's a real letting go demanded at this stage. They can't always tell which pieces Stipe will choose, says Buck in describing the fallout of this arrangement in R.E.M., and it's not easy to persuade him to finish a song that he's not moved by. But his bandmates have been known to urge him to complete tracks that are dear to their hearts.

Thinking that Stipe wouldn't be interested in "Saturn Return," a favorite of Buck's, the guitarist recalled on *HMV.com* asking the singer to make a supreme effort to find lyrics for it. Similarly, the band was enamored with "Man on the Moon" but Stipe couldn't come up with any words to accompany the music. So they begged him to give it another try just before they had to complete the album. During a long walk on the streets of Seattle, Stipe had a brainwave that rescued this key track in the R.E.M. discography from oblivion. From time to time, Stipe or Kiedis bring a set of verses to the band in the hopes of having them set to music and *they* are then in the position of entreating their partners to turn them into a song. "Californication" was a poem Kiedis wrote after a trip to Borneo, and for which he requested a soundtrack from his partners. Bored by the piece and unable to find the right arrangement for it, the band set it aside after several fruitless months. But Kiedis refused to let it go. Much to his relief, Frusciante eventually took the lyrics home and worked out a gorgeous guitar part that put the song back on the group's radar screen, Chad Smith revealed in *Mix*.

So, just as the songs change dramatically once lyrics are added, the album itself is shaped by the singer's sway in terms of what makes it to the next level and what gets left behind. *Automatic for the People* was filled with soft and slow tracks because these are the ones Stipe chose to work on, Mills commented in *The Chicago Tribune* (1992). The Red Hot Chili Peppers' *By the Way* features few heavy songs, not, Frusciante explained to *Chart Attack*, because the band isn't writing them, but because Kiedis wasn't feeling them and wrote lyrics mainly for the more melodic material the group produced. The singers/lyricists may have a lot of control over the album selections, but they are also under tremendous pressure because they complete the collaborative songwriting cycle.

Since they are at the end of the assembly line, so to speak, it's up to them to ensure that the lyrics don't become the bottleneck in the process by dragging their feet (which happened to R.E.M. with *Up* and to the Chili Peppers with *One Hot Minute*). *Up* was so stressful for Stipe, with his bandmates hovering over him and a deadline hanging over his head, that the band decided to ease the burden by dispensing with schedules, thus giving the singer some much-needed leeway. In *Addicted to Noise* (1998) Buck drew attention to the fact that Stipe is also faced with the intimidating task of generating vocals that live up to music the band has toiled for months to perfect, and declares that he wouldn't want to be in such a tough position.

Another issue is whether the singers feel that the lyrics and the themes sown in the album, which serve to focus the music and push it in a particular direction, must, in some way, speak for the group. Stipe explains that since a lot of weight is put on the words, he has to keep himself in check when writing for the band. "I'm representing four people and not just myself."[34] This doesn't preclude writing from personal experience or expressing one's innermost feelings, but, Stipe continues, if he has a particular viewpoint—political or religious, for instance—that the others don't share he has to tread very carefully. On their part, Stipe's bandmates have faith in him, notes Scott Litt. "They trust Michael implicitly with where he's going with stuff."[35] Seldom do they find his lyrics objectionable, adds the producer, but they don't hesitate to voice their disapproval when they do.

Bono has a very collective take on his position as U2's wordsmith, so he feels that his lyrics are inevitably reflective of the band as a whole. His job is, in effect, to translate the music that the group has come up with into language. "I try to put into words what I felt from the music. We spend most of our time working on the arrangements and the melodies, and then at the last minute, I try to articulate the feeling we found while we were improvising."[36] It's all about developing an image that captures the mood of the piece they worked on together. With "New Year's Day," for example, the notes Edge played on the piano struck Bono as icy, hence the winter motif. It's the same with Anthony Kiedis, who remarked after completing *Californication* that the music told him what to sing. So, in a sense, the lyrics emerge from, and embody, a collaborative effort. For Stipe, it varies. Sometimes he will have lyrical ideas for an album from the outset (and modify them to fit the music). At other times, he listens to the demo tapes and goes where the music beckons.

The lyrics do tend to reflect the mood and feelings of the band at a given moment. "It's been pointed out to me," says Stipe, "that many of the songs are about particular times in the life of [R.E.M.]."[37] Yorke noted in *NME* (1994) that "My Iron Lung" and other songs on *The Bends* relate to what the group went through when "Creep" stormed the charts. He expressed the frustration they *all* felt during this period. On *Achtung Baby*, Bono's lyrics revolve around the concept of relationships gone sour, tying in with the divorce Edge was dealing with as well as the divisions in the group itself. That the songs reflect Edge's situation stems from the profound emotional connection between the band members, claimed the guitarist in *Hot Press* (2002). The implication is that Bono is able to pick up on what is in their hearts and in the collective air because they are such close friends. While the singer insisted in *Musician* (1987) that he doesn't really agree with the notion that he is obligated to write on behalf of the band rather than himself, Edge pointed out that there's such a deep commitment and bond within the group that nearly all of Bono's lyrics could have been written as if they were actually meant to represent the group. So, whether or not Bono purposely tries to give his words a collective resonance, that's the end result. Besides, adds the guitarist, in U2 they discuss the lyrics, so there is always input from all four of them.

In both R.E.M. and U2, other band members have indeed started pitching in on the versification front in order to take some of the weight off the singer and speed up the process. Edge now contributes lyrics regularly and has received co-credit alongside Bono. In 1997, the guitarist remarked in *Guitar World* that he has come to share the overwhelming responsibility of coming up with all the lyrics at the tail end of the sessions, after the whole band has worked hard on the music. It was a function that evolved quite naturally, beginning with Edge replacing Clayton as Bono's soundboard, a role the bassist had assumed during the sessions that led to *The Unforgettable Fire*. During the *Achtung Baby* period, the guitarist became Bono's editor and gradually began inserting phrases and introducing thematic ideas. This represents quite a change of tack given the band's initial practices. No one took much interest in the lyrics, which Bono ad-libbed frantically at the microphone, on the first two or three U2 albums. As the quartet grew more cognizant of the importance of lyrics, they understood that it's incumbent upon them to give the singer, who had been on his own until then, a hand. Buck and Mills have also become more than just lyric editors in R.E.M. Stipe now feels he can turn to them for more substantial assistance.

Radiohead is the only band among the four profiled in this book in which the lyrics are typically ready at the outset of the songwriting process. Yorke hands out lyric sheets to his bandmates and his words, in large part, mold the songs. "No Surprises" is probably the best example. Its childlike sentiment smacked of nursery rhymes, which is why the band ultimately couched them in chiming sounds reminiscent of a music box. "The lyrics have really helped us as a band, helped us find a route, you follow the lyrics and the vocal," said Ed O'Brien in an effort to explain why the group felt lost without these signposts when making *Kid A* (the first time Yorke didn't have lyrics, or anything else, prepared).[38]

Surprisingly, understanding Stipe's enigmatic lyrics isn't a priority for the other members of R.E.M. It doesn't really matter to him and Buck whether the lyrics make sense to them or not, says Mills, because they concentrate on the music. If they really want to figure out a particular phrase or image, they ask Stipe what he means, Mills told *Q* in 1996. On the whole, however, they are content to let him cast his magic spell without trying to decode it. This is partly because they enjoy interpreting his words for themselves, explains Stipe, who believes they don't find the lyrics all that perplexing anyhow because they know him so well. "They have a pretty clear idea about my references," he asserts.[39] Over the years, Stipe's bandmates have indeed grown more accustomed to his manner of expressing himself, but they still find much of his material baffling, Mills informed *The Guardian* (2001). The songs on *Murmur* still make sense to them mostly on a sonic level, and some of those written afterwards, such as "The Sidewinder Sleeps Tonight," they still find puzzling.

Anthony Kiedis' bandmates don't think too hard about his (often cryptic) lyrics either. "I'm not really someone who tries to take something poetic and turn it into a literal meaning," said Frusciante, excusing himself from deciphering "Californication."[40] Little attention was paid to Bono's lyrics when U2 first started out. His bandmates didn't even grasp at first that songs like "Tomorrow" and "I Will Follow" actually dealt with Bono's agonizing experience of his mother's death. It was quite a bit afterwards that they started to realize what Bono had actually been writing about, reveals Edge. "We didn't really talk about that sort of stuff much in those days," he adds, implying that their outlook has since changed.[41] *Kid A* marked the first time in Radiohead's history that Yorke's bandmates didn't know what he was singing about. He didn't open up about the lyrics to the rest of the band, Ed O'Brien divulged to *The Sydney Morning Herald,* intimating that such discussions normally occur and serve to apprise everyone of the singer's intentions.

CONTRIBUTIONS

This brings us to the subject of songwriting contributions and how they are viewed. Larry Mullen asserts that there is no pressure on any individuals in U2 to contribute a set amount to a song or album. That goes for Radiohead as well. They put in as much as they want to put in and get involved at different points in the process, says O'Brien. Being in a band requires a delicate balancing act. On the one hand, each member has to pull his own weight, Mullen commented in *Hot Press* (2000). On the other, there's no sense contributing for the sheer sake of throwing something into the pot. With five musicians in the group, this is a lesson Radiohead, in particular, couldn't avoid learning. In the past, all of them wanted (and expected) to play on every song, says Selway. "We don't do that anymore. By now we are self-confident enough to not contribute to a song if it is good for it. Sometimes nothing can be a very valuable contribution."[42] The key is to have a certain level of reverence for the music, Jonny Greenwood remarked when asked if he ever feels marginalized in Radiohead. "I'm not as good a musician as I think 'Pyramid Song' is a good song. And it's a great song. So that's enough for me, to be part of that."[43]

They are quite prepared to be idle for half a song, Greenwood confirms. If they're only needed for ten seconds in the middle of it, that's acceptable. Putting one's head down and just playing for an hour isn't the point of being in a band, he adds. But this approach has limits. "Naturally, if there's not enough for you to do it ceases to feel like a group project," notes Selway judiciously.[44] Defining what's enough is the tricky part. The interdependency of the band members and the one-person-per-instrument configuration of the four-piece go a long way towards ensuring that each musician has an opportunity to participate. And it's not like one person ever does everything, Buck asserts. In R.E.M.'s case that would be impossible because he doesn't sing and Stipe doesn't play any instruments. Needless to say, not all contributions are tangible and quantifiable; as mentioned earlier, ideas and suggestions count and need to be taken into consideration in the ultimate assessment of who did what.

The music bears the stamp of the way in which the individuals perceive their input and its purpose. Members of all four bands claim that their goal is to *serve the song* rather than their own interests. Essentially, this means not making contributions for the sake of gaining notice or acclaim (or simply for the sake of having a tangible contribution), but purely for the benefit of the music. So, for instance, when the tracks are being finalized, the band members look for the best mix instead of seeking to have their parts turned up louder than everyone else's, Phil Selway reflected in *The Sydney Morning Herald* with respect to Radiohead's operation. And, as Jonny Greenwood noted above, they hold the songs in such esteem that they're content to have participated in any way at all.

For the Chili Peppers, the song also comes first, but the band members are also concerned with helping each other express themselves. "I wanted to choose things that would propel the groove yet still leave enough space so everybody else's part could speak," is how Chad Smith describes his approach on *Californication*, adding that he tries to play in a style that supports both the song and the other musicians in the band.[45] More than ever, they're trying to work as an integrated ensemble. It's not about getting himself across, John Frusciante clarified in *Guitar Player* (1999), but about the part he plays in getting everybody across. This philosophy represents quite an about-face for Flea, who confessed in *Bassist* that he once strove to show off his considerable prowess on the bass at every opportunity (for personal glorification) and is now content to play the simplest lines as long as they're the right lines (to glorify the music and the band).

An interesting sidebar to this discussion: Rick Rubin observed in an interview with *Drum* that it's not wise for band members to concentrate on their own parts to such an extent that they fail to take into account the bits contributed by their collaborators. The various elements of the track don't end up interacting as they should if the musicians don't constantly keep in mind how their part fits into the bigger scheme of the song and respond to what their bandmates have put forward. With the Chili Peppers, they put a lot of stress on the song, he says. By thinking of it that way, instead of concentrating on individual parts, what they do together works.

OWNERSHIP OVER THE MUSIC

What sense of ownership do the band members have over the music, given that they write together? Anthony Kiedis proclaims in *Scar Tissue* that by the time the song goes through the process of each person adding his bit, they all own the piece equally. Even in R.E.M. and Radiohead, where one songwriter normally lays down the foundation of a track, the key is that the contributions of the other members turn it into a group song. The extent and nature of the contributions doesn't really matter, because ultimately, everyone has a hand in shaping the final track. Somewhat ironically, while there is a feeling of proprietorship over the song as a whole, the band members don't lay any claims to their own part. For the Red Hot Chili Peppers that's because they believe it would never have existed had it not been for the others and what they brought to the piece. "When Anthony writes his vocals, he doesn't feel like he's responsible for the vocals for a song that he wrote," Frusciante clarifies. "He feels like it was our music that made him sing that way and that made those words come to him."[46] Bono would likely make the same claim.

The same attitude is evinced by U2's Larry Mullen, who remarks about his drum sound: "Nothing that I do is really my own; everything is influenced by the others."[47] As collaborative as these bands are, each member is responsible for and has a lot of space to come up with his own parts, but at the same time, they're very open to input and criticism from the others. So Mullen may work out a particular beat, but more likely than not, his bandmates will make consequential remarks about it. In that sense, even their own bits of the songs are not *truly* their own because the collaboration is too pervasive to allow for this kind of partitioning. Also, when the musicians don't zero in on their own part and are involved in the song as a whole, their sense of ownership naturally extends to the entire piece. Related to the topic of ownership is how close the band members feel to the music. During an Australian radio interview, Jonny Greenwood stated that he, personally, has a sense of detachment from Radiohead's recordings precisely because they are communally-generated. "You don't feel like they're anything to do with you. There's four other people involved, not like you're listening to yourself."[48]

Part II: Facilitating collaboration

RECEPTIVITY

So far, this chapter has provided a fairly in-depth account of the four bands' respective creative practices and principles; the concern now is to get a better understanding of how the members interact in order to facilitate collaboration. Receptivity and openness are concepts that surface repeatedly. In one sense, that implies being receptive to suggestions regarding one's own part, which means that the drummer has to be willing to accept advice about his drumming from the guitarist or the singer and vice versa. The musicians must see not just the validity but also the value of any view expressed by their partners, Chad Smith explained in *Batteur*, where he remarked that listening to the other Chili Peppers pays off because it takes him out of the stock drummer's thought pattern. As we saw in Chapter 7, in U2 the band members propose approaches to one another all the time, with little regard for their formal roles.

On a broader level, there is a need to be open to various suggestions with respect to the songs or the project at hand. This is one of several behaviors that U2 would classify under generosity of spirit, a comprehensive code of conduct (encompassing tolerance, empathy, support and respect) that has been crucial to the band's longevity and to fostering a fruitful collaborative environment within it. It's a key term in accounting for how any band functions harmoniously. So, in Radiohead, for example, Phil Selway says the five friends are "very tolerant in recognizing good ideas in each other."[49] It's easy enough when everyone agrees that an idea has merit. The hard part is if they don't. When they can't see the value in something, the trick, Yorke explained in *The Chicago Tribune* (2001), is to allow whoever is interested (or the band as a whole) to pursue it rather than shoot it down instantly. A willingness to explore even seemingly dubious paths is how Adam Clayton expresses this notion. He speaks of committing to whatever is happening musically, whether it's just a concept for a song or the actual arrangement of a track. "You have to say that there's enough of an idea here that is worth pursuing, that is worth investing time in."[50] It's crucial to flesh out all the possibilities and be willing to try anything because you can't foresee which idea will prove beneficial to the piece, Rick Rubin and Chad Smith noted in a joint interview with *Drum*.

Along with a desire to serve the song, faith in and respect for one another breeds the requisite receptivity. They've simply learned to trust each other's instincts and judgment in R.E.M., Bill Berry said in 1991, adding: "If somebody suggests something, we'll try it. No matter how wacky it is."[51] Of course, Berry points out that no one is arrogant enough to present ideas in a way that clearly doesn't admit of dissension and thus provokes defiance. "Rarely do we come to rehearsal and say, 'Look, I'm convinced that this arrangement, from beginning to end, is perfect.'"[52] If, after weighing an idea, any member of the group continues to be adamantly against it, there's no point trying to pour it down his throat, Chad Smith observed in a 1999 interview with *Modern Drummer*.

That results in conflict (and could prompt the opposed member to exercise his veto—an even more unpleasant scenario), but Smith provides two additional reasons to avoid pushing the objectionable plan: for one thing, the piece will never work if one of the musicians isn't into it, and secondly, the band has lots of ideas so there's no need to get fixated on any of them. Getting too attached to any one approach or idea counteracts receptivity and causes problems given the collaborative setup. Recording *Hail to the Thief* was an unusually untroubled experience for Radiohead, until it came to deciding on final mixes. There was a "long sustained period during which we lived with it but it wasn't completely finished," says Yorke, "so you get attached to versions and we had big rows about it."[53] In this context, Anthony Kiedis remarked in his memoirs that the Face-Offs never lead to disputes because both Flea and Frusciante submit themselves to the group vote and neither of them holds out for the bit he came up with.

The expectation of openness on the part of one's bandmates is cardinal in fostering the relaxed atmosphere and comfort level that allow for candid personal expression. As the Chili Peppers worked on *Blood Sugar Sex Magik*, to take one example, Rick Rubin stumbled across a heartfelt poem Kiedis had written and encouraged the singer to share it with his bandmates. It was an off-putting thought for Kiedis because "Under the Bridge" expressed such intimate feelings and cast him in a most un-macho light (in what was, at the time, a group prone to displays of bravado). But he felt sufficiently at ease within the band to overcome his trepidation. That was largely due to Frusciante's presence. "I felt like anything was possible with this kid. I could show him my most sentimental writings, and he didn't stop to judge them once," declares Kiedis in *Scar Tissue*, describing how the band changed after the teenaged guitarist joined. "Now I didn't have to second-guess myself or be afraid to show something or try something new."[54] The reception that "Under the Bridge" received from all of Kiedis' bandmates, who entered fully into the spirit of his verses, was enough to wipe away any lingering doubt he may have had regarding what he can and cannot share with the group. The Chili Peppers were never the same again.

CRITICISM

There is a lot of criticism to endure within the context of a collective creative process engaged in by equals. Being passionate about their work and with each member having a commensurate stake in it, the band members can be quite hard on one another. But they strive to both dole out and accept criticism as constructively as possible. At the heart of the matter lies faith in the purity of everyone's intentions. Bono, for instance, knows that his bandmates won't attribute his censorious comments to base motives like spite or jealousy. In addition to the prevailing generosity of spirit in the band, they know the singer is impelled by a sincere desire to serve the song and that he has tremendous respect for his partners. This gives him the liberty to speak his mind without fearing a backlash. "I can say to The Edge: 'I don't like that thing you've just played' and he doesn't go: 'And I don't like what you've done,' he goes: 'You must be right otherwise you wouldn't have said it.'"[55]

When it comes to giving criticism, there seem to be certain guidelines each band (or band member) follows in order to prevent it from becoming too rampant, damaging or just pointless. In U2, says Mullen, "the party line is, if you don't have a better idea, shut the fuck up."[56] Phil Selway reported in *Kulturnews* that they have become more openly critical in Radiohead over the years, but they have learned to balance censure with compliments (that goes for the perennially exacting Thom Yorke as well). State what you think without fear, is the Red Hot Chili Peppers' motto, but be prepared to provide reasons and explanations. There's nothing worse than saying something sucks, Smith proclaimed in *Modern Drummer*, without being able to state why. A healthy balance with regards to the source of the criticism also prevents it from causing major blowups. In other words, it works best when there isn't one individual constantly criticizing everyone else and the band members are more or less equally critical of one another, as Mullen claims is the case in U2 (*msn.com*). And empathy is also crucial, says Clayton. "It's not easy to be the person to say 'I don't think we are there yet,' and it's not easy to be the person receiving that information."[57] When the recipient of the criticism knows it hasn't been easy for his bandmate to deliver it, he's less likely to become annoyed or upset; when the individual expressing criticism is keenly aware of how difficult it is to bear it, he won't voice disapproval lightly or callously.

DISPENSING WITH DIPLOMACY

One would think that tact and diplomacy are essential aspects of teamwork, but they can actually be impediments in this setting. U2 scores music in what Larry Mullen refers to as a brutally honest environment. As he explained to *USA Today* (2000), diplomacy has no place in the studio because if they beat around the bush and try to not hurt somebody's feelings, it would take four years to make a record instead of two. So they are very blunt and clear, which is, admits the drummer, hard on the ego but necessary. Stipe also makes the point, as we've seen, that hurt feelings have to take a backseat to the music. If shielding people from the sometimes-injurious effects of trenchant criticism comes before the good of the songs, the band's output will be compromised. (Going back to an earlier chapter, speaking directly should not be interpreted as displaying callous disregard for the feelings of others.) Conceivably, since it's assumed that everyone in the group is open-minded and unbiased, and considering the closeness of the band members, diplomacy is probably more dispensable in these outfits than it might otherwise be.

Collaboration can be nerve-wracking even when band members feel comfortable and fairly certain that their ideas won't be abruptly slagged, because their partners are free to criticize every move and don't pull any punches when doing so. Journalists like Robert Hilburn, who have spent time in the studio with U2, have remarked that Bono's vulnerability is evident when he is waiting for his bandmates to cast their vote after he has read them a lyric or finished a vocal take. Stipe admits to being at his most nervous and vulnerable when the band is writing and recording. He's so susceptible under these circumstances that his bandmates can hardly breathe without affecting him one way or another. It's as if he has antennae that automatically pick up on his partners' thoughts, which is enough to make anyone jumpy. "Whatever I present, with those guys I can sense across the room what they think about what I've put on tape. I don't even need to look at them to know what they feel."[58] He goes on to state that, given this reality, it's particularly important for the band to be close and cohesive during the creative stages, presumably in order to assuage this anxiety.

Understanding one another's needs

Not only do musicians in these communal situations need to deal with pressures from management, the record company and their own muse, they can sometimes face enormous pressure from their bandmates, particularly if they're working at a different pace or inspiration level than others in the group. Because the creative collaboration is such an integrated process, if one person's building block isn't in place, often, his partners can't do their job. Phil Selway confessed to *Modern Drummer* (1996) that working in the studio can be nightmarish for him at times, as the session can't go ahead until he gets the drum part down and he is stressed by the fact that his bandmates are waiting (however patiently) on him. As noted in an earlier chapter, working together can, at the same time, alleviate strain because no one has to come up with all the material on his own, so from a pressure perspective, the band is something of a two-edged sword.

Frustration—rarely absent from any artistic enterprise—engenders tense relations among the band members. When U2's recording sessions are proceeding well, Mullen stated in *The Los Angeles Times* (2004), the studio feels like a playground, but if things are going badly, it turns into a boxing ring. Tellingly, Ed O'Brien confided to *Rolling Stone* in 2003 that *Hail to the Thief* represented the first Radiohead album where, upon its completion, the members didn't want to kill each other. What helped (in addition to the fact that they were far less confused this time around) was that the band emerged from *Kid A* with a clearer understanding of each member's individual needs in the studio. Similarly, R.E.M. realized after the *Up* crisis that Stipe's needs were not being met, specifically, that he could do with more space than they were giving him. The trio subsequently introduced what the singer called "a new, relaxed and less pressurised way of working."[59] When they reconvened for *Reveal*, they talked a lot about how to ensure that each of them has a positive experience this time.

Part III: Redirections and reinventions

It's one thing for solo artists to reinvent themselves and drastically overhaul their style, but for a band like any of these four, such actions have unique implications because of the equality of the collective set-up. Obviously, some changes are unintentional and unplanned. The Chili Peppers have undergone mostly organic and accidental metamorphoses, mostly brought about by lineup shuffles. The most notable example is how the addition of Frusciante ushered into the group a different creative strategy and style. Kiedis was able to work one-on-one with the guitarist—particularly when he had lyrics prepared, as with his tribute to Hillel Slovak, "Knock Me Down"—in putting a melody and some basic music to the words (reminiscent of U2's attempts at formal songwriting). In *Scar Tissue* the singer admits this was a real epiphany for him because, previously, every shred of music the band produced came out of a group context, without much emphasis on the various elements of a song (chorus, bridge, etc.). Using this structured songwriting technique, the two were able to develop more "proper" songs, but the group largely incorporated this ability into its jam-based approach, producing similarly pop-oriented material by improvising as a group. So an unfamiliar methodology helped the band arrive with one leap at a brand of music it had been inching towards, but neither the sonic nor the operational left-turns had been actively sought.

For many long-lived bands, there comes a point or points when the members feel they have reached the end of a particular road and have to either actively seek new avenues to explore together or go their separate ways. This is not to imply that adjustments aren't made every time a band readies a new album, but the focus in this section is on radical shifts precipitated by fairly serious dissatisfaction with the group's previous methods or material. R.E.M., U2 and Radiohead have all found themselves in this position and ended up undertaking fairly calculated group transformations in pursuit of a different sound. But deliberate changes in direction can be difficult to orchestrate *en masse*. Some members can be more insistent on change than others, and fierce disagreements can arise with regards to where the band should go. *Achtung Baby* is a case in point.

Bono and Edge were pushing to take the band's sound into radically different terrain, reflecting their newfound interest in industrial and heavy techno dance music. Clayton and Mullen weren't sure if this was the right path to follow, and the two factions were butting heads when they desperately needed to make headway. "The music ideas Bono and I presented were not receiving a wonderful reaction from Adam and Larry. They worried that we might be taking off in a direction that could prove to be a mistake," Edge explained a decade later.[60] Never before or since has the group been so divided. The bandmates were completely out of sync, observes Mullen, while everyone who was there recalls that the atmosphere in the studio was very tense.

The band accomplished very little during the early days of the strained sojourn in Berlin. Enter producer Brian Eno and a song appropriately named "One." Eno's presence alleviated some of the unsettlement within the group while the relatively easy birth of this key track in U2's discography seemed to blow open the floodgates of creativity. And with Eno essentially in favor of the electronica exploration, the drummer and bass player came around to the thinking of the band's other half, and everyone was on the same page again.

Often, achieving a new sound requires developing another songwriting methodology, or the customary methods of composing music have simply become tiresome to the group and have to be shaken up. For Radiohead, the post–*OK Computer* era marked a significant dual turning-point of this sort. A keen desire to completely revamp the band's sound coincided with a determination to revolutionize its mode of operation in the studio. Thom Yorke, in particular, felt utterly alienated from the band's early recordings, so much so that he considered changing the group's name to escape its musical history. Melody, guitars, his own radio-familiar voice had become tedious to him. Inspired by the work of pioneering electronic artists like Aphex Twin and Autechre, Yorke felt that Radiohead should incorporate similar elements into its own music and instigated a shakeup (though he didn't have a clear direction in mind). It would mean abandoning the traditional instruments of the four-piece rock group as well as its cherished verse-chorus song structure, replacing drums and guitars with programmed elements that would push rhythm and texture, rather than melody, to the foreground. Although the rest of the group agreed that, after more than 10 years together, it was time for a sharp break with past, the direction in which Yorke was pushing didn't strike his bandmates as ideal. Like U2, the band spent the initial period fractiously groping for consensus and came close to calling it quits.

What they all agreed on was that in order to develop a dramatically different sound, they would have to adopt an unfamiliar methodology. And, after touring *OK Computer*, they felt as though they had reached the end of a particular phase of the band, elaborates Phil Selway. "There was a certain fatigue about the way that we were playing, the ideas that we were generating between the five of us in the set-up as it was." They wanted to "rewrite" the way the band worked together but had no idea what form that would take.[61] Yorke made the same point more abrasively. "You can't just sit in a room together and play like that for the rest of your fucking lives and expect it to be wonderful."[62] Apparently, even chemistry needs to be stoked once in a while. So, throwing all the procedural precedents to the wind, the band tried out various songwriting tactics, such as working together in pairs or trios and starting dozens of tracks at the same time then abandoning them as soon as they hit a wall. They tried out new instruments and composed with computers. It was liberating to discover alternate ways of collaborating, but very hard on the band at the same time.

These episodes in which the group makes a decided break with the past, especially by transforming how the members create together, essentially amount to reforming it with the same members. "We've broken our band up so many times internally," says Bono. "When we started working with Brian Eno early on, in a way we had to break up and start over. We did it again with *Achtung Baby*."[63] Thom Yorke used the same terms when discussing with *Q* (2000) the dramatic permutation Radiohead underwent just prior to making *Kid A*. To some extent, the band breaks up at the end of each album cycle and *reunites* in the name of a worthwhile venture, Bono points out. In other words, U2 essentially reunites whenever the four feel like they have promising ideas to develop together. "I think you've got to justify every record by its own merits," says the singer. "In one sense, every time we go in to make an album, we break up the band and reform it."[64]

Adam Clayton doesn't go so far as to label such events a reunion or reformation, but he agrees that there is a process of recommitment to the band and to one another each time they embark on a new project (*Live!*). It's followed by a re-acclimatization to the studio and to the collective situation, which can be difficult in some circumstances. One of the reasons U2 decided to make *Passengers* rather than charge full-steam into a new U2 record is because, after such a long break, they knew it would be challenging to resume working together again—and they didn't want to do their adapting to one another in a high-pressure situation. The experimental album with Brian Eno serving as the band's fifth member made for a fairly stress-free warm-up, Edge told *Guitar World* in 1997.

CREATIVE UNITY

Every artist knows that there's no rushing the creative process. Inspiration strikes when it strikes. For bands, which rely on collaboration, there's another factor to take into consideration. As Anthony Kiedis points out perceptively, "there's a natural flow of creative unity and that doesn't happen according to a schedule or a deadline."[65] The artistic consonance requisite for musicians in bands to write music together cannot, in itself, be forced or hurried.

In an article about Radiohead for *The New Yorker*, journalist Alex Ross draws attention to the intriguing fact that the five together essentially form a single artist: the Radiohead composer, who can never be met face-to-face because it only exists in the music. The concept applies to the three other bands, and any like them. Ask Bono and he'll tell you that's where a band like U2 trumps The Beatles. They were the ultimate group, he says of the Fab Four. "But we're more of a group in one sense because we're a co-op. Everything is shared. They didn't share their songwriting."[66] Many of the outfits that meet the description of a group, he remarked back in 1984 (*U2 Magazine*), are actually singers/songwriters and their accomplices, rather than a fully integrated ensemble in which each individual plays a significant role and has an equal voice in the creative process. That's why, in the case of a group like U2, it's the band that is the real work of art, he told *Rolling Stone* in 1989.

9

"Road Trippin'": Onstage and on the Road Together

Being in the studio and being onstage are discrete experiences with unique objectives and requirements. "The studio is a beautiful place to make music and to experiment with ideas," says John Frusciante, drawing one distinction. "Onstage, it's completely different. It's getting in touch with the energy in the room, and putting everything that happened to you that day into your head and into your hands."[1] Likewise, the relations within a band change considerably onstage (and, by extension, on the road) versus the studio. Not only do creation and performance require a completely different mentality and set of skills for a band, each task calls for, and no doubt inspires, a unique group dynamic and working relationship. The first part of this chapter will discuss performing together and what that means for U2, R.E.M., Radiohead and the Red Hot Chili Peppers. The second part discusses life on the road in these outfits given the tedious migration from one venue to another and the close quarters occupied by members for long periods of time.

Part I: Onstage

APPROACHES TO PERFORMANCE

A band's philosophy with regards to its live shows has a tremendous impact not only on what happens onstage but also on what transpires between the members. U2's ambitious productions, most notably the Pink-Floyd-topping Zoo TV and Popmart tours, essentially turned the band members into co-directors behind the scenes. In the planning stages for the 1993 campaign, the four, operating as what Bono once dubbed the Zoo Board, spent many late nights brainstorming and evaluating concepts and props. Since they are also the "actors" in this production, one that reflects on both themselves and the band in which they have such a profound stake, this can undoubtedly get hairy. (One imagines the words "Forget it. I'm not doing *that*" or "No, that will make us look ..." coming up repeatedly.)

Some members take on functions that make it possible for the band to put on a certain kind of concert, one that meets the group's specific performance goals. Edge says his job is to hold the band together on stage so that Bono can relax and focus solely on making the connection with the audience that the band deems supremely important. He tends to be constrained, he told *Propaganda* (1987, issue 6), because a lot depends on him if Bono is to be so carefree. While many bands leave the showmanship to the frontman, this has never been the Red Hot Chili Peppers' practice—probably a good idea because they have always striven to be the wildest rock band around, claims Flea. No matter how energetic and entertaining a singer you have, that just won't cut it. So, from the start, Flea took on a headlining role in order to do his bit for wildness. "My position goes beyond that of just a bass player, I also consider myself an entertainer," says the bassist. "I buy into the show-bizz aesthetic of giving a dazzling performance, and I'm into putting on a show."[2]

Smith and Frusciante also make a significant effort to turn the band's gigs into memorable spectacles. As a result, Kiedis often steps back and lets his bandmates carry the banner of showmanship, a rather unique situation. "I don't feel like the focal point," he declares. "If ever there was a band that had four equal members that all exist as one on stage, it's us. That's when we are at our best, working as a team, free of self. I depend heavily on those guys and that, I think, is mutual."[3] R.E.M. has traditionally had a powerful main attraction in Stipe, who shouldered most of the theatrical burden with the aid of his natural charisma, offbeat makeup, oddball outfits (unless togas are all the rage somewhere) and kinky dance moves. In the '90s, Mike Mills purposely took to dressing more like a rock star (think a notch or two below Elton John) in order to up the entertainment quotient. It can't all be left up to Stipe after all, and, in particular, Mills felt that the members of the audience on the bassist's side of the stage, which tends to be rather humdrum in any band, might feel shortchanged. So he took it upon himself to inject a little color into the bassist's berth.

If there's anything the four bands discussed in this book have in common when it comes to their approach to shows, it's a belief that their live performances should be unpredictable, raw, unrehearsed. "We're not staging *Cats* on tour here," Stipe quipped in 1999. "That's never been our way of doing things. Our energy as a band is very kind of loose and

floppy. I like the idea that kind of anything could happen at any time."[4]
That goes for their interpretation of the album tracks, which needn't be
played note-for-note, as well as the spontaneity of the performance itself.
Jonny Greenwood, for instance, informed *Rolling Stone* in 1995 that he
refuses to play premeditated solos because then the performance
wouldn't be dangerous as there would be no chance of his doing anything wrong. The musicians in these groups leave plenty of room for surprises—but what surprises the audience can sometimes take their
partners in the band aback as well.

Bono admits that he often gets carried away on stage and ends up
taking discretionary actions or making impromptu speeches that land
him in hot water with the rest of the group. While the world watched
U2 give one of its most thrilling shows at 1985's Live Aid concert, the
band—along with billions of viewers around the globe—believed they
were witnessing its deathblow. An overly zealous Bono leapt into the vast
audience and didn't return to the stage until the band's 15-minute set
was over. His spontaneous attempt to reach out to the audience, which
seemed to have gone terribly awry, incensed the singer's bandmates.
After nearly a decade together, Mullen, Edge and Clayton had come to
expect (and accept) the unexpected from the impulsive and audacious
singer (who had ventured into the audience on many previous occasions) but they felt that pulling the stunt under these circumstances was
completely misguided, particularly as it seemed to have ruined their big
moment. They nearly fired him, Bono confided to journalist Michka
Assayas. *Creem* reported in 1987 that Bono was so dismayed he nearly quit
of his own accord. As it turned out, the singer's heartfelt gesture res-
onated strongly with viewers, making U2 the standout act of the historic
benefit.

This is only the most notorious instance of a series of events frequently replayed in U2. "Whenever the performance was sagging I'd
throw the proverbial stick of gelignite into the audience and it would
freak the band. I've had to face the firing squad on late-night phone calls
from the band as a result," remarks Bono, hinting at how regularly he
steps out of line during gigs.[5] From climbing the scaffolding to wrapping
himself in a white flag to pontificating about global politics or throwing
Mullen's drumkit into the audience, adrenaline constantly gets the singer
into trouble with his partners. It came to blows on one occasion, but usually, Bono explained in *Vanity Fair*, there is an ominously silent drive
back to the hotel, followed by a phone call from the diplomatic Clayton
asking if the band can have a word with him. In the course of the ensu-
ing discussion, Bono's bandmates typically advise him to let the music
speak for itself and try to make him realize that he doesn't have to resort
to such extreme measures to get the band's message across to the audi-

ence. Their admonitions, if they can be called that, consist of asking him to maintain greater self-control.

On the whole, however, they admire Bono's nerve and understand that his impulsive exploits contribute significantly to the excitement of a U2 show—for everyone in attendance. He makes gigs as colorful and thrilling for the band as they are for the audience. "There's always a surprise in working with U2 for all of us. I suppose when we come to play live it's that sense of spontaneity and jeopardy that is so much a part of Bono as a performer," says Edge, noting that the singer consistently flies without a parachute.[6] So even his own bandmates get a kick out of watching him paint himself into a corner and then find his way out somehow, or fall flat on his face. And while it may seem as if the singer uses the stage as a pulpit to air his personal views on politics and religion, more often than not, he's expressing the band's collective feelings. His partners may give him flak for his headline-grabbing expressions or the length of his discourses, but generally, Clayton stressed to *Rip It Up* (1989), they share the singer's basic sentiments.

Another performer who is full of surprises onstage is Anthony Kiedis. His legendary antics are aimed purely at putting on a good show, surrendering to the music and letting go of inhibitions. "I still let that wind take me where it will," he said in 1996 about his attitude toward live performance.[7] But even in a group where anything goes, especially in front of an audience, an objectionable caper sometimes catches the others unawares. During one memorable gig, when he was high on heroin and cocaine, Kiedis launched into a rambling soapbox oration about the pitfalls of doing drugs. As he tells it in *Scar Tissue*, the other band members gave him dirty looks all the while and, afterwards, he could hardly bring himself to face them, knowing they must be livid.

Personal escapades aside, live shows are filled with unforeseen situations ranging from the comical—such as when the U2 quartet were trapped inside the mechanical lemon from which they emerged each night on the Popmart tour—to the infuriating. When the latter occur, the band members are there to help one another keep their cool. Radiohead's landmark 1997 performance at Glastonbury was riddled with technical problems. The high-strung Yorke was ready to storm off the stage as the crisis reached an intolerable peak, but O'Brien managed to talk the singer out of it (he told him he'd regret the rash move for the rest of his life).

Just as each band member's perspective on studio work needs to jive (more or less) with that of his partners, they have to agree on some basic principles with respect to gigs. The Red Hot Chili Peppers are such a high-spirited live act that it hasn't been easy for the group to find musicians who share their no-holds-barred attitude. Asking Dave Navarro to don a rather outlandish lightbulb costume for his first outing as a Chili Pepper—at none other than the momentous Woodstock festival held in 1994—has been interpreted by some critics as an initiation or test the band decided to put the newbie through. Whether or not that was their intent, Navarro, who obviously didn't share the zany sense of humor they bring to their performances or their views on showmanship, hated it. In that regard, his outlook on performing jarred with the rest of the group's, as did that of Hillel Slovak's first stand-in, Jack Sherman.

With scarcely-concealed disdain, Kiedis writes in his memoirs about Sherman's uptight and frigid (or so it seemed to him) approach to shows, which contrasted sharply with what the band felt its gigs were all about. Flea and Kiedis believed in expressing their passion for the music with their bodies, which often had them careening manically around the boards. But Sherman couldn't bear such wildness, especially when Kiedis encroached on the guitarist's block of the stage with his wild dances. In an attempt to carve out an inviolable space for himself, Sherman formed lines on the floor using tape and instructed Kiedis not to cross them, a move nothing short of anathema among musicians who fervently hold that there should be no boundaries onstage—least of all between the performers. "Why would you want to cut yourself off from your bandmate, spiritually or physically?" Kiedis asks in *Scar Tissue*.[8]

BONDS AND NEEDS ONSTAGE

This incident makes it abundantly clear that the band members need to take one another's unique onstage needs into consideration and put themselves in their partners' shoes. Larry Mullen is quite content to play live without any frills and trappings. At the same time, he understands Bono's need for props, seeing as he's the frontman and can feel very exposed on a bare stage. "When you're a singer—you gotta remember I'm the drummer so I'm at the back, I've got this kit of drums surrounding me so I'm protected—but for him, there is a certain amount of fear with standing in front of an audience and not having anything else. That's kind of scary."[9] For John Frusciante, it's important that the band members pay attention and respond to one another during gigs. The fact that the Chili Peppers weren't doing so on the Blood Sugar Sex Magik tour made it practically impossible for him to enjoy the shows or feel fulfilled as a musician. At that time, he relied solely on the reaction of his bandmates for a measure of his performance, so their self-engrossment and consequent obliviousness to his actions onstage made him feel as if his tremendous efforts were pointless. "The only people that [sic] could have made me feel good about what I was doing were the people in the band, but they weren't doing that," he explains.[10]

On his part, Dave Navarro informed *Guitarist* in 1996 that he and the Chili Peppers have incompatible needs when it comes to communing onstage; he likes to look down at his guitar and just sense the other players while Flea and Smith prefer to make direct eye contact. How the members bond during shows varies, of course, from one group to another. The telepathic link the Chili Peppers boast is palpably reinforced by shared glances and, as it turns out, their theatrical antics. What is almost universally regarded as a clever publicity stunt, the socks-on-cocks routine, was actually, Kiedis insisted during a backstage interview in Singapore, a rite of passage and means of strengthening the onstage bond between the band members (though it started off as an extemporaneous lark). Venturing before an audience with Dave Navarro for the first time, the band may very well, then, have chosen the bizarre lightbulb get-up to establish a sense of solidarity between the three veterans and their new guitarist. In U2, a strong offstage ethic of togetherness engenders in-concert synergy. While some bands feed off their aggression and animosity onstage, U2 plays well when the four friends can look each other in the eye, Bono asserted in *The Sun* (2001).

Prior to every show, the Chili Peppers enact a casual group bonding ritual called the Soul Circle. They join hands and sing songs (campfire classics, Chad Smith joked when *Kerrang!* requested details), say a few words or recite a short prayer, which is slightly more civilized than the mutual face slapping the founding lineup used to engage in but which served the same purpose. The other bands observe no such practices. In fact, Phil Selway says that he and his four mates in Radiohead try to give each other plenty of space so everyone can be calm and centered when they take the stage. In R.E.M., Mills and Buck hang around together, soothing each other's nerves, but Stipe keeps his distance. He and Buck have individual rituals that make each other anxious—the singer says he's very vacant and the guitarist intensely jittery—so they avoid one another. Buck has to be at the venue several hours in advance of going onstage, Stipe reported in 2003 (*VH1.com*), adding that he then proceeds to warm up his fingers by playing a lot while making repeated trips to the bathroom to pee. The singer told *Q* (2001) that, by contrast, he goes crazy if he's reminded of what lies ahead of him, so he arrives shortly before he's due onstage, locks himself in his dressing room and paces until he's called to the microphone. To save his voice and energy, Bono often keeps to himself before gigs as well. He tends to go into a sort of trance on his own, he revealed to *Propaganda* in 1987 (issue 5), because performing takes so much out of him.

WHEN SOMEONE ISN'T INTO IT

Obviously, the whole group is affected whenever anyone in the ranks isn't really into the show. There's nothing worse than playing in front of a huge throng, says Colin Greenwood, when someone (in this case, he meant Yorke) doesn't want to be there "and you can see that hundred-yard stare in his eyes. You hate having to put your friend through that experience."[11] Sympathy for that individual isn't always the reaction that attends emotional withdrawal from the experience. Bono admits that he gets very angry when any member of U2 seems to be taking a gig too lightly or isn't displaying tremendous enthusiasm for the performance, partly because it makes his own job that much harder. "For me to sing on stage, the only way I can do it is if I'm really committed to it and if I sense anything less than complete commitment from the others, then I get very antagonistic towards them and occasionally this had led to a bit of fracas."[12]

This has a lot to do with how the band perceives its live shows. For U2, "being onstage is like the sacred moment," Larry Mullen observed, so it's imperative that everyone be present in body *and* spirit.[13] (Clayton wasn't chastised for missing a date in Sydney because it demonstrated to the others the depth of his distress whereas a lazy performance might have merely aroused their ire). The Chili Peppers were furious with Frusciante in 1992 when he grew increasingly apathetic about their concerts—particularly as, in this case, it wasn't just a detachment his partners sensed but which could be hidden from the audience. His performances visibly suffered. In his memoirs, Kiedis describes confrontations the infuriated band had with the guitarist over his halfhearted appearances, like one evening when he strummed lethargically in a corner of the stage while they gave their all. It wasn't long before Frusciante started actively sabotaging the shows. The situation was coming to an undeniable head when he resolved it by quitting.

EXCITEMENT OF PLAYING TOGETHER

When the band puts on a good show (or tour), there is a sense of excitement about, as well as joy and confidence in, the unit that is an important source of momentum. Radiohead and R.E.M., most notably, have been able to recover from paralyzing blows (the one-hit wonder stigma, the departure of Bill Berry) by re-experiencing the thrill of playing gigs together. Exhausted and downcast by Berry's absence and the ordeal of making their first album as a trio, the members of R.E.M. quickly regained their assurance and enthusiasm as an ensemble once they hit the road and were able to "rediscover the sheer fun of playing together."[14] Thom Yorke and his partners saw their faith in Radiohead restored by a short tour in the middle of the arduous and problematic sessions for *The Bends*. Bono says that U2 derives constant inspiration from putting on concerts that prove to them what a great band they have because their combustible four-way chemistry is most perceptible when they're performing. "There's a certain thing that happens to us onstage, a certain spark, a certain electricity. It's impossible to describe but it's sort of like, that is the show, you know?"[15]

The Red Hot Chili Peppers talk more about how elated they are by one another onstage. "It's so exciting for me every night," Kiedis stated in reference to touring with Frusciante again in 1999. "Every night is different, largely because of his solos and his improvisational vibe. I feel like a spectator sometimes. I'm very uplifted by his space, and his color."[3] Getting off on each other's performance and feeling their connection to each other makes the stage a uniquely stimulating medium for the members of this band. Restorative and stirring, the live shows are also very pure in a way, showcasing the ensemble and really bringing to the fore the interaction between the members. "It is when we are playing that we are at our most U2yness!," says the term-coining Clayton. "It is to an extent a celebration of sorts, but there is a simplicity about it, everyone doing what they do best for the greatest effect—that is a pure situation."[17]

For U2, having additional musicians onstage with the band can taint that purity. They have an almost sentimental attachment to the four-piece, says Edge. "I don't know why, but it just seemed like four people on stage is what it's about for us."[18] There is a fear, Bono remarked in an earlier BBC interview (1988), that extra people onstage would interfere with what goes on between the band members, which is so crucial to a U2 show. Radiohead and the Chili Peppers also tend to stick with the band's integral lineup for concerts. But since 1995, and especially since Berry left, R.E.M. has routinely fleshed out its live ensemble with musicians like Ken Stringfellow, Scott McCaughey and Joey Waronker. They don't worship the core-piece and frequently claim that the guest musicians have helped reinvigorate their unit both on the road and in the studio. It's certainly not unreasonable to argue that guest musicians no more dilute the pure magic of the ensemble performance than elaborate props.

Part II: Touring

MAKE OR BREAK IT

Nightly performances combined with the daily grind of touring and its attendant camaraderie can take a set of musicians and turn them into a close-knit band. On a professional level, playing concerts together regularly has a highly unifying effect on the group, gradually merging the individual musicians into a singular artistic entity, as Kiedis points out. "It's always at the end of a tour that you become this organic vessel. You're tight and it's effortless and you become one heart beating together."[19] Meanwhile, the personal bonds between the band members are frequently strengthened by the connection they make onstage as well as the sense of fellowship engendered by traveling and undertaking a major campaign together. The gang mentality that forms or deepens on tour is the natural product not just of living in close quarters but going through intense emotional experiences together over a long period of time. (At the very least, these shared experiences are the basis of many unifying in-jokes, as Phil Selway told *NME* in 1994.) These bonds are often viewed as an integral part of the interconnectivity that defines a "real" band, and many musicians believe that they can't develop fully if the band doesn't tour.

R.E.M. admit that the group didn't feel much like a "real" band after a few years off the road, especially with Buck living in Seattle, which was one of the primary motivations for touring *Monster*. "Bill was the first one to pick up on the fact that as a band, we were a little bit falling apart," says Stipe. "We realized we were not going to be our idea of a band if we didn't tour again. In a way, it was a little bit of an effort to pull us back together."[20] In 1991, Buck remarked in *The Los Angeles Times* that they're more committed to the idea that a band involves writing and recording songs together, not necessarily going on stage together. But by 1995, they realized that the tightness and esprit de corps of a touring band is indeed essential to their ethic of togetherness. "I believe playing live is the thing that makes a band a band," Mills stated unequivocally in 1996.[21]

Shortly after Berry's departure in 1998, Stipe told *The New York Times* that he's not sure R.E.M. is a band anymore, what with the members living apart, touring rarely, minus a drummer and recording (at that time, under fractious circumstances) with other musicians. But Buck later proclaimed in *Rolling Stone* that the tour they undertook as a trio in 1999 made them realize that R.E.M. is a different band than it was in the past, but it's still very much a "real" band. Colin Greenwood agrees with this attitude towards the band-defining force of touring and staging live shows. "I think if we didn't play concerts then we wouldn't really be Radiohead anymore."[22]

The *Mother's Milk* tour the Chili Peppers undertook in 1989 with new members Smith and Frusciante undeniably helped cement the relationships in the group, which, in turn, proved beneficial to the group's subsequent work in the studio. Thanks to the tour, there was a cohesion and musical telepathy in the band that provided the quartet with the impetus to make *Blood Sugar Sex Magik*, their breakthrough album. In Chad Smith's view, its successor, *One Hot Minute*, failed to live up to the Navarro-lineup's true potential precisely because the four didn't have a chance to tour extensively and acquire the type of chemistry (personal and professional) that playing together night after night confers on a band. "Nothing can really replace that," he declared.[23] Consequently, they weren't very intimate with or attuned to one another when they embarked on the sessions (despite buying matching motorcycles and cavorting around Hawaii together).

Not every tour has served to boost the solidarity of these groups. Being on the road has been known to undermine it by exacerbating existing problems or by giving birth to tour-specific tensions. Both Radiohead and the Red Hot Chili Peppers saw their unity and fraternity crumble in the midst of their first jaunts as rock stars. Warped by the overshadowing success of "Creep" and dragging on longer than anyone expected, Radiohead's *Pablo Honey* tour was hardly conducive to robust internal dynamics. Resentment towards their situation, which was aggravated by the frustrating crusade, nearly destroyed the band members' relations. The victorious tour the Chili Peppers undertook in support of the blockbuster *Blood Sugar Sex Magik* had disastrous consequences for their unit. Frusciante didn't want to be there, which gave rise to the intra-group friction discussed earlier, and, given how antithetically he and Kiedis reacted to becoming rock stars (a status that becomes very evident during a tour), it was the worst possible time for the two to contend with the enforced togetherness of such a venture.

THE TEST OF TOGETHERNESS

As it is, touring is an emotional test for the members of any band. "It manifests itself in different ways," Flea once remarked on this subject. "Mainly with us being sick of each other, little things that get on our nerves get magnified by about 50 billion times."[24] That statement was delivered in 1987, before the Red Hot Chili Peppers made it big. Success has a huge impact on touring arrangements, with significant consequences for bands in particular. Traveling in a cramped van and sharing motel rooms entails far more compulsory contact between the members than does a cavalcade of luxury buses, separate dressing rooms and individual hotel suites.

The claustrophobic nature of low-budget tours really got to R.E.M. by 1985, nearly causing the band to break up in London while recording *Fables of the Reconstruction*. Says Buck: "Everyone was tired of being away from home and broke and always in each other's company." They stayed in cheap motels, he recalls, and roomed together, so they didn't have a minute to themselves (not even in the shower, because someone would frequently be at the sink shaving at the same time). "Sometimes you'd get a quart of beer and sit on your own in the parking lot. That would be the only time you could be alone for a week. Five years of that and everyone was really worn out. The lack of privacy was mind-boggling."[25] By 1988, they were so fed up that they decided to forego touring altogether in order to maintain their sanity and preserve the group. When they went back on the road in 1995, they were a headlining act able to afford far more clement accommodation.

Fledgling and small-time groups have no choice but to tour, and much more extensively than high rollers, simply in order to survive. For the first decade of R.E.M.'s existence, the band was on the road at least half the year, reports Mike Mills. "That's how we lived. I wouldn't have been able to eat otherwise."[26] Like most bands of their stature, R.E.M. doesn't need to tour nonstop anymore or submit to an unremitting itinerary. Once the slog aspect of touring is alleviated by more pleasant conditions coupled with a humane schedule, privacy becomes less of an issue and nerves are less frayed, so it's somewhat easier to maintain harmony within the collective. But new factors come into the picture. Well-known bands make the trek in a sort of isolated bubble, Thom Yorke observed in *Rolling Stone* (1995), which means that they tend to rely more heavily on one another for company.

Touring in style means the musicians have space to give one another and, by this stage of their career, usually realize they need to give it, but Radiohead learned on the long *OK Computer* haul that it's no good constantly trying to stay away from each other either. Flea, meanwhile, claims that the Chili Peppers still manage to "get in each other's hair" after all these years.[27] The fact is that the band members now seem to walk a precarious tightrope between too much and too little togetherness on tour— and the amounts undoubtedly differ for each group. Extended tours are particularly difficult to abide, no matter how carefully the group strives to maintain a comfortable level of fraternity. Bryce Edge, one of Radiohead's managers, told *The Face* in 2001 that by the end of a prolonged campaign, the five members can barely look each other in the eye. However, the U2 frontman pointed out during a 2002 radio interview that he and his bandmates tend to get more tired of one another in the studio than they do while traveling; the atmosphere can get quite suffocating when they're recording, but the variety on the road provides some relief from the general claustrophobia.

The band as surrogate
family on the road

The band members—even those like Bono and Stipe, who tend to spend a lot of time on their own in this context—say they feel like part of a family or gang on the road. In U2, the four see a lot of each other in social situations on tour. They end up doing various activities together, such as clubbing, often with other members of the crew along for the ride. It goes some way towards mollifying the loneliness and homesickness that's an inevitable part of the experience. Forming a tight-knit little village, something of a surrogate family, is what gets you through a long campaign, Edge told *MAX* in 1997. It certainly helps, agrees Bono, but it's not a cure-all. Asked if he gets lonely during these outings, the singer replied that he does, although he realizes that this is somewhat unwarranted in a band like U2. "It's the sort of loneliness a *spoilt* brat has that's been put outside the door. We've got this small town on the road and I *love* a lot of these people and I think each and every one of them would let me in if I knocked on their door. That's not loneliness is it?"[28] It's paradoxical, he noted in an earlier BBC1 interview (1988), that he can still feel lonely with his closest friends just down the hall.

Bringing one's loved ones on the road, at least for parts of the journey, is one way to stay emotionally healthy, but some bands, like the Red Hot Chili Peppers, aren't keen on girlfriends, for instance, tagging along for extended periods of time because it allows individuals to withdraw from the pack. John Frusciante's sweetheart joined him for the group's 1992 trek and her presence interfered with the quartet's communion because the guitarist often secluded himself with her. Obviously, a particular sense of fellowship and unity are extremely important for the Chili Peppers when they are on the road, so opportunities for members to isolate themselves are limited or discountenanced in order to protect that dynamic. On their 2006 tour, girlfriends and wives accompanied the band, signifying, perhaps, greater confidence in its cohesiveness among the longtime collaborators. But with families, responsibilities and, to some extent, identities, left at home, and feeling more like rock stars than ever in this situation, the band members appear to be called upon to keep one another in check moreso on tour than at any other time. People can get a bit out of control on tour, Bono explains, "and forget where they've come from and who they've left behind."[29] On the road, they are also constantly surrounded by numerous individuals whose job it is to keep them happy, notes Mike Mills. "And that'll warp your mind in no time flat."[30]

Touring and creativity

Some musicians find that touring boosts their creativity while, for others, an extended trek is artistically stifling. Being on the road at least provides the band members with opportunities to throw around ideas and play together simply because they're in one another's company and have time to kill—at soundcheck and sometimes in other situations. Radiohead develops some of its material on the road. During the interminable tour in support of *Pablo Honey*, they alleviated their itchiness to get back into the studio by bringing equipment on the bus and working on new music as they clocked mileage. The documentary of the *OK Computer* tour, *Meeting People Is Easy*, shows the band taking a stab at some fresh material along the way, with Yorke experimenting on his own then taking advantage of his bandmates' presence to further the piece by jamming on it as a group.

Some R.E.M. tracks were conceived on tour, often as an offshoot of the band's camaraderie, reports Buck, who says these songs tend to "start as hootenannies on the bus at four in the morning."[31] R.E.M. also decided to harness the powerful energy and unity generated during a tour by recording an album on the road (*New Adventures in Hi-Fi*). Although *Zooropa*, unlike *New Adventures*, was written and recorded in the studio, U2 also effectively exploited (as was their explicit intent) the momentum and tightness bestowed on the band by the Zoo TV tour they were in the midst of at that time. As for writing on tour, Edge told *The Mirror* in 2001 that he gets a lot of ideas for songs, but the band (including himself) finds it exceedingly difficult to develop music under these circumstances.

10

"Otherside": External Influences on Band Dynamics

"Insular" and "clannish" are terms that have frequently been used to describe R.E.M., particularly because the band closes ranks, shutting out the world and thereby fiercely protecting its autonomy. In this sense, the unit becomes impermeable to industry pressures and directives. Colin Greenwood has similarly characterized Radiohead as "hermetic."[1] Like R.E.M., they claim to stick together and not listen to anyone outside their immediate circle. Beyond that, the quintet has always felt somewhat secluded from the rest of the world. Jonny Greenwood told *B-Side* that there is a sense of detachment from others being in Radiohead. Even members of U2 admit that the quartet is sealed-in to a certain degree. Clayton: "As the band has become more successful and achieved more, you find that the people who still know the most about what you do are the other three guys in the band. Now you could say, 'That's terribly sad, they're cut off in their own world,' but it really is the most exciting combination of people for any member of the band."[2]

Though every group is its own microcosm and, to a certain extent, closed-off from the rest of the world, a variety of external forces do have an undeniable impact on its internal dynamics. The Red Hot Chili Peppers nearly fell apart after *Blood Sugar Sex Magik* turned them into superstars. U2 was beset by moral conflict as a result of members' religious affiliations, and later confronted by image-related issues and the hype surrounding the band. Radiohead's initial struggles as a unit stemmed primarily from the group's efforts to stay afloat in the treacherous waters of the media and corporate music business. R.E.M. spent years running up against the blockades set by mainstream music programmers, coped with the Cult of Stipe and saw members of the band take on fairly significant side-projects. This chapter will assess how various events that take place outside the strict confines of the group impact its mechanics, and the way in which persistent extrinsic factors like fame, the media, and the realities of the music business affect it.

Part I: Band adjustment to fame

PONDEROUS BIGNESS

U2, R.E.M., and the Red Hot Chili Peppers thank their lucky stars that they didn't see fame and riches overnight, as many groups (including, some would argue, Radiohead) have. The adjustment to mainstream success is complicated for bands, and they usually benefit from having time to lay down a cooperative foundation that keeps the outfit intact when the storm hits. For one thing, becoming a "big" band brings changes to the work that have an impact on the unit's internal mechanics because there's more weight attached to each album and tour. The band's ventures have to match its magnitude, as Bono points out: "You can't tour on a wooden stage with a paper backdrop anymore," which for U2 has meant organizing major productions that require, as we saw, a lot of intra-group deliberation and boardroom cooperation.[3]

A huge hit album that is a crowning achievement of sorts often prompts shifts in direction, which can be a struggle, as discussed earlier, to undertake in unison. After releasing the landmark *Joshua Tree* album, U2 found itself in a position where the band had to fight for its musical life and ended up drastically overhauling its sound. "The bigness of U2 had become a distraction," Larry Mullen revealed in 1992. "We could have either split up or poured all of our confusion into a different kind of music."[4] Clayton added that, given their rock royalty status, they had to make an album they were apprehensive about, that was far from a sure bet, otherwise there would have been no reason to carry on. The watershed moment ultimately led to significant fracas within the group, as the members struggled in search of a new aesthetic they could all rally around. An argument can be made (and many critics have made it) that Radiohead was in a similar position after *OK Computer* brought the group superstardom, and that the members reacted to it by reinventing the band. However, they have offered a different rationale (which we'll get to in the next chapter) for their desire to break with the past.

The more successful the group becomes, the more people tend to hang on its every word and note, leaving little room for throwaway material, which adds strain to the creative process. In addition, the weight of public and media expectation is tremendous and can frequently translate into intra-group tensions. Bono reports that the immense expectations U2 faced in the early '90s had the four of them "tearing at each other" until they decided to start playing around with the idea of rock stardom.[5] Radiohead also appears to have been acutely affected by the hype surrounding the band at times. There was certainly a lot of internal turmoil when the quintet was burdened with proving that its music has substance (following "Creep") and later, getting past an album as wildly acclaimed as *OK Computer.*

Making it to the top (and afterwards)

While the media puts the heat on bands by propagating hyped-up expectations, success largely removes the onerous and often divisive pressure to make it to the top. Countless bands have broken up in the quest to gain an audience or crack the mainstream. It takes hard work, thick skin and, at least in the past, nonstop touring (on a shoestring budget). Unknown groups also tend to face tremendous industry and record company pressures. When they bow down to them unwillingly, frustration is the result and it can seep into the internal relations in the unit. Many of Radiohead's early problems within the group stemmed from the fact that the five friends frequently heeded external directives, against their better judgment. "There's an awful lot that's just horrible about the process of the music business, and when you're a young band, you can't do much about it," says Colin Greenwood, in an effort to justify some of the band's initial missteps.[6] They were pissed off with the industry during the *Pablo Honey* era—having to extend their tour, capitalize in unsavory ways on their hit single, and put out an embarrassing version of "Stop Whispering"—and took it out on one another, Ed O'Brien admitted in 1999. "We were forced on tour to support ["Creep"], and it gagged us, really," confirms Yorke, who adds that they were on the verge of breaking up as a result.[7] By 1997, Radiohead was selling millions of albums and playing arenas, which put the members in a position to ignore dictates they didn't want to follow.

With the pressures involved in "making it" effectively eliminated, a major source of stress falls out of the picture. The band can ease up a bit. "Throughout our career we've been struggling and fighting for survival," said Edge in 1992, "to get out of Ireland in the first place, to get a deal, to just make it happen. And I think we've finally got to a stage where we realized we could relax a bit. It's still not easy, but it doesn't have to be quite so much do-or-die."[8] Being in a 'big' group is, in fact, much easier, he told *Spin* in 1989, admitting that U2's first few albums were the hardest to make and that there used to be arguments about everything. Less hustle and more artistic freedom should, in theory, translate into more peaceful internal relations. However, with each album, particularly successors to those that received flak or weren't as well-received as others (like *Rattle and Hum* and *Pop*) U2 has had to re-justify its position. In a sense, the pressure to conquer the world was quickly replaced by the exigent necessity to remain a dominant musical force. As such, the group's mandate for the '90s occasioned as much (if not more) commotion within the unit as its mission to reach superstar-dom. With the benefit of hindsight that Edge didn't have in 1989, Bono remarked in 1997 (*The Guardian*) that staying relevant has proven to be an even greater challenge than breaking the band.

Similarly, for Radiohead, "arriving" was a mixed blessing in terms of the group's internal dynamics. Like U2, they were more at ease, Yorke confessed to journalist Ian Fornam in 1997, after *The Bends* and *OK Computer* validated the band and everything didn't seem like such a battle anymore. On the other hand, beefs they hadn't had time to deal with in the past came to the fore. Slowing down gave them the opportunity to clear the decks in terms of issues that had arisen in their five-way rela-tionship, Selway reported in 2000. There was, in addition, a sense that the band had earned the right to call the shots—and indeed doing things their own way became the group's highest priority (in contrast to U2's aim to stay ahead)—but figuring out how to exercise this new freedom led to factionalism. "We were going in so many different directions and ironing out problems that we hadn't had time to address before," the drummer sums up.[9]

He believes that the recession of externally generated pressure and tribulation was partly to blame for the internal tumult that erupted in 1999: "I think what was happening back then was that for the first time we didn't have anything to push against as a group, and so we pushed against each other."[10] According to Colin Greenwood, Radiohead thrives on adversity and playing the underdog (*Hot Press*, 1995). But, as O'Brien informed *The New Zealand Herald* in 2001, the momentum the quintet derived from being in that position and lurching from crisis to crisis had them constantly hovering on the verge of implosion. Still, once the chal-lenge of breaking the band had been overcome, other tensions initially surfaced.

STAYING LOYAL TO THE COLLECTIVE

Celebrity also introduces a whole roster of temptations for the band to succumb to, any one of which can lead to internal fracas or bring about a split. Withstanding them is tough, as the parties involved need to share the spotlight, curb their greed, check their egos, stick to their communal principles and maintain their closeness amidst the circus that surrounds them. Loyalty to the group can be one of the first things to go when someone gets a taste of stardom. According to Edge, the status U2 attained with *The Joshua Tree* and *Rattle and Hum* forced the members to reassess their need for the collective. "We all individually stopped and looked around and said, 'Yes, we need one another. No, I, personally, am not a star.' None of us are bigger than the band—not Bono, not myself, not Adam and not Larry."[11] Perhaps it was this realization that held the band together during the tumultuous recording sessions for *Achtung Baby*.

Thom Yorke confesses that he went through a period after *Pablo Honey* when he thought himself a little too special (in homage to the song that got him there) to be in a band and considered opting out of Radiohead. "I thought I could go it alone, I thought I didn't need anybody. As soon as you get any degree of success, you disappear up your own arse and you lose it forever." In Yorke's case, he was only momentarily blinded by a sophistical perception of what it takes to be a "great" artist, and felt he had to live up to the reputation that supposedly comes with it. "You start to believe you are this sensitive artist who has to be alone, and you have to become this tortured melodramatic person to create wonderful music."[12] The camaraderie and mutual dependency in a band seemed at odds with the solitary life one generally associates with serious artists.

Achieving widespread recognition as a band can have the opposite effect, in that it reinforces the members' faith in the value of their chemistry and collaboration. "All of us have been given great belief in ourselves," Yorke declared in 1996, obviously reacting to fame differently than he had the first time around (i.e., dwelling on the band's collective power). "It's like a flash of relief more than inspiration. I know we can do it now." (By "it," he presumably means something to the effect of "make worthwhile music").[13]

CONFLICTING RESPONSES TO FAME

Other problems arise when individuals in the group respond in incompatible ways to its celebrity. While Anthony Kiedis basked in the glory the Chili Peppers attained with *Blood Sugar Sex Magik*, John Frusciante bewailed it. The singer valued mass attention, as long as it was accorded for the right reasons, and thought that the world had legitimately come around to the band. But the guitarist, who eschewed stardom in any form, was particularly disgusted by the notion of courting it and believed the band was doing just that: selling out to be popular. "I felt like they thought to be successful they had to pretend to be something, to make funny faces and jump around and be silly and make weird jokes, because that's what was going to make them successful."[14] Frusciante's contempt for "the whole rock star thing" made the singer feel guilty and ashamed for reveling in the band's victory, as if embracing mainstream success proved that he lacked integrity. Consequently, Kiedis ended up concealing his real sentiments. "He was scared to say anything like he usually did which was his thing and so it was just awful," remarked a rather incoherent Frusciante in 1994.[15] And while the rest of the band fanned the flame with loads of press and glitzy television engagements, the guitarist subverted their efforts by refusing to give interviews and ruining their momentous *Saturday Night Live* appearance.

There were other discrepancies in the group. The Chili Peppers' rise to global prominence seemed, for a time at least, to really satisfy the singer and bring him tremendous contentment. It left Flea, who had expected the same, empty and cold. They were finally in the position every band dreams of being in, but he was miserable, he confided in *Rolling Stone* (1995). He didn't scorn the band's status as Frusciante did, but it didn't make him nearly as happy as it did Kiedis. In an interview with *VH1.com*, the bassist admitted that in his withered state, he felt bitter towards his euphoric friend and that they, too, were distanced by how contrarily the situation affected them. It took them a while to get back together, he said. Fame and fortune simply left the group off-balance, confirms Kiedis.

Bill Berry also didn't embrace rock stardom to the same extent as his partners in R.E.M. and, in Buck's view, likewise resented the fact that the band welcomed it with open arms (*Q Special Edition R.E.M.*). His decision to leave R.E.M. stemmed partly from these mutually exclusive ambitions. Berry preferred that the group remain an underground sensation. Like Frusciante, he couldn't stay committed to the band once it became a global phenomenon—it wasn't what he had signed up for. *OK Computer*'s astounding success was taken more or less in stride by Yorke's bandmates in Radiohead, but Colin Greenwood later confided to *NME* that all the hoopla "did Thom's head in."[16] Although they all felt dismayed by the celebrity tornado the record unleashed on them, Yorke took it harder than anyone else. It left him confused, disillusioned, angry that his life had spun out of control and, ultimately, in a different headspace than the rest of the band. They had gained a belief in themselves and seemed to have found their footing, while Yorke felt completely discombobulated and needed to question everything, which is largely why their internal relations were so fraught during this period. With time (and some mentoring from Stipe), Yorke grew more comfortable with his position, which gradually put the five on an even plane again and helped bring harmony to a band that seemed likely, at times, to be destroyed by an iconic stature that the singer, in particular, couldn't deal with.

Band makes it easier to cope with fame

Being part of a group can often make fame easier to cope with on an individual level simply because a number of other people are in the same boat as you. Thom Yorke revealed during a 1998 radio interview with Triple J that he would really freak out if he had to face the rock and roll circus on his own, as would, he predicts, any of his bandmates. Discussing the challenges of fame, Edge remarks that the collective provides comfort, sanity, and support. It must be hard being a soloist, he muses, because "there's no one else you can check with and see how they're feeling or who can keep an eye on you when you're going through a rough period." In this regard, having bandmates is a "good feeling," he says. "There are just those four people—but it makes it a lot easier to handle, no matter what happens."[17]

Having the option of discussing his feelings with someone who understands makes a big difference, Bono observed in *Rolling Stone* (1987), because he knows he can always drag one of his three partners out of bed to talk when a celebrity-related issue arises. And, just as good press and groupies meet with valuable ego checks and reality monitors courtesy of the others in the group, unfavorable media doesn't need to be absorbed alone—whether it's directed at the group or a single individual—so its impact is somewhat diminished. At least there are others with whom to commiserate. "We're very close knit and every member takes the criticism personally," said Colin Greenwood in 1995 with regards to stinging comments made about the band and Thom Yorke specifically.[18]

Part II: Life in the limelight

Sharing the spotlight

One aspect of fame that has been a problem for many bands—but isn't in these four—is the jealousy that can arise when one member (usually the frontman) gets more attention than the others. It's the way their partners respond to the disproportionate attention they receive that separates U2, R.E.M., Radiohead and the Red Hot Chili Peppers from groups in which this causes problems. It's understood and he bears in mind, Clayton told *The Dallas Morning News*, that as far as the media spotlight is concerned, there's a typical hierarchy, so inevitably the singer and guitar player (especially the talented and charismatic ones) are going to bask in it more than the other members of the band. Similarly, Mike Mills testified in *The Vancouver Sun* that he doesn't mind flying under the radar while Stipe and Buck are glorified because it's a well-known fact that bassists are a really low priority for the press. Given the history of rock and roll, he argued, everyone assumes (mistakenly) that the singer and guitar player write all the music, and the bass player is therefore irrelevant. Meanwhile, Edge accepts the fact that though guitarists get a lot of attention in the relative scheme of things, they are just sidemen (unless they're also on lead vocal) and the singer's the main attraction.

One way in which R.E.M. has avoided conflict over this issue is by openly discussing it, particularly the attention Stipe receives, so that everyone's feelings about the situation are clear. They also recognize that his high profile benefits the group to some extent. "The thing we never wanted as a band was for our personalities, our celebrity as people, to eclipse the music. But that's happened to a degree, especially for me," confesses the singer, adding that they talk about it a lot and everyone in the band is "cool with it."[19]

Most importantly, the members accorded less notice claim they wouldn't want it any other way. They don't crave the attention lavished on their more famous bandmates. This is another sense in which the various parties in these outfits are well-matched. U2 works, says Edge, because "[Bono] loves nothing better than being in the spotlight and I don't think anyone else is that interested in it. I'm the perfect sideman."[20] Being in the public eye is actually hard on him and Mullen in particular, says the guitarist, because they're not very gregarious, so they're quite happy to let Bono bear the brunt of the band's renown. Echoing this sentiment, Jonny Greenwood says he doesn't mind seeing Yorke alone on magazine covers because it means the rest of them get bothered less.

Peter Buck once remarked, with a hint of wicked delight, that he actually enjoys being mistaken for Stipe's bodyguard. It's not like he's losing anything by it. "I make as much money as anybody else and I have all the artistic satisfaction I want because I help write the songs," he stated.[21] Celebrity isn't what Buck wants to get out of the group, so he maintains a sense of humor about the inequalities inherent in collective stardom. So does Chad Smith, who is amused, not angry, he relayed to *El Pais*, when people stare at him, obviously wondering: who is the tall guy hanging out with the Chili Peppers? Similarly, Larry Mullen laughs at how unwitting fans have asked him to hold their personal belongings while getting Bono's autograph and Adam Clayton jokes that he's famous only because he knows Bono.

Being appropriately valued within the unit is equally crucial in maintaining a healthy perspective on sharing the spotlight. The inner mechanics of the band often aren't accurately represented in the media, but the real relations are what count. "Although in the outside world it's inevitable that Bono should have all the attention thrust upon him, among the four of us there's an equality there which is still respected," observes Clayton.[22] Rock and roll tradition (or narrow views of it), as Mills notes, coupled with media biases create a false impression of the internal dynamics in groups like R.E.M. The perception is that certain members (the singer and guitarist) run the band and write all the songs, he charged in an early *Los Angeles Times* interview (1984). That's why, says Buck, people tell him all the time, "'I know it's credited to all four of you, but of course Michael and you do it all.'"[23] But outsiders would be surprised at how many songs he actually has little to do with because one of his bandmates has taken the lead, contends the guitarist.

It's also essential for the individual musicians to recognize the significance of their own part in the whole. "I know what I contribute to the band so the hell with everybody else," shrugs Mike Mills.[24] The result is that this unavoidable discrimination doesn't breed resentment and toxic forms of competitive attention-seeking don't rear their ugly heads. The only ones who seem at all annoyed by the inequity are the fêted singers. Bono was disappointed with the Live Aid book because it failed to reflect the fact that there are four people in U2 (i.e., it focused on him). For a time after *The Joshua Tree* became a global phenomenon, the U2 frontman also refused to give interviews because he was sick of being seen as the MVP of the band and worried about the potential implications of his growing personal fame.

PRESENTING A UNITED FRONT

From the start, the members of R.E.M. thought of themselves as an ensemble from which no individual stuck out and made it a point to let others know that it's a four-piece band in which each member is of equal significance. During an early appearance on *The David Letterman Show,* Letterman invited the band's "leader" to join him at his desk for a chat, but R.E.M. refused to appoint one and instead had the host speak with all four of them in the performance area. They have taken other subtle steps to present a united front to the world. Upon releasing a new album, they frequently make a show of solidarity by involving the whole band in photo sessions and having Buck or Mills conduct interviews instead of Stipe. Since *Out of Time,* they began making primarily group appearances in their videos, rather than letting Stipe star on his own. Buck insists that they also avoid playing up their individual characters so that none of them will stand out or eclipse the collective.

U2 claim that they have similarly striven to put the focus on the band rather than individuals within it. One of the reasons they made the *Rattle and Hum* film, the singer flagged in *Propaganda* (1989, Issue 9), was to give his bandmates an opportunity to come to the forefront by doing more of the talking, while Clayton told *Sunday Express Magazine* (1988) that one of the project's goals was to capture the quartet's closeness and unity, or in other words, to present U2 as a real group. He hoped the film's lasting message would be that he and his bandmates were four people committed to looking after one another and making music together. These efforts to push the group forward instead of themselves stem partly, as we know, from a desire for personal anonymity, at least in some cases, but also from a determination to portray the band as a composite entity.

The media and the group's internal communication

What individual members choose to let the media in on can occasionally become a bone of contention within the unit. Anthony Kiedis was nonplussed when Chad Smith told *Rolling Stone*, while the Chili Peppers slogged away on *One Hot Minute*, that the band's frontman was suffering from writer's block and identified it as the cause of the record's delay. In 2006, Kiedis was similarly exasperated that Flea informed the press of his desire to quit the band following the 2002/03 tour. The singer's bandmates likewise resented what *he* revealed about the group in his autobiography, much of which, claims Frusciante, they had vowed not to discuss publicly. Another facet of the relationship between these bands and the media that is particularly intriguing is how the latter can intrude upon the group's internal dialogue. What this means is that individual members have, on occasion, heard one of their partner's views or ideas indirectly, through the press. For instance, it's a well-known fact that Ed O'Brien revealed in a post–*OK Computer* interview that he foresees Radiohead throwing off the prog-rock label that some critics had affixed to the band by making a record full of three-minute pop songs. But Yorke, who had something entirely different in mind, learned of O'Brien's vision for the album from a journalist rather than his bandmate. Chad Smith only learned during a *Stadium Arcadium* interview about Flea's near defection after *By the Way*. In the foreword to the collected articles from *Propaganda*, Bono observes that reading the publication over the years was a useful way of keeping tabs on one another in U2, particularly during periods when they weren't on speaking terms! "It was a revelation to discover what Larry thought of the *Passengers* album," he writes. "I had no idea!"[25]

As R.E.M.'s conceptual instigator, Peter Buck has often used the media to set a direction for the group, by announcing what tack its next album will take—often without discussing it with the others first. The most interesting incident of this nature happened during a promotional junket for *Monster* in 1994. The quartet gave interviews in pairs: Berry and Buck in one room, Mills and Stipe in another. The first two told interviewers that they would record the next R.E.M. album live on the road. The journalists then asked the other duo about it, but it was news to them. "Eventually they came over and said 'What is this about us doing a live record?'" Buck told *Reuters* with evident amusement.[26] But the media sometimes enters without invitation into the band's vision- or direction-establishment efforts, so that it's almost as if there are other voices at the table. "If you read the papers you're obviously aware of where other people want you to go," points out Colin Greenwood. "And if that's not where Thom is comfortable, it causes a lot of tension and it can impact upon the creativity as well."[27]

Given that there are already so many differing views to take into consideration in a democratic collective, media involvement can make it even more difficult to arrive at a consensus. "The three of us already manage to have five opinions," says Buck, who contends that this is one reason they avoid listening to suggestions from external sources (the other is that they don't want to forfeit artistic control).[28] In Yorke's case, media observations tend (or tended) to creep insidiously into his perception of himself and his relationship with his bandmates, such as the time *Melody Maker* compared him to the troubled Richey James of the Manic Street Preachers (who abruptly ditched the band one fine day and subsequently disappeared), after which Yorke was wary of giving interviews. "My whole thing about it is, if it's going to affect my work— the way we can work together, how we see each other—then fuck them," he snapped.[29]

Part III: Producers and personal lives

We've looked at fame, the media, the industry, and the ways in which each of these affects the internal mechanics of the groups. Changes in members' personal lives have an impact equally worthy of discourse. Members becoming family men has had a big influence on most of these bands. U2 and Radiohead, for example, have slowed down in order to spend more time at home with their young children instead of putting out an album every year and touring nonstop. In the studio, they are more motivated than ever before to work quickly and effectively, with as little angst as possible to impede them. When asked how fatherhood has changed Yorke, Colin Greenwood replied that the singer has indeed displayed greater pragmatism in putting the band's time to good use. The time spent away from one's kids needs to be worthwhile, he explains, which has benefited the band because everyone wants to see the work progress smoothly and with as few holdups as possible. His brother Jonny added succinctly: "all that pain and the unproductive side gets avoided."[30]

The eagerness to put in a productive day at the studio and return to the homestead has, on one notable occasion, been deleterious in R.E.M.'s case. Far from his wife and daughters in Seattle during the recording of *Up*, Buck was rather antsy to wrap up the sessions in Athens as quickly as possible, but Stipe experienced a bout of prolonged writer's block that held up the process. Buck's evident frustration only made the singer indignant, so the already fractious atmosphere in the studio was further soured by the mutual resentment that arose between the two.

As honorary members of the group for brief periods, producers understandably influence the dynamics of the unit. The contrasting styles of John Leckie (*The Bends*) and Nigel Godrich (*Kid A, Amnesiac, Hail to the Thief*) created very different collaborative environments for Radiohead. Being a very hands-off producer, Leckie left the five to their own devices quite frequently, which forced them to work as a tight team, and gave them the confidence to produce *OK Computer* themselves (with a little help from then-friend Nigel Godrich). They decided to attempt producing their third album because they enjoyed figuring out the recording process together, with little outside intervention, and wanted to take the experience a step further. "The times we most got off on making [*The Bends*] were when we were just completely communicating with ourselves and John Leckie wasn't really saying much and it was just all happening," explains Yorke.[31] So, in a sense, they didn't want anyone else to enter into the fruitful creative relationship between the five of them. They wanted to stretch the unit's self-sufficiency farther.

The much more hands-on Godrich interjects himself into the group rather than standing to the side as Leckie did. He seems to be the de facto manager in the studio, bossing the band around and making them hold midday meetings, as Yorke informed *MTV.com* in 2000. They obviously like his style, since he has produced the band's last three albums (besides assisting with *OK Computer*). Frequently, Colin Greenwood remarked, Godrich also acts as a mediator. "He has an overall sense of fair play which he brings to Radiohead as well which is a really important quality when you're dealing with a group of five people who have their own power-based relationships and political relationships built up over working together for 15 years."[32] R.E.M. claim that their longest-serving producer, Scott Litt, played a similar role, arbitrating disagreements. "We turn to him when the four of us are so bound up in what we're doing that we can't see clearly."[33]

Part of the reason producers act in this capacity, Rick Rubin points out in *Mix*, is because they aren't concerned with any specific part of the song (such as the bass line)—as the band members, with their distinct

roles, inevitably *are* to some extent—but with the whole. They are genuinely free of bias. But to do their job effectively, especially when it comes
to mediating, they need to understand the band's dynamic and where
they fit in. Having been at the controls for most of U2's albums, Brian
Eno and Daniel Lanois have a clear understanding of when they should
speak up during band disputes and when to let the band members duke
it out themselves, Mullen told *Hot Press* (2000).

Since a multi-way democratic collaboration can easily bog down the
writing and recording sessions, the producers who work with these bands
are frequently responsible for keeping the process moving forward.
"There are four of us and while we love starting songs we hate finishing
them and democracy is a pain in the hole to be around," stated Bono
while discussing the making of *Pop*. "But Flood was amazing at pushing
things through."[34] This is a particularly important function when the
recording sessions are fraught. That's why Stipe has referred to Pat
McCarthy as R.E.M.'s secret weapon in the struggle to complete *Up*. As
the group fell apart in front of his eyes, he was the mortar that kept it
together and drove the project through to the end. Nigel Godrich also
strives to expedite what tends to be a protracted pursuit—the creation
of new music—for Radiohead.

Part IV: The band's impact on life outside of it

IS A BREAK EVER A BREAK?

Being in a band is an all-consuming full-time job. Even when you're
not touring or in the studio, you're still in a band, Stipe proclaimed during an AOL chat with fans. How does participation in the collective affect
the individual's life outside of it? Are there ever any real breaks from the
group? These are some of the questions this section attempts to answer.

When the R.E.M. clan resided in Athens together, time off meant
time spent at home rather than time spent away from group business,
Buck informed *East Coast Rocker* in 1988. According to the guitarist, in
the first decade of R.E.M.'s existence, they spent nearly every "unofficial"
moment rehearsing and writing songs together. Now that they're living
in different cities, that has changed, of course. To this day, the U2 clan
tends to keep *the group* together even when *the band* isn't working. For
one thing, the four members take joint vacations in adjacent residences
located in the south of France. It just makes sense for them to go away
together, explains Mullen, because if someone has an idea, it doesn't
have to be put on hold. "It is unusual and it can be a little trying, because
a break is never really a break with us," he concedes, adding that that's
just how they work.[35]

Within the democratic set-up—particularly one characterized by tire-less discussions—band business can also take up a great deal of the members' so-called personal time. "Sometimes I think being in U2 is being in one long meeting," Clayton consequently jokes. "Your own life is just a tea break between meetings."[36] They have gone their separate ways on the rare occasions when U2 has been on extended hiatus, as was the case in 1994, a year the quartet took off partly in order to get away from each other for a while. There was minimal contact between them during this period, the bassist revealed, adding that seeing less of each other was healthy for a group that had spent nearly two decades joined at the hip.

PERSONAL IDENTITY AND
BAND IDENTITY BOUND UP

"Being in a band is like being a parent," says Clayton. "You're never really out of the role."[37] This implies that even when the group's members are away from one another, the band is never far from their minds, and that a lot of their extracurricular activities do come back to the band in some way. It also means that everything you do reflects upon the group (as it would on a family), and that you always represent it in some way. In this vein, the members of U2 have compared being in a band to join-ing a street gang or the priesthood, largely because you're constantly affiliated with the organization in which you participate.

This is another way in which the band infringes on personal lives. When Peter Buck was charged with air rage and Adam Clayton picked up for possession of marijuana—both events occurring while they were off-duty—the *band's* reputation was very much on the line. To a certain extent then, the members, at least in R.E.M. and U2, try to avoid PR inju-rious to the group in order to maintain its upstanding image. The indi-viduals need to be very careful about how they present themselves in general, always thinking about the impact on the band. In 1987, Stipe tellingly confided to *Melody Maker* that he doesn't like to discuss his mys-tical side with the press because it reinforces a perception of R.E.M. the members wish to discredit. "Well, you know it's really outside the band and I think it would infuriate them [his partners] if I talked about it. We get enough shit about being hippies already, especially now my hair's long again."[38]

At a time when U2 was after a less puritan and more rock-star-wor-thy image, Clayton's party-boy profile and engagement to supermodel Naomi Campbell made just the right mark on the group, whereas, in their more somber days, his hedonistic tendencies (which wouldn't have been out of sync in any other band, as he pointed out himself), clashed with how the others wanted (consciously or subconsciously) the outfit to be seen. These days, it's Bono's high-profile activism that rubs off on U2, and the foursome is very conscious of its impact. Although they staunchly support his work, the singer's bandmates wish he would tread more carefully sometimes, as they worry about the effect his actions have on the group's image.

"It doesn't necessarily help our band that Bono is so well known now as a political activist. It's great on one level, but being photographed with George W. Bush and the Pope—I don't like it particularly and he knows it," stresses Edge, who apparently begged the frontman not to be snapped alongside the U.S. president.[39] (Mullen didn't like seeing him with Vladimir Putin.) While appreciating their tolerance for his unhip auxiliary career, the singer continues to do whatever is necessary to further his cause, only hoping it doesn't look *too* bad on the band. It appears to have become a central conversation piece amongst the four. They're always discussing it, the guitarist asserted in a 2004 *Time* feature on U2.

SIDE-PROJECTS

Some members of these bands have fairly substantial and ongoing side-gigs, musical and otherwise. Bono has his politics, Stipe runs two movie production companies in addition to being a published photographer, John Frusciante has a budding solo career, Peter Buck participates in several Seattle-based bands, and Jonny Greenwood is (at the time of writing) the BBC's composer in residence.

While onlookers often frown upon side-projects or consider them gratuitous at best (deleterious at worst), many of the band members insist that they are generally beneficial to the collective, which is strengthened and invigorated by the knowledge and experience acquired through experiments tackled outside of the fold and then incorporated into it. The most exciting thing about a band, Bono observed astutely in *Propaganda* (1990, Issue 13), is that it is a melting pot for the ideas of a collection of individuals. Since members of all four bands claim that their primary artistic influences are each other, it's easy to see why the group profits when the individuals involved have a finger in other pies. Furthermore, it stands to reason that if the members are fulfilled and fueled by these other efforts, their other gigs will ultimately serve the band. When Bono is criticized for devoting too much time to non–U2 projects, these are precisely the arguments his partners bring forward in his defense. They also claim that since *the group* has always been politically involved, Bono's work is almost an extension of that rather than something separate from it.

Supplementary ventures have always been encouraged in R.E.M.

Defining the band's structure as loose in *The Athens Daily News* (1997), Mills explained that they've never had a problem with any outside work any of them have wanted to do. In fact, Peter Buck believes the longevity of the group is at least partly attributable to the fact that the members have the freedom to get involved in diverse projects (*The Seattle Times*, 2002). In order for this system to work, it's essential, Stipe says, for the individuals never to lose sight of the fact that the band is, as he calls it, the mothership, or to cease focusing on it. As occasional-actor Anthony Kiedis once told *Rhythm and News*, you have to recognize no matter what else you're working on that the cornerstone of your career is the band. In a 2004 interview with *CD:UK*, Bono indeed referred to U2 as his day job and the political campaigning as his paper round—not with the intention of trivializing his activist efforts but to indicate where his priorities lie. Stipe believes particular benefit can be derived from solo endeavors, especially artistic ones like his photography sideline, because they provide an often much-needed channel for non-communal personal expression. It's important, he says, to have "something that is selfishly your own—your own vision that is not particularly collaborative."[40]

There's no doubt, however, that making room for considerable side ventures of any sort taxes the band. As if the difficulties R.E.M. encountered while making *Up* weren't overwhelming enough, the fact that Stipe had three movies in production at that time added significant strain. There were days they had to have "throw-down therapy sessions," Stipe later confided, because he was spending so much of his time in the studio on the phone conducting film-related business.[41] Bono's work requires that he frequently absent himself from rehearsals and recording sessions and it does interfere with the band, admits Mullen. "It's a four-legged table, and with one leg missing even for short periods of time the thing becomes a little unstable."[42]

Necessity was the mother of invention when the four novices from Dublin started out and that's the attitude they've taken to dealing with the current handicap. They don't just work around Bono's absences but try to use them to their advantage. Edge insists that Bono's time away has given the others an opportunity to work at their own parts and that the music has benefited. Judging by the accolades heaped on his guitar work on 2000's *All That You Can't Leave Behind* and 2004's *How to Dismantle an Atomic Bomb*, the group has indeed found a way to turn the singer's truancy into a collective strength. They also focus on the positive aspects of the situation. It makes the rest of them realize that what they do is important to the group, Clayton told *Rolling Stone* in 2002, where he proceeded to point out that they have also had to learn to use the time they are all together more wisely. Ultimately, they realize that Bono gets frustrated when he's tied to the studio and feels like he could be doing more important things with that time, so they wouldn't get more out of him if they tried to keep him put when it's not absolutely necessary. That's one reason they have striven to make it work.

The singer is keenly aware of the demands his political agenda have put on the band and grateful for the sacrifices his partners have made in order to accommodate it. When he's not around to finish a song, or when an album that should take one year to complete ends up taking two because of his other commitments, everyone's life is on hold. "In the end, it's their time I'm spending," he acknowledged in *The Hollywood Reporter*.[43] The band's support structure is evident, says a grateful Bono, in the way his partners have furthered his campaign to drop third world debt by giving him time off and by making financial contributions, while taking the heat from his unhip duties as third world ambassador.

From a public perspective, no issue is thornier than musical side ventures. For one thing, many groups begin to splinter as soon as the members develop side projects and solo gigs. The resulting fragmentation of a previously more close-knit and single-minded band is regarded as a precursor to an out-and-out split. Indeed, when Thom Yorke released his first independent album (*The Eraser*) in 2006, he was reluctant to even call it a solo effort because of the term's negative connotations. To some observers, significant extracurricular pursuits also signify a lack of creative satisfaction with the group or one's role in it. Edge conceded in *The Chicago Sun Times* that it can be difficult to justify, even to oneself, devoting time to an extracurricular musical enterprise, like a solo album, when you know you could be more effective in the band and that it's where you do your best work (that's why you're in it).

Along these lines, Peter Buck suggests that if one feels sufficiently fulfilled within the group, it neutralizes the impetus to seek other musical outlets. "If I want to do something, a particular thing musically, I could bring it to the band and we'll do it," he adds, harking back to the notion of receptivity within the unit.[44] This is a rather odd statement coming from a musician with myriad non–R.E.M. projects. Buck regularly records and performs with bands like Tuatara and Minus 5. With regards to his full slate of extracurricular activities, the ubiquitous guitarist contradicted his earlier statement, admitting that "a lot of things I come up with just aren't appropriate [for R.E.M.], and now I have plenty of places to go with the stuff that doesn't fit my band."[45]

The truth is, as versatile and diffuse as the band may strive to be—and R.E.M., like the other three groups, has toyed with many different styles and sounds—Buck's remark implies that there are, nevertheless, certain boundaries that one must look elsewhere in order to overstep. Stipe confirmed as much in an interview with *Melody Maker* in which he stated that his position within the band is very set in certain ways and that he could never, for instance, bring a sledgehammer onstage and "hit metal" in R.E.M.[46] The group's collective vision, artistic direction, basic setup and image all impose some limitations. There are also divergent tastes among the individuals involved preventing members from delving as deeply into a particular genre or sound as they would like if their bandmates aren't equally interested.

No one in Radiohead is as excited about French horns as Jonny Greenwood. If he is to *seriously* explore this instrument, it has to be outside of the band (in his case, by working with an orchestra). Similarly, when R.E.M. took its five-year break from the road, Mike Mills, who missed performing live, said he might try to find another outfit to gig with if his bandmates continue to eschew touring. So sidestepping the inevitable limitations entailed by the group is one reason to get involved in other musical projects. On a purely practical level, some musicians, like Peter Buck, John Frusciante and Jonny Greenwood, simply don't need as much downtime as their partners, so they quite legitimately use the band's periods of inactivity to embark upon additional musical projects.

For Buck, the primary distinction between R.E.M. and the other bands he works with has to do with whose vision is represented therein. In R.E.M., it's (partly) his own, but that's not the case in Tuatara, for example. "I always go to pains to stress that I'm a side guy [there]," he says. "I'm working to help other people find their vision and to bring ideas to it."[47] In that sense, there's little overlap, certainly no conflict, between the two ventures. One could say that he feels a degree of ownership over R.E.M.—because his own vision is expressed within this group and he was involved in laying down its founding principles—that he doesn't feel outside of it. The supplementary musical activities of individual band members can really enrich the group. The moonlighting musician picks up not merely ideas, but concrete techniques, styles and approaches that then feed back into the band. Playing with other ensembles has not only introduced Buck to various ways of working and composing songs, but has also helped him appreciate the democracy and camaraderie that prevail in R.E.M. by enabling him to get a voyeur's eye-view of what it's like to be in a less functional or egalitarian outfit. "There's one guy making decisions, the other guys don't like it. I wouldn't want to do that," he declares.[48]

Generally, when a band member strikes out independently to make a solo album, it's regarded as a prelude to an imminent breakup. But a few artists (such as Jerry Garcia of The Grateful Dead) manage to balance parallel careers, and John Frusciante appears to be one of them. *Niandra LaDes & Usually Just a Tshirt*, Frusciante's first solo effort, came out in 1994, shortly after he exited the Chili Peppers. But since rejoining the group, he has, alongside his participation within it, put out solo albums at an ever-more frenzied pace, culminating in six separate discs issued monthly throughout a particularly prolific period for the musician in 2004. He requested a six-month break from the group following its 2002–2003 tour in order to devote himself to his solo pursuits, and that's when he wrote and recorded much of the material featured on these back-to-back releases. However, many of the tracks that appeared on his acclaimed 2003 LP, *Shadows Collide with People* (the album that kicked off the deluge), were actually written while he was composing songs with the band for 2002's *By the Way*.

In interviews, Frusciante is often asked why he pulls double-duty, recording on his own as well as with the band. The response is that he tends to be more of a workaholic than the other three, but more importantly, he is driven by distinct creative impulses. What he does in the Chili Peppers, he explained to *Guitar* in 2004, is write bits of songs, generally the guitar part. But there's no outlet in the group for the complete songwriter in him (he's been cranking out full-scale tunes since he was 11 years old). Since Kiedis contributes the lyrics and vocal melodies for the Chili Peppers, a substantial chunk of the tracks is out of Frusciante's hands. Yet, songs (music *and* words) seem to pour out of him, and it's a shame, he explains, not to share them with others. "I have two musical lives," he thus declares, adding that the Peppers' recordings chart his growth as a guitarist while his solo works reveal how he has progressed as a songwriter.[49]

Like Peter Buck and Jonny Greenwood, Frusciante is also motivated by a desire to explore musical genres that aren't really part of the group's agenda, amongst them punk and electronica, he explained in *Amplifier*. With the Chili Peppers, Frusciante also knew he'd never have a chance to speedily record unvarnished material (essentially in one take) as he has done on his own. This quick-and-dirty approach greatly appealed to him but big bands rarely put out such albums in these days of the momentous and built-up next effort. In addition, the democratic collaborative process, as we know, and as the guitarist pointed out in the German publication *Spiegel*, prolongs the writing and recording sessions, making it extremely difficult to cut new tracks in a matter of days as Frusciante wanted to do (even if a band as big as the Chili Peppers could put out such an album without taking a lot of flak).

For Frusciante the two settings in which he operates are very much separate. When writing for the group, he told *Guitarist*, he concentrates almost exclusively on the guitar parts, whereas with his own songs, the guitar may be the least interesting feature for him, and he tends more carefully to the lyrics, vocals or synthesizer segments. He also regards his music as quite different from that of the band's. Occasionally, his ideas have cross-over potential, but usually, he insists, it's very clear to him what belongs in the Chili Peppers and what is better suited to his own music. That answers the charge leveled by a few cynics that he must be keeping the best bits for himself. The group is free to, and occasionally does, appropriate pieces he has earmarked as John Frusciante material. He described in *Rock Mag* in 2001 how he played a surf music-inspired piece for Kiedis, who immediately asked to work on it. At that point, reported the guitarist, it ceased to belong to him and became the property of the Chili Peppers. (Yorke told *The Sydney Morning Herald* that when the pieces on *The Eraser* began to sound like real songs, he experienced serious qualms about working without the band, but decided to carry on.)

There's also a tremendous difference, Frusciante points out, between realizing one's own vision versus a collective one. In the Chili Peppers, he writes the guitar part for the whole song, but he still doesn't know where the track is going. When he works on his own, he's responsible for all the parts and knows exactly where he's heading with the song, he explains, adding that every strand of music contributed by anyone he's working with on his solo material has to fit into his own pre-laid plan for the song. "In the Chili Peppers, I'm more interested in seeing it go in directions I didn't expect."[50] Frusciante claims to enjoy both experiences equally. On their part, Frusciante's bandmates are happy that he has found an arena in which to pursue his independent artistic aims and assume roles unavailable to him in the band.

TWO MORE THINGS

This chapter began with various declarations about how insular these bands are, but clearly their internal dynamics are greatly affected by the external world, which also tends to intrude on the creative process. That's why bands occasionally opt to go into isolation when they're recording. It allows them to both immerse themselves in the music and commune with one another. Radiohead retreated to a remote mansion to prepare new material for its third album. Ed O'Brien confided in *Addicted to Noise* (1997) that working close to home, as they did initially, distracted them, so they decided to go somewhere far away and cloister themselves together to record it. Similarly, the Red Hot Chili Peppers rented a mansion in the Hollywood Hills from which they emerged after two months of enforced exile with *Blood Sugar Sex Magik*. Living together and creating an enclosed environment in the home restricted to the band and necessary crew members reduced the tension that generally attends studio sessions and allowed the four to communicate with one another more fluidly than ever before.

A final note: Radiohead, U2 and R.E.M. hail from areas that, on the pop-rock map, couldn't be more off the beaten path. They all chose to remain in their hometown—be it Oxford, Dublin or Athens—rather than move to a music capital to pursue their career. In doing so, they avoided many of the external pressures that have strangled other bands at birth. Playing in a city like New York, points out Buck, fledgling groups face immediate scrutiny and have to fight their way onto the bottom of a bill whereas he and his partners were able to play in front of an audience virtually every night of the week, without reading a make-it-or-break-it review of the show in a major paper the next morning. In a big city, it would never have happened, he told *East Coast Rocker* (1988) in reference to the band's gradual development and ascent. Being away from all that gave R.E.M. an opportunity to develop at its own pace and become a tight-knit, mutually-attuned unit before facing the world at large. For these reasons, Larry Mullen says U2 couldn't have come from anywhere but Dublin, where the band was "protected and away from the circus of rock 'n' roll culture."[51] Had Radiohead moved to London, Yorke once told *Vox* with assurance, the band wouldn't have lasted a month.

11

"Another Time, Another Place": Evolution of the Unit's Communal Life

The maturation process each of the four bands discussed in this book has undergone is evident in their music, for their recordings chart their growth as artists. Not captured on tape (not directly, at least) is the evolution of the collaborative entities themselves. As their output metamorphosed over the years, so did their inner workings and relationships. Long-lived bands have an opportunity to establish a consistent interchange, the musicians to cement their connection and mature alongside one another. But longevity in an insulated creative partnership likewise raises the specters of monotony and predictability, obstacles the group must overcome if it is to survive. These are a few of the themes taken up in this chapter, which looks at some of the ways in which the dynamics in the groups have changed over time.

Part I: Changes

GROWING PAINS AND SURVIVING ADOLESCENCE

Like individuals, bands experience significant growing pains in their early years, and many don't survive this tumultuous period. As these outfits tend to be started by musicians who are in their teens and early twenties, the dynamics of the unit reflect their own pubescent struggles. Radiohead's Ed O'Brien points out, for instance, that many of the internal problems the band experienced during its nascent years can be attributed to the pimple-prone life stage the members were at and the hang-ups that come with it. "[T]here's a lot of shit in your late teens, a lot of angst and insecurity and paranoia that kind of oozes out. And when you're with people as much as we are, it comes out sometimes."[1] The difficulties involved in making their first three albums, he explained in 2000, stemmed from "personalities clashing and individual neuroses," as well as insecurity, "the way it is with five people in their 20s."[2] To some extent, then, much of what they went through in the initial stage of their career was unavoidable because of their age.

About the frictions pervading R.E.M. in 1985, Mills similarly commented that the squabbles arose partly because he and his bandmates were very young and still in the process of figuring out who they are. In fact, he and Stipe didn't get along at all in the beginning, but their relations improved, he told biographer David Buckley, when they stopped behaving immaturely. Without pointing to any particular culprits in the juvenile psyche, Anthony Kiedis alludes to the strain of maturing aboard the rock and roll rollercoaster while strapped to three other people. "Growing up together in the band with all of the crazy psychotic shit that happens along the way is not easy. Sometimes the ship goes down."[3] He should know. Not only did he spend his own youth in the Red Hot Chili Peppers, but later witnessed John Frusciante's struggle to cope with *his* growing pains while taking part in a successful rock band.

Alongside the inherent frictions that arise among adolescents, there is the age-irrelevant adjustment to being in a band and what that collective arrangement entails both professionally and personally. For instance, as noted in an earlier chapter, competition was a factor early on in U2 not only because the band's four founders were testosterone-driven teenagers but because it took a while to settle into a certain structure, for the members to feel confident in their roles and to learn how to govern the group jointly. Mike Mills remarks that he and his bandmates did a lot of growing up in the two years between *Murmur* and *Fables of the Reconstruction*. "We were on the road constantly, dealing with what it meant to be a band, and it was a very rugged learning experience."[4] In 1989, Bono stated quite aptly during a press conference that he and his bandmates had spent ten years essentially learning *how to be* in U2 and that they would spend the next decade seeing what U2 can *do*.

PERSONAL MATURATION AND EVOLUTION OF BAND DYNAMICS

One of the advantages of studying the inner workings of rock bands whose core lineup (plus or minus one member) has been in place for more than a decade is that it's possible to examine how the increasing maturity of the parties involved affects the unit. Adam Clayton notes that the relations within U2 have changed dramatically with the passing years primarily because they have all mellowed and developed greater self-assurance. "I think there's much more acceptance and understanding of people's positive things. And by and large the negative aspects of anyone have actually kind of disappeared as people matured."[5] They are also much more secure in themselves, he noted in another *Hot Press* interview (1998).

The result, according to Edge, is that they don't argue over every little thing anymore. But, by Bono's account, it hasn't gotten any easier to get along with one another or maintain their togetherness as they've grown older because with age you "lose the malleability" to fit around others.[6] That's why, he contends, during the 1990s, the band members became too independent of each other and had to rediscover how to be close. These conflicting observations suggest that the personal aging process can be simultaneously conducive and detrimental to concord and unity. Mike Mills seems to focus on its positive aspects. Things are calmer now that the R.E.M. clan is older, he told *Rolling Stone* in 1994, noting that the band members haven't so much changed as their personalities have solidified, which likely translates into less volatility in the group's inner workings.

If there's any band whose members have evolved significantly, it's the Red Hot Chili Peppers—and they make no bones about it, nor about the impact this has had on their relations, which have gone from legendarily dysfunctional to enviably harmonious. Flea speaks frequently of his own and bandmate Kiedis' metamorphosis over the past few years. In a 2002 *Kerrang!* feature, Flea admitted that he's learned to cope with his anger instead of flying off the handle as he used to do. He confided to *Oor* that he has, in fact, spent a decade striving to become someone he can like, an inner search his bandmates also embarked on around the time of *Californication*, he reckons, adding that their mutual bond has grown stronger as a direct result of these efforts. "Anthony is getting nicer as well, even humbler," says the singer's longtime pal. "He has really shed his ego now and is much more considerate of the world around him."[7] In another interview from this period, Flea again drew attention to his friend's positive transformation. "Anthony's changed like crazy. He realizes the power he has to hurt people or to nurture them. Before, you never knew—one day he was your friend, the next day he wasn't."[8]

Describing the negative aspects of his character unsparingly in his autobiography, Kiedis readily confesses that his controlling and self-centered nature often interfered with the band's operation, as did his insecurities (which Rick Rubin incidentally informed *LA Weekly* have, by and large, disappeared). He now realizes how tough it must have been for the others to be in a band with him when he thought he had all the answers and that everyone in the group should fall in line with his actions. For him, the art of acceptance meant coming to terms with the fact that his bandmates react to various developments in their own way, he told *Celebrity Café*. His big faux pas lay in failing to understand how they could behave differently from himself in certain situations. "Just accept that people deal with things from their own place. That allows the band to keep existing," is the conclusion his "big learning curve" has led him to.[9]

He is especially aware of the part he played in driving Frusciante from the band, owning up to the fact that he behaved very callously towards the sensitive guitarist and that he abused their friendship in certain ways. The singer confided to *Australian Rolling Stone* in 2002 that he learned a lot about how to treat people from that relationship. By all accounts, Thom Yorke—the self-confessed erstwhile tyrant—is also treating his partners in a more conciliatory and regardful manner.

OUTGROWING DELETERIOUS COLLECTIVE PRACTICES

Each band has outgrown certain collective practices and tendencies that once destabilized the unit. Many specific problems were documented in previous chapters, so this section is, by default, more of a summary. In the Red Hot Chili Peppers, there used to be battles of ego and pride, unacknowledged competitiveness, cliquishness, grudge-holding, and a noxious tendency for members to get caught up in themselves and their own concerns (to the exclusion of everything going on around them) that all contributed to the band's once less-than-healthy internal environment.

The older and wiser Chili Peppers conduct themselves, in a word, more selflessly, which has eliminated many of the relationship issues they struggled with in the past. They claim to now show great concern for and tend to one another's happiness far more than they ever did in the past. This new mode of operation is in stark contrast to their erstwhile me-centered, narcissistic and inconsiderate attitude. It goes without saying that the group's drug-free lifestyle has also had a positive effect on its internal dynamics. Flea admitted to *Kerrang!* (2002) that he also had, in the past, a recurring habit of floating off or being mentally absent from the group. But now that he is aware of the cost to the Chili Peppers, he is making a bigger effort to be there in mind and spirit, as well as body, at all times. The same can be said of Kiedis, who, as we saw, let his bouts of psychosis interfere, on occasion, with his full participation in the band and admitted in an *MTV.com* interview (1999) that he hasn't always been very present in the group.

The Radiohead quintet has learned to tone down the hysteria and curb the propensity to overreact that, on more than one occasion, led to major falling-outs or a near split. They took everything too seriously, from the ramifications of the hype surrounding "Creep" to their inability to agree on a common direction when it came time to record the follow-up to *OK Computer* (and the fear that that they had exhausted the band's ideas which it instilled in them). "We had a lot of growing up to do," Yorke admitted in retrospect.[10] Excessive intensity also made U2 a more volatile outfit during its formative period. Edge recounts a show during which Bono attacked Mullen and his drum kit after the latter stopped playing due to technical problems. "Everything we did, it was like our lives depended on it," the guitarist proffers as an explanation for this over-the-top strife-inducing behavior.[11]

On the whole, R.E.M. and U2 appear to have had fewer bad habits to turf. Most of their internal frictions stemmed from creative disagreements or trying circumstances rather than standard conduct injurious to the group. The relations in all four bands seem to have improved or remained relatively amicable over decades, whereas many of their predecessors, some of whom define band-hood (The Beatles, The Byrds, Cream, Pink Floyd, Fleetwood Mac, The Police, The Smiths, to name a few), started out on relatively good footing, but saw their relationships (creative and personal) deteriorate with the passing years. In short, the amelioration trajectory is rather unusual as bands go. The next few sections look specifically at some of the contributing factors in terms of beneficial collective habits the groups have formed, as opposed to imprudent ones they've left behind.

Improved communication skills

Collectively, as opposed to personally, the members of all four bands claim, not surprisingly, that they have developed better communication skills over the years, which, more than anything else, has helped the group run smoothly. However, the communication problems that needed fixing were different for each band. Since they lacked musical training and the appropriate terminology with which to express their ideas, the members of U2 couldn't discuss the music calmly during the group's early years, making collaboration a strained affair. "We fistfight over the music. We don't speak over the music. Remember, we were 14, 15, 16 when we met and we didn't even have any [musical] vocabulary," explained Bono in 1992. "Now we are learning to communicate to each other without throwing the drum kit into the audience or gagging the singer."[12]

As noted in earlier sections of the book, the five friends in Radiohead were reluctant to speak their minds or confront issues squarely, so they have had to learn to be more open with one another. When they *were* actually addressing concerns, they had a problem being direct with each other. This was partly because of their reserve and desire not to fight, but also on account of their insecurities. Candor wasn't possible so long as they took every comment personally and consequently felt compelled to pussyfoot around each other. "But now we do speak our mind, and we know it's not going to be anything personal."[13] These days, they have the confidence to be straight with one another. Everything is on a more realistic footing now, Selway proclaimed in *Melody Maker* (2000). Incidentally, this is one communication problem U2 never seemed to have. Edge told *Trouser Press* back in 1983 that there are no sensitive or vulnerable relationships in U2 precisely because the members are *not* afraid of speaking frankly to one another.

The communication breakdown that plagued R.E.M. after Berry left gave way to a new brand of unrestricted forthrightness. Even more so than before, they fearlessly call each other on questionable behavior (like Lead Singer Syndrome) all the time now, Stipe revealed to *People* in 2003. Buck claims that another significant hump they had to get over was that, having been in R.E.M. for over two decades, they had fallen into the habit of neglecting to speak their mind. One consequence of knowing one another for so many years, he explains, is that "you tend to sometimes skip saying the things you need to say and I think we kind of figured out, with some help, that you have to say what you mean."[14] He remarked in *The Los Angeles Times* (2003) that, though the band had been together so long, there was, in fact, a lot that they had never expressed to one another, and that came as something of a surprise to them. It took the deterioration of their relationships after Berry left to make them realize that there had been gaps in their communication all along (a situation they were now able to rectify).

For the Chili Peppers, significant changes on the communication front have involved not letting issues slide and not getting so self-engrossed that they can't relate to one another. "At this point, we all are very aware of each other and we all want the others to be happy, so if there's any weird energy sensed by anybody we try and get to the bottom of it," says Frusciante.[15] This concern for one another and determination to keep the air clean is what keeps them together, he asserts. They've stopped holding grudges, get over things more quickly and now realize they need to discuss problems that arise in their relationship before they fester insidiously inside them.

Of course, communication is a two-way street. Listening to others is as essential as verbalizing one's own sentiments, and it's another skill the members of Radiohead have struggled to acquire. During a 1998 Much-Music interview, Selway sounded off about how much more effectively they were working as a unit since learning how to really listen to each other. Kiedis states in his memoirs that the Chili Peppers have also developed this ability over the years, whereas each of them used to be too caught up in himself to genuinely listen to his bandmates.

FIGURING OUT AND
UNDERSTANDING ONE ANOTHER

The band members tend to figure one another out as time goes by, so behavior that may have led to friction at some point becomes less contentious once the motives are clear. Some of Bono's actions, such as his highly symbolic (but often controversial) stage antics and his tendency to embroider stories instead of sticking to the facts, used to bother him, Edge admitted in 1985, quickly adding, "I've learned about Bono recently." He grasped, essentially, that Bono cares more about having an effect by telling a good story than he does about accuracy. "And now," said the guitarist, "I've applied that to what he's like onstage and I feel a little more happy. In some sort of intuitive way, not in a cynical way, he's very aware of performance and whether it's powerful and effective. He's not really worried about justifying it, it's always heartfelt, but he will always intuitively go for the thing that works."[16] In short, understanding Bono made the singer's previously maddening actions more acceptable to Edge.

CONFIDENCE IN AND
APPRECIATION OF THE BAND

With the passage of time, U2 and Radiohead developed faith in the band that they didn't have at first. According to Edge, this strengthened the foursome's commitment to the alliance, which had wavered in the early '80s, because at least they no longer had doubts about its merit. Confidence helped Radiohead relax, making the group less volatile. The longer the group exists, the more the musicians also seem to appreciate it. Edge and his partners realize how rare it is to be in a great rock band and that's been an important lesson for them. "None of us is taking that for granted right now."[17] The decades behind U2 shape its current dynamics, Clayton commented in *The Sunday Times* (2004), because looking back on what the band has achieved increases the members' perception of its value. That's another reason the group is operating more harmoniously than in the past, concludes the bassist. Having been in R.E.M. since he was 19, Stipe says he has come to regard it as his life's work, and cherishes the partnership accordingly. Like the Chili Peppers, he and his bandmates are grateful for every day they are still together because they came so close to disbanding.

BANDS JUST WANNA HAVE FUN

Another noticeable trend, as irrelevant as it may seem, is that the four bands have, over time, placed an increasing emphasis on enjoying themselves—usually once they've firmly established their position and can afford to relax a bit and do as they please. Asked in 2004 on Triple J how the older Radiohead differs from the younger one, Jonny Greenwood replied that they now appreciate what they do and have more fun doing it. His brother Colin confirmed in *The Age* that fun, which didn't seem to be in the British quintet's vocabulary once upon a time, has become a key term in the band's operation.

By now, says Peter Buck, being in R.E.M. is mostly fun—even taking into consideration the occasional blip, like the *Up* slog. "We're able to do away with the things that are less fun the longer we go at it," is his explanation (similar to Yorke's stating during a radio interview that they want to jettison the dull aspects of being in Radiohead as they go along).[18] Indeed, when the trio convened to start work on *Reveal*, making the process enjoyable was their primary concern. There's no band having more fun than U2, Bono declared in 2001, and while fun was in short supply in the Chili Peppers for most of the '90s, they've been having a blast since Frusciante returned to the fold and, like R.E.M., are making an effort to ensure that the band never again feels like a job. It's obviously much easier to cooperate with one another under these circumstances, so band relations tend to improve when fun is high on the list of priorities.

Part II: The implications of longevity

SUSTAINING THE EXCITEMENT
OF THE PARTNERSHIP

Keeping the excitement alive and the partnership inspiring is one of the principal tests of an enduring collaboration. Since the enthusiasm—whether for the band or making music or both—tends to weaken when youth and novelty are no longer fueling it, it has to be deliberately buoyed. This is a subject to which Peter Buck repeatedly draws attention. "The way to manufacture it for us," says Buck, "is to keep things liquid and keep them really fluid."[19] While he and Mills claim that they continue to find the act of songwriting exhilarating, their interest in the three-way partnership is proactively maintained by diversifyng their individual projects, abstaining from grinding tours, and most importantly, taking risks and exploring a wide variety of musical terrains.

Being too sure of what you're doing is the kiss of death, according to the members of these bands, so despite the temptation for established acts to play it safe, they must actively court a certain level of artistic confusion and precariousness—primarily by constantly breaking new ground. "We don't care about what we did last year or the year before. We care about what we're doing now. We want to find new cosmic beasts," declares Anthony Kiedis, adding that the Chili Peppers have no intention of revisiting their past and, indeed, thrive on uncertainty.[20] His bandmate, Chad Smith, spoke in *Batteur* about the importance of avoiding routines and promoting spontaneity in keeping the partnership vital. In Chapter 8 the difficulty of changing sonic directions as a group was discussed at length. But, like a landmark album, an extended career often makes these shifts necessary. Having been in Radiohead for 15 years, it would have been pointless to carry on in the vein of *OK Computer* or *The Bends*, remarked Phil Selway in an effort to justify the fairly dramatic artistic transition represented by *Kid A* and *Amnesiac*. This was a juncture at which Radiohead, like U2 around the time of *Achtung Baby*, wondered if there was any point carrying on, unless the band could find new ground to cover.

It's a catch-22 in some cases, as these bands need to frequently change course for their collective endeavors to retain their vitality and sparkle, but the partnership itself can be prohibitive, making radical departures tricky. "Radiohead is very challenging," contends Selway. "You are working with the same people you've been working with since school. Not that we've become set in our ways, but it can be a little difficult to see other ways at some points."[21] Colin Greenwood made a similar statement in *The New York Times Upfront*, indicating that it's getting harder for the group to do anything new because they've been together so long. The Chili Peppers have largely been spared this dilemma because of the procession of guitarists that have graced the group's lineup. They've been accidentally helped along, says Kiedis, by having different musicians in the band over the years, "which presents a whole new, exciting set of circumstances to write music under."[22] Tellingly, in 2003 the singer remarked that he feels as if he's just joined the band, partly, it's safe to assume, because their sonic orientation has changed substantially and partly because the collaboration with Frusciante is relatively fresh. R.E.M. seems to have experienced something of a rebirth upon becoming a trio. "It's nice to be confused, especially after all this time," Buck commented in 1998, hinting at how problematic it can be for an inveterate band to reach this surprisingly enviable state.[23]

THE ELEMENT OF SURPRISE

Despite knowing each other intimately, it's crucial that the relationships between the band members don't become trite and monotonous.

"I don't think we're that predictable as people," says Buck. "One of the reasons we're still together is we tend to surprise one another."[24] When asked by Michka Assayas if he finds his three bandmates predictable by now, Bono replied that what keeps him interested in working with them is their sly sense of humor and an integrity that never ceases to astonish him (in other words, a circuitous "no"). Colin Greenwood once denied that this is the case in Radiohead. "We've known each other for a ridiculous amount of years so nothing surprises me anymore," he stated in 1993.[25] If his assessment is accurate, this is not a feature the members of Radiohead, unlike the R.E.M. crew, deem vital to the band's durability.

To sustain their passion for the alliance on a professional level, the band members must display a continuous ability to foil the expectations of their partners. It's simple: if someone's ideas and manner of playing become too wonted, the collaboration ceases to be electrifying. "I Don't Sleep, I Dream" is a track Buck cites as a specific example of how deliciously incalculable he finds his bandmates' approaches. He figured that Stipe would come up with something "very amorphous" for the simple one-chord jam and was bowled over when the singer presented him with "this really concise, melodic thing over the top that totally changed the song."[26] The guitarist told *Melody Maker* in 1992 that they get very excited at the mere thought of surprising one another with unexpected or uncharacteristic material. Edge, too, feels that his bandmates have a unique ability to surprise him when they're making music together. In the *Chicago Sun Times*, he called Clayton the most avant-garde and unorthodox musician in the group, who always comes up with a part no one else would have thought of in their wildest dreams. Mullen, meanwhile, dumbfounds them with his musical clairvoyance and gift for nailing his parts with one take. Often, while the other three deliberate about a piece, Mullen will play something that turns out to be precisely what it required, and thereby sews the song together with a single stroke—to the amazement of his bandmates. Bono is a fount of unexpected ideas. Musical wild cards (as Adam Clayton, Jonny Greenwood and Bill Berry are reputed to be) are thus a particularly valuable asset to the group in terms of preserving its appeal.

In addition to certain deliberate attempts to fan the flame, these bands possess inherent features that do their part in preventing the alliance from becoming stale. The mysterious chemistry is one. "There's something really unusual and magical that happens when we start playing," notes Anthony Kiedis. "And it's something that doesn't diminish, doesn't get boring or old."[27] In a long-term collaboration, witnessing the artistic growth of one's partners is also highly stimulating. These infusions of ardor play an important part in sustaining the musicians' zest for the job and the group. And, often, when one member of the group is fired up, it reinvigorates everyone, as was the case when U2 recorded *All That You Can't Leave Behind* and the whole group was inspired by Edge's "rediscovery" of the guitar. Since reuniting with music fanatic John Frusciante, all the Chili Peppers feel renewed passion for the band. Finally, it's likely that the band provides a broad enough artistic scope— within the limitations of an enclosed unit—to maintain the members' zeal on account of their highly divergent creative points of view. "The only real constraint, creatively, is ourselves—and that's enough," says Stipe, implying that there's plenty of room to maneuver nonetheless by noting in the next sentence that he and his bandmates are very different from one another.[28]

DOES IT GET ANY EASIER?

Harmony aside, does being in the band get easier as the years add up? Not according to Edge, who informed *USA Today* in 2002 that it gets harder as you get older and conveyed to *Revolver* that only the work justifies the difficulties of being in a band in one's thirties and forties. Bono, meanwhile, avers that U2 has not become "warm and fuzzy," that there's still plenty of hardship and conflict involved.[29] The group's bass player takes a similar stance, contending that U2 is "as difficult as ever. I don't think it ever suddenly becomes easy." He adds: "You still have to work as hard to complete things."[30] Peter Buck sides with Edge, claiming that R.E.M. has become *more* challenging with time. "It's easy to be a band when you're 20, when you're first starting out, because you're all just full of energy." But later on, when everyone is an adult, he says "getting together and inventing something, and compromising something" isn't as easy.[31] In 1996, after battling through *Monster*, Buck was so worried by the fact that each album seemed harder than the last one to complete, for this and other reasons, that he was afraid the band would eventually start a record and not be able to finish it. So he suggested informally recording a bunch of tracks on the road (for *New Adventures in Hi-Fi*) to make the process less daunting.

Aside from how difficult it becomes to do something new and bend one's spirit to compromise, the creative process grows increasingly belabored for the individual songwriters, claims Buck, and therefore for the group as a whole. When he and his partners were in their early twenties, they knocked out new tunes quickly, without thinking about it much, he said in 2003, noting how timorous they have become in comparison. "We did something in half an hour and that was fine. Nowadays, you tend to work a little harder and you tend to doubt yourself a little bit more."[32]

From one perspective, knowing each other well is a creative advantage due to the musical telepathy (as the Chili Peppers would say) that springs up between longtime collaborators. As Phil Selway declared with respect to Radiohead in 1996, "The intuitive side has benefited very much from ten years of playing together."[33] Speaking for himself, Clayton revealed to *Q* in 2004 that adding his bass parts has become fairly painless of late, compared to how complicated it was in the past, because the band members are so attuned to one another by now. They don't need to talk about their individual chops as much to ensure they complement one another and they don't feel like they have to overplay, he said in an interview with *Bass Player* (2000). That makes it possible to just get on with the task at hand and work on a much more instinctive level.

WORKING TOGETHER LESS FREQUENTLY

Many established bands, especially successful ones, gradually slacken the pace so that they end up working together less frequently than young groups trying to make their way in the business, who are perpetually together. Side ventures and families, in many cases, start taking up more of the members' time, and with the band firmly entrenched at the top, there's no need to work constantly in order to generate momentum, only to maintain its position with the occasional album and clutch of shows. Essentially, then, at some point in a lengthy life cycle, certain bands staffed by older musicians cease being a gang and become something best described as a periodically renewed collaboration—especially if they don't tour extensively anymore. R.E.M. (and an argument can be made for Radiohead as well) fits this model to a large extent, U2 and the Red Hot Chili Peppers slightly less so primarily because they still play the massive live circuit between sporadic releases.

Edge told writer and band confidante B.P. Fallon back in 1992 that the worst part about being in U2 is the pressure to continue, not to let it fizzle out. Presumably, that pressure increases exponentially when the group isn't permanently convened. But, according to members of R.E.M., that hasn't been their experience, though they live apart, have other consuming pursuits and rarely tour the globe. It's not difficult to keep the band going under these circumstances, they claim. They just need to remember to get together every few years to make a record. And, having been in this band for so long, it doesn't take much to maintain their relationship, according to an earlier quote from Stipe. However, the singer draws attention to the fact that the band shouldn't cease being their top priority or be taken lightly—nor should they let less frequent gatherings turn into rare ones. "I do think it's good for us to keep working on a regular basis and not turn this into a kind of hobby. It has to be something important in your life that you work on."[34]

One interesting repercussion is that breaking up is rendered almost irrelevant by this intermittent partnership coupled with abstention from touring. "Except for the fact that we've made two records in the '90s, most people would consider us as having already broken up," Buck acknowledged halfway through the decade, indicating that there is a certain perception of bands that the new R.E.M. doesn't fit and is therefore considered—by some—effectively dissolved.[35] These views don't seem to bother the group. They scarcely had any time off throughout the '80s, says Buck, but they couldn't carry on that way. The band has prevailed precisely because they have backed off from it and given everyone more breathing space. Sometimes it doesn't feel much like a band though, he admits, especially when they've been "off" for a while. It's not the way it is in U2, he remarks. "You feel like the guys in U2 live for it. Every second of their lives is about the band." R.E.M.'s Irish contemporaries have also continued to do "all the stuff that you feel like a band should do," he says, such as (presumably) hanging out together, jamming a lot and touring extensively. But ultimately, he and his partners have found it liberating not to be "really bound by the band thing anymore."[36]

A more irregular band schedule also seems to suit Radiohead. Jonny Greenwood told *The Face* in 2002 that it has a positive outcome because it's both more productive and exciting when they do work as a group than it was when they were always focused on the band. However, on the band's blog site, Dead Air Space, Colin Greenwood logged an entry on August 21, 2005, wherein he mentioned how difficult it is to kickstart the group's momentum after a lengthy break, though it can be creatively healthy to start from scratch because it's easier to avoid covering old ground. It's certainly hard to believe that any member of the British Quintet would now declare that the band represents nearly one hundred percent of his life, as Yorke proclaimed in *Alternative Press* in 1995. No one in either of these outfits is likely to contend that there are no real breaks from the band given their current setup.

Conclusion: band longevity rare

If there's one deposition that few would quibble with, it's that the longevity these bands (including Radiohead, who have been together since their teens) boast is rare. Each group has, in its own way, earned the title of sonic pioneer, but their lasting vital creative alliance and sustained popularity render them trailblazers on a broader scale. Few, if any, bands have been in such a financial, creative and critical situation more than two decades into their career, says Adam Clayton with respect to U2. And, like a snowball, the band—primarily its chemistry and internal bonds—have accumulated power over the years, claims Bono, who said in 2001: "I don't know quite how to explain that to you, but just having been in the band for a while, I've never felt this kind of force."[37] They are in a very unique position as far as their internal dynamics go, considering as their friendships have endured for nearly 30 years and that jealousy, resentment, greed and control issues haven't cropped up over time—which enables them to continue devoting their energy to the music.

Perhaps no one but a member of a band is in a position to really appreciate the achievement that a long-lived alliance of this sort represents. Tipping his hat to a group that's been around nearly a decade longer than his own, Ed O'Brien says, "I love the dynamic of musicians working together and all the voodoo shit that comes with it. It's a complicated thing to do over the expanse of time, which is why I respect U2 so much."[38]

12

"It's the End of the World as We Know It (And I Feel Fine)": Challenges to the Band Paradigm

This chapter describes how various circumstances and pursuits test the collaborative paradigm in these four groups, or to put it simply, make their customary form of collaboration inherently more challenging by introducing factors that are not conducive to it—and ultimately forcing them to develop new ways of working together. R.E.M. is pushing the limits of the collective through geographic dispersal in addition to shifting away from the customary instruments and practices of rock bands, as U2 and Radiohead have done with much greater fanfare. Meanwhile, the Red Hot Chili Peppers have dealt with multiple lineup changes, a condition not favorable to meaningful cooperation. This book began by talking about how the interdependency of musicians, especially in a live setting, promotes groupwork, to which contemporary rock bands like the four profiled herein have given a profound meaning by taking integration to its highest level. Yet these groups have also gone (or been pushed) down paths that clash either with an ensemble approach in general and/or with the close-knit band ideal they helped propagate.

Part I

TRIAL BY ELECTRONICA

At various points in the 1990s, U2, R.E.M. and Radiohead decided to flout the limitations of the traditional four-piece rock band by turning to electronic instruments like synthesizers, drum machines and music-generating software—the type of gear used to produce techno, industrial and dance music. In doing so, they encountered a number of problems in adapting their collective approach to forms of music that don't accommodate it, let alone necessitate it. As producer Nigel Godrich puts it, the British quintet was after a sound that just doesn't tend to be made by bands. The members of Radiohead have gone into great detail about why this switchover was so complicated for them given the group setup. And there were many factors. First of all, working with computers is a rather solitary activity, Ed O'Brien explains. "It's not something that you can all huddle around and do collectively. It's essentially a lonely affair—inevitably, a lot of the stuff starts out with one or two people."[1] Since the five weren't really able to generate electronic music by working together in one room and wanted to steer away from that conventional configuration at any rate, they split into teams—quite often Thom Yorke and Jonny Greenwood in one room, the remaining three in another. Some of the band members had misgivings about being divided by the new aesthetic. But the level and manner of collaboration they had grown accustomed to seemed impossible under the circumstances.

Electronic sound manipulation also renders it almost impossible for the musicians to interact spontaneously and simultaneously. "Somebody's on a computer coming up with something, then everybody reacts to it," O'Brien detailed, adding that an ensemble playing approach (let alone jamming) can be replicated only if the set-up is such that everyone is "firing off" samplers and drum machines at once, which isn't commonly done.[2] In pursuit of more programmed music and with Yorke too lost in his search for a new direction to prepare any material beforehand, the band was obliged to create from scratch in the studio without significant prior rehearsals. Usually, Colin Greenwood stated in *Mojo* (2003), the big studio record turns out to be a disaster. As many groups have learned the hard way, there's enough pressure in the studio without the added weight of manufacturing the material. Occasionally that can be stimulating, says Selway, but more often than not, it's just daunting. That's when groups tend to become mired in a chaotic process, frustrated by the lack of progress and finally, turn on each other—basically what happened to Radiohead (except that the band emerged intact).

Perhaps the most consequential upshot of working in this genre was that traditional instruments weren't required (at least initially), effectively annulling everyone's sanctioned role in the group. The fundamental band blueprint had been rendered inapposite, so each of the members was left to grope in search of his function within the vastly altered outfit. O'Brien unabashedly confided that he didn't feel he had a role to play, and some of his bandmates—the other pair who were very skeptical about the new process—were no less discombobulated. "Phil, Colin and I went through some major dilemmas at various stages. How could we contribute to this new music? We all wondered if it wasn't better to just walk away. It was a very scary thing at first."[3] Not being a multi-instrumentalist, O'Brien revealed on *Planet Sound,* the boycott on guitars came as a real blow for him. Not only was he not sure what he should be doing, but he couldn't actually *do* anything else. He later admitted that feeling like he had no part in the sessions was "massively depressing."[4]

Eventually, O'Brien and the other members of the band learned to use the gear demanded by the group's latest sonic aspirations—a situation that harkened back to Radiohead's early days, when they were figuring out their instruments together. The main difference between the two periods was that, until they found their feet this time, the three felt sidelined. In other words, quite often it didn't seem like a poetic communal apprenticeship, but like an impossible test of one cell in the group by the controlling faction. Colin Greenwood compared the experience to being an "underpowered" middle-manager in a shoe company whose bosses are trying to edge him out by setting him up to fail. "So they tell you they're moving you to Tokyo and you have to learn Japanese in a week, or else. And you're on the language course, and you haven't got a hope in hell, but you have a go."[5] At times, he added, that glimmer of hope made them stick around, and at their lowest moments, they hung in out of a sense of duty.

It should be pointed out that this was merely the trio's impression at the time, and not one that Yorke or Greenwood intended to produce. The singer seems to have been largely unaware of his partners' fears, probably because he never did consider the other musicians gratuitous or think he was ahead of anyone else. It was a learning curve for all of them, he insists. "It wasn't like I was standing there waiting for everybody to catch up."[6] So the only real (though purely circumstantial) test inherent in the transition to an electronic aesthetic was whether a guitarist or drummer's ego could survive the musical castration it entailed. What made the experience different for Yorke (and to some extent, Jonny Greenwood) as compared with the three remaining members of the band is that while they felt crippled, the singer felt, from the start, *empowered* by casting off the familiar (including many of his own roles)— it's what he sought at all costs.

He may not have realized, fully, what a dilemma his partners were in, banned as they were from their instruments. They were even more lost with their leader not playing his usual part in providing the group with demos or lyrics to kickstart the process. This time, he simply didn't have a plot (aside from avoiding anything that sounded like the 'old'

Radiohead), so, ultimately, the others didn't know which instruments to play *nor to what end.* "Even when guitars were needed, I was bereft with ideas about what to play," O'Brien reflected.[7] The subsequent months-long stalemate, accentuated by this profound sense of displacement and aimlessness, was soul sapping, Colin Greenwood observed.

With a completely revamped methodology and corresponding roles to be defined (or left undefined), the group went through a lengthy term of what amounted to a substantial internal restructuring. As Phil Selway described it in *The Toronto Sun* (2000), it largely came down to finding the pith—or what it is about the creative relationship between the five of them that produces great music—then, presumably, applying that within a radically different paradigm for the same effect (kind of like a marrow transplant). It was no simple feat. According to *The Wire*, Ed O'Brien's online diaries charting Radiohead's progress draw a picture of "a group almost tearing itself to pieces in the struggle to achieve total aesthetic renewal."[8] In addition to mastering unfamiliar equipment and deciding what kind of music they actually want to make with it (while in the studio), the quintet had to develop new collaborative practices in accordance with its new musical orientation, one which doesn't really accommodate the ensemble approach. Is it any wonder the sessions were stormy? From Thom Yorke to Nigel Godrich, neither Radiohead members nor their accomplices have minced meat about the fact that this venture was punctuated by a lot of arguing, drama, confusion and general insanity.

Although U2 had been creating with studio tools since Brian Eno took the producer's chair in 1984, *Achtung Baby* marked the band's first serious foray into computer- and machine generated sounds. They took this aesthetic further on *Zooropa,* and then to an extreme on the avant-garde and spacey *Passengers* and the techno-influenced *Pop.* The idea, explained Edge in numerous interviews, was to explore the outer limits of what a band can do and abstract the whole idea of a rock group. Their usual instruments weren't off-limits and the band wasn't nearly in the same disarray as Radiohead, but as the Irish quartet delved further and further into dance-inspired drum-loops in particular, Larry Mullen, quite naturally, contemplated the possibility that the machines would render him obsolete.

Asked if Mullen thought he was being fazed out of the band, Edge allowed that the drummer had experienced some anxiety on that score, not because his position had ever really been endangered but on account of the territorial instinct that comes with being in a collective of this sort. "I think we all guard our corner of what it is to be in U2 quite jealously, and I think Larry might have felt a little threatened when we started using drum machines," although, emphasized the guitarist, they never considered touring or recording without him.[9] Adam Clayton admitted to *Q* in 2002 that he, too, felt somewhat insecure about his position and, at times, uncomfortable with where the band was heading because of the possible implications for the collaboration and its output. As in Radiohead's case, the transition to a new medium involved a great deal of conflict and confusion. An expression used by members of both bands to describe the shifts and unsettlement their group underwent is that everything, including their established relationships with one another, was "up for grabs."

What did it take for each band to overcome the trials it faced at this juncture? Ed O'Brien believes that he and his bandmates had simply reached a level of personal maturity that enabled them to surrender their "corner." At the age of 32, one ought to able to let go of his ego, but had they tried this when they were just 22, he, for one, would have likely "gone off in a sulk."[10] Edge talked in *Hot Press* (2002) about an unshakeable commitment to the collective and strong sense of togetherness as U2's saving grace in situations that put the band's collaborative structure to the test. Above all, radical shifts of this nature, especially those that can potentially dispense with the usual mode of collaboration, demand that every member of the group feel secure in the realization that his value to it depends on more than his ability to throw in a bass line or some other instrumental bit.

BREAKTHROUGHS

Meaningful breakthroughs in going the electronica route *as a band* put an end to the turmoil in Radiohead. To use Ed O'Brien's oft-quoted account, they learned how to be a participant in a song without playing a single note—and that changed everything. The very notion of being a band member was evolving, journalist Gerald Marzorati wrote in a *New York Times Upfront* article. What counted now were taste and ideas for song arrangement and direction. It did, however, take a while for everyone to feel comfortable with tracks they hadn't played on, O'Brien admits. "You know the nature of bands; you want to put *your* thing in. But sometimes on this record you just didn't. You were part of the production committee, if you like, and you talked openly about what you thought about the song, but you might not necessarily play on it. It's a really good place to get to."[11]

Phil Selway agrees that, once he put his personal anxiety aside, the new methodology was very liberating and all the hurdles had been worthwhile in order to get to a more enlightened place as artistic partners. The goal is to take the definition of a band beyond musicians playing and writing music together, putting the emphasis on other creative functions they perform in unison. "We're working towards the idea that we work almost as a production or creative team, and the important thing is making the decisions, rather than us trying to stamp our individual voices all over it."[12] Roles would now be determined mainly by the requirements of the song rather than vice versa. As Jonny Greenwood spelled out in *Undercover*, the idea is to play any instrument (or use any device) one is capable of if the song demands it. It's a loose role structure Radiohead has been moving towards for years, and the *Kid A* sessions provided the real breakthrough. Recognizing a collective achievement of another sort, in addition to this evolution as a unit, shored up the besieged sense of bandhood in Radiohead. "I think we managed somehow to bend the machines to our will—that's what we did together, as a band," Colin Greenwood boasts.[13] But, having admitted that certain members weren't involved in some of the tracks on the album and that Thom Yorke largely drove the proceedings, the band had to make it a point to stress to the media that it isn't a glorified solo album, that they all, in fact, contributed.

LESSONS AND DISCOVERIES

Like all experiments, those set in motion by U2 and Radiohead led to a series of discoveries. Although they first felt cast adrift without their bit of ground to stand on and the sense of security provided by the long-standing band setup, the Radiohead clan learned that defending one's own "musical patch," as Yorke refers to it, is simply restrictive.[14] According to Nigel Godrich, they also realized that forcibly imposing an external aesthetic on the music generally fails (i.e., the song should dictate the treatment). Meanwhile, staring at laptops and twiddling knobs proved to be far less exciting and rewarding than playing in a more traditional fashion as a band, Yorke admitted in *The Chicago Tribune*, claiming that the process got quite boring at times.

For both groups, the most important finding pertains to what it means to be in a rock band. To boil it down to a single statement: they grasped the inimitable value of the collective. "We discovered that there are certain tasks that you have to do on your own, but basically, the best stuff comes out of collaboration with other people," Yorke testified.[15] In 2003, he went on to say that they had developed tremendous confidence in the band and are into celebrating the way they play together as a unit. Recorded at the same time as *Kid A*, the group's subsequent release, *Amnesiac*, featured a mix of band arrangements and programmed tracks, since the musicians ultimately ended up alternating between the two approaches. On the next LP, *Hail to the Thief*, Radiohead successfully married the distinct mediums on many of the tracks. Of course, for live shows, all the songs that had been created with studio tools—and not always in a communal fashion—had to be "translated" into a format which allowed them to be performed by the full contingent.

On *Pop*, U2 realized it had taken the foreign formats too far and that the band sound is more precious than any other. With Mullen recovering from a back injury, it seemed like a perfect opportunity to actually build songs up from samples and drum loops. As Flood pointed out in *Q* (2002), this was the first time, even with all the experimentation the band had previously engaged in, that the tracks hadn't been grounded in the four musicians playing together in a room. That threw off the album and its creators, who, partway through the album, suddenly longed to recover the element that was obviously missing from the music: the group. The machines were taking over, obliterating the band and the very qualities that made it U2.

An uncharacteristic lack of vitality and spontaneity had crept into the music, so the quartet tried to revert to ensemble playing. In fact, the band approach proved to be the most interesting treatment for almost all the tracks, says Edge. "We always knew that was what was special about anything we would release, but we went on quite a roundabout journey to come back to some essential U2 arrangements and productions."[16] The organic sound, he told *Guitar Player*, is what made their outfit unique in the first place, and it now became clear that it should never be taken for granted or absented from the music. "We're a band, we have something that we must protect," was the lesson Bono imparted in 1997, adding that electronica can inform their work but should never overpower it.[17]

The group's attention shifted squarely back to the collaboration at its core, in a desire to unleash its power. "Previously, we would have been exploring the outer limits of what a band can do as a band, where the band could go as a band and still hold the center. Now we're happy to explore the center, what it's all about, the band itself, what it can do," explained Edge.[18] There are certain feels and sounds that only a band can produce, he notes, and would likely agree that U2's music is even more distinctive because it's the product of a group graced by a special alchemy and long history. Indeed, while Edge tended to talk about rediscovering the essence of the four-piece rock band in general, Bono typically referred to delving into the heart of U2 specifically. Mullen and Clayton play their instruments so differently from all their counterparts, he pointed out in an interview with *CDNow.com*, and Edge is unlike any other guitarist. It's that unparalleled combination—the thing that separates them from all other outfits—that the singer became intrigued with plumbing. No longer were they envious of dance music's seemingly infinite possibilities, but ready to rejoice in and exploit the comparative limitations of a rock band, *their* band.

U2's next two albums captured the musicians' hungry return to the basic four-piece rock band format. (Their own feelings aside, there wasn't really any alternative, admits Edge, as they had taken the band as far in the other direction as it could go.) They were thrilled to "discover it was still inspiring to work together in a very simple way, where the chemistry of the musicians playing together was really the glue, and the idea behind the sessions and the songs came out of simply playing together."[19] In the end, the guitarist remarked, their chemistry is what the band has to offer that can't be imitated, so they started pushing it back to the forefront of the music. It had been a long time since the band had collaborated this way (simply playing as an ensemble), Mullen observed in *Revolver* in 2000, and it felt odd at first, but they were relieved to see the old spark return. They made what they call a band-centric record, meaning that the foundation of the tracks was laid down by the four members writing and playing together (as opposed to writing songs using electronic gear and then trying to superimpose a band arrangement over them). Albums like this have a distinct feel, insists Edge, implying that the methodology—or more precisely, the collective effort—comes through in the material.

What great rock bands have in abundance is personality, a distinct identity. Once they start dabbling in electronica they dilute or efface it, contend critics of such experimentation. Edge agrees that it's practically impossible to carry through the band's personality when the musicians go down the sampling and programming route. "You might persuade yourself that you're doing that but there's something about the here and now, the actual performance of the musicians unadulterated, which is at the core of what a band is."[20] U2 came close to losing to technology what's special about the band, Mullen corroborated in *Reverberation*, which is why they had to pull back. While Thom Yorke agrees that electronic elements de emphasize personalities, he seems to believe that Radiohead's identity inevitably brands the music, no matter what equipment is involved in creating it. "*Kid A* and *Amnesiac* was [sic] us trawling around finding other things to do—but saying that, the end result is always us. We could trawl around for years, and still sound like us."[21]

The middle road U2 has opted for is to combine the best of both worlds, using electronic tools to embellish tracks laid down in a more conventional fashion by the band. By and large, Radiohead seems to have done the same. Both groups insist they wouldn't have reached this stage without first going through a more radical exploration of technology. That's doesn't seem to be the case in the Chili Peppers. The band has an interest in electronica, says Frusciante, but he maintains that going more than half-way is basically out of the question. He told *Wall of Sound* in 2001 that the band is toying with the idea of incorporating more programmed elements on a future album, but that it would be a waste for him and his three partners to make music that is predominantly electronic on account of their sheer talent as musicians and the inimitable way they play together.

THE FUTURE OF BANDS

One of the reasons underlying both U2 and Radiohead's electronica turn was the belief that this is the cutting-edge sound, and that the rock band product (even at its most contemporary) sounds tired in comparison. "While the band format is still valid, the really exciting things going on in music now are created in people's bedrooms," Ed O'Brien stated in 2001.[22] U2 eventually rationalized their return to the more conventional four-piece methodology by contending that it sounded radical and progressive to their ears as the airwaves became increasingly crammed with manufactured music and the electronic age marched forward. Drawing attention to a surprising reversal, Bono noted in 2001 that, suddenly, bands sound futuristic and machines old-fashioned. During a *Yahoo!* chat, he claimed that what's become a rare commodity is "the presence of humanity and the feeling of people in a room playing off each other."[23] The group that, more than any other, had come to represent bandhood thus proudly declared that it has faith in the future and continuing relevance of these collectives.

Part II

TRIAL BY TRIO

R.E.M.'s collaborative paradigm was shaken to the core when Bill Berry departed in 1997 and the three remaining musicians decided not to hire another drummer in his place—putting an end to the traditional and clear-cut band lineup. Lineup changes usually involve adjusting to a new band member, but in R.E.M., the three remaining musicians had to adapt to working with *one another* within a new band structure very different from the one they were familiar with. The basic system the unit had relied upon to write and record music for nearly two decades was no longer valid in the context of the ambiguous outfit the members were left with. Berry's shell-shocked partners didn't sit down to discuss how they would function as a trio or how their group dynamic would be affected before launching into sessions for a new album because they simply didn't know what awaited them. They just dealt with issues as they came up and figured out how to work together as they went along. In retrospect, claims Mills, it might have been wiser had they reconstructed their working relationship and only then resumed their career because going through such a serious transition in a high-pressure studio situation proved hellish.

As they quickly learned, the most fundamental change was that they couldn't generate or lay down material through performance (the sacred playing-in-a-room-together), since it's practically impossible to do that without a drummer. On their own, a guitarist and bassist can do little in the way of rehearsing and live tracking, Buck often reiterated. "R.E.M. always prided ourselves on the fact the four us could walk in a room play a song, walk out, and it'd sound like a finished record," he remarked in 1998. "You know, no overdubs, no extra side musicians. But we couldn't do that this time around."[24] Instead, Mills and Buck cut rough demos of songs in their individual home studios, and when they convened to work on them, pieced together the final tracks by layering elements on top of one another.

Ultimately, then, there were only a couple of tracks on which more than one musician played at one time, and the group struggled to collaborate in this unfamiliar fashion. "It was real non-performance oriented, and that's an equally valid way of making records," said Buck, "but I'm used to getting people together in a room and feeling each other out. There wasn't a huge amount of that."[25] Normally, he, Mills and Berry would improvise, without much call for discussion, and the songs—or whatever part was missing from a piece one of them had brought in—would essentially write themselves. "Without all of that structure, with Bill gone, not sitting there cueing each other, nodding at each other, it was kind of like Alice in Wonderland."[26] R.E.M. had already been gravitating towards programmed music when Berry decided to trade in his drumstool for a tractor seat, but, as a drummerless three-piece unit, the band had little choice but to employ non-human replacements. The music embodied the new methodology, not only because it pushed computerized strands (which the band had always used to add color and texture) to the forefront but because the musicians found it very difficult to really rock without being able to play together and because of their heavier reliance on machines. That's why the songs were moodier, and more static, the guitarist explained to *Newsweek*.

For R.E.M, there had never been any rules governing how they create, Buck told *The New York Times* in 1998, except that, if you're a four-piece band, you operate as a four-piece. Once they no longer had to abide by that dictum, there were no limitations on their collaboration at all—and the group felt very liberated by this surprising turn of events. "We are more of a collective now than a rock band. We could do anything. There's potential to really push the boundaries," gushed Stipe in 1997.[27] As such, the group's role structure, which wasn't very rigid any-

how due to the musicians' practice of instrument-swapping, collapsed
entirely in Berry's absence. On *Up*, neither Mills nor Buck occupied their
customary stations. Ultimately, then, the band's eleventh album was
experimental on every level, but particularly from a co-writing perspective.

    Confusion remained even after the band managed to finish it—there
was still so much to sort out. "I'm not sure how we'd play this stuff live,"
wondered the guitarist shortly after the LP was released. "I mean, I played
all the bass on the record, so am I now the bass player? Does that mean
Mike's the keyboard player and we'll have to hire a guitar player too?"[28]
They had defined the album somehow, but not the parameters of the
new R.E.M. nor how the trio could stage a tour. Redesigning the band
would be a longer and more complicated process than anyone had anticipated. Eventually, the three certified band members teamed up with
some of Buck's Seattle buddies to flesh out their collective sound both
inside and outside the studio, although R.E.M. is still a closed shop as
far as songwriting goes. On the group's next album, *Reveal*, R.E.M., like
U2, returned to the performance style of writing and recording, playing
together as a six-piece with guest musicians.

Part III

TRIAL BY DISPERSAL

    This internal revolution followed in the wake of the major adjust-
ments R.E.M. had to make after Peter Buck moved to Seattle a few years
earlier. As far as collaboration goes, what could be a greater spanner in
the works than the dispersal of the collaborators? In this case, the uncommon geographic distance between the band members represented a particularly poignant inversion. The foursome had, after all, occupied the
same house when the band first formed and later had separate dwellings,
but in and around the relatively small community of Athens. Their collective habits reflected their proximity to one another during R.E.M.'s
first decade. They would often go to someone's house or to the band's
offices/rehearsal space and write songs together when they all lived in
the same town. Indeed, Buck told author Jim Greer in 1992 that they
practice a lot and generate new material on a regular basis just by virtue
of the fact that they are all in the same place. Even when the band was
supposed to be on a break, like after *Out of Time*, the four inevitably gath-
ered to rehearse and hammer out new songs. "That's something that
never stops," Mills declared in 1992.[29]

    Towards the end of Buck's residency in Athens, they were already opting to write independently, according to Mills (*MTV.com* 2001), but that ceased to be a choice once the guitarist flew the coop. Since then, the group's collective efforts involve the individual musicians writing separately in their home studios and presenting demos to one another. While they then refine the tracks together, there is less collective input in the music's formative stages. "We used to get into a room and everyone would present ideas, and then, just by the other guys being there, those ideas would change and refigure," says Stipe, but under other circumstances, it became simpler to exchange tapes with songs that have been more or less blueprinted.[30] It's not as if they never write together anymore, Mills points out (*VH1.com*, 2003). He and Buck still take advantage of opportunities that arise when they're in the studio with instruments in hand. Inevitably, they end up composing a few pieces jointly.

The current setup has given rise to a new breed of intensity. While the band used to rehearse five days a week, two hours a day for eight months, says Buck, they now periodically unite for a defined interval but put in longer days. "Now, I'll fly to Athens and we'll spend 10 hours a day in the studio for three weeks, so it's much more focused," but, he adds, "you don't get that organic growth feeling."[31] He also noted in an interview with *Neumu* that there's less spontaneity now that they live in different parts of the country. They don't jam regularly (especially since Berry left, making jamming virtually impossible) and can't just decide to take the stage together on the spur of the moment (as they often did in the past). Of course, the physical distance between the band members is one of the reasons they work together infrequently.

Part IV

TRIAL BY LINEUP SHIFTS

Lineup changes, such as those weathered repeatedly by the Red Hot Chili Peppers, are yet another factor that can imperil a band's unity and ability to collaborate or dramatically alter the nature of their communal creative process. "We've always strived [sic] to become one single-cell unit," remarks Flea, implying that this is the necessary condition for the group's optimal performance.[32] But the frequent influx of new members rendered that ideal state unattainable for much of the Chili Peppers' career. They often tried to force it, admits the bassist, but to little avail given the lack of stability in the group's ranks. Although some personnel shifts can be beneficial for a group—an infusion of fresh blood and ideas—a revolving door of musicians can be lethal for the band, as the Chili Peppers learned. Flea told *The Sunday Herald* that, after plowing through a succession of failed replacements for John Frusciante between 1992 and 1998, the group reached a point where it could not sustain any further turnover simply because "the internal bond had been breached once too often."[33] The implication is that, had Frusciante not resumed his place in the lineup, the band wouldn't have been able to carry on with someone else.

It's no easy feat to incorporate new members into such a close-knit alliance under any conditions. As we saw earlier, the Chili Peppers have a collective vision and approach to their work that is particularly difficult to impress upon outsiders, as well as a distinct spirit (especially onstage) to which few musicians have been able to truly relate. Every time a new musician entered the band's circle, there was a period not only of disjunction, but also of tremendous *uneasiness* that made it hard for the musicians to work together. Both John Frusciante and Dave Navarro have talked about how long it took them to feel part of the group and be themselves rather than trying to please or impress their new bandmates. The rest of the band, meanwhile, struggled to accommodate and adapt to the newcomers. Most of the new recruits in the Chili Peppers didn't last long enough for the group to even attempt getting past the initial stage of discomfort. Frusciante and Smith did, and the band seemed to get over any preliminary awkwardness relatively quickly. The young guitarist may have been nervous, at the outset, about rubbing shoulders with his idols, but they seemed to feel at ease with him almost right away, perhaps, as Kiedis suggested in *Rock & Folk*, because he was so young, zealous and completely in tune with the band.

In contrast, Navarro's debut was marked by a high degree of unsettlement within the unit—and it never really went away. During his first year, there was an extreme sense of discomfiture on both sides, Navarro and Flea remarked in 1995 (*Guitar Player*). Their relations improved when they stopped worrying so much about what wasn't working, started playing what they wanted (rather than pandering to perceived expectations of one another), and concentrated on finding common ground. But the fact remained that the new guitarist, like others the band had tried to assimilate in the past, couldn't adapt to their free-flowing and telepathy-dependent improvisational methodology, preferring to meticulously work out his parts on his own and hold tactical discussions about how to approach each song. Collaboration was a whole different ball game with Navarro in the group, and no one was really reconciled to the process that evolved as, essentially, a compromise between the two styles.

While Navarro was fairly well-suited to the band on a personal level (better than, say, the introspective Arik Marshall), they never managed to truly embrace each other emotionally or develop the kind of bond that the group had enjoyed with both Slovak and Frusciante, which prevented the four from achieving the kind of fraternity they needed in order to operate effectively. In an episode of VH1's *Behind the Music*, Kiedis provided another explanation as to why this lack of closeness bothered the group as much as it did—it has to do with settling for less after you've had more. "When you have that experience, that ultimate intimacy experience, as we had with John, I think you always crave it. We didn't know what to do. Something was amiss." The core trio in the Chili Peppers naturally compared their experiences with different guitarists and many came up short of the superlative partnership (the out and out brotherhood) they had known and subconsciously set as a standard, making it extremely challenging to find a satisfactory (let alone equivalent) lineup. That's one of the reasons the band went through so many cast configurations, and endured all the volatility that comes with them. At any rate, there was no point trying to record another album with Navarro, with whom they continued to be musically and emotionally out of sync. With Frusciante back in the band, Kiedis remarked with assurance, in a way that tactfully accounts for the switch, "This is the chemistry at which the Red Hot Chili Peppers are meant to function the best."[34]

The band members claim that the profound connection and fluid musical communication they managed to establish with Frusciante resulted from having had a relatively lengthy period to become attuned to one another as musicians and people, but, clearly, time wasn't the differential factor. They had six years with Navarro, during which they never achieved the comprehensive synthesis they desired; it took just two years with Frusciante (1988–1990, the years before they recorded *Blood Sugar Sex Magik*) to become what they fondly call a "team of telepathic bastards."[35] That's not to discount the idea that something special happens between musicians who have known one another and played together a long time, but there has to be a solid interpersonal alchemy for the years to build on. They didn't have that with Navarro. It does take some time to form a cohesive unit and develop a musical kinship even when the basic chemistry is right. In Frusciante, the Chili Peppers finally found the ideal partner, but it still took a while for everyone to gel the way they ultimately did, Kiedis noted in his autobiography.

As far as the creative process goes, a variable lineup has particular disadvantages. For one thing, writing music together is a big step and a newly formed collective needs to be ready to undertake it. *One Hot Minute* was such a difficult album to make, claims Navarro, because the band rushed headlong into songwriting too soon after he joined (despite the bonding attempts) and everyone consequently felt overwhelmed. "It's like meeting a girl at a club and the very next morning going to brunch with her parents, grandparents, brothers and sisters."[36] Their relationship wasn't ripe enough for the type of communion that mutual effort required. Since a fruitful collaboration can't be instantly resumed in many cases where a band member has been replaced, an alternative is to take it slow, maybe tour for a while, before going into the studio. One way or the other, the group's collective creative momentum is interrupted. And even when the musicians are finally at a stage where they feel they can undertake new material together, it often takes more than one effort for the group to reach its true potential as a songwriting unit. The Chili Peppers had a chance to put this theory to the test while recording the band's fourth and fifth albums.

With Frusciante and Smith having been in the band just a few months, *Mother's Milk* was a strained affair, as the four disparate musicians tried to forcibly impose a certain level of unity on their roughhewn alliance. *Blood Sugar Sex Magik*, however, was the second album this quartet worked on together—and the first time the band had the luxury of recording a follow-up with the same lineup. It was created not only in a far more relaxed atmosphere, but was the product of a fully integrated group, a real *band* characterized by an intense telepathic exchange between the musicians (which is crucial to their jam-oriented approach). And it showed, says Frusciante. *Mother's Milk* bore the individual signatures of each member. But its substantially superior successor was the work of the Red Hot Chili Peppers. One album was a collage of contributions from four people, he observed in *Guitare & Claviers*, and the other created by a singular entity.

Not every group is able to cope with incorporating new members or even engaging new associates. R.E.M. couldn't bear the idea of replacing Bill Berry, and Thom Yorke told *Spin* in 2001 that it's even difficult for him to shoot videos with a different director each time because he finds it destabilizing to constantly work with new people. He needs a more secure network around him. Flea points out that even without member changes, bands tend to be unstable and uncontrollable by nature. In particular, the chemistry and collective creative flow Kiedis mentions are subject to fluctuations beyond the musicians' satellite of influence, and that's what makes it a rock band.

Final Remarks

Ultimately, then, what separates a band such as the four discussed in this book from other configurations of musicians playing together are the impenetrable chemistry, the musical intuition or telepathy between the members, the deep commitment and loyalty to the partnership, and, some would say, the camaraderie as well. It can be argued that longevity, a togetherness that spans multiple years and experiences, is another distinguishing factor, or at least one that enhances the collective's innate bandhood.

"The real thing that makes a rock 'n' roll band is the relationship that goes on between the individuals," Bono said in 2003, adding "and when we walk onto a stage, we're a band that formed before we could play, that had been through shit together and come out the other side. That's a very powerful thing."[37] U2's frontman has also contended that equality, particularly equal voices in and equal contributions to the music and the group, separate a band from a soloist or songwriting duo and their accomplices, who perform and record music together, but don't *create* collectively or govern the band in unison. Equal ownership over the band and its output are key, in other words. It's about functioning as a unit, in the truest possible sense.

As musicians and individuals, nothing compares to being in this kind of outfit, the members declare. "To be in a band is an amazing feeling, both in its fraternity and fun and frolics, as well as its musical achievement," exclaims Bono.[38] For Peter Buck, the best thing about being in R.E.M. is "working with the other guys, being able to grow up with guys I respect and like, learn from them, work with them well."[39] It takes tremendous effort and devotion to the band ethic to maintain such an all-encompassing unity, but the rewards are many.

Notes

PREFACE

1. Dave Bowler and Bryan Dray, *Documental* (London: Boxtree, 1995).
2. Jon Wiederhorn, "The Secret Sauce," MTV.com, Jul. 2002.
3. Allison Stewart, "Red Hot Chili Peppers Interview," CDNow.com., Sept. 2000.

INTRODUCTION

1. Hunter Davies, *The Beatles: The Authorized Biography* (New York: W. W. Norton, 1968).
2. John Densmore, "Riders on the Storm," *The Nation*, 8 Jul. 2002.

CHAPTER 1

1. Olaf Tyaransen, "Pushing the Envelope," *Hot Press*, 7 Nov. 2002.
2. Jim DeRogatis, "The Day's Still Beautiful for U2," *The Chicago Sun Times*, 6 May 2001.
3. Robert Hilburn, "How R.E.M. Spells Success," *The Los Angeles Times*, 27 Feb. 1994.
4. Debbie Gilbert, "R.E.M.: Why They're Still Around," *The Memphis Flyer*, 2 Nov. 1995.
5. "Interview with R.E.M.," *Melody Maker*, 15 Jun. 1985.
6. Robert Hilburn, "How R.E.M. Spells Success."
7. Michael Goldberg, "Reinventing R.E.M.: The Michael Stipe Q&A," *Addicted to Noise*, Nov. 1998.
8. Dave Di Martino, "Nowhere to Go But Up," Yahoo! Launch.com, 13 Apr. 1999.
9. John Harris, "R.E.M.—One Week in South America," *Q*, May 2001.
10. Gary Terratzo, "R.E.M.," *Muse*, 1998.
11. Chris Heath, "Michael in the Middle," *Details*, Feb. 1995.
12. Catherine Yates, "Get Up and Jump," *Kerrang! Legends*, Issue No. 4. (Red Hot Chili Peppers).
13. John Aizlewood, "Red Hot," *The London*

Evening Standard, Metro Life section, 7 Mar. 2003.
14. "One Red Hot Minute with the Red Hot Chili Peppers," *Rhythm and News*, 1995.
15. John Albert, "Sons of the City," *LA Weekly*, 6–12 Dec. 2002.
16. David Fricke, "The Naked Truth," *Rolling Stone*, 25 Jun. 1992.
17. "Anthony Kiedis: Blood Synergy Sex Meltdown," VH1.com, 30 May 2002.
18. David Fricke, "The Naked Truth."
19. David Fricke, "Red Hot Reunion," *Rolling Stone*, 1 Apr. 1999.
20. David Fricke, "Red Hot Reunion."
21. Chris Douridas, interview with Anthony Kiedis for AOL's *Sessions*, 16 May 2002.
22. Nisid Hajari, "Tales From The Creeps," *Entertainment Weekly*, 19 May 1995.
23. Steve Malins, "Scuba Do," *Vox*, Apr. 1995.
24. Andy Richardson, "Boom! Shake the Gloom!," *NME*, 9 Dec. 1995.
25. David Fricke, "Making Music That Matters," *Rolling Stone*, 2 Aug. 2001.

CHAPTER 2

1. "Unforgettable Fire," CNN.com, 12 Dec. 2001.
2. Gavin Martin, "Kings of the Celtic Fringe," *NME*, 14 Feb. 1981.
3. Terry O'Neill, "U2," *In Fashion*, 1 Jan. 1988.
4. J.D. Considine, "R.E.M.: Subverting Small Town Boredom," *Musician*, Aug. 1983.
5. Liam Mackey, "Articulate Speech of the Heart," *Hot Press*, 22 Jul. 1983.
6. Michael Heatley, liner notes to Red Hot Chili Peppers interview CD. Sound and Media (Virgin Publishing), 1997.
7. John Kelly, "Taking Music to Strange Places," *The Irish Times*, 15 Sept. 2001.
8. Jason Pettigrew, "Red Hot Chili Peppers—Funkin' Up the Milky Way," *Alternative Press*, Nov. 1989.

9. James Henke, "The Edge: The Rolling Stone Interview," *Rolling Stone*, 10 Mar. 1987.

10. Tony Fletcher, *Remarks Remade: The Story of R.E.M.* (New York: Omnibus Press, 2002).

11. Bill Wyman, "How R.E.M. Woke Up Rock 'n' Roll in the '80s," *The Chicago Tribune*, 5 Dec. 1989.

12. Terry Allen, "The First Gig," *Q Special Edition (R.E.M.)*, 2001.

13. Nick Kent, "Happy Now?" *Mojo*, Jun. 2001.

14. Phil Sutcliffe, "Death Is All Around," *Q*, Oct. 1997.

CHAPTER 3

1. Jeff Apter, *Fornication: The Red Hot Chili Peppers Story* (New York: Omnibus, 2004).

2. Bill Flanagan, "Soul Revelation and the Baptism of Fire," *Musician*, 1 Feb. 1985.

3. Paulo Hewitt, "Getting Into U2," *Melody Maker*, 13 Sept. 1980.

4. Ethlie Ann Vare, "At War with Mediocrity," *ROCK!*, 1 Sept. 1983.

5. Dermod Moore, "Ace of Bass," *Hot Press*, 29 Aug. 2001.

6. Dave Bowler and Bryan Dray, *Documental* (London: Boxtree, 1995).

7. Phil Sutcliffe, "The Band That Tried to Kill Themselves," *Q*, Oct. 1999.

8. Peter Paphides, "Into the Light," *Mojo*, 2003.

9. Chrissy Iley, "U2 Interview: Group Therapy," *The Sunday Times Magazine*, 7 Nov. 2004.

10. Dorian Lynskey, "Socks Away!," *Q*, Jun. 2002.

11. "R.E.M. Talks About Breaking Up, Making Up, and New Album," *AllStar*, 23 Apr. 2001.

12. *U2 in Quotes* (England: Babylon Books, 1986).

13. Jon Wiederhorn, "The Secret Sauce," MTV.com, Jul. 2002.

14. Phil Alexander, "Some Like It Hot," *Raw*, 21 Feb.–6 Mar. 1990.

15. "Interview with Flea," Guitarcenter.com, Oct. 2001.

16. David Fricke, "Making Music That Matters," *Rolling Stone*, 2 Aug. 2001.

17. Andy Richardson, "Boom! Shake the Gloom!," *NME*, 9 Dec. 1995.

18. Ted Kessler, "We Never Wanted to Be the Biggest Band in the World," *NME*, 13 Dec. 1997.

19. Tom Doyle, "Out of Time?" *Q*, Sept. 1999.

20. Nancy Price, "Radiohead on Their Band Dynamic," *The Musician's Exchange*, 23 Jun. 1999.

21. Josh Tyrangiel, "Top of the Rock 'n' Roll Heap," *Time*, 9 Jun. 2003.

22. Johnny Black, *Reveal: The Story of R.E.M.* (San Francisco: Backbeat, 2004).

23. Edwin Pouncey, "R.E.M.: Deconstructing the Fables," *Sounds*, 18 Oct. 1986.

24. Jon Wiederhorn, "The Secret Sauce."

25. John Soeder, "Band of Brothers," *Plain Dealer Pop Music Critic*, 7 Feb. 2003.

26. Gregory Isola, "Reluctant Rock Star: How U2's Adam Clayton Learned to Play—And Conquer the World Onstage," *Bass Player*, 11 Nov. 2000.

27. Bob Gulla, "Radiohead—At Long Last, A Future for Rock Guitar," *Guitar World*, Oct. 1997.

28. Barney Hoskyns, "Four Guys Working for the Sainthood," *NME*, 21 Apr. 1984.

29. Peter Ross, "Shinier, Happier People," *The Sunday Herald*, 15 Jun. 2003.

30. Sarah Rodman, "Chili Peppers on a Red Hot Streak," *The Boston Herald*, 17 Jul. 2000.

31. John Walshe, "Bang a Gong," *Hot Press*, 24 May 2002.

32. Mac Randall, *Exit Music: The Radiohead Story* (New York: Delta, 2000).

33. John Harris, "Renaissance Men," *Select*, Jan. 1988.

34. Garry Mulholland, "Interview with Michael Stipe," *Time Out*, 23 Jun. 1999.

35. Brantley Smith, "R.E.M. Love Song '91," *Details*, Apr. 1991.

36. Dave Di Martino, "Nowhere to Go But Up," Yahoo! Launch.com, 13 Apr. 1999.

37. Clare Kleinedler, "Radiohead Programmed for Success," *Addicted to Noise*, Jul. 1997.

38. Caroline Sullivan, "Bridges and Sighs," *The Guardian*, 16 May 1997.

39. Stuart Clark, "Transistor Act," *Hot Press*, 12 Jul. 1995.

40. Brad Kava, "An Edge-y Quality," *The San Jose Mercury News*, 13 Apr. 2001.

41. Mark Edwards, "He Learnt to Sing from His Soul By Accident," *The Sunday Times*, 7 Dec. 2003.

42. "Fornicating California Style," *Metal Hammer*, Jun. 1999.

43. Stuart Bailie, "Viva la Megabytes!" *NME*, 21 Jun. 1997.

44. Liam Fey, "Back to the End of the Beginning," *Wales on Sunday*, 23 Jul. 1995.

45. Mac Randall, *Exit Music: The Radiohead Story*.

46. Mark Sutherland, "Return of the Mac!" *Melody Maker*, 31 May 1997.

47. David Buckley, *R.E.M. Fiction: An Alternative Biography* (London: Virgin, 2003).

48. Chris Ahrens, "Survival Mechanisms," *Risen*, Vol. 2, No. 2 (2005).

49. Harold De Muir, "There's No Reason It Shouldn't Be a Hit," *East Coast Rocker*, 7 Oct. 1987.

50. Chris Chandar, "Love Loss Life Magik," *Pulse!*, Aug. 2002.

51. Niall Stokes, "Matter of Life and Death," *Hot Press Annual 2002*, 1 Dec. 2001.

52. Iain Shedden, "Red Alert," *The Australian*, 29 Nov. 2002.

53. Gil Kaufman, "Red Hot Chili Peppers: Back in the Saddle," *Addicted to Noise*, Jan. 1999.

54. "Rattle and Humble," CNN.com, 27 Oct. 2000.

55. Video Conectate Interview With John Frusciante. 15 Oct. 2002.

56. Simon Young, "Green Peppers," *Kerrang! Legends*, Issue No. 4. (Red Hot Chili Peppers).

57. Paulo Hewitt, "Getting Into U2," *Melody Maker*, 13 Sept. 1980.

58. "U2 at the R.D.S.," *U2 Magazine*, No. 2, Feb. 1982.

59. Dave Bowler and Bryan Dray, *Documental* (London: Boxtree, 1995).

60. Gerald Marzorati, "The Post-Rock Band," *The New York Times Upfront*, 30 Oct. 2000.

61. Elianne Halbersberg, "Interview: Peter Buck of R.E.M.," *East Coast Rocker*, 30 Nov. 1988.

CHAPTER 4

1. Jim DeRogatis, "The Day's Still Beautiful for U2," *The Chicago Sun Times*, 6 May 2001.

2. G. Brown, "R.E.M.: Rockin' Even More," *The Denver Post*, 12 Sept. 2003.

3. Jon Pareles, "Searching for a Sound to Bridge the Decades," *The New York Times*, 9 Feb. 1997.

4. Jared H. Bailey, "Mike Mills: Producer Of Sorts," *Flagpole*, 8 Sept. 1993.

5. Sheryl Garratt, "The Band Played On," *The Guardian*, 14 Feb. 1997.

6. Johnny Black, *Reveal: The Story of R.E.M.* (San Francisco: Backbeat, 2004).

7. Mark Blake, "U2's Bono: Rumors of His Demise Have Been Greatly Exaggerated," *Q*, 1 Jan. 1998.

8. Tom Doyle, "10 Years of Turmoil Inside U2," *Q*, 10 Oct. 2002.

9. Neil McCormick, "Twenty One Years of Pop Music," *Propaganda*, Issue 26, 1 Jun. 1997.

10. Neil McCormick, "Twenty One Years of Pop Music."

11. Tony Fletcher, *Remarks Remade: The Story of R.E.M.* (New York: Omnibus Press, 2002).

12. Mac Randall, "The Golden Age of Radiohead," *Guitar World*, Apr. 1998.

13. Dave Bowler and Bryan Dray, *Documental* (London: Boxtree, 1995).

14. Tamara Conniff, "Dialogue with Bono," *The Hollywood Reporter*, 21 Feb. 2003.

15. David Fricke, "Making Music That Matters," *Rolling Stone*, 2 Aug. 2001.

16. Lisa Y. Garibay, "Phil Selway (Radiohead)," Thenitmustbetrue.com *(TIMBT)*, Jun. 2001.

17. Stephen Dalton, "Are We Having Fun Yet?" *The Age*, 11 Apr. 2004.

18. Michael Goldberg, "Reinventing R.E.M.: The Peter Buck/Mike Mills Q&A," *Addicted to Noise*, Nov. 1998.

19. Robert Hilburn, "How R.E.M. Spells Success," *The Los Angeles Times*, 27 Feb. 1994.

20. Dave Bowler and Bryan Dray, *Documental*.

21. Tony Fletcher, *Remarks Remade: The Story of R.E.M.*

22. Yoichiro Yamazaki, "Thom Yorke Interview," *Q Special Edition (Radiohead)*.

23. Lisa Robinson, "U2's Unforgettable Fire," *Vanity Fair*, 25 Oct. 2004.

24. U2 Interview CD, *Bono Talks in Philadelphia*, Baktabak 1987 (CBAK 4006).

25. J.D. Beauvallet, "Nigel the Nihilist," *Les Inrockuptibles*, 25 Jan. 2000.

26. Bob Gulla, "Radiohead—At Long Last, A Future for Rock Guitar," *Guitar World*, Oct. 1997.

27. John Aizlewood, "Red Hot," *The London Evening Standard*, Metro Life section, 7 Mar. 2003.

28. Richard Cromelin, "Pop Beat," *The Los Angeles Times*, 8 Jan. 2005.

29. Raoul Hernandez, "Music: Me and My Friends," *The Austin Chronicle*, 26 Nov. 2004.

30. Kim Curtis, "Radiohead Goes Where No Other Band Has Gone," *The Bergen County Record*, 29 Oct. 2003.

31. David Fricke, "Bitter Prophet," *Rolling Stone*, 25 Jun. 2003.

32. Rob Jovanovic and Tim Abbott, *Adventures in Hi-Fi: The Complete R.E.M.* (London: Orion, 2001).

33. Jim Irvin, "R.E.M.," *Mojo*, Nov. 1994.

34. Don Snowden, "The Reckoning of R.E.M.," *The Los Angeles Times*, 18 Jul. 1984.

35. Niall Stokes, "Matter of Life and Death," *Hot Press Annual 2002*, 1 Dec. 2001.

36. Bert Van De Camp, "Angels and Devils," *Music Express*, 1 Jul. 1992.

37. "Red Hot Chili Peppers Interview," *El Pais*, 27 Jul. 2002.

38. Dave Thompson, *Bono: In His Own Words* (New York: Omnibus Press, 1989).

39. Olaf Tyaransen, "The Final Frontier," *Hot Press*, 26 Oct. 2000.

40. Brian Hiatt, "U2's Beautiful New Day," Sonicnet.com, 2001.

41. Susan Black, *Radiohead … In Their Own Words* (London: Omnibus, 2002).

42. Michael Goldberg, "The Making of R.E.M.'s *Monster*," *Addicted to Noise*, Feb. 1995.

43. Andrew Smith, "Sound and Fury," *The Observer*, 1 Oct. 2000.

44. Dave Di Martino, "Nowhere to Go But Up," Yahoo! Launch.com, 13 Apr. 1999.

45. Toby Manning, "Oddfellows Local," *Q Special Edition (R.E.M.)*, 2001.

46. David Fricke, "The Wizards of Pop," *Rolling Stone*, 29 May 1997.

47. Anthony Kiedis, *Scar Tissue* (New York: Hyperion, 2004).
48. Alan Di Perna, "Getting Better All the Time," *Guitar*, Aug. 2002.
49. *U2 in Quotes* (England: Babylon Books, 1986).
50. Barbara Jaeger, "U2 Rocks the Boat with Unorthodox Style," *The Bergen County Record*, 12 Apr. 1985.

CHAPTER 5

1. "The Elastic Bono Band," *Q*, 1 Nov. 2000.
2. Christine Sams, "Hot Reception," *The Sydney Morning Herald*, 25 Nov. 2002.
3. "Unforgettable Fire," CNN.com, 12 Dec. 2001.
4. Jim DeRogatis, "The Day's Still Beautiful for U2," *The Chicago Sun Times*, 6 May 2001.
5. Andrew Mueller, "Kid B," *Amazon.co.uk*, Jun. 2001.
6. Robyn Flans, "Serving Up a New Red Hot Brew," *Modern Drummer*, Aug. 1999.
7. Tony Woolliscroft, "Riders on the Storm," *Kerrang!*, 11 Jul. 1998.
8. Jim Macnie, "In the Studio with R.E.M., The Return of Mumbles and the Love Gods," *Musician*, Apr. 1991.
9. Robert Hilburn, "Their Reckoning," *The Los Angeles Times*, 1 Jun. 2003.
10. Michael Goldberg, "Reinventing R.E.M.: The Peter Buck/Mike Mills Q&A," *Addicted to Noise*, Nov. 1998.
11. Olaf Tyaransen, "Closer to the Edge," *Hot Press*, 4 Dec. 2002.
12. Alan Light, "Band of the Year: Rock's Unbreakable Heart," *Spin*, 1 Jan. 2001.
13. Dominic Mohan, "'NY Showed Us Heroes,'" *The Sun* [UK], 8 Dec. 2001.
14. Howard Johnson, "U2 People: Larry Mullen," *Uncut Legends*, Vol. 3. (U2).
15. Anthony Kiedis, *Scar Tissue* (New York: Hyperion, 2004).
16. Edna Gundersen, "Alive and Ticking," *USA Today*, 18 Nov. 2004.
17. Chris Heath, "R.E.M.: More Songs About Death and Anxiety," *Rolling Stone*, 17 Oct. 1996.
18. Jeff Giles, "Number One with an Attitude," *Rolling Stone*, 27 Jun. 1991.
19. Joan Anderman, "For R.E.M., Time Is Finally Right to Tour Again," *The Boston Globe*, 3 Oct. 2003.
20. Sarah Rodman, "Chili Peppers on a Red Hot Streak," *The Boston Herald*, 17 Jul. 2000.
21. Jay Cocks, "Band on the Run," *Time*, 27 Apr. 1987.
22. Ian Shedding, "Red Alert," *The Australian*, 29 Nov. 2002.
23. Lauren Zoric, "I Think I'm Meant to Be Dead ...," *The Guardian*, 22 Sept. 2000.
24. Jim Sullivan, "From Boys to Men," *The Boston Globe*, 2 Feb. 1996.
25. "Red Hot Chili Peppers Latest Album," *Rolling Stone*, 21 Jun. 1995.
26. Bill Flanagan, "The View from the Edge," *Musician*, 1 Mar. 1992.
27. Liam Mackey, "I Still Haven't Found What I'm Looking For," *Hot Press*, 1 Dec. 1988.
28. Bill Graham and Niall Stokes, "U2 Give Themselves Away," *Musician*, 1 May 1987.
29. Elianne Halbersberg, "Interview: Peter Buck of R.E.M.," *East Coast Rocker*, 30 Nov. 1988.
30. Anthony Kiedis, *Scar Tissue*.
31. John Soeder, "What's 'Up' with R.E.M.?" *The Cleveland Plain Dealer*, 20 Aug. 1998.
32. Mike Zwerin, "R.E.M. Is Alive and Well with Album No. 11," *The International Herald Tribune*, 22 Jan. 1999.
33. Krista Desens, "Adam Clayton on U2's Longevity," BuzzFM.com, 12 Apr. 2005.
34. Timothy White, "Bono," *Rock Lives* (New York: Henry Holt, 1990).
35. Mark Blake, "Like Spinning Plates," *Q Special Edition (Radiohead)*.
36. Tom Doyle, "Out of Time?" *Q*, Sept. 1999.
37. Jon Regardie, "Red Hot Chili Peppers: Return of the Century," *Alternative Press*, Jul. 1999.
38. Chuck Klosterman, "Meeting Thom Is Easy," *Spin*, Jun. 2003.
39. Bill Flanagan, "Soul Revelation and the Baptism of Fire," *Musician*, 1 Feb. 1985.
40. Brendan McAndrew and Eileen Threlfalls, "From L.A. to New Yorke," *The Trigger*, 4 Nov. 1995.
41. Nancy Benecki, "An Interview with U2's Larry Mullen: No More 40-Foot Lemons," Music.com, 2 Nov. 2000.
42. Aidin Vaziri, "Q&A with Anthony Kiedis," *The San Francisco Chronicle*, 26 Dec. 1999.
43. Edna Gundersen, "Bono Honored As 2003 MusiCares Person of the Year," *Grammy*, 20 Feb. 2003.
44. "Absolute McGuinness," *Propaganda*, 1 Oct. 1987 (issue 7).
45. Tony Wadsworth, "The Making of *OK Computer*," *The Guardian*, 20 Dec. 1997.
46. Tony Wadsworth, "The Making of *OK Computer*."
47. Russell Smith, "U2: Rock 'N' Roll for the '80s," *The Dallas Morning News*, 25 Feb. 1985.
48. Bill Flanagan, "Soul Revelation and the Baptism of Fire."
49. Adrian Deevoy, "Welcome to the Funny Farm," *Q*, Dec. 1988.
50. Gerald Marzorati, "The Post-Rock Band," *The New York Times Upfront*, 30 Oct. 2000.
51. Steve Roeser, "Conversation with Kiedis," *Goldmine*, 22 Nov. 1996.

52. Gary Graff, "Split Personality: Radiohead Gives Its Fans a Double Dose," *The New York Times*, 25 Jun. 2001.

53. Peter Murphy, "How Radiohead Learned to Loathe the Bomb," *Hot Press*, 11 Oct. 2001.

CHAPTER 6

1. Russell Baillie, "Ed O'Brien: Turning Up, Tuning In," *The New Zealand Herald*, 7 Apr. 2001.

2. Tom Doyle, "Party On," *Q,* Jun. 1997.

3. Russell Baillie, "Ed O'Brien: Turning Up, Tuning In."

4. Clare Kleinedler, "Radiohead Programmed for Success," *Addicted to Noise*, Jul. 1997.

5. "Press Release for *Green*," *Warner Brother Records*, Oct. 1988.

6. John Harris, "R.E.M.—One Week in South America," *Q,* May 2001.

7. David Buckley, *R.E.M. Fiction: An Alternative Biography* (London: Virgin, 2003).

8. Jill Kipnis, "Red Hot Chili Peppers' *By the Way* Due in July," *Billboard*, 22 Jun. 2002.

9. "Interview with Flea," CNN.com, 27 Jun. 2003.

10. Mike Pattenden, "Phil Selway," *Q Special Edition (Radiohead)*.

11. Allison Stewart, "Red Hot Chili Peppers Interview," CDNow.com, Sept. 2000.

12. Anthony DeCurtis, "Monster Madness," *Rolling Stone*, 20 Oct. 1994.

13. Elianne Halbersberg, "Interview: Peter Buck of R.E.M.," *East Coast Rocker*, 30 Nov. 1988.

14. John Hutchinson, "Luminous Times," *Musician*, 1 Oct. 1987.

15. Murray Cammick, "Interview with Adam and Edge," *Rip It Up*, Dec. 1989.

16. Tabitha Soren, "R.E.M.'s New Adventures," *MTV Online*, 13 Sept. 1996.

17. Jim Irvin, "R.E.M.," *Mojo*, Nov. 1994.

18. Paulo Zollo, "R.E.M.," *Songwriting*, 4th ed. (Cincinnati: Da Capo Press, 2003).

19. Flea's Liner Notes, *Red Hot Chili Peppers Greatest Hits CD*, Warner Brothers, 2003.

20. "An In Depth Interview with Anthony Kiedis in Glasgow," *Vibe*, Mar. 2003.

21. Clare Kleinedler, "Don't Call 'Em Britpop," *Addicted to Noise*, May 1996.

22. Barney Hoskyns, "Four Guys Working for the Sainthood," *NME*, 21 Apr. 1984.

23. Gregory Isola, "Reluctant Rock Star: How U2's Adam Clayton Learned to Play—And Conquer the World Onstage," *Bass Player*, 11 Nov. 2000.

24. Thom Yorke of Radiohead Talks to BBC World Service, *BBC Press Release*, 21 Apr. 2003.

25. Paul Lester, "From the Bedroom to the Universe," *NME*, 25 Oct. 1995.

26. Sean O'Hagan, "Another Green World," *NME*, 24 Dec. 1988.

27. Gary Terratzo, "Interview with R.E.M.," *Muse*, 1998.

28. Paul Martin, "I'm Living on the Edge," *The Mirror*, 20 Aug. 2001.

29. Alan Light, "Band of the Year: Rock's Unbreakable Heart," *Spin*, 1 Jan. 2001.

30. Tom Gliatto, "Bono's World: Part Rocker, Part Policy Wonk, U2's Singer Calls Himself 'The Thinking Man's Perry Como,'" *People*, 25 Feb. 2002.

31. Mary Gaitskill, "Radiohead: Alarms and Surprises," *Alternative Press*, Apr. 1998.

32. John Harris, "R.E.M.—One Week in South America."

33. Brantley Smith, "R.E.M., Love Song '91," *Details*, Apr. 1991.

CHAPTER 7

1. Harry Wylie, "Radiohead," *Total Guitar*, Nov. 1997.

2. Harry Wylie, "Radiohead."

3. Gregory Isola, "Reluctant Rock Star: How U2's Adam Clayton Learned to Play—And Conquer the World Onstage," *Bass Player*, 11 Nov. 2000.

4. John Platt, "R.E.M.," *Bucketfull of Brains*, Dec. 1984.

5. Paulo Zollo, "R.E.M.," *Songwriters on Songwriting* 4th ed. (Cincinnati: Da Capo Press, 2003).

6. Gary Graff, "Interview with R.E.M.," *Wall of Sound*, 31 Oct. 1998.

7. John Kelly, "Taking Music to Strange Places," *The Irish Times*, 15 Sept. 2001.

8. Lyndsey Parker, "Two Sides to Every Story," *Guitar One*, Jan. 2003.

9. Bill Flanagan, "Introduction," *U2: The Complete Songs* (London: Wise Publications, 1999).

10. Mark Cunningham, "The Larry Mullen Jr. Interview," *Propaganda*, 1 Apr. 1995 (issue 22).

11. Michael Goldberg, "R.E.M.'s Peter Buck Can't Get No Satisfaction," *Addicted to Noise*, Sept. 1996.

12. Russell Smith, "U2: Rock 'n' Roll for the '80s," *The Dallas Morning News*, 25 Feb. 1985.

13. Steve Roeser, "Conversation with Kiedis," *Goldmine*, 22 Nov. 1996.

14. Dorian Lynskey, "Socks Away!" *Q,* Jun. 2002.

15. Robyn Flans, "Serving Up a New Red Hot Brew," *Modern Drummer*, Aug. 1999.

16. Dorian Lynskey, "Different Class," *Q,* 2 Aug. 2001.

17. Tony Fletcher, *Remarks Remade: The Story of R.E.M.* (New York: Omnibus Press, 2002).

18. David Buckley, *R.E.M. Fiction: An Alternative Biography* (London: Virgin, 2003).

19. "R.E.M. Star Reveals Future Plans," *NME*, 6 Sept. 2001.

20. Aidin Vaziri, "Q&A with Anthony Kiedis," *The San Francisco Chronicle*, 26 Dec. 1999.

21. Kurt Loder, "Red Hot Chili Peppers: Californication," MTV.com, 8 Jun. 1999.

22. Zev Borow, "The Difference Engine," *Spin*, Nov. 2000.

23. Lowri Williams, "Radiohead Go All Classical on Us," Gigwise.com, 22 Mar. 2005.

24. Stephen Dalton, "Are We Having Fun Yet?" *The Age*, 11 Apr. 2004.

25. Lauren Zoric, "Fitter, Happier, More Productive," *Juice*, 25 Sept. 2000.

26. Tom Doyle, "10 Years of Turmoil Inside U2," *Q*, 10 Oct. 2002.

27. Fred Schruers, "A Visit to Dublin—Home of U2," *U2 Magazine*, No. 7, May 1983.

28. "Red Hot Chili Peppers' Latest Album," *Rolling Stone*, 21 Jun. 1995.

29. Alex Ross, "The Searchers: Radiohead's Unquiet Revolution," *The New Yorker*, 20 Aug. 2001.

30. Anthony DeCurtis, "Zoo World Order," *Rolling Stone*, 14 Oct. 1993.

31. Stuart Bailie, "In the Beginning," *Uncut Legends*, Vol. 3 (U2).

32. Dermod Moore, "Ace of Bass," *Hot Press*, 29 Aug. 2001.

33. Chrissy Iley, "U2 Interview: Group Therapy," *The Sunday Times Magazine*, 7 Nov. 2004.

34. Josh Tyrangiel, "Mysterious Ways," *Time*, 14 Nov. 2004.

35. Josh Tyrangiel, "Mysterious Ways."

36. Dan Aquilante, "A Word Edge-Wise—U2 Sideman Is Definitely Pro Bono," *The New York Post*, 18 May 2005.

CHAPTER 8

1. Patrick Runkle, "Drummer on Top: The RHCP's Chad Smith on the New Album, *By the Way*," *ArtistPro*, May 2002.

2. John Williams, "The Red Hot Chili Peppers Q&A," *Jam!*, 8 Aug. 2002.

3. J.D. Considine, "Good Time Boys," *Guitar World*, Jul. 1999.

4. Don Zulaica, "LiveDaily Interview: Producer Rick Rubin," LiveDaily.com, 17 Mar. 2004

5. "Interview with Jonny Greenwood," [unidentified radio source], 29 Jan. 1998.

6. Sam Vicchrilli, "Radiohead Is Tuned in to Messages, But the Music Comes First," *The Salt Lake Tribune*, 22 Aug. 2003.

7. Patrick MacDonald, "Radio Wave: Britain's Band Rides Crest of Superstardom with Low-Wattage Egos," *The Seattle Times*, 2 Apr. 1998.

8. Tim Cashmere, "Jonny Greenwood Interview," *Undercover*, 2003.

9. Chuck Klosterman, "Meeting Thom Is Easy," *Spin*, Jun. 2003.

10. Mac Randall, *Exit Music: The Radiohead Story* (New York: Delta, 2000).

11. David Fricke, "People of the Year: Thom Yorke," *Rolling Stone*, Dec. 2000.

12. Stephen Dalton, "Are We Having Fun Yet?," *The Age*, 11 Apr. 2004.

13. Tom Doyle, "Out of Time?" *Q*, Sept. 1999.

14. Parry Gettelman, "R.E.M. Has a Monster on Its Hands," *The Orlando Sentinel*, 10 Nov. 1995.

15. Lynne Thompson, "Coming Up for Air," *Scene*, 8 Jun. 1995.

16. Paul Zollo, "R.E.M.," *Songwriters on Songwriting*, 4th ed. (Cincinnati: Da Capo Press, 2003).

17. U2 Interview CD. *Sound and Media 1995 (SAM 7003)*. [Interviews 1985/1986.] Issued 1995.

18. Gary Graff, "In Excess," *Guitar World*, Sept. 1997.

19. Darrin Fox, "The Edge Brings U2 Back to Basics," *Guitar Player*, Jan. 2001.

20. *U2 in Quotes* (England: Babylon Books, 1986).

21. Billy Corgan, "U2 Q&A," *Live!*, 1 May 1997.

22. "The Edge of the Zoo," *Propaganda*, 1 Nov. 1993 (issue 18).

23. "Frusciante Talks About Chili Peppers' New Album," *AllStar*, 26 Apr. 2001.

24. Lisa Robinson, "Interview with Michael Stipe," *The New York Post*, 7 Nov. 1998.

25. Edwin Pouncey, "Deconstructing the Fables," *Sounds*, 18 Oct. 1986.

26. Jim DeRogatis, "The Day's Still Beautiful for U2," *The Chicago Sun Times*, 6 May 2001.

27. Brian Eno, "Bringing Up Baby," *Rolling Stone*, 28 Nov. 1991.

28. Tom Forsythe, "Laughing All the Way," *Guitar*, Feb. 1991.

29. Jim Irvin, "R.E.M.," *Mojo*, Nov. 1994.

30. John Robinson, "It's Clear and Pretty—But I Think People Won't Get It," *NME*, 3 May 2003.

31. Mikael Wood, "Spinning Plates: Radiohead Doesn't Make Albums. It Has Accidents," *Denver Westword*, 14 Jun. 2001.

32. Robert Hilburn, "The Songwriters—U2—'Where Craft Ends and Spirit Begins,'" *The Los Angeles Times*, 8 Aug. 2004.

33. Jim Greer, *R.E.M.: Behind the Mask* (Boston: Little, Brown, 1992).

34. Tom Morton, "Southern Accents," *Melody Maker*, 6 Sept. 1986.

35. Michael Goldberg, "The Making of R.E.M.'s Monster," *Addicted to Noise*, Feb. 1995

36. Erik Philbrook, "Keeping the Peace," *ASCAP Playback*, 28 Nov. 2001.

37. Barney Hoskyns, "Four Guys Working for the Sainthood," *NME*, 21 Apr. 1984.

38. Stephen Dowling, "Interview with Ed & Phil," *Music365.co.uk*, 29 Sept. 2000.

39. Dan Aquilante, "'Up' and Running," *The New York Post*, 3 Sept. 1999.

40. Sarah Rodman, "Chili Peppers on a Red Hot Streak," *The Boston Herald*, 17 Jul. 2000.

41. "Postscripts from the Edge," *NME*, 31 Oct. 1998.

42. Steffen Rüth, "The Heavy Nothing," *Kulturnews*, Jun. 2003.

43. Andrew Mueller, "Kid B," *Amazon.co.uk*, Jun. 2001.

44. Michael Odell, "Silence! Genius at Work!," *Q*, Jul. 2003.

45. Robyn Flans, "Chad Smith: Serving Up a New Red Hot Brew," *Modern Drummer*, Aug. 1999.

46. James Black, "Interview with John Frusciante," *Canadian Musician*, May–Jun. 2001.

47. John Hutchinson, "Luminous Times," *Musician*, 1 Oct. 1987.

48. Triple J Interview with Jonny Greenwood, 16 Apr. 2004.

49. Bruce T. Wittet, "Phil Selway," *Modern Drummer*, Aug. 1996.

50. Dermod Moore, "Ace of Bass," *Hot Press*, 29 Aug. 2001.

51. Jeff Giles, "Number One with an Attitude," *Rolling Stone*, 27 Jun. 1991.

52. Robert Santinelli, "The Back Door of Success," *Modern Drummer*, 1987.

53. Will Self, "All Hail Yorkie Boy," *GQ*, Jul. 2003.

54. Anthony Kiedis, *Scar Tissue* (New York: Hyperion, 2004).

55. *U2 in Quotes.*

56. Paul Rees, "Riders on the Storm," *Q*, Nov. 2004.

57. "Adam Speaks to U2.com," U2.com, 28 Dec. 2004.

58. Mark Edwards, "Pop: He Learnt to Sing from His Soul by Accident," *The Sunday Times*, 7 Dec. 2003.

59. Sean O'Hagan, "The Laughing Cavalier," *The Guardian*, 14 Apr. 2001.

60. Edna Gundersen, "U2's Second 'Best' Evolves from Raucous '90s," *USA Today*, 15 Nov. 2002.

61. Sean Plummer, "Everything in Its Right Place.... At last," *Access*, Jun.–Jul. 2003.

62. Lauren Zoric, "Fitter, Happier, More Productive," *Juice*, 25 Sept. 2000.

63. Billy Corgan, "U2 Q&A."

64. Brian Hiatt, "U2's Beautiful New Day," Sonicnet.com, 2001.

65. "Red Hot Chili Peppers," Artistdirect.com, 1995.

66. Steve Turner, "U2: The Rock of the Irish," *Sunday Express Magazine*, 16 Oct. 1988.

Chapter 9

1. Tom Forsythe, "Laughing All the Way," *Guitar*, Feb. 1991.

2. Scott Malandrone, "Flea Starts from Scratch," *Bass Player*, Feb. 1996.

3. Ian Shedden, "Red Alert," *The Australian*, 29 Nov. 2002.

4. Jane Stevensen, "4 Minus 1 Still Equals R.E.M.," *The Toronto Sun*, 21 Aug. 1999.

5. Gavin Martin, "U2 People: Bono," *Uncut Legends*, Vol. 3 (U2).

6. Jim DeRogatis, "The Day's Still Beautiful for U2," *The Chicago Sun Times*, 6 May 2001.

7. Steve Roeser, "Conversation with Kiedis," *Goldmine*, 22 Nov. 1996.

8. Anthony Kiedis, *Scar Tissue* (New York: Hyperion, 2004).

9. Nancy Benecki, "An Interview with U2's Larry Mullen. No More 40-Foot Lemons," Music.com, 2 Nov. 2000.

10. Gil Kaufman, "Red Hot Chili Peppers: Back in the Saddle," *Addicted to Noise*, Jan. 1999.

11. Chuck Klosterman, "Meeting Thom Is Easy," *Spin*, Jun. 2003.

12. Dave Thompson, *Bono: In His Own Words* (New York: Omnibus, 1989).

13. Tom Doyle, "10 Years of Turmoil Inside U2," *Q*, 10 Oct. 2002.

14. Mark Harden, "R.E.M. Comes to Red Rocks," *The Denver Post*, 13 Aug. 1999.

15. Bill Flanagan, "The View from the Edge," *Musician*, 1 Mar. 1992.

16. Roger Coletti, "Red Hot Chili Peppers: A Conversation with Anthony Kiedis," MTV.com, Aug. 1999.

17. "Adam Speaks to U2.com," U2.com, 28 Dec. 2004.

18. DJ Mark Goodier, BBC Radio 1 Interview with U2, 13 Feb. 1992.

19. Anthony Kiedis, *Scar Tissue*.

20. David Browne, "R.E.M.: Road Worriers," *Entertainment Weekly*, 17 Mar. 1995.

21. David Cavanagh, "The Arenas of the Unwell," *Q*, Jan. 1996.

22. Jim Sullivan, "Radiohead Remembers the Pleasantries," *The Boston Globe*, 1 Jun. 2001.

23. Dominique Dujean, "Vicious Rumour," *Hard 'n' Heavy*, 26 Jul. 1996.

24. Justin Mitchell, "It's Red Hot for the Chili Peppers," *The Orange County Register*, 25 Dec. 1987.

25. Dave Bowler and Bryan Dray, *Documental* (London: Boxtree, 1995).

26. Cat Mantione-Homes, "Everything's Looking 'Up' for R.E.M.," *The Athens Daily News*, 25 Oct. 1998.

27. Gavin Edwards, "Are We Not Men? We Are Peppers!," *Rolling Stone*, Apr. 2000.

28. B.P. Fallon, *U2 Faraway So Close* (New York: Virgin, 1994).

29. Liam Mackey, "I Still Haven't Found What I'm Looking For," *Hot Press*, 1 Dec. 1988.

30. Jim Irvin, "R.E.M.," *Mojo*, Nov. 1994.

31. Mat Snow, "R.E.M.: Touched! Chuffed! Etc.!," *Q*, Jan. 1992.

CHAPTER 10

1. David Fricke, "Making Music That Matters," *Rolling Stone*, 2 Aug. 2001.
2. Adrian Deevoy, "I Had Too Much to Dream Last Night," *Q*, 1 Sept. 1993.
3. "An Interview with U2: Album, Tour, and More," Interference.com, Sept. 2004.
4. Sean O'Hagan, "U2 Anew," *Details*, 1 Sept. 1992.
5. Edna Gundersen, "U2 Strikes Again," *USA Today*, 30 Oct. 2000.
6. Zev Borow, "The Difference Engine," *Spin*, Nov. 2000.
7. "Rejuvenated Radiohead Is on the Rise," *The Denver Post*, 12 Jun. 1995.
8. Bill Flanagan, "The View from the Edge," *Musician*, 1 Mar. 1992.
9. "We're Not So Uptight Now ... Thom Yorke's Happy Return," *Melody Maker*, 21–27 Jun. 2000.
10. Gerald Marzorati, "The Post-Rock Band," *The New York Times Upfront*, 30 Oct. 2000.
11. Kevin Connal, "Exclusive Interview: The Edge," *Hit Parader Presents U2*, 1 Jun. 1992.
12. Stuart Bailie, "The Lung and Whining Road," *NME*, 1 Oct. 1994.
13. Jim Shelley, "Nice Dream?" *The Guardian*, 13 Jul. 1996.
14. John Albert, "Sons of the City," *LA Weekly*, 6–12 Dec. 2002.
15. VPRO Interview with John Frusciante, 1994. [Available on Frusciante.net.]
16. James Oldham, "Radiohead: Their Stupendous Return," *NME*, 24 Jun. 2000
17. James Henke, "The Edge: The Rolling Stone Interview," *Rolling Stone*, 10 Mar. 1987.
18. Susan Black, *Radiohead ... In Their Own Words* (London: Omnibus, 2002).
19. Mark Blackwell, "Meet Ze Monster," *Huh*, Nov. 1995.
20. Dorian Lynskey, "Different Class," *Q*, 2 Aug. 2001.
21. Don Snowden, "The Reckoning of R.E.M.," *The Los Angeles Times*, 18 Jul. 1984.
22. B.P. Fallon, *U2 Faraway So Close* (New York: Virgin, 1994).
23. Don Snowden, "The Reckoning of R.E.M."
24. Dave Bowler and Bryan Dray, *Documental* (London: Boxtree, 1995).
25. "Introduction," *U2: The Best Of Propaganda* (New York: Thunder's Mouth, 2003).
26. Gary Graff, "R.E.M. Set off on Another Sonic Adventure," *Reuters New Media*, 3 Sept. 1996.
27. Peter Murphy, "How Radiohead Learned to Loathe the Bomb," *Hot Press*, 11 Oct. 2001.
28. Edna Gundersen, "R.E.M.'s Upheaval Has Its Upside," *USA Today*, 10 Dec. 1998.
29. "Radiohead Master," *Microsoft MusicCentral*, 2 Sept. 1997.
30. Peter Murphy, "How Radiohead Learned to Loathe the Bomb."
31. Mac Randall, *Exit Music: The Radiohead Story* (New York: Delta, 2000).
32. Martin Turenne, "Interview with Colin," *The Georgia Straight*, 21 Jun. 2001.
33. Jim Irvin, "R.E.M.," *Mojo*, Nov. 1994.
34. Niall Stokes, *Into the Heart: The Stories Behind Every U2 Song* (London: Carlton, 2002).
35. Olaf Tyaransen, "The Final Frontier," *Hot Press*, 26 Oct. 2000.
36. Lisa Robinson, "U2's Unforgettable Fire," *Vanity Fair*, 25 Oct. 2004.
37. "Adam Talks," *Propaganda*, 1 Sept. 1989 (issue 11).
38. Mat Smith, "Welcome to the Occupation," *Melody Maker*, 12 Sept. 1987.
39. Lisa Robinson, "U2's Unforgettable Fire."
40. Gil Kaufman, "Michael Stipe on Photography," Sonicnet.com, 9 Apr. 1999.
41. Allison Adato, "The Stipe Man Cometh," *The Los Angeles Times*, 26 Mar. 2000.
42. Vicki Mabrey, "60 Minutes II: BONO," CBCNews.com, 20 Feb. 2002.
43. Tamara Conniff, "Dialogue with Bono," *The Hollywood Reporter*, 21 Feb. 2003.
44. Michael Goldberg, "R.E.M.'s Peter Buck Can't Get No Satisfaction," *Addicted to Noise*, Sept. 1996.
45. Bob Gulla, "Buck of All Trades," *Guitar*, Jul. 1997.
46. Mat Smith, "Welcome to the Occupation," *Melody Maker*, 12 Sept. 1987.
47. Michael Roberts, "The Buck Stops Here," *The Dallas Observer*, 23 Jul. 1998.
48. Johnny Black, *Reveal: The Story of R.E.M.* (San Francisco: Backbeat, 2004).
49. Kieran Grant, "Water Muse Surfaces," *The Toronto Sun*, 17 Feb. 2001.
50. Patrick Berkery, "Perfect from Now On," *Magnet*, No. 65, Oct.–Nov. 2004.
51. Howard Johnson, "U2 People: Larry Mullen," *Uncut Legends*, Vol. 3 (U2).

CHAPTER 11

1. Nancy Price, "Radiohead on Their Band Dynamic," *The Musician's Exchange*, 23 Jun. 1999.
2. Jack Rabid, "What the A? The Oxford Powerhouse Shocks the World with an Oblique, Obtuse, Impressionistic, Artistic, Total Curveball of a New LP. But Will It Stick?," *The Big Takeover*, Issue No. 47.
3. "Anthony Kiedis: Blood Synergy Sex Meltdown," VH1.com, 30 May 2002.
4. Greg Kot, "R.E.M.'s Best Album Side?," *The Chicago Tribune*, 27 Nov. 1994.
5. Olaf Tyaransen, "U2: A Bass Odyssey," *Hot Press*, 25 Nov. 1998.
6. Niall Stokes, "Matter of Life and Death," *Hot Press Annual 2002*, 1 Dec. 2001.

7. Britt Stubbe, "No to Drugs, Yes to Religion," *Oor,* Jun. 2002.

8. Kate Sullivan, "Icons: Red Hot Chili Peppers," *Spin,* Aug. 2002.

9. Dominick A. Miserandino, "Kiedis, Anthony—Lead Singer for the Red Hot Chili Peppers," Celebritycafe.com, Jan. 2005.

10. David Cavanagh, "I Can See the Monsters," *Q,* Oct. 2000.

11. David Fricke, "The Wizards of Pop," *Rolling Stone,* 29 May 1997.

12. Robert Hilburn, "Soul Searching for a '90s Sound," *Newsday,* 8 Mar. 1992.

13. Ted Kessler, "We Never Wanted to Be the Biggest Band in the World," *NME,* 13 Dec. 1997.

14. P.J. Morel, et al., "R.E.M. Peter Buck Talks About the Passion," *Pulse of the Twin Cities,* 11 Sept. 2003.

15. "Q&A," *Kerrang! Legends,* Issue No. 4. (Red Hot Chili Peppers).

16. Barney Hoskyns, "Flags and Penance: U2's American Dream," *NME,* 22 Jun. 1985.

17. Alan Light, "Band of the Year: Rock's Unbreakable Heart," *Spin,* 1 Jan. 2001.

18. "R.E.M. Artist of the Month," HMV.com, May 2001.

19. Michael Goldberg, "R.E.M.'s Peter Buck Can't Get No Satisfaction," *Addicted to Noise,* Sept. 1996.

20. Jon Bream, "Chili Peppers Frontman Talks Tour, Lakers," *Wall of Sound,* 24 Mar. 2000.

21. "Airheads," *Rip It Up,* Jun.–Jul. 2001 (issue 281).

22. Steve Roeser, "Conversation with Kiedis," *Goldmine,* 22 Nov. 1996.

23. Mac Randall, "Now We Are Three," Yahoo! Launch.com, 17 Nov. 1998.

24. Dave Di Martino, "Nowhere to Go But Up," Yahoo! Launch.com, 13 Apr. 1999.

25. Risa Bryan, "Anyone Can Play Cards," *The Island Ear,* 16–29 Aug. 1993.

26. Jim Irvin, "R.E.M.," *Mojo,* Nov. 1994.

27. "An In Depth Interview with Anthony Kiedis in Glasgow," *Vibe,* Mar. 2003.

28. Anthony DeCurtis, "Monster Madness," *Rolling Stone,* 20 Oct. 1994.

29. Chrissy Iley, "U2 Interview: Group Therapy," *Sunday Times Magazine,* 7 Nov. 2004.

30. "U2 Q&A on *How to Dismantle an Atomic Bomb,*" BestBuy.com, 24 Nov. 2004.

31. Gary Graff, "Interview with R.E.M.," *Wall of Sound,* 31 Oct. 1998.

32. P.J. Morel, et al., "R.E.M. Peter Buck Talks About the Passion," *Pulse of the Twin Cities,* 11 Sept. 2003.

33. Bruce T. Wittet, "Phil Selway," *Modern Drummer,* Aug. 1996.

34. "R.E.M. Star Reveals Future Plans," *NME,* 6 Sept. 2001.

35. Jud Cost, "R.E.M. Interview: Breakfast with Buck," *The Bob,* 1995.

36. Michael Goldberg, "R.E.M.—The Band That Sometimes Isn't," *Neumu,* 2001.

37. Brian Hiatt, "U2's Beautiful New Day," Sonicnet.com, 2001.

38. Chuck Klosterman, "Meeting Thom Is Easy," *Spin,* Jun. 2003.

CHAPTER 12

1. "A Spy in the House of Music," *MC,* Jan. 2001.

2. Tom Moon, "Radiohead: Companion to *Kid A* Sessions," *The Philly Inquirer,* 3 Jun. 2001.

3. Nick Kent, "Happy Now?," *Mojo,* 2001.

4. Peter Paphides, "Into the Light," *Mojo,* 2003.

5. Peter Paphides, "Into the Light."

6. David Cavanagh, "I Can See the Monsters," *Q,* Oct. 2000.

7. "Radiohead Recall *Amnesiac,*" Planet Sound Channel 4 (UK) Teletext, 19 May 2001.

8. Simon Reynolds, "Walking on Thin Ice," *The Wire,* Jul. 2001.

9. Olaf Tyaransen, "Closer to the Edge," *Hot Press,* 4 Dec. 2002.

10. John Davidson, "New Kid on the Block," *The LiNK,* Nov. 2000.

11. Gary Graff, "Ed and Colin Interview," *Music Connection,* 16 Jul. 2001.

12. Stuart Berman, "Fitter, Happier, More Productive: Radiohead Emerge from the Dark Side," *Eye,* 12 Oct. 2000.

13. Gerald Marzorati, "The Post-Rock Band," *The New York Times Upfront,* 30 Oct. 2000.

14. Greg Kot, "Alluring Otherworldliness," *The Chicago Tribune,* 19 Aug. 2001.

15. Lauren Zoric, "Fitter, Happier, More Productive," *Juice,* 25 Sept. 2000.

16. Gary Graff, "In Excess," *Guitar World,* Sept. 1997.

17. Richard Harrington, "U2's 'Pop' Arch," *The Washington Post,* 26 May 1997.

18. Martin Wroe, "Under Construction," *Propaganda,* Issue 30, 2000.

19. Gary Graff, "U2, As Big As Any Rock Band," *United Press International,* 1 Nov. 2002.

20. Niall Stokes, *Into the Heart: The Stories Behind Every U2 Song* (London: Carlton, 2002).

21. John Robinson, "It's Clear and Pretty—But I Think People Won't Get It," *NME,* 3 May 2003.

22. Susan Black, *Radiohead … In Their Own Words* (London: Omnibus, 2002).

23. Yahoo.com Chat with Bono, 12 Mar. 2000.

24. "'Up,' with People," *The Boston Globe,* 25 Oct. 1998.

25. David Sprague, "Buck on *Up,*" *Guitar,* Dec. 1998.

26. Gary Graff, "Interview with R.E.M.," *Wall of Sound,* 31 Oct. 1998.

27. Edna Gundersen, "R.E.M.'s Upheaval Has Its Upside," *USA Today,* 10 Dec. 1998.

28. Bill Forman, "Diminished But Unafraid, R.E.M. Talk about the Passion," *Pulse!*, Nov. 1998.

29. David Fricke, "Living Up to *Out of Time*/Remote Control," *Melody Maker*, 26 Sept.–3 Oct. 1992.

30. Andrew Mathis, "Interview with Michael Stipe," RockDaily.com, 4 Apr. 1999.

31. Adam Sweeting, "Highs and Lotus," *The Age*, 9 Nov. 1998.

32. Tony Fletcher, "Rap's Rudeboys Hang Tough," *Newsday*, 6 Oct. 1991.

33. Fraser Middleton, "Back from the Brink: Red Hot Chili Peppers Beat Their Addictions to Return Even Stronger," *The Sunday Herald*, 2 Jan. 2003.

34. John Bream, "Kiedis Talks Peppers Tour, L.A. Lakers," *Wall of Sound*, 24 Mar. 2000.

35. Red Hot Chili Peppers Interview CD, Baktabak 1991 (CBAK 4091).

36. Jeff Apter, *Fornication: The Red Hot Chili Peppers Story* (New York: Omnibus, 2004).

37. Dublin Press Conference Backstage at the 2003 Meteor Awards, 4 Mar. 2003.

38. David Breskin, "Bono: U2's Passionate Voice," *Rolling Stone*, 8 Oct. 1987.

39. Elianne Halbersberg, "Interview: Peter Buck of R.E.M.," *East Coast Rocker*, 30 Nov. 1988.

Bibliography
(works cited and works consulted)

ARTICLES AND BOOKS

Aaron, Charles. "Strange Currencies: R.E.M. Comes Alive!" *Spin*, Aug. 1995.

Abbot, Tim. "Live Adventures in Hi-Fi." *Record Collector*, Aug. 1997. [REM]

"Absolute McGuinness," *Propaganda*, 1 Oct. 1987 (issue 7).

"Adam Speaks to U2.com." U2.com, 28 Dec. 2004.

Adams, Noah, and Rick Karr. "R.E.M." *All Things Considered*. NPR. 28 Oct. 1998.

Adato, Allison. "The Stipe Man Cometh." *The Los Angeles Times*, 26 Mar. 2000. [REM]

Ahrens, Chris. "Survival Mechanisms." *Risen*, vol. 2, no. 2 (2005). [RHCP]

"Airheads." *Rip It Up*, Issue 281 Jun.-Jul. 2001. [RH]

Aizlewood, John. "Red Hot." *The London Evening Standard*, Metro Life section, 7 Mar. 2003. [RHCP]

Albert, John. "Sons of the City." *LA Weekly*, 6–12 Dec. 2002. [RHCP]

Alexander, Phil. "Some Like It Hot." *Raw*, 21 Feb.–6 Mar. 1990. [RHCP]

Allen, Terry. "The First Gig." *Q Special Edition (R.E.M.)*.

Anderman, Joan. "For R.E.M., Time Is Finally Right to Tour Again." *The Boston Globe*, 3 Oct. 2003.

"Anthony Kiedis: Blood Synergy Sex Meltdown." VH1.com, 30 May 2002. [RHCP]

Apter, Jeff. *Fornication: The Red Hot Chili Peppers Story* (New York: Omnibus, 2004).

Aquilante, Dan. "R.E.M. Sleep Is Over." *The New York Post*, 26 Sept. 2003.

_____. "'Up' and Running." *The New York Post*, 3 Sept. 1999. [REM]

_____. "A Word Edge-Wise—U2 Sideman Is Definitely Pro Bono." *The New York Post*, 18 May 2005.

Ascott, Phil. "John Frusciante—Universally Speaking." *Guitarist*, Jun. 2003. [RHCP]

Assayas, Michka. *Bono: In Conversation With Michka Assayas*. New York: Riverhead, 2005. [U2]

Bailey, Jared H. "Mike Mills: Producer of Sorts." *Flagpole*, 8 Sept. 1993. [REM]

Bailie, Stuart. "The Lung and Whining Road." *NME*, 1 Oct. 1994. [RH]

_____. "Motley Crew." *NME*, 13 Feb. 1993. [RH]

_____. "Viva La Megabytes!" *NME*, 21 Jun. 1997. [RH]

Baillie, Russell. "Ed O'Brien: Turning Up, Tuning In." *The New Zealand Herald*, 7 Apr. 2001. [RH]

Baker, Brian. "John Frusciante." *Amplifier*, Issue No. 44, Sept.-Oct. 2004. [RHCP]

"Band's Melancholy Music Elates Fans." *The Plain Dealer*, 7 Jun. 1995. [RH]

Bannour, Férid, and Christophe Rossi. "Chad Smith: Californibatteur." *Batteur*, Jul.-Aug. 1999. [RHCP]

_____. "Lust for Life." *Batteur*, Jun. 1998. [RHCP]

Barret, Ed. "Rock's Winston Churchill—Profile: Bono." *The Sunday Independent*, 21 Feb. 1999. [U2]

Barringer, Holly. "All You Need Is Loathe." *NME*, 11 Jun. 1996. [RH]

Beauvallet, J.D. "Nigel the Nihilist." *Les Inrockuptibles*, 25 Jan. 2000. [RH]

Bell, Max. "Five Men and *Achtung Baby*." *Vox*, Dec. 1991. [U2]

Bell, Mike. "All Hail Radiohead." *The Calgary Sun*, 3 Jun. 2003.
Benecki, Nancy. "An Interview with U2's Larry Mullen: No More 40-Foot Lemons." Music.com, 2 Nov. 2000.
Bento, Debbie. "Red Hot Chili Peppers Yearn to Be with God." *Chart Attack*, 16 Aug. 2002.
Berkery, Patrick. "Perfect from Now On." *Magnet*, Issue No. 65, Oct.-Nov. 2004. [RHCP]
Berman, Stuart. "Fitter, Happier, More Productive: Radiohead Emerge from the Dark Side." *Eye*, 12 Oct. 2000.
Berrera, Sandra. "R.E.M.'s Awakening." *The Long Beach Press Telegram*, 4 Sept. 2003.
"Berry, R.E.M. Want Fans to Let Band Move Ahead." *The Athens Daily News*, 1 Nov. 1997.
Bill, David. "R.E.M. Having 'A Blast,' Stipe Says." *The Athens Daily News*, 27 Aug. 1999.
Black, James. *Canadian Musician*, May-Jun. 2001. [RHCP]
Black, Johnny. *Reveal: The Story of R.E.M.* (San Francisco: Backbeat, 2004).
Black, Susan. *Radiohead ... In Their Own Words*. (London: Omnibus, 2002).
Blackett, Matt. "Return of the Prodigal Son: John Frusciante Fires Up the Chili Peppers." *Guitar Player*, Sept. 1999.
Blackwell, Mark. "Meet Ze Monster." *Huh*, Nov. 1995. [REM]
_____, and Greer, Jim. "Three's Company." *Ray Gun*, Dec. 1998. [REM]
Blake, Mark. "Like Spinning Plates." *Q Special Edition (Radiohead)*.
_____. "U2's Bono: Rumors of His Demise Have Been Greatly Exaggerated." *Q*, 1 Jan. 1998.
Blashill, Pat. "Band of the Year: Radiohead." *Spin*, Jan. 1998.
Block, Adam. "Pure Bono." *Mother Jones*, 1 May 1989. [U2]
"Bono Talks about the New Album." *U2 Magazine*, Oct. 1984. No. 12.
Booth, Philip. "Two Decades of One Life ... One Band ... U2." *The Sarasota Herald-Tribune*, 30 Nov. 2001.
Borow, Zev. "The Difference Engine." *Spin*, Nov. 2000. [RH]
Bowler, Dave, and Bryan Dray. *Documental* (London: Boxtree, 1995). [REM]
Boyd, Brian. "Closer to the Edge." *The Irish Times*, 21 Oct. 2000. [U2]
_____. "Meet the Bomb Squad." *The Irish Times*, 23 Dec. 2004. [U2]
_____. "A Tough Gig, This Messiah Business." *The Irish Times*, 3 Mar. 2002 [U2]
Bradman, E.E. "Flea: At Your Service." *Bass Player*, Aug. 2002. [RHCP]
Bream, Jon. "Chili Peppers Frontman Talks Tour, Lakers." *Wall of Sound*, 24 Mar. 2000.
Breskin, David. "Bono: U2's Passionate Voice." *Rolling Stone*, 8 Oct. 1987.
Bronson, Fred. "Radiohead Upgraded from 'OK' to 'A.'" *Billboard*, 21 Oct. 2000.
Brown, G. "R.E.M.: Rockin' Even More." *The Denver Post*, 12 Sept. 2003.
Browne, David. "Road Warriors." *Entertainment Weekly*, 1996. [REM]
_____. "Stipe's Rich Pageant: R.E.M's Main Man Riffs on Sex, Music, and Big-Screen Dreams." *Entertainment Weekly*, 14 Jul. 1995.
Bryan, Risa. "Radiohead: Anyone Can Play Cards." *The Island Ear*, 16–29 Aug. 1993.
Buckley, David. *R.E.M. Fiction: An Alternative Biography* (London: Virgin, 2003).
Byrne, George. "Interview with Michael Stipe." *The Irish Independent*, 18 Mar. 1999. [REM]
Calvet, Vincent. "Red Hot: La Confession Exclusive." *MCM.net*, Sept. 1999. [RHCP]
Cammick, Murray. "Interview with Adam and Edge." *Rip It Up*, Dec. 1989. [U2]
Campbell, Alastair. "Bono Interviewed." *Five*, 27 Oct. 2004. [U2]
Cantin, Paul. "Jam! Interviews Radiohead." *Jam!*, 17 Oct. 2000.
_____. "R.E.M. Album 'Lush,' 'Melodic.'" *Jam!*, 24 Aug. 2000.
Carducci, Joe. *Rock and the Pop Narcotic*. (Chicago: Redoubt, 1990).
Carroll, Jim. "U2: The Muse Interview." *Muse Online*, 18 Dec. 1998.
Cashmere, Tim. "Jonny Greenwood Interview." *Undercover*, 2003. [RH]
Cavanagh, David. "The Arenas of the Unwell." *Q*, Jan. 1996. [REM]
_____. "I Can See the Monsters." *Q*, Oct. 2000. [RH]
_____. "Tune In, Cheer Up, Rock Out." *Q*, Oct. 1994. [REM]
"Certains L'Aiment Show." *Rocksound*, Jun. 1996. [RHCP]
"Chad on Rock 'N' Roll Back." *Rolling Stone*, 2002. [RHCP]
Chandar, Chris. "Love Loss Life Magik." *Pulse!*, Aug. 2002. [RHCP].
"Change of Tune for Radiohead." *The Record*, 1 Jun. 1995.
Charlton, Matt. "Radiohead Welcomes the Rock." *Exclaim!*, 30 May 2003.
Chat with Michael Stipe. Zoogdisney.com, 1 Feb. 1999. [REM]
Chat with R.E.M. *AOL Live*, 31 Oct. 1997.
"Chili Peppers to Try Drum Machines, Loops." *Wall of Sound*, 7 Mar. 2001.
Clark, Stuart. "Transistor Act." *Hot Press*, 12 Jul. 1995. [RH]

Clarke, Martin. *Radiohead: Hysterical and Useless* (London: Plexus, 2000).

Clayton-Lea, Tony. "Arms Around the World." *The Irish Times Magazine*, 25 Aug. 2001. [U2]

Cocks, Jay. "Band on the Run." *Time*, 27 Apr. 1987. [U2]

Cohan, John. "In the Studio with the Red Hot Chili Peppers' Drummer and Producer." *Drum*, May-Jun. 2002.

Cohen, Jonathan. "Greenwood Produces His Own 'Body' of Work: Radiohead Guitarist Scores Film." *Billboard*, 14 Feb. 2004.

_____. "Web Leak Fails to Derail Capitol's Radiohead Setup." *Billboard*, 14 Jun. 2003.

Coletti, Roger. "Red Hot Chili Peppers: A Conversation with Anthony Kiedis." MTV.com, Aug. 1999.

Connal, Kevin. "Exclusive Interview: The Edge," *Hit Parader Presents U2*, 1 Jun. 1992. [U2]

Connelly, Christopher. "Keeping the Faith." *Rolling Stone*, 14 Mar. 1985. [U2]

Conniff, Tamara. "Dialogue with Bono." *The Hollywood Reporter*, 21 Feb. 2003. [U2]

Considine, J.D. "Good Time Boys." *Guitar World*, Jul. 1999. [RHCP]

_____ "R.E.M.: Subverting Small Town Boredom." *Musician*, Aug. 1983.

Cook, Richard. "A Dreamboat Named Desire." *NME*, 27 Feb. 1982. [U2]

Copely, Richard. "One on One." *The Athens Daily News*, 31 Oct. 1997. [REM]

_____. "R.E.M. Drummer Calls It Quits." *The Athens Daily News*, 31 Oct. 1997.

_____. "R.E.M.'s Newest, Huge in Europe, Is Much More Than Just a Hit Single." *The Athens Daily News*, 20 Oct. 1996.

Corgan, Billy. "U2 Q&A." *Live!*, 1 May 1997.

Cornell, Rick. "Mike Mills Speaks *Up.*" *The Music Monitor*, Nov. 1998. [REM]

Cornwall, Hugh. "Adam Talks to Hugh Cornwall of the Stranglers." *U2 Magazine*, no. 14, 1 Mar. 1985.

Coryal, Karl. "Flea! Red Hot Chili Pepper." *Bass Player*, Feb. 1992.

_____. "Mike Mills Climbs the Charts with R.E.M." *Bass Player*, Sept. 1991.

Cost, Jud. "R.E.M. Interview: Breakfast with Buck." *The Bob*, 1995.

Crabb, Annabel. "Thom Out of Tune." *The Sydney Morning Herald*, 14 Aug. 2006. [RH]

Crandall, Bill. "R.E.M. Recharged on *Reveal.*" *Rolling Stone*, 9 Apr. 2001.

_____. "U2 Hope to Reawaken America." *Rolling Stone*, 27 Oct. 2000.

Cromelin, Richard. "Pop Beat." *The Los Angeles Times*, 8 Jan. 2005. [RHCP]

Curtis, Kim. "Radiohead Goes Where No Other Band Has Gone." *The Bergen County Record*, 29 Oct. 2003.

Dalton, Stephen. "Are We Having Fun Yet?" *The Age*, 11 Apr. 2004. [RH]

_____. "In the Name of Love." *Uncut*, 1 Nov. 1999. [U2]

"Dandy's Inferno." *NME*, 22 May 1993. [U2]

Davidson, John. "New Kid on the Block." *The LiNK*, Nov. 2000. [RH]

Davies, Hunter. *The Beatles: The Authorized Biography* (New York: W. W. Norton, 1968).

Davies, Laura Lee. "Wings of Desire." *Time Out*, 8 Aug. 2001. [U2]

Davis, Tim C. "Talk about the Passion." *Creative Loafing Charlotte*, 5 Feb 2003. [REM]

DeCurtis, Anthony. "Interview with R.E.M." CDNow.com, 31 Dec. 1998.

_____. "Monster Madness." *Rolling Stone*, 20 Oct. 1994. [REM]

_____. "Raw Power." *Revolver*, 1 Dec. 2000. [U2]

_____. "U2's Edge and Adam Clayton Look Back on Two Decades of Hit Albums with Few— If Any—Regrets." *Revolver*, 2000.

_____. "Zoo World Order." *Rolling Stone*, 14 Oct. 1993. [U2]

Deeds, Michael. "A Lesson in Rock Longevity." *The Mercury News*, 16 Aug. 2006. [RCHP]

Deevoy, Adrian. "I Had Too Much to Dream Last Night." *Q*, 1 Sept. 1993. [U2]

_____. "U2 Walk on Water!" *Blender*, 17 Oct. 2004.

_____. "Welcome to the Funny Farm." *Q*, Dec. 1988. [REM]

De Muir, Harold. "There's No Reason It Shouldn't Be a Hit." *East Coast Rocker*, 7 Oct. 1987. [REM]

Densmore, John. "Riders on the Storm." *The Nation*, 8 Jul. 2002.

DeRogatis, Jim. "The Day's Still Beautiful for U2." *The Chicago Sun Times*, 6 May 2001.

_____. "R.E.M.: What Happened?" *The Chicago Sun Times*, 20 Aug. 1999.

Desens, Krista. "Adam Clayton on U2's Longevity." BuzzFM.com, 12 Apr. 2005.

Dietrich, Hans-Peter. "Airplane Man." *Flagpole*, 30 Jun. 1999. [REM]

Di Martino, Dave. "Give Radiohead Your Computer." Yahoo!Music.com, 2 May. 1999.

_____. "Nowhere to Go But Up." Yahoo!Launch.com, 13 Apr. 1999. [REM]

Di Perna, Alan. "Dave Navarro: Red Hot Chili Stranger." *Guitarist*, Feb. 1996.

_____. "Getting Better All the Time." *Guitar*, Aug. 2002. [RHCP]

_____. "The Red Hot Chili Peppers." FenderEurope.com, 2002.

_____. "Shock Exchange." *Guitar World*, Nov. 1997. [RHCP]

Dixon, Guy. "Mike Mills." *The Globe and Mail*, 12 Nov. 2004. [REM]

Domellöf, Maria. "Bono: Up in the Blue with the Feet on the Ground." Unknown Source. 2002. [U2]

Dougherty, Steve, and Anne Driscoll. "Band of Brothers." *People*, 24 Nov. 2003. [REM]

Douridas, Chris. Interview with Anthony Kiedis for AOL's *Sessions*. 16 May 2002. [RHCP]

_____. Interview with Thom Yorke. *Morning Becomes Eclectic*. KCRW [Santa Monica], 9 Jun. 1997. [RH]

Dowling, Stephen. "Interview with Ed & Phil." *Music365.co.uk.*, 29 Sept. 2000. [RH]

_____. "Radiohead: Hail to the Thief." *The New Zealand Herald*, 1 Jun. 2003.

Doyle, Tom. _____. "Out of Time?" *Q*, Sept. 1999. [REM]

_____. "Party On." *Q*, Jun. 1997. [RH]

Doyle, Tom. "10 Years of Turmoil Inside U2." *Q*, 10 Oct. 2002.

Drake, Damian, and C. Bottomley. "R.E.M.: Time After Time." VH1.com, 10 Oct. 2003.

Droney, Maureen. "Rick Rubin: Life Among the WildFlowers." *Mix*, Oct. 2000. [RHCP]

Dubigeon, Manuel. "Chad Smith: Red Hot Funky Drummer." *Batteur*, Sept. 1995. [RHCP]

Dublin Press Conference Backstage at the 2003 Meteor Awards, 4 Mar. 2003. [U2]

Dujean, Dominique. "Vicious Rumour." *Hard N' Heavy*, 26 Jul. 1996. [RHCP]

Du Noyer, Paul. "Let's Hear It for ... Us!" *Q*, 1 Jan. 1993 [U2]

Eccleston, Danny. "Radiohead Interview." *Q*, Oct. 2000.

_____. "There's Life in the Old Knees Yet!" *Q*, Jul. 1999. [REM]

Edgar, Mike. "Pop: The Questions." *Hot Press*, 20 Aug. 1997. [U2]

The Edge. "The Edge Looked at Johnny." *Hot Press*, 30 Sept. 2003. [U2]

Edwards, Gavin. "Are We Not Men? We Are Peppers!" *Rolling Stone*, Jun. 2000. [RHCP]

_____. "Radiohead Swagger on *Thief*." *Rolling Stone*, 9 May 2003.

Edwards, Mark. "Pop: He Learnt to Sing from His Soul By Accident." *The Sunday Times*, 7 Dec. 2003. [REM]

Ehrlich, Dimitri. "Anthony Kiedis." *Interview*, Dec. 2000. [RHCP]

"The Elastic Bono Band." *Q*, 1 Nov. 2000. [U2]

Elder, Robert K. "Re-Energized R.E.M." *The San Jose Mercury News*, 12 Aug. 1999.

"Elevate Thyself—The Ten Commandments of Bono." *Q*, 7 Feb. 2002. [U2]

Eno, Brian. "Bringing Up 'Baby.'" *Rolling Stone*, 28 Nov. 1991. [U2]

Fallon, B.P. *U2 Faraway So Close* (New York: Virgin, 1994).

_____. Zoo TV Tour Programme. 1992.

Fanning, Dave. "Here's Looking at You, Kid." *Hot Press*, 28 Sept. 2000. [RH]

Farley, John. "Monster Music." *Time*, 26 Sept. 1994 [REM]

Fey, Liam. "Back to the End of the Beginning." *Wales on Sunday*, 23 Jul. 1995. [REM]

Finn, Timothy. "Last Band Standing." *The Kansas City Star*, 27 Nov. 2001. [U2]

_____. "R.E.M. Looks Back to the Future." *The Kansas City Star*, 12 Sept. 2003.

Fitzmaurice, Eddie. "U2's Larry's Shock Statement on Band's Future." *The Irish Sunday Mirror*, 8 Dec. 2002.

Fitzpatrick, Rob. *Give It Away—Red Hot Chili Peppers: The Stories Behind Every Song* (New York: Thunder's Mouth, 2004).

Flanagan, Bill. "Soul Revelation and the Baptism of Fire." *Musician*, 1 Feb. 1985. [U2]

_____. "U2 on the Tube: The Rock Superstars Conquer Prime Time." *TV Guide*, 25 Apr. 1997.

_____. *U2: The Complete Songs* (London: Wise Publications, 1999).

_____. "The View from the Edge." *Musician*, 1 Mar. 1992. [U2]

Flannigan, Erik. "Northwest Interview: R.E.M." *The Rocket*, 25 Aug. 1999.

Flans, Robyn. "The Red Hot Chili Peppers Still Cookin.'" *MIX*, Jul. 1999.

_____. "Serving Up a New Red Hot Brew." *Modern Drummer*, Aug. 1999. [RHCP]

"Flea: Bass Specters Sex Madness." VH1.com, 30 May 2002. [RHCP]

Flea. Email to Redhotchilipeppers.com from St. Louis, Missouri. 27 Apr. 2000.

Flea on *Virgin Superstars*. Virgin Radio. [UK]. Mar. 2003. [RHCP]

Flea's Liner Notes, *Red Hot Chili Peppers Greatest Hits* CD. Warner Brothers, Nov. 2003.

Flea's Liner Notes, Reissued *Red Hot Chili Peppers* Album. Capitol Records, Mar. 2003.

Fletcher, Tony. "Rap's Rudeboys Hang Tough." *Newsday*, 6 Oct. 1991. [RHCP]

_____. *Remarks Remade: The Story of R.E.M.* (New York: Omnibus Press, 2002).

Flick, Larry. "Exclusive: U2 Tour To Begin March 24 In Miami." *Billboard*, 5 Jan. 2001. [U2]
Foege, Alec. "Once Death-Defying Clowns, The Red Hot Chili Peppers Grow Up to Be Sensitive White Males." *Rolling Stone*, 19 Oct. 1995.
Folkerth, Bruce. "Radiohead: Ignoreth The Hype." *Flagpole*, 13 Aug. 1997.
"For Anthony Kiedis, What Doesn't Kill You Only Makes Your Book Longer." MTV.com, 7 Oct. 2004. [RHCP]
Forman, Bill. "Diminished But Unafraid, R.E.M. Talk about the Passion." *Pulse!*, Nov. 1998.
"Fornicating California Style." *Metal Hammer*, Jun. 1999. [RHCP]
Forsythe, Tom. "Laughing All the Way." *Guitar*, Feb. 1991. [RHCP]
Fortnam, Ian. "Radiohead's Back Pages." Unpublished article, 1997. Article available (for a fee) online at www.rocksbackpages.com.
"40 Most Important Bands: Interview with Thom Yorke." *Spin*, Apr. 2001. [RH]
Fox, Darrin. "The Edge Brings U2 Back to Basics." *Guitar Player*, Jan. 2001.
Fricke, David. "The Bassman Speaks." *Rolling Stone*, 25 Apr. 2002. [U2]
_____. "Bitter Prophet." *Rolling Stone*, 25 Jun. 2003. [RH]
_____. "Living Up to *Out of Time*/Remote Control." *Melody Maker*, 26 Sept.–3 Oct. 1992. [REM]
_____. "Making Music That Matters." *Rolling Stone*, 2 Aug. 2001. [RH]
_____. "The Naked Truth." *Rolling Stone*, 25 Jun. 1992. [RHCP]
_____. "People of the Year: Thom Yorke." *Rolling Stone*, Dec. 2000. [RH]
_____. "Q&A Bono." *Rolling Stone*, 8 Jan. 1998. [U2]
_____. "Radiohead Talk *Amnesiac*." *Rolling Stone*, 24 May 2001.
_____. "Red Hot Reunion." *Rolling Stone*, 1 Apr. 1999. [RHCP]
_____. "Tattooed Love Boys." *Rolling Stone*, Jun. 2006. [RHCP]
_____. "U2 Finds What It's Looking For." *Rolling Stone*, 1 Oct. 1992.
_____. "The Wizards of Pop." *Rolling Stone*, 29 May 1997. [U2]
"Frusciante dans le 4eme Dimension." *Rock Mag*, Mar. 2001. Issue No. 5 [RHCP]
"Frusciante Talks about Chili Peppers' New Album." *AllStar*, 26 Apr. 2001.
Fulkerson, Ginger. "What's the Frequency, Michael?" *Ego Miami*, Aug. 2004. [REM]
Gabarini, Vic. "Reconstruction of the Fables." *Guitar World*, Nov. 1996. [REM]
_____. "Stark Side of the Moon." *Guitar*, Jun. 1993. [REM]
Gabriella. "The Californication of John Frusciante." *NYRock*, Jul. 1999. [RHCP]
_____. "Radiohead and Their New *Kid A*." *The Inside Connection*, Dec. 2000.
Gaitskill, Mary. "Radiohead: Alarms and Surprises." *Alternative Press*, Apr. 1998.
Galan, Olivier. "Red Hot Chili Fever." *Guitarist*, Jun. 1999.
Gale, Daisy. "Transcript of Interview with U2 in South of France." *CD:UK*, 16 Oct. 2004.
Garcia, Sandra A. "Radiohead Creeps Past Early Success." *B-Side*, Jul.–Aug. 1995.
Gardner, Elysa. "Chili Peppers, Hot Again." *USA Today*, 11 May 2006.
_____. "Is Rock Dead?" *USA Today*, 23 Apr. 1999. [REM]
Garibay, Lisa Y. Phil Selway (Radiohead). Thenitmustbetrue.com, Jun. 2001.
Garratt, Sheryl. "The Band Played On," *The Guardian*, 14 Feb. 1997. [U2]
Gee, Mike. "Bill Berry: Perfect Circle." *iZine*, 1994. [REM]
_____. "The Radical Reinvention of Radiohead." *The Sydney Morning Herald*, 6 Oct. 2000.
Gettelman, Parry. "R.E.M. Has a Monster on Its Hands." *The Orlando Sentinel*, 10 Nov. 1995.
Gilbert, Debbie. "R.E.M.: Why They're Still Around." *The Memphis Flyer*, 2 Nov. 1995.
Giles, Jeff. "Number One with an Attitude." *Rolling Stone*, 27 Jun. 1991. [REM]
Gill, Andy. "Greenwood Breaks Out." *The Hamilton Spectator*, 5 Nov. 2003. [RH]
Gillespie, Ian. "Radiohead Embraces Technology, Both on the Video and Sonic Side of Things." *The London Free Press*, 17 Aug. 1997.
Gittins, Ian. "The Story of Tchocky." *Q*, 2003. [RH]
_____, and U2. *U2: The Best of Propaganda—20 Years of the Official U2 Magazine* (New York: Thunder's Mouth, 2003).
Gliatto, Tom. "Bono's World: Part Rocker, Part Policy Wonk, U2's Singer Calls Himself 'The Thinking Man's Perry Como.'" *People*, 25 Feb. 2002. [U2]
Glover, Adrian Gregory. "Radiohead Getting More Respect." *Circus*, Aug. 1997.
Gold, Jerry. "R.E.M. Now a Veteran in Influential Music." *The Vancouver Sun*, 27 Aug. 2003.
Gold, Kerry. "Radiohead's Secret Weapon." *The Vancouver Sun*, 28 Aug. 2003.
Goldberg, Michael. "The Making of R.E.M.'s Monster." *Addicted to Noise*, Feb. 1995.
_____. "Reinventing R.E.M.: The Michael Stipe Q&A." *Addicted to Noise*, Nov. 1998.
_____. "Reinventing R.E.M.: The Peter Buck/Mike Mills Q&A." *Addicted to Noise*, Nov. 1998.

_____. "R.E.M.—The Band That Sometimes Isn't." *Neumu*, 2001.
_____. "R.E.M.'s Peter Buck Can't Get No Satisfaction." *Addicted to Noise*, Sept. 1996.
Goodier, Mark. Interview with U2. BBC Radio 1 [London]. 13 Feb. 1992.
Goodman, Dean. "R.E.M Looking Ahead with An Eye on the Past." *Reuters*, 5 Sept. 2003.
Gore, Joe. "Red Hot Chili Peppers—Au Travail." *Guitare & Claviers*, May 1995.
_____. "The Red Hot Chili Peppers: Gods of Sex Funk." *Guitar Player*, Oct. 1991.
Graff, Gary. "Adam Clayton Discusses the Next U2 Album." *Reuters*, 16 Jun. 1996.
_____. "Ed and Colin Interview." *Music Connection*, 16 Jul. 2001. [RH]
_____. "In Excess." *Guitar World*, Sept. 1997. [U2]
_____. "Interview with Michael Stipe." *Wall of Sound*, 1 Jul. 1999. [REM]
_____. "Interview with R.E.M." *Wall of Sound*, 31 Oct. 1998.
_____. "R.E.M. Set Off on Another Sonic Adventure." *Reuters New Media*, 3 Sept. 1996.
_____. "Split Personality: Radiohead Gives Its Fans a Double Dose," *The New York Times*, 25 Jun. 2001.
_____. "U2, As Big As Any Rock Band." *United Press International*, 1 Nov. 2002.
_____. "U2: Audio Interview." CDNow.com, 7 Sept. 2001.
Graham, Bill. "Band on the Run." *Hot Press*, 17 Dec. 1987. [U2]
_____, and Niall Stokes. "U2 Give Themselves Away." *Musician*, 1 May 1987.
Grant, Kieran. "Chili Pepper Guitarist Two-Timing." *The Toronto Sun*, 14 Aug. 2002.
_____. "Chillin' Out." *The Toronto Sun*, 8 Aug. 2002. [RHCP]
_____. "Water Muse Resurfaces." *The Toronto Sun*, 17 Feb. 2001. [RHCP]
Greer, Jim. *R.E.M.: Behind the Mask* (Boston: Little, Brown, 1992).
Grobel, Lawrence. "Anthony Kiedis: The Playboy Conversation." *Playboy*, 7 Oct. 2004. [RHCP]
Gulla, Bob. "Buck of All Trades." *Guitar*, Jul. 1997. [REM]
_____. "Radiohead—At Long Last, a Future for Rock Guitar." *Guitar World*, Oct. 1997. [RH]
Gundersen, Edna. "Alive and Ticking." *USA Today*, 18 Nov. 2004. [U2]
_____. "Bono Honoured As 2003 MusiCares Person of the Year." *Grammy*, 20 Feb. 2003. [U2]
_____. "Bono Takes His World Issues Seriously." *USA Today*, 4 Dec. 2001. [U2]
_____. "R.E.M.'s Upheaval Has Its Upside." *USA Today*, 10 Dec. 1998.
_____. "U2 Strikes Again." *USA Today*, 30 Oct. 2000.
_____. "U2's Second 'Best' Evolves from Raucous '90s." *USA Today*, 15 Nov. 2002.
Haggerty, Beth. "R.E.M. Begins Recording with Substitute Drummer." *The Red and Black*, 4 Feb.1998.
"Hail to Radiohead." *ICCoventry.co.uk*, Jun. 2003.
Hajari, Nisid. "Tales from the Creeps," *Entertainment Weekly*, 19 May 1995. [RH]
Halbersberg, Elainne. "Interview: Peter Buck of R.E.M." *East Coast Rocker*, 30 Nov. 1988.
Hale, Jonathan. *Radiohead: From a Great Height* (Toronto: ECW, 1999).
Harden, Mark. "R.E.M. Comes to Red Rocks." *The Denver Post*, 13 Aug. 1999.
Harding, Nigel. "Radiohead's Phil Selway." *Consumable Online*, 5 May 1995.
Harrington, Richard. "After the Show It Had to Be U2." *The Washington Post*, 28 May 1997.
_____. "Chili Peppers—Red Hot & New." *The Washington Post*, 9 Feb. 1996.
_____. "U2's 'Pop' Arch." *The Washington Post*, 26 May 1997.
Harris, John. "Finally Friends Again." *The Telegraph*, 29 Mar. 2001. [REM]
_____. "R.E.M.—One Week in South America." *Q*, May 2001.
_____. "Renaissance Men." *Select*, Jan. 1998. [RH]
Hayes, Dermott. "Do You Know This Man?" *Select*, 1 Jun. 1993. [U2]
"The Heat Is On." Dec. 2002. [Pre-Show Interview at the Singapore Indoor Stadium]. [RHCP]
Heath, Chris. "Michael in the Middle." *Details*, Feb. 1995. [REM]
_____. "R.E.M.: More Songs About Death and Anxiety." *Rolling Stone*, 17 Oct. 1996.
Heatley, Michael. Liner notes to Red Hot Chili Peppers interview CD. Sound and Media (Virgin Publishing), 1997 (SAM 7028).
Helms, Colin. "Interview with the Edge." *College Music Journal*, 30 Oct. 1998. [U2]
Hendrickson, Matt. "Dream Weavers." *Rolling Stone*, 16 Oct. 1997. [RH]
Henke, James. "Blessed Are the Peacemakers." *Rolling Stone*, 9 Jun. 1983. [U2]
_____. "The Edge: The *Rolling Stone* Interview." *Rolling Stone*, 10 Mar. 1987. [U2]
Hernandez, Raoul. "Music: Me and My Friends." *The Austin Chronicle*, 26 Nov. 2004. [RHCP]
Hewitt, Paulo. "Getting Into U2." *Melody Maker*, 13 Sept. 1980.

Hiatt, Brian. "U2: Biting Pop's Arse." MTV.com, Jan. 2001.
_____. "U2's Beautiful New Day." Sonicnet.com, 2001.
Hilburn, Robert. "Bill Berry Is Leaving R.E.M., But Band Will Continue As Trio." *The Los Angeles Times,* 31 Oct. 1997.
_____. "Building the Beast." *The Los Angeles Times,* 20 Apr. 1997. [U2]
_____. "Far Down the Road, a Sudden U-Turn." *The Los Angeles Times,* 29 Oct. 2000. [U2]
_____. "How R.E.M. Spells Success." *The Los Angeles Times,* 27 Feb. 1994.
_____. "The Lowdown on Hi-Fi." *The Los Angeles Times,* 8 Sept. 1996. [REM]
_____. "R.E.M. Renews Its Dedication to Excellence." *The Los Angeles Times,* 1 Nov. 1995.
_____. "The Songwriters—U2—'Where Craft Ends and Spirit Begins.'" *The Los Angeles Times,* 8 Aug. 2004.
_____. "Soul-Searching for a '90s Sound." *Newsday,* 8 Mar. 1992. [U2]
_____. "Their Reckoning." *The Los Angeles Times,* 1 Jun. 2003. [REM]
_____. "U2 Looking Ahead But Keeping the Future Open." *The Los Angeles Times,* 5 Nov. 1998.
_____. "U2's Mysterious Way." *The Los Angeles Times,* 1 Dec. 1996.
The History of Rock & Roll. Time Life Video, Time (Inc.), and Warner Bros. Domestic Television. 1 Jan. 1995. [U2].
Hoare, Chris. "The Prodigal Son Returns." *Australian Guitar,* Oct. 1999. [RHCP]
Hodgkinson, Will. "New Adventures in Hi-Fi." *The Guardian,* 10 Sept. 2004. [REM]
"Hollywood Can Be Deadly (Hollywood Kann Todlich Sein)." *Musikexpress,* May 2006. [RHCP]
Hoskyns, Barney. "Be Seeing You?" *Mojo,* Aug. 1996. [REM]
_____. "Flags and Penance: U2's American Dream." *NME,* 22 Jun. 1985.
_____. "Four Guys Working for the Sainthood." *NME,* 21 Apr. 1984. [REM]
_____. "No Surprises: Radiohead and Their Kind." *The Guardian,* 14 Apr. 2000.
Howell, Georgina. "Fame." *Vogue* (British), 1 Dec. 1992. [U2]
Hughes, Kim. "Radical *OK Computer* Disc Boots Up UK's Magnificent Five." *Now,* 14 Aug. 1997. [RH]
Hutchinson, John. "Luminous Times." *Musician,* 1 Oct. 1987. [U2]
Iley, Chrissy. "Luck of the Irish." *The Sunday Times,* 25 Feb. 2001. [U2]
_____. "U2 Interview: Group Therapy." *The Sunday Times Magazine,* 7 Nov. 2004.
"An In Depth Interview with Anthony Kiedis in Glasgow." *Vibe,* Mar. 2003. [RHCP]
Interview with Flea. CNN.com, 27 Jun. 2003. [RHCP]
Interview with Flea. Guitarcenter.com, Oct. 2001. [RHCP]
Interview with Jonny Greenwood. Triple J Radio. [Australia]. 16 Apr. 2004. [RH]
Interview with Jonny Greenwood. Unidentified Radio Source. 29 Jan. 1998. [RH]
Interview with Michael Stipe. *Razor Cuts.* Virgin Radio. [UK]. Dec. 2003. [REM]
Interview with Michael Stipe. *Access,* 1 Oct. 1998. [REM]
Interview with Michael Stipe. *TV Guide,* 1996. [REM]
Interview with R.E.M. *Melody Maker,* 15 Jun. 1985.
"An Interview with U2: Album, Tour, and More." Interference.com, Sept. 2004.
Irvin, Jim. *R.E.M. Mojo,* Nov. 1994.
_____, and Barney Hoskyns. "We Have Lift-Off." *Mojo,* Sept. 1997. [RH]
Irwin, Colin. "Glory Days." *Spin,* 1 Jun. 1987. [U2]
Isler, Scott. "Operation Uplift." *Trouser Press,* 1 Jul. 1983. [U2]
Isola, Gregory. "Reluctant Rock Star: How U2's Adam Clayton Learned to Play—and Conquer the World Onstage." *Bass Player,* 11 Nov. 2000.
Jackson, Laura. *Bono: The Biography* (London: Piatkus, 2001). [U2]
Jaeger, Barbara. "U2 Rocks the Boat with Unorthodox Style." *The Bergen County Record,* 12 Apr. 1985.
Jennings, Dave. "Creepshow." *Melody Maker,* 25 Sept. 1993. [RH]
Jennings, Nicholas. "From Street Punks to Rock Idealists." *Maclean's,* 2 Nov. 1987. [U2]
"John Frusciante." *Guitarist,* Apr. 2004. [RHCP]
"John Frusciante Interview." *Mucchio Selvaggio,* Ma. 2004. [RHCP]
Johnson, Howard. "U2 People: Larry Mullen." *Uncut Legends,* vol. 3 (U2).
Johnson, Neala. "R.E.M. Frontman Michael Stipe Elects to Get Serious with Neala Johnson." *The Herald Sun,* 15 Apr. 2004.
Jordan, Brianne. "'Head Music." *Access,* Dec. 2000. [RH]
Jovanovic, Rob, and Tim Abbott. *Adventures in Hi-Fi: The Complete R.E.M.* (London: Orion, 2001).

"Just Like The Beatles!" *Select,* Jul. 1995. [RH]

Kara, Scott. "Faith in What They Do." *The Electric Newspaper,* Jun. 2001. [RH]

Kaufman, Gil. "Guitarist John Frusciante Ready to Funk Up Chili Peppers." Sonicnet.com, 20 May 1998.

_____. "Michael Stipe on Photography." Sonicnet.com, 9 Apr. 1999. [REM]

_____. "Red Hot Chili Peppers: Back in the Saddle." *Addicted to Noise,* Jan. 1999.

_____. "R.E.M. Stretches Sound with Off-Beat Experiments." Sonicnet.com, 12 Mar. 1998.

Kava, Brad. "An Edge-y Quality." *The San Jose Mercury News,* 13 Apr. 2001. [U2]

Kelly, John. "Taking Music to Strange Places." *The Irish Times,* 15 Sept. 2001. [RH]

Kent, Nick. "Happy Now?" *Mojo,* Jun. 2001. [RH]

Kerrang! Legends (Red Hot Chili Peppers). Issue No. 4.

Kessler, Ted. "Radio Daze." *NME,* 27 May 1995. [RH]

_____. "We Never Wanted to Be the Biggest Band in the World." *NME,* 13 Dec. 1997. [RH]

Kiedis, Anthony, with Larry Sloman. *Scar Tissue* (New York: Hyperion, 2004). [RHCP]

Kingsmill, Richard. Interview with Thom Yorke. Triple J Radio. [Australia]. Feb. 1998. [RH]

_____. Interview with Thom Yorke. Triple J Radio. [Australia]. 25 Apr. 2004. [RH]

Kipnis, Jill. "Chili Peppers Take the Long 'Way' Back." *Billboard,* 20 Jun. 2002.

_____. "Red Hot Chili Peppers *By the Way* Due in July." *Billboard,* 22 Jun. 2002.

Kleinedler, Clare. "Don't Call 'Em Britpop." *Addicted to Noise,* May 1996. [RH]

_____. "Radiohead Programmed for Success." *Addicted to Noise,* Jul. 1997.

Klosterman, Chuck. "Meeting Thom Is Easy." *Spin,* Jun. 2003. [RH]

Knapp, Keven. "U2 In America: Pop Morality Vs. the Irish Way." *Creem,* 1 Sept. 1983.

Kot, Greg. "Alluring Otherworldliness." *The Chicago Tribune,* 19 Aug. 2001. [RH]

_____. "Killing 'Em Softly." *The Chicago Tribune,* 4 Oct. 1992. [REM]

_____. "Pulling the Plug." *The Chicago Tribune,* 24 Mar. 1991. [REM]

_____. "Radiohead: Making Records Is Easy." CDNow.com, Jun. 2001.

_____. "R.E.M Against the World." *The Chicago Tribune,* 27 Nov. 1994.

_____. "R.E.M.'s Best Album Side?" *The Chicago Tribune,* 27 Nov. 1994.

Krulle, Von Stefan. "Kreativ-Berserker John Frusciante." *Spiegel Online,* 21 Aug. 2004. [RHCP]

Kula, Geoffrey. "R.E.M.'s Alternative Reality." *U,* 1992.

LaGambina, Gregg. "Out of His Radiohead." *Filter,* 23 Mar. 2004.

Lamacq, Steve. Interview with Anthony Kiedis. BBC Radio 1. [London]. 2 Jul. 2002. [RHCP]

Lamb, Gordon. "Twenty-First Century Boys." *Flagpole,* 6 Oct. 2004.

Lee, Soo Yin. Radiohead Interview. Muchmusic. Chum Television Network. [Toronto]. 12 Apr. 1998.

Lester, Paul. "From the Bedroom to the Universe." *NME,* 25 Oct. 1995. [RH]

Levin, Eric. "Dublin's U2 May Be the Only Band Whose Sound Says Let's Get Physical— And Spiritual, Too." *People,* 1 Apr. 1985.

Levy, Doug. "Radiohead: The Band Who Stole the World." *CMJ,* Jun. 2003.

Liberman, Rachel. "'Head'Case." *The Marquette Tribune,* 22 Feb. 2002. [RH]

Light, Alan. "Band of the Year: Rock's Unbreakable Heart." *Spin,* 1 Jan. 2001. [U2]

Loder, Kurt. "Radiohead: Ice Age Coming." MTV.com, 2000.

_____. "Red Hot Chili Peppers: Californication." MTV.com, 8 Jun. 1999.

Long, Colleen. "Q&A: Red Hot Chili Peppers' Anthony Kiedis." *Associated Press,* 13 Oct. 2004.

Lowe, Steve. "Praise Be!" *Q,* Aug. 2000. [RH]

Lowe, Zane. Interview with R.E.M. XFM Radio [UK]. 2001.

Lynskey, Dorian. "Different Class." *Q,* 2 Aug. 2001. [U2]

_____. "Socks Away!" *Q,* Jun. 2002. [RHCP]

Mabrey, Vicki. "60 Minutes II: BONO," CBCNews.com, 20 Feb. 2002. [U2]

MacDermott, Diarmaid, and Elaine Edwards. "I Can Be Obnoxious, But I Don't Think I'm Boring." *The Mirror,* 18 Jul. 2002. [U2]

MacDonald, Patrick. "Radio Wave: Britain's Band Rides Crest of Superstardom with Low-Wattage Egos." *The Seattle Times,* 2 Apr. 1998. [RH]

Mackey, Liam. "Articulate Speech of the Heart." *Hot Press,* 22 Jul. 1983. [U2]

_____. "I Still Haven't Found What I'm Looking For." *Hot Press,* 1 Dec. 1988. [U2]

Macnie, Jim. "In the Studio with R.E.M., the Return of Mumbles and the Love Gods." *Musician,* Apr. 1991.

Malandrone, Scott. "Flea Starts from Scratch," *Bass Player*, Feb. 1996. [RHCP]

Malins, Steve. "Scuba Do." *Vox*, Apr. 1995. [RH]

Manning, Toby. "Oddfellows Local." *Q Special Edition (R.E.M.)*, 2001.

Mantoine-Holmes, Cat. "Everything's Looking 'Up' for R.E.M." *The Athens Daily News*, 25 Oct. 1998.

Martin, Gavin. "Kings of the Celtic Fringe." *NME*, 14 Feb. 1981. [U2]

_____. "Look Back in Anger. Are R.E.M.'s Glory Days Behind Them? No Way Says An Indignant Michael Stipe." *The Mirror*, 5 Dec. 2003.

_____. "U2 People: Bono," *Uncut Legends*, Vol. 3.

Martin, Paul. "Bono's Tower of Dublin." *The Mirror*, 13 Nov. 2002. [U2]

_____. "I'm Living on the Edge." *The Mirror*, 20 Aug. 2001. [U2]

_____. "We Two Are the Brains Behind U2; Adam and Larry's Back-Seat Role." *The Mirror*, 23 Aug. 2001.

Marzorati, Gerald. "The Post-Rock Band." *The New York Times Upfront*, 30 Oct. 2000. [RH]

Masuo, Sandy. "Subterranean Aliens." *Request*, Sept. 1997. [RH]

Mathis, Andrew. "Interview with Michael Stipe." RockDaily.com, 4 Apr. 1999. [REM]

McAndrew, Brendan, and Eileen Threlfalls. "From L.A. to New Yorke." *The Trigger*, 4 Nov. 1995. [RH]

McCollum, Brian. "Disconcerting." *The Detroit Free Press*, 5 Nov. 1997. [REM]

McCommons, Molly. "Interview with Michael Stipe." *Flagpole*, 21 Sept. 1994. [REM]

McCormick, Carlo. "Creating the Modern Rock 'n' Roll Lifestyle Was the Easy Part. The Trick Was Surviving It." *Interview*, 1 Aug. 2002. [RHCP]

McCormick, Neil. "Twenty One Years of Pop Music." *Propaganda*, Issue 26, 1 Jun. 1997.

McLean, Craig. "Karaoke. Champagne. Shopping. The Funk ... Radiohead: How They Took on 2001. And Won." *The Face*, Jan. 2002.

McNee, Brian. "Thoughts of U2." *Hit Parader Presents U2*, 1 Jun. 1992.

Micallef, Ken. "I'm OK, You're OK." Yahoo!Music.com, 17 Aug. 1997. [RH]

Mico, Ted. "Hating U2." *Spin*, 1 Jan. 1989.

Middleton, Fraser. "Back from the Brink: Red Hot Chili Peppers Beat Their Addictions to Return Even Stronger." *The Sunday Herald*, 2 Jan. 2003.

Milano, Brett. "Pete and Pals." *The Boston Phoenix*, 22 May 1997. [REM]

Miller, Edwin. "Rocking with U2." *Seventeen*, Aug. 1985.

Milne, Richard. "Michael Stipe: That's Me in the Spotlight." *The Financial Times*, Nov. 2003. [REM]

Miserandino, Dominick A. "Kiedis, Anthony—Lead Singer for the Red Hot Chili Peppers." Thecelebritycafe.com, Jan. 2005.

Mitchell, Justin. "It's Red Hot for the Chili Peppers." *The Orange Country Register*, 25 Dec. 1987.

Mohan, Dominic. "'New York Showed Us Heroes.'" *The Sun* [UK], 8 Dec. 2001. [U2]

Moody, Paul. "Creeping Up with the Joneses." *NME*, 11 Sept. 1993. [RH].

Moon, Tom. "Eno: The Story Behind Original Soundtracks 1." *Knight Ridder News Service*, 5 Nov. 1995. [U2]

_____. "How R.E.M. Recorded in a Spectrum Bathroom." *The Philadelphia Inquirer*, 8 Sept. 1996.

_____. "Radiohead: Companion to *Kid A* Sessions." *The Philadelphia Inquirer*, 3 Jun. 2001.

Moore, Dermod. "Ace of Bass." *Hot Press*, 29 Aug. 2001. [U2]

Moore, Lisa M. "Michael Stipe's Photo Exhibit Debuts in Boston." *Allstar*, 18 Sept. 1998. [REM]

Morel, P.J., et al. "R.E.M. Peter Buck Talks about the Passion." *Pulse of the Twin Cities*, 11 Sept. 2003.

Morris, Gina. "You've Come a Long Way Baby." *Select*, Apr. 1995. [RH]

Morton, Tom. "Southern Accents." *Melody Maker*, 6 Sept. 1986. [REM]

Mueller, Andrew. "Kid B." *Amazon.co.uk*, Jun. 2001. [RH]

_____. "The Year of Living Dangerously." *The Independent*, 31 Dec. 1997. [U2]

Mulholland, Gary. "Interview with Michael Stipe." *Time Out*, 23 Jun. 1999. [REM]

Munro, Ronan. "Talking Head." *Nightshift*, Jul. 2001. [RH]

Murphy, Peter. "A Reconstruction of the Fables." *Hot Press*, 23 Jul. 1999. [REM]

_____. "Blood Sugar Sex + Spontaneous Ejaculation." *Australian Rolling Stone*, Dec. 2002. [RHCP]

_____. "How Radiohead Learned to Loathe the Bomb." *Hot Press*, 11 Oct. 2001.

Myers, Caren. "Dork Radio." *Details*, Nov. 1993. [RH]

Needs, Kris. "The Unforgettable Band: A U2 Overview." *Creem Collectors Series*, 1 Aug. 1987.

Nickson, Liz and Judy Ellis. "More at Home in Dublin Than On the Big Screen." *Life*, 1 Nov. 1988. [U2]

Niesel, Jeff. "On Tour: R.E.M." *Hear/Say*, Sept. 2003.

Nolan, Tom. "On the Edge of Success." *U2 Magazine*, May 1982. [U2]

_____, and Jas Obrecht ."The Edge of U2." *Guitar Player*, 1 Jun. 1985.

Notorious Stuart Brothers. "A Date with Peter Buck." *Bucketfull of Brains*, Dec. 1987. [REM]

Obrecht, Jas. "Close to the Edge." Guitar.com, 27 Jun. 2001. [U2]

Odell, Michael. "Silence! Genius at Work." *Q*, Jul. 2003. [RH]

O'Hagan, Sean. "Another Green World." *NME*, 24 Dec. 1988. [REM]

_____. "Billion-Dollar Dreams." *The Guardian*, 4 Mar. 2000. [U2]

_____. "The Laughing Cavalier." *The Guardian*, 14 Apr. 2001. [REM]

_____. "Saint Bono Defrocked." *The Face*, 1 Apr. 1992. [U2]

_____. "U2 Anew." *Details*, 1 Sept. 1992.

"One Red Hot Minute with the Red Hot Chili Peppers." *Rhythm and News*, 1995.

O'Neill, Terry. "U2." *In Fashion*, 1 Jan. 1988.

Oldham, James. "'People Basically Want Their Hands Held Through Twelve Mull of Kintyres... .'" *NME*, 23 Dec. 2000. [RH]

_____. "Radiohead: Their Stupendous Return." *NME*, 24 Jun. 2000.

_____, and Lauren Zoric. "'I Was a Complete Fucking Mess When *OK Computer* Was Finished.'" *NME*, 30 Sept. 2000. [RH]

Paphides, Peter. "Into the Light." *Mojo*, 2003. [RH]

_____. "We're Going to Save Pop Music!" *Melody Maker*, 6 Feb. 1993. [RH]

Pareles, Jon. "Searching for a Sound to Bridge the Decades." *The New York Times*, 9 Feb. 1997. [U2]

Parker, Lyndsey. "Putting the Music Biz in Its Right Place." Yahoo!Music.com, 28 Jul. 2003. [RH]

_____. "Two Sides to Every Story." *Guitar One*, Jan. 2003. [RHCP]

"Passionate Friends." *Melody Maker*, 1 Dec. 1984. [REM]

Pattenden, Mike. "Phil Selway." *Q Special Edition (Radiohead)*.

Patterson, Sylvia. "We Have 1976 Tattooed on Our Psyche." *NME*, 14 Oct. 2000. [U2]

"The People's Choice." *Indie-cator*, Oct. 1992. [REM]

Petit, Jade. "Red Hot Chili Peppers: Baroque Bordello." *Rocksound*, Jun. 1999.

Pettigrew, Jason. "Red Hot Chili Peppers—Funkin' Up the Milky Way." *Alternative Press*, Nov. 1989.

Philbrook, Erik. "Keeping the Peace." *ASCAP Playback*, 28 Nov. 2001. [U2]

Phillips, Julie. "Friends, Colleagues Saddened, But Support Berry's Decision." *The Athens Daily News*, 31 Oct. 1997. [REM]

Pierce, David. "Interview With Michael Stipe." *Tasty World*, Feb. 1985. [REM]

Platt, John. "R.E.M." *Bucketfull of Brains*, Dec. 1984.

"Players: Radiohead Biography." FenderEurope.com.

Plummer, Sean. "Everything in Its Right Place ... at Last." *Access*, Jun.-Jul. 2003. [RH]

Pond, Steve. "Now What?" *Rolling Stone*, 9 Mar. 1989. [U2]

"Postscripts from the Edge." *NME*, 31 Oct. 1998. [U2]

Pouncey, Edwin. "R.E.M.: Deconstructing the Fables." *Sounds*, 18 Oct. 1986.

Powers, Ann. "The Future Sound of U2." *Spin*, Mar. 1997.

Price, Nancy. "Radiohead Interview." *Consumable Online*, Sept. 1997.

_____. "Radiohead on Their Band Dynamic." *The Musician's Exchange*, 23 Jun. 1999.

Q Special Edition (Radiohead).

Q Special Edition (R.E.M.)

Rabid, Jack. "What the A? The Oxford Powerhouse Shocks the World with an Oblique, Obtuse, Impressionistic, Artistic, Total Curveball of a New LP. But Will It Stick?" *The Big Takeover*. Issue No. 47. [RH]

Radiohead Interview CD. Baktabak Recordings. London. 1998. (CBAK4115).

"Radiohead Master." *Microsoft MusicCentral*, 2 Sept. 1997.

"Radiohead on New Wave on and off Stage, Radiohead Seems At Peace." *The Guide*, 30 Apr. 2004.

"Radiohead Raises Profile Opening for Morissette." *The Baltimore Sun*, Oct. 1996.

Radiohead Recall *Amnesiac*. Planet Sound Channel 4 (UK) Teletext. 19 May 2001.

Randall, Mac. *Exit Music: The Radiohead Story* (New York: Delta, 2000).
_____. "The Golden Age of Radiohead." *Guitar World*, Apr. 1998.
_____. "Now We Are Three." Yahoo!Launch.com, 17 Nov. 1998. [REM]
Randee, Dawn. "Modulation Across the Nation." *Alternative Press*, Oct. 1995. [RH]
Raphael, Amy. "Interview with Michael Stipe." *Esquire*, Jun. 1999. [REM]
"Rattle and Humble." CNN.com, 27 Oct. 2000. [U2]
Raymaker, Derek. "Stipe Still Discarding Pop Formulas." *The Globe and Mail*, 24 Aug. 1999. [REM]
Rayner, Ben. "Thom Yorke, Optimist." *The Toronto Star*, 3 Jun. 2003. [RH]
"Red Hot Chili Peppers." Artistdirect.com, 1995.
Red Hot Chili Peppers Interview CD. Baktabak Recordings, London. 1991. (CBAK 4091).
"Red Hot Chili Peppers Interview." *El Pais*, 27 Jul. 2002.
"Red Hot Chili Peppers Latest Album." *Rolling Stone*, 21 Jun. 1995.
Red Hot Chili Peppers. Personal Appearance. MuchMusic. Chum Television Network. [Toronto]. 7 Aug. 2002.
Rees, Paul. "Riders on the Storm." *Q*, Nov. 2004. [U2]
Regardie, Jon. "Red Hot Chili Peppers: Return of the Century." *Alternative Press*, Jul. 1999.
"Rejuvenated Radiohead Is on the Rise." *The Denver Post*, 12 Jun. 1995.
"R.E.M. Artist of the Month." HMV.com, May 2001.
R.E.M. documentary. *The Making of Up*. [Available at REMHQ.com].
"R.E.M. Feeling 'Strong As Ever.'" CNN.com, 23 Oct. 2003.
"R.E.M. Reveal Themselves." MTV.com, 7 May 2001.
"R.E.M. Star Reveals Future Plans." *NME*, 6 Sept. 2001.
"R.E.M. Talks About Breaking Up, Making Up, and New Album." *AllStar*, 23 Apr. 2001.
"Remember Us?" *Q*, Nov. 1996. [REM]
Reynolds, Simon. "Walking on Thin Ice." *The Wire*, Jul. 2001. [RH]
Richardson, Andy. "Boom! Shake the Gloom!" *NME*, 9 Dec. 1995. [RH]
Robbins, Ira. "R.E.M." *Pulse!* Oct. 1992.
Roberts, Michael. "The Buck Stops Here." *The Dallas Observer*, 23 Jul. 1998. [REM]
Robinson, John. "'It's Clear and Pretty—But I Think People Won't Get It.'" *NME*, 3 May 2003. [RH]
Robinson, Lisa. "Interview with Michael Stipe." *The New York Post*, 7 Nov. 1998. [REM]
_____. "U2's Unforgettable Fire." *Vanity Fair*, 25 Oct. 2004.
Rodman, Sarah. "Chili Peppers on a Red Hot Streak." *The Boston Herald*, 17 Jul. 2000.
_____. "Out of Time? No Way! After Rough Period, R.E.M. Returns Stronger Than Ever." *The Boston Herald*, 4 Oct. 2003.
Roeser, Steve. "A Conversation with Kiedis." *Goldmine*, 22 Nov. 1996. [RHCP]
Rollings, Grant. "True Story of Rockers U2." *The Sun* [UK], 27 Aug. 2001.
Rose, Charlie. "Interview with Michael Stipe." *Charlie Rose*, 4 May 1998. [REM]
Rosen, Craig. "Red Hot Chili Peppers Say the Road Ain't Easy." Yahoo!Launch.com, 6 Jun. 2000.
_____. "Retail, Radio Expect R.E.M.'s Warner Set to Be a 'Monster.'" *Billboard*, 10 Sept. 1994.
Rosenthal, Joe. "Pepper Mill Grinds On." *Rolling Stone*, 6 Apr. 1998. [RHCP]
Ross, Alex. "The Searchers: Radiohead's Unquiet Revolution" *The New Yorker*, 20 Aug. 2001.
Ross, Peter. "Shinier, Happier People." *The Sunday Herald*, 15 Jun. 2003. [REM]
Runkle, Patrick. "Drummer on Top: The Red Hot Chili Peppers' Chad Smith on the New Album, *By the Way*." *Artistpro*, May 2002.
Rüth, Steffen. "The Heavy Nothing." *Kulturnews*, Jun. 2003. [RH]
Sakamoto, John. "Michael Stipe Talks Shop." *Jam!*, 18 Oct. 1998. [REM]
Sams, Christine. "Hot Reception." *The Sydney Morning Herald*, 25 Nov. 2002. [RHCP]
Sandall, Robert. "The Red Hot Chili Peppers Are Still on Fire." *The Times Online*, 22 Apr. 2006.
Sanghera, Sathnam. "U2's Fifth Member." *The Financial Times*, 4 Sept. 2001.
Santelli, Robert. "The Back Door of Success." *Modern Drummer*, 1987. [REM]
Savage, Jon. "R.E.M.: Post-Yuppie Pop." *The Observer*, 21 May 1989.
Saxberg, Lynn. "Everybody Hurts: Only the Rich Won on Election Day, Says R.E.M.'s Mike Mills." *The Ottawa Citizen*, 11 Nov. 2004.
Scaggs, Austin. "Q&A Michael Stipe." *Rolling Stone*, 6 Oct. 2004. [REM]
Scanlon, Tom. "R.E.M.'s Peter Buck: Talking about the Passion." *The Seattle Times*, 9 Jul. 2002.

Schlosberg, Karen. "The Roots of U2." *Creem Collectors Series*, 1 Aug. 1987.
Schoemer, Karen. "R.E.M. Reinvents Itself." *Newsweek*, 26 Oct. 1998.
Scholz, Martin. "The Edge Q&A." *Rolling Stone Germany*, Nov. 2002. [U2]
_____, Jean-Francois Bizot, and Bernard Zekri. "Even Bigger Than the Real Thing." *Spin*, 1 Aug. 1993. [U2]
Schruers, Fred. "U2." *Musician*, 1 May 1983.
_____. "A Visit to Dublin—Home of U2." *U2 Magazine*, No. 7, May 1983.
Scott, Roger, and Annie Nightingale. Interview with U2. BBC Radio 1. [London]. 30 Oct. 1988.
Sculley, Alan. "R.E.M. Regains Creative Chemistry." *The Herald [Snonomish]*, 29 Aug. 2003.
Secher, Benjamin. "Rock's Biggest Small Band." *The Telegraph*, 4 Sept. 2004. [REM]
Self, Will. "All Hail Yorkie Boy." *GQ*, Jul. 2003. [RH]
"Sex, Steak and Insanity." *Q*, May 2006. [RHCP]
Sexton, Paul. "Radiohead Won't Play By the Rules." *Billboard*, 16 Sept. 2000.
Shedden, Ian. "Red Alert." *The Australian*, 29 Nov. 2002. [RHCP]
Sheffield, Rob. "38 Special." *The Village Voice*, 28 Oct. 1998. [REM]
Shelley, Jim. "Nice Dream?" *The Guardian*, 13 Jul. 1996. [RH]
Silverman, David. "R.E.M. Revs Up." *Chicago Tribute*, 22 Jan. 1989.
Simmons, Carol. "The Whole Enchilada." *The Dayton Daily News*, 24 Mar. 2000. [RHCP]
Simmons, Sylvie. "California Love." Yahoo! Music.com, 29 Jun. 1999. [RHCP]
_____. "Conference Call: Mike Mills Talks to 10cc!" *Mojo*, 1995. [REM]
Simpson, Dave. "It's Great To Go Straight." *The Guardian*, 14 Feb. 2003. [RHCP]
Smith, Andrew. "Sound and Fury." *The Observer*, 1 Oct. 2000. [RH]
Smith, Brantley. "R.E.M., Love Song '91." *Details*, Apr. 1991.
Smith, Mat. "Welcome to the Occupation." *Melody Maker*, 12 Sept. 1987. [REM]
Smith, Russell. "U2: Rock 'N' Roll for the '80s." *The Dallas Morning News*, 25 Feb. 1985.
Sng, Susanne. "U2 Still Rocks." *Malay Mail*, 10 Nov. 2000.
Snow, Mat. "R.E.M.: Touched! Chuffed! Etc.!" *Q*, Jan. 1992.
Snowden, Don. "The Reckoning of R.E.M." *The Los Angeles Times*, 18 Jul. 1984.
Soeder, John. "Band of Brothers," *Plain Dealer Pop Music Critic*, 7 Feb. 2003. [U2]
_____. "What's 'Up' with R.E.M.?" *The Cleveland Plain Dealer*, 20 Aug. 1999.
Soren, Tabitha. "R.E.M.'s New Adventures." *MTV Online*, 13 Sept. 1996.
Sprague, David. "Buck on *Up*." *Guitar*, Dec. 1998. [REM]
Staunton, Terry. "Review of *Out of Time*." *NME*, 16 Mar. 1991. [REM]
Stern, Jeremy. "Radiohead Interview." *BBC.co.uk*.
Stevensen, Jane. "4 Minus 1 Still Equals R.E.M." *The Toronto Sun*, 21 Aug. 1999.
_____. "*Kid A*'s Conception." *The Toronto Sun*, 28 Sept. 2000. [RH]
_____. "Marching to No Drummer." *The Toronto Sun*, 26 Oct. 1998. [REM]
_____. "Radiohead of State." *The Toronto Sun*, 3 Jun. 2003.
_____. "U2's Bono Flying High." *The Toronto Sun*, 1 Oct. 1997.
Stewart, Allison. "Red Hot Chili Peppers Interview." CDNow.com, Sept. 2000.
Stokes, Niall. "The Big Picture." *Hot Press*, 29 Aug. 2001.[U2]
_____. *Into the Heart: The Stories Behind Every U2 Song* (New York: Thunder's Mouth, 2001).
_____. "Matter of Life and Death." *Hot Press Annual 2002*, 1 Dec. 2001. [U2]
The Story of ... Radiohead. Hosted by Bill Welychka. MuchMoreMusic. Chum Television Network. [Toronto].
Stoute, Lenny. "Radiohead Is Touring Till It Drops." *The Toronto Star*, 30 Oct. 1993.
_____. "Runaway Hit a Mixed-Blessing for UK's Radiohead." *The Toronto Star*, 1 Jun. 1995.
Strauss, Neil. "The Pop Life: Feeling the Beat of No Drummer." *The New York Times*, 28 Oct. 1998. [REM]
Strickman, Andy. "Stipe Says New R.E.M. Album Is Far-Out." *Wall of Sound*, 5 Feb. 2001.
Stubbe, Britt. "No to Drugs, Yes to Religion." *Oor*, Jun. 2002. [RHCP]
Stubbs, David. "The Right Stuff." *Uncut*, Aug. 1999. [REM]
Sturges, Fiona. "Michael Stipe: Who Are You Calling an Elder Statesman?" *The Independent*, 20 Oct. 2003. [REM]
Sullivan, Caroline. "Bridges and Sighs." *The Guardian*, 16 May 1997. [RH]
Sullivan, James. "R.E.M.'s New Adventures in the City." *The San Francisco Chronicle*, 2 Apr. 1998.
Sullivan, Jim. "From Boys to Men." *The Boston Globe*, 2 Feb. 1996. [RHCP]
_____. "Radiohead Remembers the Pleasantries." *The Boston Globe*, 1 Jun. 2001.

Sullivan, Kate. "Icons: Red Hot Chili Peppers." *Spin*, Aug. 02.
Sutcliffe, Phil. "The Band That Tried to Kill Themselves," *Q*, Oct. 1999. [RHCP]
_____. "Boys to Men." *Q*, 1 Dec. 1998. [U2]
_____. "Death Is All Around." *Q*, Oct. 1997. [RH]
_____. "U2: 1980–1990—The Edge Looks Back." *Q*, 1999.
Sutherland, Mark. "Return of the Mac!" *Melody Maker*, 31 May 1997. [RH]
Sweeting, Adam. "Highs and Lotus." *The Age*, 9 Nov. 1998. [REM]
_____. "R.E.M.: The Band Who Saved American Music." *Uncut*, Aug. 2005.
_____. "Still Shiny After All These Years." *Electronic Mail & Guardian*, 26 Nov. 1998. [REM]
Terratzo, Gary. "Interview with R.E.M." *Muse*, 1998.
Thielke, Lars. "Tonal Telepathy." *Guitar*, Aug. 2002. [RHCP]
Thom Yorke of Radiohead Talks to BBC World Service. BBC Press Release, 21 Apr. 2003.
Thompson, Dave. *Bono: In His Own Words* (New York: Omnibus, 1989). [U2]
Thompson, Lynne. "Coming Up for Air." *Scene*, 8 Jun. 1995. [REM]
Toombs, Mikel. "Chili Peppers Emerge Whole from Punkless Funk." *The San Diego Union Tribune*, 6 Jun. 1999.
Trakin, Ray. "Five Years on with U2." *Creem Collectors Series*, 1 Aug. 1987.
_____. "The Red Hot Chili Peppers Eat It Raw." *Musician*, Dec. 1989.
Turenne, Martin. "Interview with Colin." *The Georgia Straight*, 21 Jun. 2001. [RH]
Turman, Katherine. "The Red Hot Chili Peppers Sock It to Ya!" *MusicMakers*, Apr. 1990.
Turner, Dale. "Red Hot Once Again!" *Guitar One*, Aug. 1999. [RHCP]
Turner, Steve. "U2: Another Day, Another Dollar." *Q*, Jul. 1987.
_____. "U2: The Rock of the Irish." *Sunday Express Magazine*, 16 Oct. 1988.
Tyaransen, Olaf. "Closer to the Edge." *Hot Press*, 4 Dec. 2002. [U2]
_____. "The Final Frontier." *Hot Press*, 26 Oct. 2000. [U2]
_____. "Pushing the Envelope." *Hot Press*, 7 Nov. 2002. [U2]
_____. "U2: A Bass Odyssey." *Hot Press*, 25 Nov. 1998.
Tyrangiel, Josh. "Mysterious Ways." *Time*, 14 Nov. 2004. [U2]
_____. "Top of the Rock 'N' Roll Heap." *Time*, 9 Jun. 2003. [RH]
"U2 at the R.D.S." *U2 Magazine*, No. 2, Feb. 1982.
U2 in Quotes (England: Babylon Books, 1986).
U2 Interview CD. *Bono Talks in Philadelphia*. Baktabak Recordings. London. 1987. (CBAK 4006).
U2 Interview. *Dazed and Confused*, May 1997.
U2 Interview CD. [Interviews 1985/1986]. Sound and Media (SAM 7003). Issued 1995.
"U2 Max Interview." *MAX*, Mar. 1997.
U2 MSN Chat with Jo Whiley. MSN.com, 2002.
"U2: The Pop Interview." *Reverberation Online Magazine*, 1 Mar. 1997.
U2 Press Conference at the Auckland Airport in New Zealand. 3 Nov. 1988.
"U2 Q&A on *How to Dismantle an Atomic Bomb*." Bestbuy.com, 24 Nov. 2004.
"The Uncut Questionnaire—Michael Stipe." *Uncut*, 7 Sept. 2004. [REM]
Uncut Legends (U2). Issue No. 3.
"Unforgettable Fire." CNN.com, 12 Dec. 2001. [U2]
Ungemuth, Nicolas. "Deux Piments sous la Pluie." *Rock & Folk*, Aug. 1996. [RHCP]
"'Up,' with People." *The Boston Globe*, 25 Oct. 1998. [REM]
Van De Kamp, Bert. "Angels and Devils." *Music Express*, 1 Jul. 1992. [U2]
_____. "Portraits of a Artist as a Young Man." *Guitar World*, Jan. 1999. [U2]
Vare, Ethlie Ann. "U2: At War with Mediocrity." *ROCK!*, 1 Sept. 1983.
Vaziri, Aidin. "British Pop Aesthetes." *Guitar Player*, Oct. 1997. [RH]
_____. "Q&A with Anthony Kiedis." *The San Francisco Chronicle*, 26 Dec. 1999. [RHCP]
Vicchrilli, Sam. "Radiohead Is Tuned In to Messages, But the Music Comes First." *The Salt Lake Tribune*, 22 Aug. 2003.
Video Conectate Interview with John Frusciante. [Panama]. 2002. [RHCP]
VPRO Interview with John Frusciante. Jan. 1994. [Available on Frusciante.net.] [RHCP]
Wadsworth, Tony. "The Making of *OK Computer*." *The Guardian*, 20 Dec. 1997. [RH]
Walshe, John. "Bang a Gong," *Hot Press*, 24 May 2002. [U2]
Warner Brothers Press Release for *Automatic for the People*. Sept. 1992. [REM]
Warner Brothers Press Release for *Green*. Oct. 1988. [REM]

Warner Brothers Press Release for *Monster*. Sept. 1994. [REM]
Warner Brothers Press Release for *Out of Time*. Mar. 1991. [REM]
Warner Brothers Press Release for Reveal. 16 Apr. 2001. [REM]
Weiss, Neal. "R.E.M. Sleepless in Vancouver." *Rolling Stone*, 13 Feb. 2003.
"We're Not So Uptight Now ... Thom Yorke's Happy Return." *Melody Maker*, 21–27 Jun. 2000. [RH]
Whiley, Jo. Live broadcast direct from Windmill Lane Studios, Ireland. Radio ProFM. [Bucharest]. 1 Mar. 1997. [U2]
White, Timothy. "Bono." *Rock Lives* (New York: Henry Holt, 1990). [U2]
Wiederhorn, John. "Radiohead Transform Emotional Turmoil Into Kinetic Pop." *Rolling Stone*, 7 Sept. 1995.
_____. "The Secret Sauce." MTV.com, Jul. 2002. [RHCP]
Wild, David. "Red Hot & New." *Rolling Stone*, 8 Jul. 2002 [RHCP]
Williams, John. "The Red Hot Chili Peppers Q&A." *Jam!*, 8 Aug. 2002.
Williams, Lowri. "Radiohead Go All Classical on Us." Gigwise.com, 22 Mar. 2005.
Williams, Simon. "I Rate Myself and I Want to Dive." *NME*, 18 Mar. 1995. [RH]
Willman, Chris. "Interview with Michael Stipe." *Entertainment Weekly*, 28 May 1999. [REM]
_____. "10 Questions: Peter Buck of R.E.M." *The Los Angeles Times*, 24 Mar. 1991.
Winfrey, Oprah. "Oprah Talks to Bono" *O Magazine*, 15 Mar. 2004. [U2]
Wittet, Bruce T. "Phil Selway." *Modern Drummer*, Aug. 1996. [RH]
Woldach, Stefan. "Flea Between Zen & Pop." *Gitarre & Bass*, Feb. 1997. [RHCP]
Wood, Mikael. "Spinning Plates: Radiohead Doesn't Make Albums. It Has Accidents." *Denver Westword*, 14 Jun. 2001.
Woodworth, Paddy. "Snap, Crackle, Pop!" *The Irish Times*, 1 Mar. 1997. [U2]
Woolliscroft, Tony. "The Last of the Mohicans." *Kerrang!*, 26 Aug. 2000. [RHCP]
_____. "Riders on the Storm." *Kerrang!*, 11 Jul. 1998. [RHCP]
Wroe, Martin. "Under Construction." *Propaganda*, Issue 30, 2000.
Wylie, Harry. "With Their Third LP, Radiohead Are in Serious Danger of Becoming the Best Band on the Planet." *Total Guitar*, Nov. 1997.
Wyman, Bill. "How R.E.M. Woke Up Rock 'n' Roll in the '80's." *The Chicago Tribune*, 5 Dec. 1989.
Yahoo.com Chat with Bono. 12 Mar. 2000. [U2]
Yamazaki, Yoichiro. "Thom Yorke Interview." *Q Special Edition (Radiohead)*.
Yates, Catherine. "Get Up and Jump." *Kerrang! Legends*, Issue No. 4. Red Hot Chili Peppers.
Young, Simon. "Green Peppers." *Kerrang! Legends*, Issue No. 4. Red Hot Chili Peppers.
Zaccagnini, Paolo. "U2 Interview." *Drums of Peace*, 1998.
Zisman, Marc. "They're Red Hot." *Guitare & Claviers*, Nov. 1991. [RHCP]
Zollo, Paul. *Songwriters on Songwriting*. 4th ed (Cincinnati: Da Capo Press, 2003). [REM]
Zoric, Lauren. "Fitter, Happier, More Productive." *Juice*, 25 Sept. 2000. [RH]
_____. "I Think I'm Meant to Be Dead." *The Guardian*, 22 Sept. 2000. [RH]
Zuel, Bernard. "Waves of Emotion." *The Age*, Jun. 2001. [RH]
Zulaica, Don. "LiveDaily Interview: Producer Rick Rubin." LiveDaily.com, 17 Mar. 2004. [RIICP]
Zwerin, Mike. "R.E.M. Is Alive and Well with Album N0.11." *The International Herald Tribune*, 22 Jan. 1999.

Websites

GENERAL WEBSITES

BBC.co.uk
Livedaily.com
Rocksbackpages.com
Mtv.com
VH1.com
Warner Music Australasia (www.warnermusic.com.au)
Yahoo! Launch.com

OFFICIAL WEBSITES

www.radiohead.com
www.redhotchilipeppers.com
www.remhq.com
www.u2.com

RADIOHEAD WEBSITES

Ateaseweb.com
Edobrien.co.uk
Followmearound.com (now defunct)
Greenplastic.com
Radiohead Article Archive (Geocities.com/SunsetStrip/Stage/9346/RAAmain.html)

RED HOT CHILI PEPPERS WEBSITES

Beeninsane.com (dedicated to John Frusciante)
JohnFrusciante.com
RHCP France (www.rhcpfrance.net)
RHCP Italy (www.redhotchilipeppers.it)
RockinFreak Central (http://www.fortunecity.com/tinpan/wuthering/26/id37.htm)
Transcending.nu
Troublekids in Funk Heaven (rhcprock.free.fr)
Universallyspeaking.org

R.E.M. WEBSITES

www.murmurs.com
www.onlineathens.com
www.remison.com
www.remrock.com
retroweb.com/rem
http://www.stud.ntnu.no/~turidbro/date.html

U2 WEBSITES

AtU2.com
www.macphisto.net
U2audio.com (U2exit.com)
http://u2_interviews.tripod.com/
http://u2intotheheart.bravepages.com/
U2station.com
U2world.com/news

Index